Bloomberg's New York

Bloomberg's New York

CLASS AND GOVERNANCE
IN THE LUXURY CITY

JULIAN BRASH

THE UNIVERSITY OF GEORGIA PRESS
Athens & London

A portion of chapter 9 appeared, in a different form, as "Re-Scaling Patriotism: Competition and Urban Identity in Michael Bloomberg's New York" in *Urban Anthropology and Studies of Cultural Systems and World Economic Development* 35 (2006): 387–423.

Designed by Walton Harris
Set in 10/13 Minion Pro

Printed digitally in the United States of America

Library of Congress Cataloging-in-Publication Data

Brash, Julian.
Bloomberg's New York : class and governance in the luxury city / Julian Brash.
    p.   cm. — (Geographies of justice and social transformation ; 6)
Includes bibliographical references and index.
ISBN-13: 978-0-8203-3566-7 (hardcover : alk. paper)
ISBN-10: 0-8203-3566-5 (hardcover : alk. paper)
ISBN-13: 978-0-8203-3681-7 (pbk. : alk. paper)
ISBN-10: 0-8203-3681-5 (pbk. : alk. paper)
1. New York (N.Y.)—Politics and government—1951–
2. Bloomberg, Michael. 3. Elite (Social sciences)—New York (State)—New York. 4. Urban renewal—New York (State)—New York. I. Title.
JS1230.B73 2010
974.7′1044—dc22   2010027198

British Library Cataloging-in-Publication Data available

CONTENTS

ILLUSTRATIONS

ABBREVIATIONS

ABNY	Association for a Better New York
CBD	Central Business District
CB4	Manhattan Community Board Four
CEO	Chief Executive Officer
CMO	Chief Marketing Officer
CPC	City Planning Commission
DCP	Department of City Planning
DSD	Draft Scoping Document
EDC	Economic Development Corporation
EFCB	Emergency Financial Control Board
EIS	Environmental Impact Statement
ESDC	Empire State Development Corporation
GPP	General Project Plan
HKNA	Hell's Kitchen Neighborhood Association
HYIC	Hudson Yards Infrastructure Corporation
IBO	Independent Budget Office
IOC	International Olympic Committee
MAC	Municipal Assistance Corporation
MSF	million square feet
MTA	Metropolitan Transportation Authority
MWBE	Minority- and Women-owned Business Enterprise
NYSCC	New York Sports and Convention Center
PACB	Public Authorities Control Board
PILOTS	Payments in Lieu of Taxes
PMC	Professional-Managerial Class
RPA	Regional Plan Association
TCC	Transnational Capitalist Class
TFA	Transitional Finance Authority
TIF	Tax Increment Financing
ULURP	Uniform Land Use Review Procedure
USOC	United States Olympic Committee

ACKNOWLEDGMENTS

It is only after producing a work such as this that one fully realizes how misconceived the notion of sole authorship is. The ultimate responsibility for the arguments, along with any errors or misconceptions, in this book is mine alone. Nevertheless, it would have been impossible to complete this work without the support and aid of many dozens of people.

First and foremost, I wish to thank the informants who granted me their time, insight, honesty, and openness, particularly Anthony Borelli, Anna Hayes Levin, John Raskin, and a number of Department of City Planning employees who will go unnamed.

Innumerable academic colleagues helped shape this book. From our first breakfast meeting at Aggie's, Neil Smith has been unfailingly helpful, kind, and supportive. He has been indispensable to this work's evolution from dissertation proposal to final product. Jeff Maskovsky has served as advocate, mentor, intellectual collaborator, friend, and (briefly) editor — I thank him for all his help. I am in deep debt to David Harvey, whose work and advice are central to this book and to my own intellectual development. I want to thank Ida Susser for both her guidance and support and her work to legitimize the anthropological study of North America and North American cities. Other current and former faculty members of the Anthropology Program of the City University of New York Graduate Center deserve my thanks, especially Michael Blim, Louise Lennihan, Jane Schneider, Cindi Katz, and Don Robotham. I am also grateful for my graduate school compatriots at the GC, including Susan Falls, Mary Taylor, Nathan Woods, Erin Martineau, Roberto Abadie, Eliza Darling, and David Vine. Others who have contributed to this work in various ways include Ellen DeRiso, Miriam Greenberg, William Sites, Anders Lund Hansen, Gary McDonogh, Marina Peterson, Arlene Dávila, Hillary Cunningham, John Clarke, Sandi Morgen, Brett Williams, Peter Wissoker, Peter Marcuse, Lionel McIntyre, and Leslie McCall.

My former colleagues at the University of Toledo have my gratitude for providing a welcoming environment in which I could convert this work from dissertation to book. Barbara Chesney was everything one could want in a first chair. I also thank Willie McKether, Patricia Case, Melissa Gregory, Sam Nelson, Ben Pryor, and Ed Lingan for their collegiality and friendship. Judy Haas and Jonas Gamso also deserve my gratitude.

Derek Krissoff of the University of Georgia Press, whose quick and supportive response made sure this book's period of homelessness was mercifully brief, has been an excellent editor. Also deserving of my thanks for their responsiveness, diligence, and professionalism are other Press staff, the editors and board members of the Geographies of Justice and Social Transformation series, and Kay Kodner. Thanks to the anonymous reviewers of this book, who provided such insightful and helpful comments, critiques, and suggestions.

Portions of chapter 9 appeared in *Urban Anthropology and Studies of Cultural Systems and World Economic Development* in 2006 (35:4). Thanks to Jack Rollwagen for permission to republish it here.

Finally, I want to thank my family and friends for their love and support. My friendships with David Auburn, Griffin Hansbury, Frank Garritano, Michele Bessey, Kevin Mialky, and T. R. Muth have all in their own ways made this book possible. I owe a profound debt to my parents, Sarah and Ed Brash, for, among other things, their unfailing encouragement; imbuing me with intellectual curiosity, a love of reading, an attention to detail, and a sense of justice; and — more practically — their babysitting. My mother- and father-in-law, Kathryn Widmer and Peter Ressler Sr., receive my deep thanks for all the support they have provided. I want to also acknowledge Kate Brash, Rachel Brash, Benet O'Reilly, Alec MacGillis, Elise Brown, Jeremy Kagan, and Jonathan Kagan for their support and encouragement. I am also deeply grateful to my two grandmothers, Jane Bennett and Sally Miller Brash, who both passed away while I was completing this book, for all they gave me.

My deepest thanks of all go to my wonderful wife and children. It is they who lived with the day-to-day trials of writing this book. To my three irrepressible children, Olivia, Leo, and Sam, I owe thanks for providing joy, love, and a reminder of what is important. And I dedicate this book to Kiry, whose love, humor, companionship, partnership, patience, generosity, and kindness during the long and arduous process of writing this book made my life full. Thanks, babe.

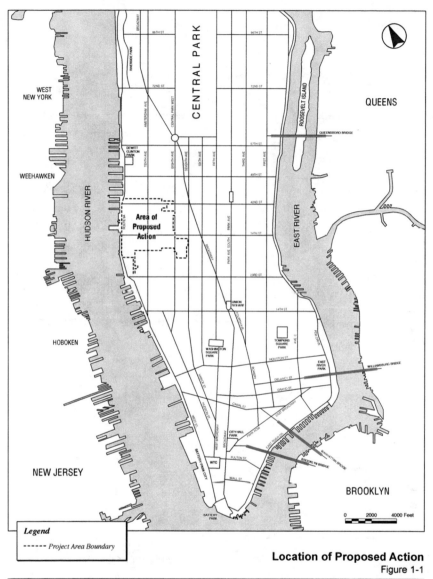

Location of Proposed Action
Figure 1-1

NO. 7 SUBWAY EXTENSION-HUDSON YARDS REZONING AND DEVELOPMENT PROGRAM

The Hudson Yards plan area. (Metropolitan Transportation Authority/New York City Department of City Planning)

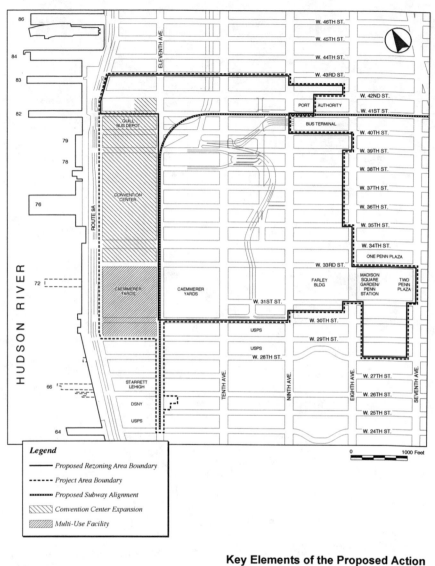

Legend

— Proposed Rezoning Area Boundary

---- Project Area Boundary

▪▪▪▪▪ Proposed Subway Alignment

▨ Convention Center Expansion

▨ Multi-Use Facility

Key Elements of the Proposed Action
Figure 1-2

NO. 7 SUBWAY EXTENSION-HUDSON YARDS REZONING AND DEVELOPMENT PROGRAM

Manhattan's far west side. (Metropolitan Transportation Authority/New York City Department of City Planning)

Bloomberg's New York

INTRODUCTION

As of early September 2001, Michael Bloomberg's campaign to be elected New York City's 108th mayor was in trouble. The billionaire ex–chief executive officer (CEO) of the media and financial services company Bloomberg LP had pitched himself to voters based on the notion that his enormous business success uniquely qualified him to be mayor. Despite the media-driven hagiography of CEOs, portrayed as individuals with extraordinary capacities for leadership and action, many New Yorkers were dubious that Bloomberg's managerial skill would translate to city hall. Among the doubters were members of the editorial board of the *New York Times*, the guardian of mainstream political opinion in New York City. In endorsing Bloomberg's Democratic opponent Mark Green, the editors laid out a lengthy rejection of the "fundamental argument behind [Bloomberg's] candidacy":

> He claims that as a successful entrepreneur, he is better qualified to be mayor than Mr. Green, a career politician. . . . Even within the annals of businessman-candidates, Mr. Bloomberg is ill matched to the job he covets. His company, a financial information service, has no stockholders, and no unions. It is a brand new business, created by Mr. Bloomberg himself, its corporate culture and decision-making structure devised to suit his character. New York City, on the other hand, is a very old business indeed, with multiple layers of interests and precedent weighing down every decision. Many of Mr. Bloomberg's greatest talents would turn out to be utterly beside the point. Others, like his penchant for saying whatever he thinks, would come back to haunt him. Other than his business successes, Mr. Bloomberg has offered little during the campaign. (*New York Times* 2001)

Despite such sentiments, Bloomberg was elected in November 2001, though by the narrowest of margins and aided by a lot of luck and even more money.

Not only was Bloomberg elected — and then reelected twice, once overwhelmingly and once narrowly and contentiously — but his mayoralty became a major phenomenon. *Time Magazine* named Mayor Bloomberg one of the country's five best big-city mayors (Gibbs 2005). Coming full circle, at the end of Bloomberg's first term the *New York Times* wrote that he might "be remembered as one of the greatest mayors in New York history" (2005). The national press touted him as a possible presidential contender in 2008 and beyond. Politicians as different as John McCain and Barack Obama have praised Bloomberg's "remarkable" tenure as mayor (Ambinder 2008; Berman 2007).

More important, the ostensibly pragmatic and apolitical corporate approach that Bloomberg touted in 2001 has emerged as a new model for urban governance, not least in New York City, where Bloomberg has become one of the city's most memorable and important mayors, dominating its politics as have few before him. Mayors of other cities have sought to learn from and associate themselves with Bloomberg's management style and perceived policy successes. For example, Los Angeles mayor Antonio Villaraigosa visited New York in early 2006 to study the Bloomberg administration's educational reforms, and Washington, D.C., mayor Adrian Fenty not only drew on these reforms but also adopted the famous "bullpen" design imported from Bloomberg LP into his city hall. Bloomberg, the "businessman-mayor," has provided a model for urban politicians around the globe. Far from being "utterly beside the point," as the *New York Times* had argued in 2001, the corporate experience that inspired Bloomberg's approach to urban governance came to be seen as a desirable trait of mayoral candidates — not just in New York (where Time Warner's chairman and CEO Richard Parsons was enthusiastically rumored to be a possible successor to Bloomberg) but in cities as far apart as Dallas and Seoul.

My book analyzes this remarkable evolution, whereby the once-challenged idea of a CEO mayor became not just accepted but widely celebrated. Along with several other aspects of Bloomberg's approach to urban governance that I discuss in this volume, I have called this phenomenon the "Bloomberg Way."[1] As we shall see, this evolution was not a smooth, conflict-free process. Indeed, one of the central paradoxes explained in this book is how the Bloomberg Way became so dominant even as central elements of its agenda stumbled. From this mix of success and failure, which saw the Bloomberg administration lose battles but win the war, so to speak, we can draw lessons about the strengths and weaknesses of the Bloomberg Way as a new and influential mode of urban governance. Moreover, analyzing this process can enhance our understanding of the sort of neoliberal and entrepreneurial urban governance exemplified by the Bloomberg Way, as it illustrates how ongoing neoliberalization both is propelled by and creates the conditions for the mobilization and formation of various class groupings. This study makes clear the role of political agency and class in the development of neoliberal urban governance.

THE BLOOMBERG WAY

Because this book makes its broader case through a close analysis of the development and structure of the Bloomberg Way, it is important to establish what I mean by this term at the outset. What was the Bloomberg Way? How should we understand Michael Bloomberg's mayoralty? How might we best characterize his approach to urban governance? Mayor Bloomberg has been the subject of a great deal of attention in the popular and political press, not just in New York but nationally and internationally as well. From my reading of this material, as well as from countless conversations about Bloomberg with New Yorkers and others, it appears that three related ideas about Bloomberg and his approach to urban governance have hardened into virtual *doxa*.

First, it is held that his approach to urban governance has been pragmatic and nonideological, with his policies praised for their moderation and nonpartisanship. Second, Bloomberg's political rise and success have been portrayed as rooted in his singular personal characteristics of candor, managerial acumen, and drive, the very characteristics that the *New York Times* once deplored. While New York City's mayors have often had outsized personalities, they have also been associated with particular social groups from which they derived both political style and support. For instance, Rudolph Giuliani and Ed Koch were both viewed as products and representatives of the white ethnic middle and working classes, while John Lindsay was closely identified with upscale Manhattan liberals. Michael Bloomberg and his mayoralty, by contrast, are seen as being defined by his *individual* experience as a CEO and manager. The perception of the Bloomberg mayoralty as characterized by pragmatism and shaped by the mayor's individual personality and experience informs a third commonly held understanding: that the Bloomberg mayoralty has been largely *apolitical*. By virtue of the mayor's wealth and political inexperience, and thus his lack of dubious political associations or commitments to special interests, he has been held to be somehow above the fray of urban politics.

My analysis rejects all of these ideas. I argue that the Bloomberg Way is deeply ideological; that it is rooted in broader political and economic processes, in particular those of post–fiscal crisis class transformation in New York City; and that it is deeply political, in that it represents an effort on the part of a specific social grouping to bring urban governance and the physical shape of the city into accord with its interests and desires and, more than this, to assert the right and beneficence of its rule. I reinterpret the Bloomberg mayoralty within the framework of a particular set of ideas concerning the relationship of class to the neoliberalization in urban governance. Thus, before providing a summary of my own interpretation of the Bloomberg Way, it is important to make this framework explicit.

NEOLIBERALISM

The concept of neoliberalism has become a central focus of geography, anthropology, and urban studies. At a high level of abstraction, there is significant agreement on the definition of the term. David Harvey describes neoliberalism as a "theory of political economic practices that proposes that human well-being can best be advanced by liberating entrepreneurial freedoms and skills within an institutionalized framework characterized by strong private property rights, free markets, and free trade" (2005, 2). It thus entails a rejection of "embedded" or "egalitarian" liberalism and the practices of social welfarism and Keynesian management that emerged in many locales after World War II (Hackworth 2007; Harvey 2005; Peck and Tickell 2002). The concept of neoliberalism is often used "to help make the crucial link between the broad economic changes often referred to as 'globalization' and the actual ideological and political practices of governance that have prompted or emerged from those changes" (Kingfisher and Maskovsky 2008, 116). Thus neoliberalism provides "a kind of operating framework" (Peck and Tickell 2002, 380) that emphasizes the importance of enhancing competitiveness and comparative advantage in a space-economy characterized by free flows of goods, services, and capital (Harvey 2001; Ward and England 2007, 7).

Neoliberalism is, therefore, a deeply spatial phenomenon, entailing the restructuring of spatial relations within and between places (Peck and Tickell 2002). Crucially, many of these changes entail shifts in the internal dynamics of cities, as well as in their relations to each other and to territorial formations of different scales. As Neil Brenner and Nik Theodore have written, "Cities are not merely localized arenas in which broader global or national projects of neoliberal restructuring unfold. On the contrary . . . cities have become increasingly central to the reproduction, mutation, and continual reconstitution of neoliberalism" (2002, 375). Some have argued that neoliberalization first gained its foothold in cities, as the regime of pro-business austerity imposed in the wake of New York City's 1970s fiscal crisis was rapidly mimicked not just by other cities in the United States, but also by the federal government and international institutions such as the International Monetary Fund (Harvey 2005, 43–48; Tabb 1982). The centrality of cities to neoliberalization since then, if anything, has intensified, as "cities have become increasingly important geographical targets and institutional laboratories for a variety of neoliberal policy experiments" (Brenner and Theodore 2002, 368).

Thus, urban governance in the United States has been transformed since the 1970s (Hackworth 2007; Sites 2003). The immediate post–World War II era was marked by a local liberalism, backstopped by relatively generous federal urban policy. These methods of governance aimed to reconcile conflicts among various racial, economic, and political constituencies via support for working-class consumption and social-welfarist redistribution as well as real estate development and corporate investment. In contrast, recent decades have seen a shift toward "entrepreneurialism," a form of neoliberal governance that prioritizes the stimulation of corporate investment and real estate development and entails speculative and activist governmental means to attain this goal (Eisinger 1988; Hall and Hubbard 1998b; Harvey 2001). This shift is generally attributed to a resurgence of the political power of capital, abetted by increased capital mobility, postindustrialization, a racialized and conservative political backlash, the rise of globalization ideology, and the decline of federal urban policy. The upshot has been that cities are (or believe themselves to be) in desperate competition for jobs, investment, and desirable residents. Enhancing competitiveness has been placed at the center of urban policy, with issues of equity and redistribution consistently deprioritized (Peck and Tickell 2002, 394).

A number of early analyses, along with a series of subsequent works (Brenner and Theodore 2002; Dumenil and Levy 2004a; George 2000; Hackworth 2007; Harvey 2005; Peck 2004; Peck and Tickell 2002), established a common theoretical reference point for the political-economic transformations that have been observed across the globe since roughly 1970. These analyses generally draw on a Marxist political-economy perspective, positing "the primary goal of neoliberal reforms [as] the restoration of capitalist power in the context of global economic crisis" (Kingfisher and Maskovsky 2008, 118). However, subsequent analysis has demonstrated the complexity of neoliberalism and generated much debate about how exactly it should be understood.

In part this discussion is the product of fundamental theoretical disagreement. Most notable was that of post-structuralists, particularly those inspired by Foucault's (1991) notion of governmentality (see also Dean 1999; Rose 1999). These scholars challenged the ostensibly structuralist, economistic, and totalizing qualities of early political-economic analyses (Ferguson and Gupta 2002; Larner 2003; Ong 2006). While some have argued that these two approaches are irreconcilable (Barnett 2005), others have argued for their mutual engagement, calling for a more flexible, grounded, and comprehensive understanding of neoliberalism that retains a focus on class, power, and global economic forces (Brenner and Theodore 2005; Clarke 2004; Hoffman, DeHart, and Collier 2006; Kingfisher and Maskovsky 2008; Leitner, Peck, and Sheppard 2007b; Liu 2006; Nonini 2008; Ward and England 2007, 8; Wilson 2004b; Wilson 2008a). Even those who advocate for structural analyses exploring the commonalities of neoliberal strategies across space acknowledge the need to address neoliberalism as contingent, processual, cultural, and context-sensitive (Hackworth 2006; Hackworth 2007; Peck 2006b).

There are still clear differences in emphasis between those who conceive of neoliberalism as "a diffuse regime of political-economic power, closely interwoven with the dynamics of globalizing financial capitalism, one that increasingly shapes the 'rules of the game' for a host of national and local actors" and those who "view neoliberalism as a much less than coherent bundle of practices and projects, contingently interwoven by agents and through networks in a wide variety of open-ended ways" (Leitner, Peck, and Sheppard 2007a, 316). But there is clearly a space for rapprochement, a space in which this book is squarely positioned. Viewing particular neoliberal projects as manifestations of a hegemonic and overarching process is clearly inadequate. What is required, instead, are contextual accounts that acknowledge contingency, political struggle, change, the articulation of neoliberalism with other processes, and culture even as they remain focused on power and political-economic factors. Of these factors, I place particular emphasis on class, as I retain the notion, drawn from David Harvey's authoritative work, that what the myriad forms and instances of neoliberalism have in common is the aim of restoring power to economic elites (2005, 19). However, before turning to the issue of class, I want to make five points concerning neoliberalism that are integral to my argument concerning the Bloomberg Way.

First, following the lead of a number of scholars (Kingfisher and Maskovsky 2008, 120–121; Leitner, Peck, and Sheppard 2007b), I treat the successful development of neoliberal projects in particular contexts not as a foregone conclusion, but as highly contingent upon local circumstances and the outcomes of particular political struggles. My focus, then, is on the political struggles that have emerged from and shaped the ongoing neoliberalization of New York City.

Second, I understand neoliberalism as *neoliberalization* — not as a stable and unchanging set of governing practices but rather as a much more fluid and dynamic phenomenon (Gledhill 2004; Peck and Tickell 2002, 383; Ward and England 2007; Wilson 2004b). Neoliberalization's internal dynamics (and its intersection with other processes) have produced emergent and often contradictory social, political, and cultural formations that represent a mix of continuity and change. That is, neoliberalization is not just a process but a *dialectical* process. Thus, I pay close attention to how both the successes and failures of neoliberalization in New York City created the conditions in which the Bloomberg Way could emerge.

Third, I understand neoliberal projects, to use John Clarke's (2004, 37) conceptualization, as "articulated ensembles": unstable and dynamic yet coherent projects that absorb practices from without, colonize and/or defuse other projects, encounter resistances, and rework institutions and that are in turn reshaped by these articulations. They are neither monolithic nor self-contained but internally diverse and in constant interaction with other processes, projects, and practices. These projects do not spring into being fully formed; instead, they are fashioned out of preexisting political, cultural, and economic materials that lie close at hand (Brenner and Theodore 2005; Kingfisher and Maskovsky 2008; Wilson 2004b).[2] They are formed and re-formed via an ongoing articulation and rearticulation of their constitutive elements, resulting in, as Edward Soja has put it, "a complex mix of continuity and change" (Brenner and Theodore 2005, 101) as new and old practices are reassembled in new ways. Thus, I pay close attention to the particular governmental, cultural, social, and political elements bound together by the Bloomberg Way, as well as its articulation with other ongoing processes and projects in neoliberalizing New York City.

Fourth, neoliberalization produces not just political-economic phenomena but "*cultural* meanings and practices related to the constitution of proper personhood, markets, and the state" — to this list we might add *cities* — "that are emergent in a contested cultural field" (Kingfisher and Maskovsky 2008, 120, emphasis added; see also Comaroff and Comaroff 2001; Duggan 2003). Neoliberalization generates new meanings, practices, and forms of subjectivity, as well as new links between these elements (Bondi 2005; Goldstein 2001). Moreover, due to its articulation with other processes and practices, neoliberal projects often involve the selective valorization of existing identities, imaginaries, and meanings (Freeman 2007; Hyatt 2001; Ruben 2001; Wilson 2004b). Neoliberal interventions would not meet with much success if they were unable to capture the imaginations and affirm the worldviews and identities of people beyond the narrow stratum of economic elites who have reaped the lion's share of their material benefits. Thus, in this book I pay close attention to both the cultural material the Bloomberg Way drew upon and reworked — in particular the figure of the charismatic CEO, which provided a crucial prop to Michael Bloomberg's initial campaign for mayor as well as his ongoing political appeal — and the urban imaginaries that animated his administration's approach to urban governance and development.

Taking all these characterizations of neoliberalism together, we arrive at a fifth point: certain social groups might experience neoliberalization as an *opportunity* rather than an assault. A number of analyses have demonstrated how particular social groupings have seized on processes of neoliberalization to further their own agendas, albeit often in contexts highly constrained by the realities of gender, class, race, ethnicity, and so on. Neoliberalization has functioned as a source of social power and mutual identification for various groups.[3] Within urban studies, there has been some work on neoliberalization that has picked up this point, addressing, for example, the ways in which neoliberal cultural marketing strategies may create opportunities for ethnic and racial advancement, if in profoundly equivocal ways (Boyd 2005; Dávila 2004). These studies also show how neoliberalization has provided urban planners and others involved in urban redevelopment with opportunities to advance their conceptions of both themselves and their cities as global and cosmopolitan (Chesluk 2008, 49–80; Gregory 1998, 193–203; Rutheiser 1996; Todd 1995).

Yet despite the widespread agreement that neoliberalization is primarily aimed at the bolstering of upper-class power, it is ironic that the agency and formation of the class groupings who might engineer and benefit from neoliberalization have rarely been addressed in the copious literature on neoliberalization in general and urban neoliberalization in particular. There has been little attention focused on the most important "constituency" of neoliberalism in cities: corporate executives, those avatars of investment who are the ultimate arbiters of a "good business climate" and thus a crucial target of neoliberal governance (for a noteworthy exception, see Nevarez 2003). While there has been some exploration of the relationship between capitalist class formation and neoliberalization, such work has been relatively abstract, with little attention either to the specific contexts in which class formation takes place or how class formation is linked to the production of space and place at a scale other than global. A good bit more attention has been paid (albeit unevenly) to another crucial constituency of neoliberalism, professionals — or "the creative class," as the boosterish Richard Florida (2002) dubs them. Before further discussing these two class groupings and their relationship to neoliberalization, let me first lay out my understanding of class and its relationship to the production of space in general and urban space in particular.

CLASS

This book is premised on the notion, central to political-economic analyses of neoliberalization, that it is "a *political* project to . . . restore the power of economic elites" (Harvey 2005, 19; see also Dumenil and Levy 2004a; Peck 2004, 396). While there is a large oeuvre building on and extending these analyses, this central feature of neoliberalization has received relatively little attention; in general, as Harvey ruefully notes, there has been a "startling . . . lack of any examination of the class forces that might be at work" (2005, 115). My aim here is precisely to examine the class forces at work in New York City's contemporary neoliberalization. In doing so, I build upon anthropological and geographical approaches to class in general, as well as work in other disciplines addressing the two class formations mentioned above, whose emergence in recent decades has been particularly important to neoliberalization in cities.

The concept of class, and especially its Marxist variants, has been subject to vigorous critique in recent decades.[4] Despite these critiques, class remains a powerful and widely used concept, and one I use here. Moreover, I follow Marxist tradition in positing that class position, if not identity, refers to one's position in relations regulating the process of social labor, and in particular to one's relationship to the means of production — whether, as Neil Smith puts it, "one owns companies or is owned by them" (1996, 106).[5] However, while the concept of class discussed here starts with this axiomatic principle, it serves not as the end of the discussion but as a beginning. I assume that the way in which class actually operates in the flux and flow of social life is processural, that is, always in the process of being constituted and never completed or final (Thompson 1964, 9–14). Moreover, it is overdetermined, meaning that class as lived and experienced is constituted not just by one's relations to the means of production but by a whole set of other processes and factors, including race, gender, and sexuality — as well as, for the purposes of this book, urban identity and governance. Thus, the Marxist conception of class should be deployed not as an objective determinant but as an entry point into the complex reality of social, cultural, and economic life (see also Dowling 2009; Gibson-Graham, Resnick, and Wolff 2001).

Thinking of class in this way is especially important in the context of ethnographic research. Ethnographers often encounter class in a wide variety of settings and in relationship to assorted social, economic, political, and cultural phenomena. What we might call the ethnographically available aspects of class usually have little direct relationship with the means of production, instead consisting of a series of explicit and implicit statements and propositions about the social world, the place of certain groups and individuals within it, and the relationships among those groups. In the process of ethnographic research and analysis, one might well discover a level of intersubjective consistency (Rotenberg 2007) in such statements and propositions among a grouping of people sharing a similar place in the production process. In such a situation, it seems reasonable to conclude that one is dealing with a class-based process or social phenomenon.

Such statements and propositions may never in fact deal with class per se. Indeed, ethnographers have found that, especially in the United States where the language and politics of class are relatively undeveloped, people tend to talk about class and express class identity in indirect and highly mediated ways. This has been most clearly seen in work excavating the "intersectionality" of race, class, sexuality, and gender, in which anthropologists have demonstrated how class identity and relationships are often displaced or mediated by gender, race, and sexuality.[6]

Most germane to this book, scholars have demonstrated how processes of class formation and identification intersect not just with race, gender, and sexuality but also with space. From Ira Katznelson's (1982) seminal work demonstrating the impact of the spatial *cum* political split between work and urban community on the development of class in the United States, to more recent work illustrating how "globality" has been a building block of identity for transnational elites and professionals (Ho 2005; Ley 2004, 159–161; Rofe 2003; Tsing 2000), this vein of work has gone beyond the truism that spatial ideologies and processes *reflect* class differences. In sum, it provides support for argument that the production of space and the formation of class identities should be seen as *mutually constitutive* — that, as Melissa Wright has put it, "class politics is inextricable from both the politics of place and the politics of identities located in particular places" (2006, 97).[7] With this in mind, let us return to our discussion of the relationship between neoliberalization and class.

CLASS AND PLACE-MAKING IN THE NEOLIBERAL CITY

There is clearly intellectual support for the idea that both neoliberalization and concomitant class processes can be linked to the production of space. As discussed at the beginning of this theoretical detour, the connection between neoliberalization and the production of *urban* space is especially tight. Thus, before returning to the Bloomberg Way, one final step is needed: to bring neoliberalization, class, and the production of urban space into relation with each other in a theoretically sensible manner. How might we accomplish this? To begin, let us take up the relationship between neoliberalization and class by returning to the two class formations mentioned above — corporate executives and professionals. Both have been linked with neoliberalization, albeit in limited sorts of ways.

The work of several scholars on the formation of a transnational elite since roughly 1970 provides an important starting point. William Robinson (2004), in his exploration of the development of a transnationalized capitalism concomitant with the development of neoliberalism, argues that this process has been in part constituted by the emergence of an increasingly coherent and self-aware "transnational capitalist class" (TCC) defined by its ownership of the globalized means of production. Harvey (2005, 31–36) briefly describes a new upper-class configuration, at least partially transnational in nature and often drawing on particular ethnic groupings and nation-state attachments. This class grouping consists of corporate CEOs, prominent corporate board members, financiers, entrepreneurs in developing sectors like biotechnology and information technology, real estate developers, and leaders in the business services industries that support the highest levels of capitalist activity. He writes that while this new class configuration clearly does "possess a certain accordance of interests that generally recognizes the advantages . . . to be derived from neoliberalization" (2005, 36), the degree to which it can act and to which it conceptualizes itself as a unified group is highly uneven and not well developed. Finally, Leslie Sklair posits the development of a cross-class global elite, including managerial and professional interests attached to the transnationalization of capitalism, and explicitly links its rise with the process of neoliberalization (2001, 24–26). Sklair, along with David Rothkopf (2008), has given the most attention to the interests and ideas binding this group together, paying particular attention to the "culture-ideology" of this group and advancing the "cautious proposition" that this class "is beginning to act as a transnational dominant class in some spheres" (Sklair 2001, 5).

There is evidently reason to believe that neoliberalization has been associated with the emergence of new elites. Moreover, it is clear that this process involves a number of different class groupings. Most obvious is the TCC, which, following Robinson in particular, I will define as including those who own and directly control transnational capital. However, as Sklair, Rothkopf, and Harvey, as well as Jamie Peck (2004, 396), point out, we must also take into account the managers, professionals, and others whose engagement in transnational capitalist activity is facilitated by their skills, credentials, and expertise, rather than their direct control of capital: that is, the professional-managerial class (PMC).[8] How might we link these two class formations with the production of (neoliberal) urban space?

In the case of the TCC, we need to reject the notion, put forward by several analysts, that this class formation is defined by its ability to transcend place, that it has, in Robinson's words, "an objective class existence and identity in the global system above any local territories and polities" (2004, 47). While it is true that the ability of the TCC to operate on a transnational scale is an important source of both class identity and power, it does not follow that it is placeless or, to use Manuel Castells's (1996) conceptualization, that it operates in the "space of flows" rather than the "space of places." Such a notion radically abstracts elites from the localized social worlds they inhabit, resulting in an overemphasis on mobility, networks, and the ability to transcend space, and a relative neglect of the sites in which production, consumption, and class formation actually "take place."

This idea is premised upon a notion of space in which different scales — the urban, the local, the regional, and the global — are distinct and separate levels arranged in a hierarchical fashion. Fortunately, there is a different understanding of scale that allows us to avoid this problem. As a number of geographers have noted, scales should be viewed not as distinct and hierarchical, but as articulated, co-constitutive, and in flux.[9] Thus, neoliberal globalization, as Neil Brenner writes, "unfolds simultaneously upon multiple, intertwined geographical scales — not only within global space but through the production, differentiation, reconfiguration, and transformation of sub-global spaces such as territorial states, regions, cities, and localities" (1999, 44; see also Inda and Rosaldo 2002; Smith 2000). Studies of the construction of transnational capitalism have made abundantly clear that the so-called global economy, far from being placeless, is constituted by and dependent on a variety of local places (Cox 1997). "Global" or "world" cities, for instance, provide crucial economic, technical, and financial infrastructures that permit transnational capitalism to function and are the site of a good deal of transnational economic activity. These locales have experienced a series of profound social, spatial, political, and cultural changes as they have been fashioned into constitutive nodes of the transnational capitalist economy.[10]

If this sort of local-global interface structures the economic workings of transnational capitalism, it seems reasonable to expect that certain local places are likely to be crucial to the formation of the TCC. Moreover, we might also expect to see the sort of place-making, including local political activity, on the part of these supposedly rootless cosmopolitans, that is often linked to class-formation processes of other types. And in fact, there is some evidence for this. A small but growing literature challenges the idea that transnationalization eviscerates the importance of sub-global places, practices, and social ties to the construction of identity even for the most cosmopolitan, powerful, and mobile (Ley 2004; Ong 2002; Tsing 2000). Even those who pose the TCC as operating "above" the local scale acknowledge that certain places are key to its constitution. These include not just the oft-mentioned World Economic Forum in Davos, Switzerland, but also global cities (and particular neighborhoods in them, such as Kensington Palace Gardens in London, the Peak in Hong Kong, or the Upper East Side in New York City), gated communities, and high-status vacation spots like the Hamptons or the Côte d'Azur. However, such places tend to be viewed as deracinated and disembedded nodes in a global network rather than as places worthy of close analysis. Moreover, the stress in discussing these places tends to be on the movement of transnational elites through these sites rather than their activity within them.[11]

This is unfortunate, because there are compelling reasons to believe that global cities like New York, as well as other key locales, are arenas not only of TCC identity formation but of TCC place-making of various kinds. The formation of the TCC has not merely taken place in cities but has actively reshaped them. Clearly this has been true in terms of economic activity, as we have seen, and consumption, as the extraordinary wealth commanded by these elites has had major effects on local consumption markets of various sorts (Sassen 2001 [1991], 284–289). However, it seems likely to be true in the realm of politics as well. This is because the globalization of capital has not rendered sub-global states irrelevant, either in general terms or to members of the TCC in particular (Brenner et al. 2003; Harvey 2005, 35). Given the importance of global cities to global capitalism and the TCC, it seems likely that the TCC would have a vested interest in influencing the actions of local government in such cities, especially given the crucial role of public action in economic development, urban planning, and the provision of cultural amenities. While there is a burgeoning literature on the participation of purely local business owners in urban politics, work on the involvement of the TCC is scanty. Indeed until recently (Lee 2005; Nevarez 2003; Smith and Graves 2005), the general consensus had been that executives of national, to say nothing of transnational, corporations played little role in local politics (Logan and Molotch 1987, 84–85), even in cities like New York (Fainstein, Fainstein, and Schwartz 1989, 78–79). The Bloomberg Way, along with several other cases discussed in the concluding chapter of this book, indicates that this consensus needs to be rethought. As Anna Tsing writes, "There can be no territorial distinctions between the 'global' transcending of place and the 'local' making of places. Instead, there is place-making . . . all around, from New York to New Guinea" (2002, 464).

Unlike the TCC, the PMC has been tightly linked to the production of neoliberal urban space. The postindustrialization of urban economies that has accompanied neoliberalization and the construction of transnational capitalism has generated numerous opportunities for the PMC, giving it an increasingly pronounced presence in cities, and especially in global or quasi-global American cities like Chicago, Miami, and New York. Indeed, the specifically urban nature of many of the industries in which PMC employment is concentrated has been crucial to the recent development of this class. For postindustrial urbanites, class and urban identity are tightly linked and mediate the synergistic relationship between postindustrial economic activity and urbanization (Currid 2007; Lloyd 2006).

However, the best-documented link between neoliberalism and PMC class formation is that of gentrification and its recent "generalization" (Smith 2002, 437). In its early stages, when it represented a rather limited process involving the reinvestment in and rehabilitation of inner-city residential neighborhoods (Hackworth and Smith 2001), gentrification provided sites of PMC class formation, as aesthetics, social networks, and consumption practices became sources of both mutual identification among PMC members and differentiation from other class formations (Butler 1997; Ley 1996; Smith 1996, 114). However, with the passage of time, gentrification has become an essential component and exemplar of urban neoliberalism (Hackworth 2007, 123–124). With the increased (and coordinated) participation of both global capital and the local state (Hackworth 2002), gentrification has metastasized. The increasing enrichment of the members of the PMC affiliated with the ascendant financial, business services, and cultural industries (often subsidized by the local state) made them a lucrative market for upscale retailers and real estate developers (Sassen 2001 [1991], 261–286), including those operating on a national or global scale. Moreover, it became neoliberal orthodoxy that the attraction and retention of members of the PMC in their roles as consumers, taxpayers, and constituents of a skilled labor force were key to cities' economic success (Florida 2002; Peck 2005). Thus, the perceived tastes and desires of this group were assigned a privileged role in the determination of urban and economic development policy (di Leonardo 2008; Greenberg 2008, 248; Ruben 2001, 438). As a result of these two processes, "whole areas [were transformed] into new landscape complexes that pioneer[ed] a comprehensive class-inflected urban remake" (Smith 2002, 443; see also Hackworth 2002; Hackworth and Smith 2001; Lees 2003). It was no longer just particular gentrifying neighborhoods that were sites of PMC class formation but much larger swaths of cities.

The neoliberalizing city has developed and has been fashioned in a way that affirms the class identity of members of the PMC, both via the cultural valorization of this identity and the provision of an urban environment where identity formation can literally take place. But while the PMC has asserted itself in a cultural and economic manner, and while its tastes are catered to by urban policy makers and business concerns, there is little evidence of this group acting politically in a self-aware or coherent manner (Boschken 2003; Boschken and Hoagland 1998). There have been glimmers of this: Richard Florida's widely read paean to the PMC was at least in part a call to political action (Florida 2002, 315–326; Peck 2005, 746–748). Indeed, in cities like Dayton, Toledo, Memphis, and Pittsburgh, local organizations sprang up that were explicitly aimed at providing opportunities for the "creative class." In some of these cases — Toledo and Pittsburgh, for instance — (unsuccessful) mayoral candidates emerged from their ranks. Steven McGovern (2009) has described how conflict over waterfront development in Philadelphia spurred "creative class" political activity, which ultimately helped bolster the successful mayoral run of progressive reformer and political outsider Michael Nutter. Indeed, Nutter is just one of a series of mayors emerging from and appealing to the PMC, who were elected in the face of opposition from well-entrenched political machines. Other examples include Gavin Newsom in San Francisco and Cory Booker in Newark. Given this, it seems likely that self-conscious and coherent political action on the part of PMC members either has emerged elsewhere and has not been documented or will emerge in the future.

Putting all this together, it seems there are good empirical and theoretical reasons to believe that contemporary neoliberal cities have been and will continue to be constitutive sites of both TCC and PMC class formation. It seems fair to expect that such processes, which heretofore have worked themselves out primarily in cultural and economic arenas, have had and will have direct impacts on politics. With so much invested (literally and figuratively) in the city, and with economic development orthodoxy attaching so much importance to the role these groups play in the city, it would hardly be surprising if members of these groups took the step of direct engagement in urban governance. It is to be expected that the exact shape and course of such engagements will vary according to the vagaries of historical and geographical context. For these urban elites, the past neoliberalization of the city will provide both the conditions of their political emergence and the grist of their governmental program. That is to say, neoliberalization and class formation will be dialectically related.

The analysis of the development and implementation of the Bloomberg Way presented in the remainder of this book explores one seminal example of this phenomenon.

THE CLASS BASIS, POLITICS, AND IDEOLOGY OF THE BLOOMBERG WAY

By approaching the Bloomberg mayoralty using this theoretical apparatus, this book both provides an alternative interpretation of the Bloomberg mayoralty and contributes to debates in anthropology, geography, and urban studies concerning the nature of neoliberalization and urbanization. Let us return to the earlier contention that it is erroneous to characterize Michael Bloomberg and his approach to governance as pragmatic, personalistic, and apolitical. I argue here that embedding the Bloomberg Way in its proper historical context of neoliberalization, postindustrialization, and, most importantly since so often neglected, class transformation permits a more robust and accurate interpretation of this mode of governance — that is, an interpretation of the Bloomberg Way as *ideological*, *class-based*, and deeply *political*.

First, I argue that the Bloomberg Way is rooted not in Bloomberg's individual experience and personality but in the broad political and economic transformation that New York City has undergone since World War II, and particularly since the fiscal crisis of the 1970s. During this time, a city emblematic of postwar liberalism and balanced economic development has developed a distorted and narrow postindustrial economy dominated by finance, business services, media, and real estate. It has also become a demonstration case for the "success" of fiscal austerity and revanchist social policy, an American "symbol of neoliberalism" (Greenberg 2008). The postindustrialization and neoliberalization of New York had an important social consequence: the development of an ascendant postindustrial elite, consisting of members of both the PMC and the TCC, who reaped so much of the economic and governmental rewards of these twin processes. Michael Bloomberg was a product of this transformation, as were the other corporate executives and professionals who worked in his city hall. His wealth, status as a rising star in the city's elite social networks, corporate and technocratic managerialism, financial acumen, and entrepreneurial success were all rooted in significant ways in the postindustrialization and neoliberalization of New York City and associated processes of class transformation. Moreover, certain internal contradictions of these processes created seemingly intractable governmental problems, to which Bloomberg's corporate and technocratic approach to governance provided potential solutions. While it would be wrong to say that a Bloomberg mayoralty, or one similar to it, was an inevitable product of these processes, they created the conditions in which such a mayoralty could emerge.

Second, this book argues that the Bloomberg Way, so often characterized as a pragmatic and nonideological approach to urban governance, was in fact profoundly ideological. It is true that the Bloomberg Way did not endorse either Democratic or Republican orthodoxy. However, it relied upon and enacted a series of implicit and explicit propositions about and imaginings of the nature of the city, political leadership, political organization, political commitment, economic and urban development, citizenship, and the relations between the state and capital. These factors were highly conditioned by the class identity and experience of the mayor and many of his fellow postindustrial elites. They can be grouped into two "urban imaginaries": collective and common, if conflictive and ideological, understandings of the city both as a whole and as an amalgamation of groups and individuals, that inform the material practices that produce, reproduce, and transform urban space.[12]

The Bloomberg Way was constituted by a particular imagining of the city as a space of government. This was an effort to appropriate the city in the imagination in order to govern and transform it (Harvey 2003, 51; Osborne and Rose 1998, 1). The annals of modern history are replete with similar attempts: Baron Haussmann's attempts to map Second Empire Paris using balloons and triangulation towers with an aim to reorganize the city according to the exigencies of a developing capitalism (Harvey 2003, 51); Lucio Costa and Oscar Niemeyer's conjuring of an efficient and just Brasilia from the wilds of central Brazil (Holston 1989); and Robert Moses's implementation of his vision of a rationalized New York metropolitan region knit together by highways and parkways, bridges, and tunnels (Caro 1975). But instead of the organic or mechanical metaphors that animated these efforts, the Bloomberg Way proposed a *corporate* vision of the city: the mayor as a CEO, the government as a private corporation, desirable residents and businesses as customers and clients, and the city itself as a product to be branded and marketed.

While a corporate-inspired approach to governance has been an important element of urban neoliberalization in many cities (Hackworth 2007, 10; Hall and Hubbard 1998a, 2), the Bloomberg Way was distinct both in the literality of the metaphor — after all, the mayor really had been a CEO! — and in the coherence and comprehensiveness of the policy interventions it inspired. From the synoptic conception of the city as a unified corporate entity in competition with other such entities flowed a program for governmental action. Viewed without reference to this broader vision, these interventions have been characterized in wildly divergent terms: as pragmatic and moderate (Ambinder

2008, inter alia); as tax-and-spend liberalism adorned by a bit of business-speak window dressing (Malanga 2003); as more of the same prodevelopment policies that have characterized the post-seventies fiscal crisis victory of "real estate over welfare state" (Moody 2007); as an instance of "continuing neoliberal hegemony" (Peck 2006a, 708); and as pragmatic progressivism by some mainstream liberals (Yglesias 2008). This book argues that these policies can only be truly understood in relation to this corporatized imagining of the city and its governance.

Ripple effects of this spatio-governmental urban imaginary flowed across municipal government. The characterization of the mayor as CEO, the city government as corporation, and the city's residents as customers had implications for governmental and mayoral accountability, citizen participation, and intergovernmental relations. These implications were not always in accord with commonly held norms of democratic process, local political mores, or fiscal prudence. The notion that the city was a product entailed the need to reshape New York City as an *urban environment* in accordance with its "brand," a fact that made urban and economic development policy a particularly salient policy area for the Bloomberg administration.[13] One redevelopment scheme, the Hudson Yards plan for the far west side of Manhattan, would become the most important element of the development strategy that flowed from the Bloomberg Way, serving as both keystone and microcosm. Moreover, the administration's efforts to finance, generate support for, and gain the necessary approvals of the plan from 2002 to 2005 would serve as the first great test of the political efficacy of the Bloomberg Way. Thus, the Hudson Yards plan will be much discussed in this book, particularly in the latter chapters.

The second urban imaginary that played a key role in the Bloomberg Way represented a particular vision of the social and cultural qualities of New York and New Yorkers that was clearly linked to class identity and experience. The city was imagined as a place of competition, elite sociality, cosmopolitanism, and luxury, populated by ambitious, creative, hardworking, and intelligent innovators. As the Bloomberg administration set about reshaping the city's landscape and economy, it did so in accordance with the qualities attributed to this imagined New York and to these imagined New Yorkers — and in conflict with those inherent in other such imaginings. This ensured that conflicts over the administration's urban and economic development policy would not be civil debates over the best technical "solutions" to the city's "problems" but pitched battles over what kind of city New York was, and what kind of city it would be.

Taken together, these two points — that the Bloomberg Way was not an expression of personality but of broader processes of class transformation, and that it was not devoid of ideology but rather brimming with it — lead directly to my characterization of the Bloomberg Way as deeply political, and to the conclusion that its most important politics were class politics.[14] Despite Mayor Bloomberg's avowed rejection of politics, and despite the commonly held idea that he and his administration were by virtue of wealth and governmental inexperience somehow "above" politics, the Bloomberg Way constituted an effort to establish the dominance of the ascendant postindustrial elite vis-à-vis other social groupings in New York City. This worked on several levels, which when taken together lead to the conclusion that the Bloomberg Way was neither apolitical nor a straightforward capture of state power by a nefarious capitalist cabal but was a rather more complex and profound undertaking: an effort to establish a new form of class hegemony in the city.[15]

The ways the Bloomberg Way proposed the city be governed and transformed ultimately satisfied the interests and desires of the members of the class alliance that played a crucial role in vaulting Michael Bloomberg to electoral victory in 2001, in staffing his administration, and in providing ongoing support for his mayoralty. By any conceivable statistical or qualitative measure, the 2000s were a good time to be a member of the city's postindustrial elite, as the industries they worked in thrived, their share of the city's income increased, and their cultural imprint on the city deepened (Bowles, Kotkin, and Giles 2009; Moody 2007; Moss n.d.; Renwick 2008). Of course, this was merely an extension of ongoing trends, as neoliberalization in New York City and elsewhere has clearly favored the interests of the PMC and TCC (Dumenil and Levy 2004b; Glaeser, Resseger, and Tobio 2008; Greenberg 2008, 227–251; Hackworth 2007). In the case of the Bloomberg Way, this was portrayed as a necessity generated by the realities of a more competitive, global space-economy, which forced cities like New York to do all they could to attract and retain well-educated and innovative people.

More distinctive was the fact that the Bloomberg Way did not just privilege the interests of postindustrial elites but was shaped in profound ways by their active participation in urban governance. The Bloomberg Way represented a remarkable episode of class mobilization. Michael Bloomberg, if the most important and catalytic, was just one of the many members of the PMC and TCC who moved into city hall in the 2000s. As they did so, they interpreted policy problems and formulated their solutions in ways consistent with their professional and class-inflected skills, desires, ideas, and experience. This injected class directly into the workings of city government, which had two effects. It "deepened" (Geertz 1973) urban governance for members of the postindustrial elite in city hall, transforming what might otherwise have been relatively bloodless areas of policy and policy conflicts into matters bearing directly on their experience, identity, and status. And since, as the saying goes, personnel is policy, this ensured that the corporatism of the Bloomberg Way went all the way down, as it were, serving not as window dressing but as blueprint.

In advancing the interests of and mobilizing the city's postindustrial elite, the Bloomberg Way reflected extant class structures in New York City. But going further, there is some evidence that the Bloomberg Way also served to solidify and perhaps even generate the identity of this postindustrial elite. Through a variety of means — describing the city the way he did, showing respect for corporate management skills and professional expertise, pitching his development policy to a "target market" of the well-educated and ambitious, drawing politically inexperienced professionals and executives into city hall — Bloomberg served as a magnetic pole of class identity. He pulled together an inchoate mass of professionals, executives, and capitalists into a politically unified and mutually recognizing group — the "best and the brightest," to use the term that he used often (though with none of Halberstam's original irony). That is to say, there is evidence that the Bloomberg Way transformed urban governance into a moment in an ongoing process of class formation.

In any case, what these various forms of class politics added up to was a twofold assertion of class prerogative. First, the postindustrial elite sought to equate its own interests with the broader interests of the city as a whole. Second, its members — and especially its TCC members — sought to portray their leadership of the city as indispensable. Thus, the Bloomberg Way as a mode of governance was crucial to establishment of a new class hegemony in New York City. This process was one of conflict and struggle, as the Bloomberg Way upset existing balances of power that had been established during the city's post–fiscal crisis neoliberalization, most notably the ongoing dominance of the city's real estate interests, which included representatives of capital, labor, and the professions. While this bloc remained powerful, the Bloomberg Way converted the local state into a vehicle by which the ascendant postindustrial elite, and again the TCC in particular, achieved a seat not just at the table of power but at its head. The Bloomberg Way, far from being above politics, was deeply implicated in ongoing struggles between various class groupings over who would lead the city into the twenty-first century.

To sum up, these are the arguments this book will make: that the Bloomberg Way represented a coherent, ideological, and radical approach to urban governance; that its emergence must be understood in the context of New York City's history, particularly its post–fiscal crisis political-economic transformation; and that it was fundamentally a class project, aimed at transforming governance and ultimately the city itself in line with a set of class-based interests, understandings, and desires. This book explores the effectiveness of the Bloomberg Way in advancing this class-based agenda, with a particular focus on its effectiveness in the contentious arena of development politics. It does so, first, by focusing on the concomitant construction of the Bloomberg administration and the Bloomberg Way during the early years of its first term and, second, by analyzing how the Bloomberg Way shaped the development and debate over the Hudson Yards plan. I argue that in these two processes the relationship between class transformation (a social process) and neoliberal urban governance (a political one) was mediated by a cultural phenomenon — the urban imaginary. It was this linking that made the Bloomberg Way, despite its limits, so powerful. Indeed, it is this linking of class, governance, and imaginary that was crucial to the process of class supersession whereby the city's postindustrial elite was able to successfully assert its leadership of the city.

METHODS AND PLAN OF THE BOOK

Having outlined this book's central arguments, let me turn to its structure, research methodologies, and data. The ethnographic research that forms the core of this book took place in New York City from September 2003 to July 2005. During this period of time, I attended conferences, city council hearings and voting sessions, community board meetings, speeches, community forums, community group meetings, strategy sessions conducted by activists, planning commission meetings, and government agency board meetings. I also conducted several dozen interviews with governmental officials and staff, researchers, advocates, activists, urban planners, journalists, businesspeople, pundits, and regular citizens involved in debates over economic development and urban redevelopment. My primary focus was on various forums in which debates took place over the city's economy, its physical form, the proper role of the municipal government and of public spending and subsidy, the distribution and redistribution of its tax burden and wealth, the nature and importance of a good business climate and of interurban competition, and a host of other issues. Interviews were primarily used to explicate what had taken place in public meetings, to draw out the understandings various actors held about economic and urban development policy, and to obtain information concerning events and processes occurring out of public view. These included internal reorganizations of government agencies, changes in the makeup and focus of advocacy groups, bureaucratic infighting and politics, and shifting relationships among various political groupings within the city. While many of these interviews were formal and "on the record," many others were not. I have cited interviews with my interlocutors who consented to being identified. In cases where they did not do so, I do not use formal citations, but rather describe their position and background in a manner general enough to protect their anonymity but specific enough to allow the reader to situate their words in the narrative.

This ethnographic research, and especially the participant observation component, coincided with public debate over the Hudson Yards plan. As a result, the latter chapters of this book, which address this debate, are more ethnographic in nature than earlier ones. Since this ethnographic research was limited to the period of time between late 2003 and mid-2005, I had to use a variety of other methods and sources to flesh out the relevant events of the first year and three-quarters of Mayor Bloomberg's first term (which began in January 2002), as well as to construct the longer-term history of development politics in New York City. Newspaper articles, transcripts of legislative hearings and conferences, published reports, government records and press releases, Web logs, and other secondary sources, as well as interviews (again both on and off the record), were used in this effort. All of these sources also provided invaluable access to a broader range of events and processes than could my ethnographic research alone.

This book is comprised of three rough sections. The first section consists of chapters 1 and 2 and establishes the short- and long-term contexts from which the Bloomberg administration emerged and which it encountered upon entering city hall in January 2002. Chapter 1 lays out the broader history of post–World War II governance and politics in New York City, with special focus on the post–fiscal crisis era. Chapter 2 describes Bloomberg's rise to political power, as well as the ways in which it was made possible by both national and local developments.

The second section of this work, consisting of chapters 3 through 5, shifts the focus to the Bloomberg administration. Chapters 3 and 4 address the Bloomberg Way itself, which explicitly conceived of the mayor as a CEO, the city as a corporation, businesses and residents as clients, and the city itself as a product. Chapter 3 lays out the ways in which the first two elements of the Bloomberg Way were manifested in city policy; chapter 4 outlines the manifestation in policy of the second two elements of the Bloomberg Way. Chapter 5 summarizes the Bloomberg Way and subjects its social, spatial, and political characteristics to theoretical interrogation.

The third section of this book, composed of chapters 6 through 9, addresses the efforts of the Bloomberg administration to gain support for and the approval of the Hudson Yards plan. Chapter 6 lays out the history of redevelopment proposals for the far west side of Manhattan, focusing on the revived elite campaigns to redevelop the area that emerged in the 1990s. The most important of these was that of NYC2012, the organization in charge of the city's Olympic bid. This chapter also lays out the details of the Hudson Yards plan as they existed in late 2001. Chapter 7 details the administration's claims that the Hudson Yards plan represented an exercise in cutting-edge urban planning shaped by the profession's best practices, along with discussion of the (largely negative) response to these claims. Chapter 8 describes how a "logic of investment" inspired the administration's efforts to justify the plan as an economic development endeavor. Chapter 9 discusses a final tactic the administration used to gain support for the plan: an appeal to New Yorkers' sense of identity through the mobilization of "urban patriotism." A final chapter outlines the development of the Bloomberg Way since 2005 and draws a number of conclusions concerning the Bloomberg Way's implications for understanding New York City politics and urban neoliberalism in general.

CHAPTER ONE

The Neoliberalization of Governance in New York City

The story of New York City's contemporary transformation is a familiar one. The prevalent mainstream narrative tells of the city's descent into disorder and crisis in the 1970s and its reemergence in the following decades as an economic powerhouse and a center of tourism, cultural production, and consumption. But critical urbanists have constructed a counternarrative of this period, which argues that the fiscal crisis of the 1970s provided an opportunity for elites to impose a regime of business-friendliness and austerity in the city. In the decades since, this neoliberal turn has resulted in a number of negative consequences: growing inequality and poverty; a drastic increase in the cost of living, particularly of housing; the loss of dignity, freedom, and occasionally life resulting from the aggressive police tactics ostensibly necessary to maintain order; and the demise of New York as a paradigm of urban grittiness and cultural ferment, symbolized by everything from the sanitization of Times Square to the shuttering of that famous 1970s incubator of punk and new wave, CBGB. Like the mainstream narrative, this counternarrative typically characterizes the fiscal crisis as a radical break in the city's history, as the era of post–World War II liberalism came to an end and the city's neoliberal era began.[1]

This chapter seeks to amend this critical narrative of New York City's recent history by drawing upon the understanding of neoliberalism laid out in the introduction. While acknowledging that the fiscal crisis period was a seminal event in the city's recent political-economic history, my argument departs from the standard critical narrative of this history in three key ways. First, I describe the city's neoliberalization not as an epochal shift in governance ushered in by the fiscal crisis but as a process that has significant continuities with the city's longer postwar history. While not without its novelties and inventions, this transformation of governance also reworked, rearticulated, disarticulated, revived, and reinvented governmental processes, understandings, and practices in order to create a coherent, if unstable, new formation. Second, while not understating the impact of neoliberalism on the city, I highlight its instabilities, contradictions, and failures. The neoliberalization of New York City has neither stamped out the political legacies of the postwar period nor set the city on a sustainable economic footing. Finally, I focus on the role of class in the neoliberalization of the city. Most critical narratives emphasize the intense class struggles that took place during the fiscal crisis; they tend to portray the city's elite in relatively static terms. In contrast, my analysis centers on the dynamics of class transformation in the city, the impact on the composition of the city's elite, and the implications of both of these for urban governance.

Using these three themes, I discuss the local conditions that made possible the election of a CEO mayor and the subsequent emergence of the Bloomberg Way. I begin by providing background on the 1970s fiscal crisis, its class protagonists, its resolution, and the new priorities for urban governance that emerged from it. Then I turn to the neoliberalization process, focusing on politics and the local state in turn. I call attention to both the successful establishment of neoliberal governmental norms and the limitations and contradictions of neoliberalization, as both were crucial to Michael Bloomberg's political rise. I then discuss the processes of class transformation that emerged in the post–fiscal crisis period, as economic transformations facilitated by shifts in the city's governance helped constitute an ascendant postindustrial elite whose members eventually became agents of the Bloomberg Way. Finally, I examine this group's initial foray into local politics, the bid for New York City to host the Summer Olympic Games.

FROM GOLDEN AGE TO FISCAL CRISIS

For a significant portion of New York City's working class, the postwar years were something of a golden age. The city during this period was characterized by labor strength, a strong and diversified economy with a large goods production and distribution sector, well-paying union jobs, and federal support for liberal urban government. All this provided the city's working class with a modicum of material comfort and social mobility, much of it channeled through the local state: decent health and pension benefits, access to adequate housing, a set of cultural institutions accessible to the public, and opportunities for higher education at little or no cost (Freeman 2000). It is important not to overstate the progressivity of postwar New York: besides deeply rooted racial inequality (Gregory 1998), many of the trends that emerged in full force after the fiscal crisis of the 1970s were in place by the 1950s. Nevertheless, it was a city notably amenable to working-class interests.

Despite its power, the city's working class was just one of three key players in the political economy of postwar New York City. The second was the city's corporate sector, which included not just finance but a large insurance sector, as well as other business services (Freeman 2000, 20–21). While Wall Street itself accounted for a relatively small slice of employment, its wealth, its role as a holder and underwriter of city bonds, and its broader economic power gave it substantial local influence. Financial elites pushed policies supportive of both their own interests and those of the broader corporate sector, including development and transportation projects that would permit the growth of the city's CBD, fiscal practices that would safeguard the value of city bonds, and lower taxes on business (Shefter 1992, 56–67).

The third player was real estate. Sharon Zukin has remarked that "New York's main business is and always has been real estate development" (2002, 16). The influence, if not dominance, of the city's real estate elite has been endemic to modern New York City. The consistently profitable real estate industry converted its wealth into political power via the provision of tax revenue to the local state, jobs to citizens, and contributions to politicians. This real estate elite is a cross-class group that derives its livelihood either directly from the profitable development of land or from creating the conditions for such development to occur. Its most prominent and powerful members are real estate developers, including the city's well-established and close-knit real estate families, and more recently national and global real estate corporations. However, it also includes urban planners, urban experts, professionals, and managers who staff the governmental, quasi-governmental, and private organizations that create the legal, political, ideological, and physical conditions for the profitable development of the city's built environment.[2]

The city's real estate elite has pursued an identifiable development strategy, though one that functions in an ad hoc and piecemeal fashion. Robert Fitch has done the most to flesh out the consistency and coherence of this strategy over time, tracing it as far back as the Regional Plan Association's (RPA) first plan for the region, published in 1929.[3] He writes that "over the last three generations, the city has had a real estate strategy—expand the CBD [Central Business District]/shrink manufacturing—which it has presented as a jobs strategy" (1993, 49). The decades-long process of creating a postindustrial landscape full of office buildings and high-end housing has consistently been presented by members of the city's real estate elite as a necessary accommodation to the realities of global economic change. In fact, this process has been to a large degree animated by the exigencies of local real estate development.[4]

While the postwar power of the city's working class forced corporate and real estate elite groups into a stable, if uneasy, ruling alliance with labor, they still had sufficient power to extract significant benefits from the local state. The high levels of income taxation and spending on various social programs and services favorable to working-class interests were accompanied by broad exemptions of property taxes, especially for office buildings (McMahon and Siegel 2005; Sanjek 1998, 87–89), and generous support of urban redevelopment that met corporate and real estate needs (Schwartz 1993; Sites 2003, 37). In short, the local state, bolstered by federal largesse, served to preserve this tripartite alliance by providing benefits all around.

This arrangement proved unsustainable. By the mid-1960s, a slowdown in economic growth created national fiscal pressures that undermined the financial basis of postwar liberalism. The "unresolved questions of racial identity and politics" (Sugrue 2005, 10) that had plagued post–New Deal federal policy from its inception came to a head in cities during the 1960s, as African Americans' demands that postwar liberalism keep its promises ran headlong into whites' demands that it defend the prerogatives of homeownership and race (Katznelson 2005). The ongoing erosion of urban tax bases, produced by federally supported inner-city disinvestment and racially exclusive suburbanization (Jackson 1987, 190–218) exacerbated this intraliberal tension, as by the late 1960s it was clear that cities would have fewer resources with which to manage conflict than in the past. Fiscal, social, and political crises had become inextricably linked in American cities (Alcaly and Mermelstein 1977; Beauregard 2003; Shefter 1992; Sites 2003, 37). Such tensions and conflicts were felt nowhere more strongly than in New York City. Granting African Americans access to the benefits that white working-class New Yorkers had long enjoyed, while meeting continuing demands for corporate and real estate subsidies, would have been difficult even if the city was flush with tax revenue. But it was impossible given the city's deteriorating fiscal situation, a product of deindustrialization and suburbanization, exacerbated by a severe recession that hit the city in 1969.

Starting with Robert Wagner in the early 1960s, New York City mayors had used a series of questionable accounting practices to avoid confronting the city's growing — and linked — budgetary and political problems (Shefter 1992, 61). Most significant was the use of long-term borrowing (generally used to pay for capital investments in infrastructure or development projects) to pay short-term expenses. From 1970 to 1974, liberal Republican mayor John Lindsay drastically increased the city's long-term indebtedness (McMahon and Siegel 2005, 103), a process that could not have occurred if not abetted by the seven New York City banks that underwrote the vast majority of the city's municipal bonds (Brash 2003, 64). By early 1974, those banks had reevaluated the wisdom of holding New York's municipal bonds, and they began dumping billions of dollars of their own holdings in city bonds onto the market, even as they continued to underwrite new city borrowing. The upshot was a glut in New York City paper, which led to the city having to pay high interest rates when it could borrow. In March 1975, there was a complete collapse of the market for city bonds. Unable to borrow to meet its financial obligations, the city plunged into technical bankruptcy (Newfield and DuBrul 1981, 34–36). This fiscal crisis was quickly seized upon by an alliance of New York City elites, led by bankers but also including other corporate elites, real estate elites, and supportive politicians and media supporters, as an opportunity to reorient municipal policy and the city's political economy, as well as to restructure the city's ruling coalition by drastically reducing the power of labor and minorities.[5]

This elite gambit to reorient the priorities of the local state, restructure power relations, and discipline the poor and working classes was aided by a hospitable political context. On the local level, by the mid-1970s the air was thick with the backlash against postwar liberalism generated by racial conflicts over key municipal services. There was a sense (mostly among whites) that an overly generous and permissive liberal state had led to urban "disorder" and that retrenchment was required (Beauregard 2003; Freeman 2000, 228–255; Smith 1996; Vitale 2008, 59–73). On the national level, ascendant neoliberals and conservatives saw in the fiscal crisis an opportunity to use New York City as an object lesson by implementing such retrenchment in the symbolic capital of postwar urban liberalism (Harvey 2005, 46–47; Sites 2003, 36–42; Tabb 1982). This led to President Gerald Ford's (in)famous withholding of federal assistance until it was clear that it would be provided, in the words of Secretary of the Treasury William Simon, on terms "so punitive . . . that no city . . . would ever be tempted to go down the same road" (Lichten 1986, 189).

With these national and local political winds at their backs (though not without wide and strenuous protest and sporadic violence), business elites, in partnership with most of the city's political leadership, imposed a set of austerity measures that slashed city jobs and spending for both basic city services and physical infrastructure.[6] First cultivated in ad hoc, private organizations, this agenda was institutionalized under the auspices of the elite-dominated Municipal Assistance Corporation (MAC), a public finance corporation that provided the city with access to capital markets when capital was otherwise not available, and the New York State Emergency Financial Control Board (EFCB), which held veto power over the city's budgeting and spending policy.

Alongside this attempt to curtail liberal policies, the fiscal crisis period inaugurated new strategies aimed to place the city on sounder fiscal and economic footing, albeit in ways amenable to elite interests. "For New Yorkers," Harvey Savitch has written, "social equality has been translated into more jobs, and more jobs have been translated into a need to entice private investment" (1988, 276). The fiscal crisis era placed the attraction of private investment at the center of development policy, if not municipal governance overall, in New York City (Sites 2003, 40–41). Let us now turn to the post–fiscal crisis neoliberalization of New York City's governance.

NEOLIBERALIZATION AND POLITICS IN NEW YORK CITY

Clearly, the fiscal crisis period marked a pivot point in the city's governance, as political, fiscal, economic, and ideological realities were reformulated. The "new urban norms" (Sites 2003, 41) that emerged from the fiscal crisis — particularly those of private-sector intervention and privatist ideology — were crucially important to the election of the CEO mayor and the emergence of the Bloomberg Way. Indeed, the Bloomberg Way intensified and expanded many of the governmental practices that characterized post–fiscal crisis governance in New York City.

However, the conditions of possibility for the Bloomberg Way were shaped by the neoliberalization of New York City in less straightforward ways. The particular strategy for stimulating private investment pursued in New York City in the final decades of the twentieth century reflected both the interests of the elite groups that had emerged victorious from the fiscal crisis period and preexisting patterns of governmental practices and ideologies. This rootedness in local context bolstered neoliberalization but also imbued it with certain contradictions and weaknesses that prevented it from achieving the necessary coherence and comprehensiveness to succeed on its own terms — to achieve fiscal health, social stability, and sustained economic and job growth. So, while the post–fiscal crisis era did see the enrichment of a small, if highly visible, slice of the city's citizenry, the record of post–fiscal crisis governance in New York prior to Bloomberg's election had been one of recurring fiscal problems, periodic social unrest, and generally lackluster economic growth (Brash 2004; Malanga 2005; Sites 2003, 46–66). Only during a brief period in the late 1990s did the city see budget surpluses, robust job growth, and high levels of economic growth, and even this period was marred by racial conflict, protest, and growing economic inequality. The election of the CEO mayor and the development of the Bloomberg Way were premised on the notion that a revitalized and revised neoliberalization might deliver on its promises.

The Bloomberg Way represented a complex reworking of post–fiscal crisis neoliberalization, rather than its straightforward extension: while certain aspects of this process were intensified or expanded, others were curtailed or even reversed. Thus, it is necessary to explicate neoliberalization's achievements and limits. As I provide such an explication, I will use the words of one key figure in the fiscal crisis as a guide. According to Felix Rohatyn, the prominent investment banker and head of MAC who led the elite campaign to restructure the city's political economy during the fiscal crisis, that period saw the "direction and philosophy of a large unit of government . . . fundamentally and permanently changed as a result of the involvement (some would say the intrusion) of the private sector" (1983b, 157). We have already seen that the fiscal crisis period altered notions of what the central aim of local governance should be. As Rohatyn's words indicate, it also had important implications for *who* could legitimately govern, for how the practice of governance *should be* conducted, and for the organization and functioning of the institutions of local governance. In other words, the fiscal crisis reworked patterns of political mobilization, political ideology, and governmental practice.

Business Intervention in Governance

As has been the case in cities across North America, business elites have long been engaged in New York City's governance. The end of the nineteenth century, for instance, saw prominent private-sector elites, spurred by economic depression and corruption, organize a "Committee of Seventy" to support the election of William Strong, a prominent merchant who promised to "run the city purely on 'business principles'" (Burrows and Wallace 1999, 1194). The next few decades saw this dynamic repeat itself as coalitions of middle-class reformers and private-sector elites periodically pushed back against the "excesses" of political machines more friendly to working-class interests and supportive of higher levels of municipal spending (Shefter 1992). In the post–World War II period this cycle ended, as the local state's placation of corporate and real estate interests preempted the necessity for direct elite intervention into urban governance.

Thus began a process of change as this period of political stability and shared economic growth came to an end. The 1960s saw the emergence of a series of direct business-elite engagements in urban governance (Shefter 1992, 56–66), culminating in the establishment of the MAC and the EFCB during the fiscal crisis. Whatever legitimacy these organizations forfeited due to their general evasion of direct political challenge and democratic accountability (Lichten 1986, 203; Savitch 1988, 59–60) was returned by their depiction as vehicles for private-sector elites to make the "unpopular but necessary" decisions to "save New York City" (Rohatyn 1983b, 157, 158).

During the fiscal crisis, private-sector elites had exercised an extraordinary degree of control over policy. Despite the continued influence of the MAC and EFCB, their influence quickly waned. This was a result of both necessity, given the reassertion of norms of democratic accountability as the immediate crisis passed, and convenience, as the new mayor, Ed Koch, placed business concerns at the top of his agenda (Moody 2007, 62–92; Shefter 1992, 175–176; Sites 2003, 46–47). Nevertheless, private-sector elites still maintained a foothold within the city's governmental apparatus under Koch and his successor, David Dinkins. One site of this participation was in the numerous public–private partnerships focused on stimulating investment, among them the 42nd Street Development Corporation, the Partnership for New York City, and the Association for a Better New York. In addition, business elites often took governmental positions related to economic development, management, and finance.[7] The election of the liberal, if moderately so, Dinkins in 1989 generated a brief and effective resurgence of elite mobilization aimed at safeguarding the city's neoliberalization. Faced with this unrest (and looming fiscal problems), Dinkins quickly capitulated, absorbing private-sector elites and their priorities into his administration (Freeman 2000, 324; Moody 2007, 122–125; Sites 2003, 51–53).

Following Dinkins as mayor was Rudolph Giuliani, whose ideological hostility to urban liberalism and commitment to the accommodation and subsidization of the city's corporate sectors rendered private-sector elite intervention in governance largely unnecessary. In fact, the highly insular Giuliani administration had very little contact with business elites; Andrew Alper, an investment banker who would enter the Bloomberg administration in 2002, told me that virtually "no relationship" existed in the late 1990s between the Giuliani administration and high-level CEOs in the city (Alper 2007; see also Steinhauer 2002a).

Even if he had been so inclined, Mayor Giuliani would have been hardpressed to find business partners to engage with, as by the late 1990s, organizations like the Partnership for New York City and the Association for a Better New York functioned more like traditional policy organizations than channels of direct engagement in governance, a result not just of their earlier successes in reorienting policy but also of generational and economic change. The private-sector elites who had been active in the fiscal crisis and its immediate aftermath were getting older, while the new generation of corporate leaders who had risen in the booming "new economy" of the 1990s now headed transnational organizations, giving them a different sort of commitment to the city. When these business elites did choose to "give back" to the city, increasingly high-pressured corporate life made them more likely to donate their money than their time (Kolker 2001). However, efforts to recruit business elites developed as the 1990s came to a close, when fiscal problems again began to rear up and there were emerging concerns that the city government was not adequately preparing for continued economic growth. These efforts included a push to reinvigorate both ABNY (the Association for a Better New York) and the Partnership for New York City (Kolker 2001, 2002), as well as two elite campaigns aimed at reinvigorating urban development in the city: the Group of 35 and the bid for the Summer Olympics.

The fiscal crisis period normalized business-elite intervention, especially by financiers, in New York City's governance. It led to the creation of new institutional bases for such intervention, such as the MAC, the EFCB, and numerous public–private partnerships. While elite intervention in the city's governance flagged in the immediate postwar period, it had played an important role in New York City's political history. Thus, the post–fiscal crisis mobilization of private-sector elites was not so much a novel development as a reawakening. Indeed, it displayed significant continuities with earlier cases in terms of both agenda and makeup. As in the past, elites intervened during the fiscal crisis and its aftermath to promote business-friendly development and fiscal policies, reductions of city spending on "unproductive" functions like social programs, and a more professionalized and managerial approach to governance. Moreover, many elites came from the same social networks, firms, and even families as their antecedents.

Ideological Changes: Scarcity and Privatism

As John Clarke has noted, a number of processes, some associated with neoliberalization and others not, have recently conjoined in such a way as to make performance a "governmental obsession" (2004, 126). Important determinants of this development include the rise of fiscal consciousness (the focus on wasteful spending, affordability, and the idea of "doing more with less"), the increasingly common conception of the citizen as consumer (in this case of public services), and a growing skepticism about the efficacy of government. A focus on performance, as well as its companion, evaluation, serves to mediate tensions between, on the one hand, doubt about government efficacy and the widespread belief in the necessity of fiscal austerity and, on the other hand, the continuing demand for public services. Clarke observes that the "performance-evaluation nexus" offers a "technical fix," through which the application of ostensibly nonpolitical expertise and management skill, often drawn from or emulating the private sector, will permit the optimal use of governmental resources (2004, 133). The governance of post–fiscal crisis New York saw just such a turn toward managerialism, with particular emphasis on the superiority of private-sector techniques and conceptions.

If the vituperative sentiments of racial and political backlash that circulated in the pages of the city's newspapers and in the streets of its white ethnic neighborhoods during the fiscal crisis period served as the id of the austerity program that emerged from it, its ego was provided by the technocratic language of fiscal management. The fact that urban crisis emerged as *fiscal* crisis led to the notion that balancing budgets, implementing cost-saving measures and financial plans, and ensuring access to bond markets were to be prioritized over all other governmental activities. Such claims depoliticized what were in fact highly political matters concerning the distribution of costs and benefits among groups, and represented one of the chief ideological legacies of the fiscal crisis period (Brash 2003; Fuchs 1992, 283–284).[8]

This ideological shift was linked to the increased participation of business in governance. Such intervention helped bolster the image of the private sector as inherently more efficient than the public sector and thus spurred the importing of private-sector practices, personnel, and conceptions into city government. While Mayor Lindsay had made limited efforts to bring private-sector management techniques into urban governance (Fainstein and Fainstein 1984, 14), the first post–fiscal crisis mayor, Ed Koch, explicitly promised to run the city "on a businesslike basis" (Macchiarolla 1986, 129). This promise was echoed by David Dinkins and to an even greater degree by Rudy Giuliani. While a focus on budget balancing has been a constant of post–fiscal crisis governance, concrete policy changes in accord with business rhetoric have been haphazard and uneven, limited to the occasional importing of certain private-sector practices like marketing (Greenberg 2000) into city government and the privatization of city services (Weikart 2001).

The depoliticizing emphasis on "management" and private-sector techniques was supplemented by and joined to an "ideology of scarcity" (Lichten 1986, 50–51) that emerged directly from the fiscal crisis period. The ideology of scarcity took as its object the *ends* rather than the means of governance, positing that the level of public services and social welfarism that had been the norm in the pre–fiscal crisis era was no longer affordable given the constraints of interurban competition and declining federal largesse. Thus, budget balancing during the fiscal crisis period and its immediate aftermath was achieved primarily through service cutting rather than through raising taxes (Tabb 1982). In the long term, the ideology of scarcity served to reorient basic notions about the role and agents of governance in New York City. Henceforth, city services would have to be justified "in a discourse that accepted governmental solvency as the highest social goal and left unchallenged the notion that there were insufficient economic resources available to undertake even the most obviously needed and beneficial government programs" (Freeman 2000, 281).

The ostensible lessons of the fiscal crisis, that government needed to act more like a business and needed to respect the limits of affordability, quickly became governmental common sense in New York City. This was true for politicians and interest groups across the mainstream political spectrum, including chastised labor and community groups (Savitch 1988, 59, 276). Thus, even when the intervention of private-sector elites declined, it became increasingly difficult to articulate a coherent alternative to the post–fiscal crisis consensus. Even David Dinkins, who proposed alternative models of community development and a renewed commitment to equality, "racial healing," and social justice, in practice demonstrated fealty to post–fiscal crisis common sense, especially after the effort on the part of private-sector elites to prevent liberal backsliding (Angotti 2008, 227; Freeman 2000, 324; Sites 2003, 52–53).

The private-sector elite intervention during the fiscal crisis period was about changing hearts and minds as much as it was about cutting services, reducing the tax burden on business, and reorienting governmental priorities. While standards of democratic accountability, however weakened, prevented direct control of the city's affairs by the MAC or the EFCB, the discrediting of liberalism and the concomitant construction of the ideologies of privatism and scarcity made such heavy-handed intervention, for the most part, unnecessary.

Liberal New York without Liberalism

The normalization and reinvigoration of private-sector intervention in governance and the development of a new governmental common sense of privatism and scarcity in the decades after the fiscal crisis both supported austerity and business-friendliness and significantly undermined liberalism's legitimacy and effectiveness. But these two elements of New York City's post–fiscal crisis neoliberalization have not been without limitations and challenges. For after a quarter decade of neoliberalization, governmental practice was still decidedly "liberal." Indeed, for an American city, New York's governance remained notably redistributive, social-welfarist, and accommodating of difference. While the post–fiscal crisis era did see a "*reorientation* of [government] spending in a new direction, and in the name of new priorities" (Greenberg 2000, 243), it did not result in sustained reductions in government spending overall. Annual spending increases have been the norm since the early 1980s, and even spending on redistribution, social services, and other "unproductive" functions has been maintained, and even expanded, in the post–fiscal crisis era (Brecher and Horton 1991; Mollenkopf 1992, 9; Mollenkopf 2003, 122; Shefter 1992, 195–199). Likewise, while municipal unions were chastened during the fiscal crisis period and had to make numerous concessions, they continued to provide their members with relatively generous wages and benefits and strong job protections (Freeman 2000, 324–325). The post–fiscal crisis period saw relatively successful efforts to integrate the civil service (Waldinger 2000, 206–253) and a general rejection of policies inimical to immigrants (Ritthichai 2003). Such liberal residuals helped create a contradictory situation whereby neoliberalizing New York City remained a symbol of profligate liberalism. Two factors account for this situation. First, many of the private-sector elites who engineered the resolution of the fiscal crisis and who were prominent in maintaining the post–fiscal crisis consensus were not free market ideologues like Ronald Reagan or Margaret Thatcher. Many, including Felix Rohatyn, were self-described "liberal Democrats," embracing a relatively prominent role for government in sparking and directing economic growth; in sustaining an effective, if scaled-back, and "affordable" welfare state; and in creating a legitimate, if again scaled-back, role for unions (Lichten 1986, 197–202; Rohatyn 1983a, 2009; Ross 1987). Their aim was a reorientation of liberalism toward corporatism and "pragmatism," rather than its eradication.

Second, even if these private-sector elites had sought to eradicate liberal state practice in New York City, they would have encountered major political obstacles. Even after the fiscal crisis period, there remained significant sources of minority and working-class power. While the power of organized labor had declined significantly and its agenda had been narrowed, unions, particularly municipal and construction unions, remained relatively powerful in the city (Freeman 2000, 324–325; Moody 2007, 288; Shefter 1992, 163–165). The electoral power of African Americans and their representation in certain portions of the political system constituted a bulwark of liberal policies, even if New York City did not, as did many other cities, see the emergence of a stable biracial liberal coalition able to place the power of the mayoralty and other citywide positions into the hands of African Americans or other minorities (Mollenkopf 2003). Advocates for the poor continued to form a politically important constituency, though they were derided by conservatives and even some white liberals as "poverty pimps" purveying victimhood, racial grievance, and dependency (Sleeper 1991). In addition, their relatively powerless constituency made them vulnerable to symbolic assuagements coupled with actual decreases in public assistance to poor people (Brecher and Horton 1991; Moody 2007, 151). Community planning, deeply rooted in the city's liberal traditions and historically linked to the anti–urban renewal, civil rights, and tenants' rights movements, remained a vibrant source of opposition to elite strategies of urban development (Angotti 2008). Finally, neoliberal governance generated its own opposition, including forms of cultural protest, ethnic organization, and labor politics.[9]

Thus, in the post–fiscal crisis period urban liberalism and tolerance existed side-by-side with austerity and revanchism. The shift toward a neoliberalization of the city's governance did curtail the ability of the working classes and minorities to push for their preferred policies. Private-sector elites, themselves generally not susceptible to the most strident free-market ideology, and mayors, now the guardians of fiscal discipline, nonetheless had to accommodate, co-opt, or confront the realities of working-class and minority political power. However, whether old or new, opposition to neoliberalization was defensive, piecemeal, reactive, and geographically isolated, and it did not coalesce to produce a coherent, comprehensive, citywide alternative approach to governance. Despite Felix Rohatyn's claim that the "direction and philosophy" of New York City governance had been "fundamentally and permanently changed," what actually emerged in the post–fiscal crisis era was a more ambiguous political situation. To use a martial metaphor, post–fiscal crisis neoliberalization had managed to push the front forward, but it had not won the class war. As we shall see, the Bloomberg Way promised to do just that.

RESTRUCTURING THE LOCAL STATE

The politics of the post–fiscal crisis period in large part centered on the distribution of costs and benefits of state policy among various social groupings within the city. Yet they also, particularly in their ideological aspects, centered on claims that the neoliberalizing of governance in New York City would deliver fiscal stability, social peace, and economic and job growth. The notion that the local state needed to become more "business friendly" was portrayed as a boon not just for business elites but for the city as a whole. Thus, restructuring the local state was imbued with political significance, as it was crucial to ensuring the efficacy, and therefore the legitimacy, of post–fiscal crisis neoliberalization.

Despite its explicit embrace of free markets and its concomitant condemnation of activist government, "neoliberalization often involves more, not less, state intervention" (England et al. 2007, 179). Accompanying the "rolling back" of state functions, aimed at redistribution or the maintenance of social welfare, has been the "rolling out" of new state forms and practices (Peck and Tickell 2002, 388–390). In the United States, this has meant that austerity and privatization have been paired with the spread and growing importance of "economic development policy," typically entailing a pronounced level of state intervention, albeit toward the end of enhancing interurban competitiveness (Eisinger 1988). Neoliberal hopes that economic development would be the yang to austerity and privatization's yin have been disappointed, as it is now clear that these two aspects of neoliberalism often generate contradictory results. While clearly supportive of elite economic interests, privatization and austerity, particularly the withdrawal of resources from the development and maintenance of physical and social infrastructure, can have the ironic effect of actually reducing the capacity of the state to act in a coherent and coordinated manner to facilitate economic development (Brenner and Theodore 2005, 102–103; Sites 2003, 17–18).

This captures the dynamic active in New York City between the fiscal crisis period and 2001. While post–fiscal crisis austerity, privatism, and privatization did make New York a more hospitable place for business, they also made it exceedingly difficult to develop and implement a long-term agenda for economic growth and development potentially able to set the city on sounder fiscal and economic footing. Moreover, this contradiction was reinforced by the fact that certain governmental practices that comprised neoliberalization — most notably the privatization and fragmentation of the state's urban development functions — predated the fiscal crisis and reflected the interests of the city's real estate elite. In other words, overcoming the contradictions inherent in the neoliberalization of the local state required actions that might well be directly opposed to the interests of one of its key constituencies.

Austerity and the Neoliberal State

Spending cuts during the fiscal crisis, the strictures of post–fiscal crisis ideologies of privatism and scarcity, and the rapid reduction of federal support for cities precluded reliance on capital spending or any other relatively expensive forms of public investment (in education or affordable housing, for example) by the local state as it sought to enhance New York's ability to attract and retain business. What emerged instead was economic development on the cheap.

A prime example of this is the fate of the capital budget during the fiscal crisis and its aftermath. Before the crisis, the capital budget, funded by long-term borrowing and intended to provide funding for productive investments in physical infrastructure, was increasingly used to finance operating expenses (that is, the day-to-day costs of running the city). This verboten and unsustainable practice damaged the city's short- and long-term finances, resulting in crushing debt service payments (which came out of the operating budget) and the siphoning off of funds from productive long-term expenses toward short-term ones, which included many of the aspects of liberal governance that the city's private-sector elites wanted to roll back. This made the capital budget a prime target during the fiscal crisis period, and it was drastically reduced from 1975 to 1978 (Shefter 1992, 138). Despite a brief recovery (and redirection toward projects related to the twin goals of economic development and ensuring urban order) during the 1980s, the capital budget never recovered from these cuts (Fuchs 1992, 131; New York City Independent Budget Office 2004a). By 2001, capital spending had been insufficient to properly maintain physical infrastructure systems like transportation and water supply, let alone to expand their capacity in line with increases in population and trade (Fainstein et al. 1989, 82; New York State Advisory Panel on Transportation Policy for 2025 2004). Moreover, the fact that the City Planning Commission (CPC) had lost control over capital spending during the fiscal crisis (Sites 2003, 45) meant that such spending during the 1980s and 1990s was typically reactive, rather than a means to proactively shape the city's physical development. Even just after the 1989 post–fiscal crisis peak in capital spending and before the 1990s erosion in such spending, Martin Shefter concluded that the "attractiveness of New York [as a place of business] has . . . been impaired by the deterioration of the city's physical infrastructure" (1992, 143).

Another example was the central role that tax policy came to play in economic development (Brash 2004, 86–90; Moody 2007, 69–70; Sites 2003, 40). Through targeted tax-incentive programs, reduced taxes on business and property, and discretionary tax subsidies to individual corporations, the local state essentially substituted the forsaking of revenue for direct expenditures. These tax reductions were consistent with prevailing ideological winds, were politically expedient for mayors dedicated to reducing city spending, and did help reduce the costs of doing business in the city. However, as well as being of questionable effectiveness in generating job growth (Brash 2004, 88–89), such use of taxes in development policy ceded the initiative for development to firms. Moreover, the billions of dollars of revenue forsaken as a result of these tax reductions deprived the local state of resources that might have been spent on more effective means toward neoliberal ends (Brash 2004, 88). The reliance on tax policy precluded a proactive, coherent, and comprehensive approach to economic development in post–fiscal crisis New York City.

There was a brief period in the second half of the 1990s where it did seem like economic development on the cheap married to revanchist social regulation might serve as a new basis for economic growth in the city. Aggressive policing strategies, punitive welfare reform, a renewed emphasis on tax incentives and reductions, and a willingness to allow private real estate development to proceed virtually unchecked came together in the context of a massive stock market bubble to create several years of economic growth, job growth, and budget surpluses (Sites 2003, 56–66; Smith 1996; Vitale 2008).

However, even this seeming fulfillment of the promises of the post–fiscal crisis consensus had terminal flaws. Alongside growing inequality, housing inaffordability, and racial unrest generated by aggressive policing strategies, fiscal overdependence on the volatile financial industries led to high budget deficits as the stock market bubble deflated toward the end of Giuliani's second term (Brash 2004, 90–91). Moreover, the limitations of tax policy as the central tenet of economic development policy became abundantly evident as it reached its zenith during the Giuliani administration. On the one hand, job retention tax breaks were flowing to corporations that clearly had no intention of leaving the city and corporations who entered into such tax incentive agreements routinely violated their terms; on the other, forgoing so much tax revenue precluded substantial investment in urban development that might support economic development or in the city's public education system, seen as a crucial resource for the development of a postindustrial work force. Finally, the Giuliani administration's antipathy toward urban planning made it difficult for the more far-sighted elements of the city's business and real estate circles to develop and implement any sort of long-term strategy that might profitably coordinate private real estate development with state actions, such as rezonings and investment in transportation, green space, and other physical infrastructure.

The Fragmentation of Development Policy and Its Beneficiaries

Along with austerity, privatization and privatism also impeded the ability of the local state to generate a coordinated and coherent economic development strategy that might fulfill neoliberalization's promises. Public–private partnerships typically were narrowly focused on particular urban or economic development projects, and so they rarely worked in coordination with each other, typically cooperating with mainline city agencies only in regards to project-specific issues. This, along with the evisceration of the power of the Department of City Planning (DCP) during the fiscal crisis, mitigated against the construction of a coherent, citywide approach to development (Savitch 1988, 59–60, 276).

Exacerbating this situation was the fact that public–private partnerships often served as arenas of private-sector elite engagement in urban governance,
since development was seen as particularly amenable to private-sector con-
ceptualizations and practices. Such organizations typically were run more like
private corporations than agencies of the city government, and their employees
had demographic backgrounds, educational achievement, social networks, and
salaries more like those of workers in the private sector (and especially the
postindustrial sectors) than in mainline government agencies. These entities
generally housed the specific private-sector practices imported into post–fiscal
crisis governance, such as branding (Greenberg 2008) or the increasingly complex financial schemes necessary to fund projects in the context of limited capital spending and decreasing federal support for urban development (Sagalyn
2001, 71–74). Relevant expertise could generally only be found among those
with significant private-sector experience. This cross-fertilization with the city's
private sector increased the isolation of these organizations from city government more broadly.

There was one public–private hybrid whose "boundaries were coextensive
with the city's" (Fainstein 2001a, 112) and thus had the potential at least to serve
a coordinating function. This was the Economic Development Corporation
(EDC), a nonprofit local development corporation that served as a broker of
sorts for particular development deals by bundling tax abatements, public
funding, and site improvements, as well as acting as a liaison to both the private sector and the state government (Fainstein et al. 1989, 71).[10] Though owned
by the city government, with a board appointed by the mayor and other city
officials, the EDC was not funded via the normal city budgeting process, instead
funding itself out of returns from its own projects. It was also not subject to the
city's Uniform Land Use Review Procedure (ULURP), which requires that major
land use changes receive the approval of the DCP and then the city council, or
to other forms of city council oversight.[11] This insulation from normal budgetary processes and direct political accountability led to the EDC often serving as
a means for mayors to implement favored deals, projects, and policies (Angotti
2008, 170). So, while EDC's citywide purview gave it the potential to coordinate
development, prior to 2001 it had not served this function. The city's leading
economic development agency remained relatively autonomous and isolated,
undercutting the ability of the local state to pursue development policy in a
coherent and comprehensive manner.

Post–fiscal crisis privatism and privatization did not cause the fragmentation of the local state, though they certainly intensified it. Public–private partnerships had played an important role in New York City since before World

War II (Fainstein et al. 1989, 56; Sites 2003, 43). Despite the perception that the Moses era saw an unleashing of the unrestrained power of the modern state to mold urban development (Scott 1998, 88), "the privatization of public decisions remained casual and pervasive throughout" the era, as Moses "offered [private interests] virtually every public subsidy that his legal draftsmen could lay their hands on" (Schwartz 1993, 304, 300). Robert Fitch notes that most planning and development schemes in New York since the late 1920s have been initiated by the private sector and then given crucial support and assistance by the local state (1993, 39–42). State-supported development typically proceeded on an ad hoc, parcel-by-parcel or project-by-project basis according to the exigencies of short-term real estate profit, rather than to broader, long-term development goals. Moreover, the use of public–private entities relatively unconstrained by accountability to legislatures or the public helped real estate interests evade the consequences of popular opposition. In short, the privatization and concomitant fragmentation of the local state's development function constituted, paradoxically, a coherent development strategy, one that served the interests of the city's entrenched real estate interests.

That is not to say that there were not periodic attempts to develop broader and more coherent approaches to the city's development. Moses, while clearly still working in league with private interests, implemented a regional program of transportation, redevelopment, and infrastructure investments that used federal money and the power of the local state to cope with automobilization, the suburbanization of both industry and the middle and upper classes, and the growing presence of agglomerations of African Americans in close proximity to the CBD. In the 1960s, in reaction to suburbanization and social and racial unrest, the Lindsay administration, working in league with members of the city's real estate elite, prominent planners, and advocates for the poor and minorities, created an ambitious master plan that sought to marry the expansion of the postindustrial CBD with community planning and high levels of support for redistribution and social welfare (Fainstein et al. 1989, 58–60).

Indeed, the contradictory position that urban planners and other urban experts occupy within the city's real estate elite has ensured both the periodic emergence of attempts to coordinate development in the city and the ineffectiveness of these attempts. On the one hand, planners' professionally ingrained commitments push them to formulate plans that might sacrifice the imperatives of real estate profitability to the rationalization of urban and metropolitan space and the "public interest" (Angotti 2008, 69). On the other hand, the privatization of development functions ensures that most New York City planners have found employment in the very public–private partnerships, private planning groups, development corporations, and public authorities through which the exigencies of real estate profitability are channeled (Doig 2002; Tobin 1953). This contradiction has been patched over in a number of ways: by equating the profitable development of real estate with the public interest, an elision that has grown particularly strong in the post–fiscal crisis era (Schwartz 1993); by denying the existence of conflicts of interest and assuming that consensus around technical solutions can be reached (Angotti 2008, 29; Marcuse 2002, 160–161); by depicting the dominant mode of planning in New York as the only possible response to broader political and economic trends (Fitch 1993, 37–55); or, more recently, by using contemporary planning orthodoxy, inspired by Jane Jacobs (1992) and centered on small-scale and focused plans, as a kind of post hoc justification for the general inattention to long-term, citywide planning. In these ways, the standard operating procedure of fragmented, privatized, and real estate development–driven planning is presented as being consistent with professional best practices, or even with a liberal concern about "saving the inner city" (Schwartz 1993, 3).

While certain aspects of plans to rationalize or coordinate development in the city, especially those consonant with the imperatives of real estate development, eventually came to fruition (Fitch 1993), more often they have been publicly celebrated and then studiously ignored (Angotti 2008, 68–69). The privatization and concomitant fragmentation of the state's planning power have supported real estate profits and thus have been the real estate elite's preferred mode of state action in the urban development arena. The contradiction between fragmentation and the fulfillment of neoliberalization's promises of economic growth, fiscal health, and social order was endemic to post–fiscal crisis New York City, as it was rooted in the key role that real estate interests played in the constitution of the elite alliance that emerged victorious from the fiscal crisis.

THE LIMITS AND POTENTIALITIES OF POST–FISCAL CRISIS NEOLIBERALIZATION

By the end of the 1990s, it was apparent that New York City's neoliberalization needed a shot in the arm. Two decades of austerity, privatization, and privatism had not set the city on sound fiscal footing, ensured sustained economic growth, or brought social peace. Even the enormous wealth that had flowed to the city's corporate and real estate elites seemed endangered, as the city was unable to provide a number of the ostensible necessities for the continued expansion of its postindustrial and real estate industries: a sound physical infrastructure, a decent school system, and support for CBD expansion.

It was unclear how these goals might be achieved. On the one hand, a further intensification of neoliberalization as currently constructed seemed politically impossible, given the continued, if lessened, power of the various constituents of liberalism. It seemed likely that the Giuliani administration had pushed that model to its limits, with the result being the (unsustainable and problematic) fulfillment of neoliberalism's promises of budget surpluses, economic growth, and social order in the late 1990s. On the other hand, any effort to deploy the power of the local state to impose a more coherent and comprehensive development agenda would threaten the interests of real estate, and thus might undermine intra-elite peace. In sum, the balance of class forces that emerged after the fiscal crisis placed serious constraints on the ability of the local state to reconstruct neoliberalization on a new, more effective basis.

Despite this political dilemma and the fact that some elements of neoliberalization had reached the end of their useful life, the potential inherent in other elements remained unmet. Private-sector management and marketing techniques had been implemented in a haphazard, short-lived, and often superficial way. After the initial burst of direct private-sector elite intervention during and immediately following the fiscal crisis, private-sector elites had generally preferred sowing the fruits of the city's booming postindustrial economy to engaging directly in its governance. In addition, there were governmental practices that had been submerged during the post–fiscal crisis period that, if excavated, had the potential to aid neoliberalization in fulfilling its promises, the most important being the practice of comprehensive and coherent urban planning. The EDC and the DCP could, if given the proper charge and invigoration, serve to coordinate the construction and implementation of a citywide development agenda, and there were certainly many planners and other real estate elites who would gladly take part in such a task.[12]

However, incubating in the supercharged postindustrial economy was a new group of elites who were slowly developing the wealth, political and social networks, and collective identity that would permit them to take a far more active role in the city's governance — and in doing so to transform its neoliberalization. It is from this process of class formation that the Bloomberg administration and its corporate approach to governance, the Bloomberg Way, would emerge, and to which we now turn.

"THE BLOODLESS REVOLUTION"

In 1977, the journalist Ken Auletta published a cover article in *New York* magazine entitled "After the Bloodless Revolution." In the article, announced on the cover by an illustration of "an enormous angry, white, baby boy toppling skyscrapers like Godzilla" (Greenberg 2008, 238–239), Auletta argued that the fiscal crisis had seen a sudden restructuring of power in New York City. Whereas the city government used to cater to poor people, African Americans, immigrants, and the electorate at large, he claimed, now it was investors and elite white-collar workers — the postindustrial elite — who were the intended beneficiaries of local state action.

Auletta was correct in identifying this shift in priorities. However, he was wrong in assuming that the "revolution" was over in 1977. As the neoliberalization of the city's governance and the postindustrialization of its economy advanced over the next quarter of a century, the numbers and wealth of the city's postindustrial elite grew, as did the impact of its aesthetic and cultural tastes, its prominence in imaginings of the city, and its share of both the attention of local politicians and the largesse of the local state, as noted by a number of scholars (Brint 1992; Greenberg 2008, 238–239; Sassen 2001 [1991], 251–289; Sites 2003, 53). While such analyses have paid some attention to the internal differences in the developing postindustrial elite, I want to focus on the specificities of its makeup in some detail. I do this because the strengths and the limits of the Bloomberg Way as a mode of urban governance derived from its ability to both reflect and reinforce a class alliance between the two class groupings that together formed the city's postindustrial elite: a New York–centered fragment of the TCC, composed of chief executives and other high-level executives of transnational corporations, particularly in the financial, business services, and media sectors; and the upper ranks of the city's PMC, the well-educated and highly paid professionals who staffed the upper ranks of these corporations and other white-collar organizations.

New York City and the Transnational Capitalist Class

New York City, as a site of financial intermediation, has been central to the construction of transnational capitalism, as the engineering of a global financial system and the globalization of finance capital was a key element of this process (Robinson 2004, 51–52). New York City's longstanding status as a center of finance gave it an advantageous position as transnational capitalism emerged, permitting it to rise to a level of prominence shared by only a few other financial centers (Moody 2007, 98; Sassen 2001 [1991]). Moreover, New York's centrality to a number of other transnationalizing industries like business services, media, advertising, and cultural production, as well as its continued status as a hub of corporate headquarters for U.S.-based transnational corporations oriented toward the global marketplace (Sassen 1997, 180–181), deepened the economic linkages between New York City and transnational capitalism — and thus between New York City and the TCC. This worked in a number of ways.

First, New York City became an important site for the accumulation of TCC wealth. If TCC members in general received a disproportionately large share of the economic benefits of the transnationalization of capitalism (Piketty and Saez 2004; Rothkopf 2008, 68–69), patterns of growing inequality demonstrate that New York TCC members were no exception. There is evidence that the increasing inequality in the city was driven not just by the well-documented capture of a disproportionate amount of city income by well-off members of the city's salaried PMC (Fiscal Policy Institute 2002a; Mitchell 2002; Sassen 2001 [1991], 229–234) but also by realized capital gains (Moody 2007, 198–204; New York City Independent Budget Office 2000). Indeed, the fact that such returns on capital have represented a crucial and growing source of income for the city's very wealthy is a strong indicator that the TCC has lodged itself in the upper reaches of the city's socioeconomic structure.

Second, as members of the TCC became more closely tied to New York City, and in turn as financial elites in New York City became more transnational-ized, the city — and specific areas and institutions within it — became sites of TCC sociality and interaction. For example, in her study of investment bank-ers, Karen Ho notes that despite claims to "globality," a strong connection to New York City has been necessary for both status and career advancement (2005, 91). Moreover, philanthropy serves to link together TCC members as stewards of the city's most important cultural, educational, and medical institu-tions (Rothkopf 2008, 45). Finally, TCC consumption habits have created spaces for class formation via their effects on markets for luxury goods, housing, and retail space (Moody 2007, 205). As David Rothkopf points out, neighborhoods like the Upper East Side have been colonized by members of the TCC, with spe-cific residential buildings and restaurants serving as hubs of TCC activity (2008, 44–45). The urban environment itself has become central to TCC formation.

The changing composition of the city's leading business group, the Partnership for New York City, also demonstrates the growing transnational-ization of the city's largest employers, as well as a willingness of TCC members to engage in local politics, if in a limited way. When founded in 1979 in re-sponse to the fiscal crisis, the Partnership was composed largely of corporate executives drawn from New York–based banks and insurance companies. Even if their firms had national or even international branches, these executives had deep social and economic roots in the city. Over time, and through a series of organizational changes, the Partnership has transmuted into an organization whose mission is to represent the largest employers in New York, including both "New York–based business organizations [and] global business entit[ies] with a presence in New York City" (Partnership for New York City 2005). The membership of this "local" business advocacy organization has come to consist primarily of CEOs and other high-level executives of transnational corporations, that is, of TCC members. Thus it has emerged as a site of class mobilization and, potentially, of class formation for the TCC in New York City.

This emergence of New York City as a center of TCC formation in economic, cultural, social, and political terms is built on older patterns. For a long time, New York has been a financial center and a site of wealth, philanthropy has been a mode of upper-class formation in the city, and the Upper East Side has been a home to the nation's richest people. Even particular residences that Rothkopf mentions in his work have an enduring history, housing Rockefellers before financiers like Henry Kravis and Stephen Schwarzman moved in (2008, 45). The Partnership for New York City, increasingly representing global corporations, was founded by David Rockefeller, the scion of perhaps the most prominent of the city's old money families. Nevertheless the TCC's emergence in New York City represents a new development in the city's status as an incubator of economic elites. While connected to well-established elites by ties of lifestyle, sociality, philanthropy, business dealings, and so on, the TCC displays a set of cultural, social, and economic characteristics that distinguishes it from earlier cohorts of the city's superrich. Whereas the fortunes of the city's old-line elite, derived from robber baron–era extractive or productive industries (à la the Rockefellers) or from real estate development, were built up over decades, most of the city's TCC members' fortunes have been accumulated in a relatively short period of time, generally through the ownership and global investment of finance capital rather than through the cross-generational building and stewardship of a corporate enterprise (Moody 2007, 198–206). The difference is also marked by variations in cultural practices: while older elites have tended to cloak their philanthropy in anonymity (at least in regard to the public at large, if not each other), members of the TCC in New York City have been far more conspicuous about their philanthropic practices, as well as, for that matter, their opulent lifestyles (Moody 2007, 204; Shachtman 2000, 9). Perhaps the most important difference regards the nature of elite — and particularly financial elite — commitment to New York City. Despite its international dealings, the city's older financial elite had been built upon a local and national foundation. As the transnationalization of capitalism proceeded in the post–fiscal crisis period, a substantial portion of the city's financial elite now derived their commitment to New York from its status as a node in transnational networks of capital rather than as an agglomeration of nationally oriented banks.

For New York's TCC, the city has been a site of personal commitment, economic enrichment, sociality, and consumption — of class formation — as a transnational *and* urban space. However, the city did not generally serve as a site of *political* action for members of the TCC, their membership in the Partnership for New York City and philanthropy aside. In contrast to the financiers and corporate executives in the 1960s and 1970s, New York's TCC members did little to engage directly with the city's governance during their ascendance from the 1980s onward. With one exception discussed shortly, they did not translate their economic and cultural power into political power in New York City until Michael Bloomberg's mayoral campaign of 2001.

The Professional-Managerial Class in Post–Fiscal Crisis New York

The growth in the city's PMC in the last decades of the twentieth century built on New York City's longstanding status as a center of finance, business and legal services, media, and cultural industries. The city had a pronounced PMC presence as early as the 1860s (Burrows and Wallace 1999, 966), but during the post–fiscal crisis period, as the local state's economic and urban development policies accelerated the city's postindustrialization, the size and impact of the PMC in New York City reached new levels (Brint 1992; Drennan 1991; Sassen 2001 [1991]). This was particularly true of "upper professionals," as Steven Brint calls them: "people with highly valued intellectual resources, who typically work for powerful organizations and are involved with the cosmopolitan side of economic and cultural life in the city. These people include, for example, many corporate lawyers, accountants in the leading . . . firms, [members] of the major architectural firms, television executives, leading artists and designers, doctors in leading medical research hospitals, and researchers involved with important civic planning activities" (1992, 156), to which one might add corporate consultants and financial professionals. Upper professionals were often affiliated with the financial, media, and business services whose agglomeration made the city a critical node in transnational capitalism (Sassen 2001 [1991], 262–264). They also received a disproportionate share of the economic benefits stemming from the city's status as such in comparison to the vast majority of its salaried and waged workers, who saw their incomes stagnate or even drop in the post–fiscal crisis period (Moody 2007, 106; Sassen 2001 [1991], 201–250).

In the introduction, I noted that the increasing enrichment of upper professionals has had important effects on such cities, with gentrification being the most obvious example. And indeed, as studies too numerous to list have described, New York City has experienced widespread and intense gentrification in the post–fiscal crisis period, much of it driven by the expansion of the numbers and wealth of the city's upper professionals.[13] As Saskia Sassen notes, "The expansion of the numbers of professionals, especially in the high-income segment working and living in Manhattan, has been a central fact in the gentrification of several parts of the city" (2001 [1991], 266; see also Moody 2007, 78). Particularly after the early 1990s, gentrification was spurred and supported by the local state, as it sought to create space for upper professionals and profitable opportunities for real estate development (Hackworth 2002). As has been the case in cities across the globe (Smith 1996, 114), gentrifying neighborhoods in New York City have become centers of class formation for upper professionals. Shared habits of consumption, aesthetics, architecture, dress, household structure, socialization, and so on embodied class distinctions and provided a sense of mutual recognition among the city's ascendant PMC (Mele 2000, 220–310; Zukin 1989).

As with the TCC, there was little direct upper-professional engagement in the city's governance during the post–fiscal crisis period. Individual upper professionals moved in and out of city government and various public–private hybrids, but they did so individually and in accordance with the contingencies of particular career paths, rather than in a collective and self-aware way. Upper professional political activity in general was marked by a lack of coherence and collectivity (Brint 1992, 172–175). This did not mean that such New Yorkers lacked political influence. Instead, their political power functioned in more subtle and systemic ways. Upper professionals had long served as a target of the long-term postindustrial urban development strategy embraced by the city's real estate elite. As neoliberalization proceeded in the post–fiscal crisis era, politicians and the local state sought to create an urban environment hospitable to upper professionals and thus to ensure that the city as a whole would benefit from its perceived cultural, economic, and intellectual resources. The confluence of these two strategies in the post–fiscal crisis period resulted in a circular pattern, whereby the creation of a postindustrial built environment, and thus a postindustrial economy, led to a growing high-level PMC population, whose high-profile presence in turn created a continued impetus for policies and development projects perceived to be in keeping with their preferences. This deepened the postindustrial transformation of the city's economy and built environment, enhancing the position and visibility of upper professionals even further.

Despite these interventions, city economic and urban development policy generally focused on corporations rather than directly on upper professionals, primarily through the use of tax incentives intended to attract and retain firms or to stimulate the construction of office space. Even when upper professionals were targeted, the Koch, Dinkins, and Giuliani administrations often seemed out of sync with their cultural sensibilities and practices. The redevelopment of Times Square, for example, was a bit too gaudy and "Disney-fied," and Giuliani's attacks on "obscene" art displayed at the Brooklyn Museum probably alienated as many upper professionals as he attracted with his support of zero-tolerance policing. While New York City of the 1980s and 1990s was hospitable to upper professionals, as of the turn of the twenty-first century they had yet to find a true political champion.

The Unfulfilled "Bloodless Revolution"

The period after the fiscal crisis of the 1970s was one of profound social change in New York City. Accompanying the oft-described transformations in the city's economy and governance during this time was a transformation of the city's class structure: the ascendance of the city's postindustrial elite, composed of both TCC members and upper professionals. As this postindustrial elite grew in numbers, wealth, power, and prominence, it shaped the city through its own collective place-making practices, comprised of gentrification, residential concentration, consumption, philanthropy, and so on. New York City qua urban environment became a space of class formation for the postindustrial elite.

However, with the few exceptions enumerated above, as of the mid-1990s, this process of class transformation had not resulted in significant engagement in the city's governance on the part of its postindustrial elite. The primary beneficiaries of the city's "bloodless revolution," to return to Ken Auletta's formulation, were not themselves revolutionaries. That role had been played in the fiscal crisis and its aftermath by politicians, members of the city's real estate elite, and an older generation of corporate leaders whose influence on urban governance was progressively reduced by the passage of time and the transnationalization of finance and business services.

We might then characterize governance during the bulk of the post–fiscal crisis period as governance *for* the postindustrial elite rather than *by* the postindustrial elite. However, by the mid-1990s this situation was ripe for change. The neoliberalization of governance in New York City resulted in an ideological, organizational, and political context conducive to elite intervention. The increasingly self-aware postindustrial elite, committed to the city in a number of ways, served as a potential wellspring for such intervention. In 1994, this marriage of conditions and agency was consummated in the form of the campaign to bring the Summer Olympics to New York City, which served a crucial and transitional role in the later formation of the Bloomberg Way.

NYC2012 AND THE POLITICAL EMERGENCE OF THE POSTINDUSTRIAL ELITE

Like all great quests, New York City's bid for the 2012 Summer Olympic Games has its own origin myth, a myth that doubles as the story of the entrée of financier Daniel Doctoroff into city politics. Doctoroff, who founded and led the bid, has said he was first struck with the idea that the city should host the Games at a 1994 World Cup soccer match in New Jersey. "I'd been to the Super Bowl, the NBA Finals, the World Series, and only a month before I'd seen the Rangers win the Stanley Cup . . . but that soccer game turned out to be the most exciting event I'd ever seen," Doctoroff has said. "I was thinking the amazing thing about the New York area is, you could play that game with almost any two countries in the world and you'd generate the same amount of excitement . . . and I started wondering how it was that the world's most international city had never hosted the Olympics, the world's most international event" (Horowitz 2004). Doctoroff, a tall, youthful man blessed with a preternatural ability to maintain both a set jaw and an ingratiating grin, often came across as a naïve, Harold Hill–like figure as, throughout the late 1990s and early 2000s, he touted the pairing of New York, multicultural city of ambitious dreamers, and the Olympics, the ultimate expression of internationalism and peaceful competition. This public persona and the story of Doctoroff's "eureka moment" at the 1994 World Cup led to the media portraying this superrich investment banker as an unlikely entrant into the rough-and-tumble world of city development politics. Upon further scrutiny, however, things look a bit more complex.

Son of a judge and a psychologist, Doctoroff was educated in government at Harvard and in law at the University of Chicago and New York University before moving into corporate finance in the early 1980s. Though Doctoroff, born in Michigan, only came to New York because his wife accepted a job in the city after receiving her MBA, he quickly climbed into the rarified circles of Wall Street. After starting out at Lehman Brothers, he managed the diverse investments of Oak Hill Capital Partners, a private equity firm controlled by Texas oilman Robert Bass, before becoming a wealthy investor in his own right through his involvement in a broad array of companies and industries. Indeed, by the late 1990s Doctoroff's diverse portfolio included city real estate: he was the co-owner of several buildings on the far west side of Manhattan.[14]

Doctoroff was linked to the world of urban development by more than his investments. His mentor at Lehman Brothers had been Peter Solomon, a man deeply involved in city development politics. Solomon had served as deputy mayor for economic development under Mayor Koch and had led a 1978 study of the feasibility of holding the 1984 Olympic Games in the city. Such interests had clearly rubbed off on Doctoroff, as by the early 1990s he was an avid student of the city's development, counting among his favorite books *The Power Broker*, Robert Caro's (1975) biography of Robert Moses; and *The American City*, a treatise on urban planning by Alexander Garvin (2002), a prominent prodevelopment planner and member of the CPC.

Doctoroff was undoubtedly aware of the key role that urban development would play in the formulation of an Olympic bid, which was housed in a private organization known as NYC2012.[15] Indeed, in the eighteen months after his revelatory afternoon at the Meadowlands, Doctoroff brought a number of prominent real estate elites into nyc2012, many of whom hoped it would give a new lease on life to projects that had foundered for years in the face of political, funding, and regulatory difficulties. In fact, a number of individuals who had been a part of the Lindsay administration, the last city administration to engage in large-scale urban planning, joined forces with NYC2012. One example was Alexander Garvin himself, who had started his career as a housing official in that administration, and who agreed to be NYC2012's chief planner. Another was Jay Kriegel, who after serving in the Lindsay administration had gone on to a long and successful career in the city's development apparatus. In 2002, Kriegel had this to say about the bid:

> The Olympics host city is always chosen seven years before the games. There's no other event like it in the world, where we would have a date certain for the entire community to know that the world is going to come here. We know how long things get delayed in this town that have to be done. Let's pick your favorite one: the expansion of the convention center, the train to the plane. This is a forcing mechanism. It sort of creates an emergency control board for public projects not financed, that gets everybody galvanized with a quarterly report on how you're doing. (2002a)

Just as the Emergency Financial Control Board had served as a vehicle of an elite program of fiscal austerity, so, it was hoped, the "forcing mechanism" of a 2012 Olympic Games would allow the imposition of a stymied elite development agenda.

So it was unsurprising that the proposal Doctoroff presented to a powerful member of the city's real estate elite, Robert Kiley, head of the Partnership for New York City and a former head of the Metropolitan Transportation Authority (MTA) in April 1996 read like an elite wish list of development projects. Most important among these was the Hudson Yards plan, which included the all-important Olympic Stadium and which would transform an area of Manhattan, the far west side, long targeted by real estate elites for postindustrial development (the details of the development of this plan are laid out in chapter 6). Kiley was intrigued, and Doctoroff went on to develop a slick presentation that gained support among prominent politicians, real estate developers, corporate executives, and planners. By 2001, the roster of NYC2012's board read like a who's who of the city's elite and the organization had raised several million dollars in private donations, including a large sum from Michael Bloomberg.

Bringing the Olympics to New York City was about more than raising real estate values alone. As Tom Angotti has written, "The Olympics proposal projected the urban ideal of global capital" (2008, 213). Certainly, this kind of globalism had been used in the past as an ideological prop to urban redevelopment in the city (Fitch 1993, 170–177). In this case, though, globalism was more than this: it reflected an urban imaginary that was a product of a particular class experience, one held by the self-consciously global members of the city's ascendant TCC. Indeed, Doctoroff often justified the bid by celebrating the city as a place of arrival for the world's most ambitious and successful people:

> New York . . . is the City that represents everything the Olympics are all about. What do we mean? Well, if you really step back and think about the Olympics, and you think about what New York lives every day, they're the same things, whether that's bringing the world together in one place, whether that is competition — anyone who sets foot in New York knows this is the most competitive place on earth. . . . Ultimately I think what really draws most people to the Olympic Games is the athletes . . . pursuing their dreams against incredible odds, usually for no financial reward, and it all coming down to a fraction of a millimeter, a point, or maybe a fraction of a second. So, too, New York more than any place on earth is a magnet for people with dreams. People come here from around the world and have for 400 years to pursue dreams of getting rich, becoming a star, or most commonly, just a better life for themselves or their families. (Doctoroff 2002)

Doctoroff's founding and leadership of the city's Olympic bid was driven by a class-bound imagining of the city as a place of ambition, meritocracy, competition, and internationalism. Such an imagining could now be expressed directly in the place-making process, where it would encounter the exigencies of real estate profitability that also animated the bid and led to its support by real estate elites. So even if the bid was not necessarily inconsistent with this older agenda, and even if Doctoroff drew on his own connections and commonalities with the city's real estate elite, his leadership of NYC2012 served as an important bridge from a development politics structured by the power of real estate to one increasingly structured by the power of the postindustrial elite, whose presence in the city had grown with the post–fiscal crisis neoliberalization and postindustrialization of New York City.

In retrospect, it is clear that at the other end of that bridge was the Bloomberg Way. Years before Michael Bloomberg's mayoral campaign, another beneficiary of the city's "bloodless revolution" had inserted himself directly into that most central element in the city's political economy — real estate development — and into the development of an area, the far west side, that had long been targeted for redevelopment. Doctoroff's arrival on the scene was a watershed in New York City's class politics, the moment when the city's TCC first asserted itself as a player in the city's governance.

THE DIALECTICS OF NEOLIBERALIZATION

In this chapter, I have put forth an analysis of New York City's post–fiscal crisis era that takes seriously the notion that neoliberalization consists of an articulated ensemble of processes and practices and is itself constantly in a state of flux. In doing so, I have argued that the fiscal crisis period served not as a hinge between a liberal epoch and a neoliberal one but as a political crucible in which ongoing and new processes and practices were disarticulated, rearticulated, and articulated anew, in accordance with a shifting balance of political power within the city and a changing external political and economic context. The upshot of the fiscal crisis was not a completely dominant and monolithic new regime of governance. Instead, what emerged was a new bundle of governing practices — austerity, privatization, postindustrial urban development, neoconservative social regulation, a reliance on tax policy, state fragmentation, corporate subsidization, aggressive policing, and so on — animated by a new ideological configuration rejecting liberalism in favor of privatism, affordability, revanchism, competitiveness, and business-friendliness. All of this was far more hospitable to the elite interests who had through the fiscal crisis and its solution managed to take the upper hand in the city's politics.

This neoliberal transformation was limited and incomplete, however. The still considerable, if reduced, power of liberalism's constituencies and advocates prevented the complete eradication of liberal governing practices, and neolib-eralization generated its own resistance, if inchoate and piecemeal. Post–fiscal crisis neoliberalization had its own internal contradictions: austerity and the fragmentation and privatization of the local state made it difficult to develop and implement a coherent development agenda, as did the entrenched power of real estate interests.

As William Sites points out, the history of New York City's post–fiscal crisis neoliberalization can be read as entailing a series of efforts to overcome these contradictions and tensions (2003, 31–68). As of the turn of the twenty-first century, they had failed: well before the terrorist attacks of September 11, 2001, fiscal crisis and recession loomed once again. Yet this history of failure did not foreclose the possibility of neoliberal success. More could be done. Three decades of neoliberalized governance not only had failed to clear away the lega-cies of liberalism but had also failed to fully capitalize on the transformational potential inherent in many of its constituent governing practices. Privatization remained uneven and partial, private-sector elite intervention was sporadic, and privatism to a large degree served as window-dressing used by business-friendly politicians. Moreover, the post–fiscal crisis consensus had precluded certain pre–fiscal crisis practices, such as the state-led coordination of develop-ment policy, that might help neoliberalization achieve its aims.

Thus, if post–fiscal crisis neoliberalization was incomplete, contradictory, and unable to meet its own stated goals, it provided a wealth of materials that might be used to construct a different, more effective form of urban governance in keeping with its central aims. What was needed was a new agent of neolib-eralization able to draw on and add to these materials in new ways. Unleashed postindustrial development in the context of a transnationalizing capitalism had created a new cohort of private-sector elites, the city's TCC and its upper professionals, whose cultural and economic clout was only beginning to be matched by their political assertiveness. While Daniel Doctoroff's Olympic bid represented a first step in this direction, it was Michael Bloomberg's 2001 run for mayor that truly thrust the city's postindustrial elite into the center of its politics. Let us now turn to that campaign.

CHAPTER TWO

Electing the CEO Mayor

Daniel Doctoroff's leadership of NYC2012 represented the first time a member of the city's ascendant TCC became directly engaged in the city's governance. However, NYC2012 operated largely out of public view, and Doctoroff's influence derived from his connections among the city's elite. He did not, in other words, translate wealth, cultural power, and social ties into a popular following. In contrast, Michael Bloomberg's mayoral campaign represented a public claim to leadership of the city by the TCC and the broader postindustrial elite of which it was a part. Candidate Bloomberg brought TCC aspirations to leadership into the open by arguing that his private-sector experience made him uniquely qualified to guide the city at a time of crisis and instability. He did so by centering his campaign on the idea that, if elected, he would be a "CEO mayor."

The election of a CEO mayor, as well as the broader corporate approach to urban governance constituted by the Bloomberg Way, was made possible by the local practices, processes, and conceptions that emerged during the post–fiscal crisis neoliberalization of New York City. These local factors created conditions in which an innovative form of neoliberal urban governance might seem attractive to many New Yorkers. However, also crucial was a specific cultural-political formation that emerged on a national scale in the last three decades of the twentieth century: the figure of the charismatic CEO. The articulation of such local and national factors created the necessary conditions for the election of the CEO mayor and the emergence of the Bloomberg Way. However, it was ultimately a series of unforeseeable events during Bloomberg's 2001 campaign that led to his unlikely election as the city's 108th mayor. This chapter describes how the neoliberalization of New York City, the figure of the charismatic CEO, and political contingencies came together to propel Michael Bloomberg into city hall.[1]

THE CHARISMATIC CEO

"By the time of the '90s boom, CEOs became superheroes, accorded celebrity treatment and followed with . . . slavish scrutiny," business journalist James

Surowiecki has written (2002). In contrast with "the professional Organization Man who toiled in anonymity during the era of managerialism capitalism" (Khurana 2002, 71), Bill Gates, Ted Turner, Jack Welch, Steve Jobs, L. Dennis Kozlowski, and the granddaddy of all these celebrity CEOs, Lee Iacocca, are household names. Their ability to turn around struggling companies, to create shareholder value, and, in some cases, to even change the course of history while still relating to common people have made them grist for the mill of both the business press and the mainstream media. The veneration of hyper-successful business tycoons has a long history in the United States — witness the celebration of Gilded Age figures like Andrew Carnegie and John D. Rockefeller — and this most recent bout of businessman-worship has drawn on long-standing strains in American culture. Nevertheless, the figure of the charismatic CEO has its own unique characteristics reflecting the particular historical-geographical context in which it has emerged: the development of neoliberalism in the United States during the last three decades of the twentieth century, which brought with it class inequalities and new forms of corporate governance.

A key spark of neoliberalism in the United States was a decline in corporate profits and upper-class wealth in the late 1960s (Goode and Maskovsky 2001; Harvey 2005). These developments generated a powerful, organized backlash from American business that aimed to reverse such trends and construct institutional, legal, governmental, and cultural arrangements more to its liking. The efforts to roll back government regulations, unionization, and labor costs at the heart of the neoliberal project were accompanied by two important developments crucial to the rise of the figure of the charismatic CEO: the internal restructuring of corporate governance and the rehabilitation of the public image of business. While the latter is the focus of this chapter, the former is worthy of brief mention to demonstrate that the rise of the figure of the charismatic CEO has not been merely a cynical effort by a unified business elite to manipulate the masses. This cultural development signifies a real shift in the way American capitalism functions, entailing a transformation of intracorporate class politics as CEOs have sought to increase and defend their compensation and power. CEO self-regard and identity has also been transformed, as members and aspirants to the highest ranks of corporate power have sought to justify their increasing wealth and status.

Management scholars have described the changes in corporate governance that have occurred since the late 1960s as part of a shift from managerial to investor capitalism (Useem 1999). Declining profits and press reports of lavish perks led to a change in the perception of professional corporate executives from one of "enlightened corporate statesmen who balanced the competing concerns of corporate constituents . . . to that of a self-interested managerial class whose primary interest was taking advantage of weak shareholders" (Khurana 2002, 55). As corporate raiders bought and restructured poorly performing firms and as the institutional investors who had been slowly growing in power since the 1950s asserted themselves, pressure was placed on corporate boards and executives to make management more accountable for corporate performance. One solution was to reform the CEO selection process. This led corporate boards, fearful of accusations of cronyism, to focus on high-level executives of other companies, often from other industries, rather than on internal candidates. The result was an overvaluation of impressive but vague personal characteristics that could transfer across companies, such as "leadership," "charisma," and the ability to effect change, and a devaluation of technical qualifications and tendencies toward stability, consensus, and working within the frameworks of established rules and policies (Guthey 2001; Khurana 2002). This in turn led to an explosion in pay and benefits for executives lucky enough to be members of the small and exclusive club of those perceived to possess the desired qualities.

Also key to the entry of the charismatic CEO into public consciousness was a broader, multipronged campaign to rehabilitate both the image and the reality of American business. This campaign included efforts not just to enhance the influence and image of business in the media, academy, and other key institutions (Harvey 2005, 43–44) but also to cultivate an image of American business as characterized by nonconformity, constant innovation and change, and a rejection of hierarchy and traditionalism (Frank 1997). These cultural and political currents, along with the empowerment of shareholders in corporate governance, aided in the emergence of a discourse that equated free-market capitalism with freedom and democracy (Harvey 2005). As powerful as this discourse has proven to be, it has proven vulnerable to the contradiction, haunting American capitalism since the days of Alexis de Tocqueville, between freedom (that is, the nearly unrestrained rights of private property) and equality (Smith 2007, 10–13). One characteristic of the figure of the charismatic CEO allowed it to respond to the contradiction: as Mark Guthey has argued, the key element of the "narrative construction" of the charismatic CEO has been its reduction of "complex phenomena [to] a heroic tale of individual agency" (2001, 119).

Personalization and Power

The radical personalization inherent in the figure of the charismatic CEO works in several ways. Guthey (2001) and Rakesh Khurana (2002) have done much to explicate one key aspect of this personalization, the inextricable linkage of the identity of the charismatic CEO with the corporation he or she heads, both in the popular imagination and in the minds of the various actors participating in the hiring and firing of CEOs. Charismatic CEOs are seen not as one piece of the large and complex organization that is the modern corporation but as its cultural personification, quite literally the human face of capital.

In this, the charismatic CEO also personifies the immense power of capital to restructure social, economic, and political relations. Key here is understanding the nature of the "charisma" that the charismatic CEO is endowed with. Max Weber famously defined this term as follows: "A certain quality of an individual personality, by virtue of which s/he is set apart from ordinary people and treated as endowed with supernatural, superhuman, or at least specifically exceptional powers or qualities. Such powers or qualities are such as are not accessible to the ordinary person, but are regarded as of divine origin or as exemplary and on the basis of them the individual concerned is treated as a leader" (1947, 358–359).[2] Weber distinguished charismatic authority from that based on tradition and especially from that based on rational grounds, that is, the control of money and expertise. Yet, he pointed out that at the highest positions of large bureaucratic organizations premised on such control, there are "'offices' for which no technical qualifications are required. . . . At the top of the bureaucratic organization, there is necessarily an element that is not purely bureaucratic" (1947, 335). Thus, while the charismatic CEO may possess a high degree of managerial skill, experience, and/or knowledge of a particular firm or industry, this is not what sets him apart (Khurana 2002, 79). As Erica Schoenberger notes, even CEOs themselves do not base their claims to power and wealth on superior management skill per se:

> It seems that [CEOs] have their positions and incomes and power because of who they are. This encompasses the whole range of characteristics they have acknowledged or attributed to themselves — intuitive yet commonsensical, creative, ambitious, born to sell, enthusiastic, energetic, etc. Yet these are not especially rare attributes. They don't quite seem to account for the dramatic success of these men. Their real secret is that they are natural catalysts. Their being in the world causes change. This is the value they create and for which they are so fabulously rewarded. (2001, 295)

This echoes Khurana's argument that the charismatic CEO is seen as "a particular kind of person" — a leader rather than merely a manager (2002, 67). Moreover, this leadership is typically proved in times of trouble, as charismatic CEOs often achieve prominence through their rescue of failing companies (Khurana 2002, 152).

The quality of being a "natural catalyst" — or a "change agent," to use the term of management-theory art — is something inherent in these men's personalities (Khurana 2002, 153). Schoenberger writes that in the typical narrative of a CEO autobiography, "here the child really is the father of the man. He just needs to grow up, overcome all obstacles, and become himself so he can undertake his true mission, which is to change everyone and everything else. In a sense, these men are born to cause change, but they themselves are still" (2001, 294). The charismatic CEO is defined not by acquired managerial experience in itself but rather by the development of the efficacy inherent in his personality. The figure of the charismatic CEO personifies the ability to effect change, and more specifically the "revolutionizing of production [and] uninterrupted disturbance of all social conditions" that Karl Marx and Frederick Engels saw as a constant of capitalist society (1994, 161).

The Charismatic CEO and the Elision of Class

The personalization of capital and its power in the figure of the charismatic CEO has served to draw attention away from structural factors and toward the individuals running the country's largest corporations. This has been a necessary condition for the charismatic CEO to generate, as Paul Smith puts it, "acceptance in the principle of equality . . . even in the face of contradictory empirical evidence" (2007, 11). But the notion that charismatic CEOs might be endowed with extraordinary capacities does not necessarily mean that their wealth and power are legitimate, at least not in the egalitarian cultural terms of American democracy. Such legitimization has required a second, seemingly paradoxical, characterization of the charismatic CEO as, in certain ways at least, an ordinary person.

A number of scholars have identified the merging of the logic of capital accumulation and the dynamics of self-government and identity as endemic to neoliberal culture (Comaroff and Comaroff 2001; Kingfisher 2002a; Martin 2002; Rose 1999). Like omnipresent stock tickers, the spread of the 401(k), the growing accessibility of business media, and the like, the incursion of charismatic CEOs into everyday life and consciousness has been a key moment in the "entrepreneurialization of the self" (Gordon 1991, 44). Everyday people have been encouraged to identify themselves as CEOs: to speak like a CEO, think like a CEO, act like a CEO, and even parent like a CEO.[3]

This is a two-way process, as charismatic CEOs often are portrayed as similar to everyday people, if ineffably different from them. They have become, like Hollywood celebrities, a familiar part of daily life, their foibles and folkways splashed across television screens and magazine covers. This steady stream of words and images in the media assures audiences that charismatic CEOs are no longer stuffy, opera-going inheritors of massive fortunes, out of touch with and contemptuous of regular people. Instead they are adventurous, quirky, self-made men and women, maybe nerdy, maybe hip, but always down-to-earth (Frank 2000). Moreover, they also, like most people, care about more than their own self-interest, as evidenced by their traditional philanthropic giving as well as their embrace of personal causes.

The two-way "theoretical melding . . . of business leaders with the people" (Frank 2000, 30) has served as the flip-side of the neoliberal era's "popular view of the poor as victims of their own individual deficiencies" (Hyatt 2001, 202). CEOs, despite their seeming everydayness, have been able to discover or develop some kind of extraordinary potency, some special ability to create change. It has been this "super personhood" that underwrites the CEO's claim to charismatic authority — and to wealth and power. The play of similarity and difference between the vast majority of Americans and charismatic CEOs serves to allay the contradiction between a belief in basic equality and the undeniable reality of growing class inequality in neoliberalizing America.

Paul Smith notes that an important effect of the belief in equality despite evidence to the contrary is "the elision of the empirical realities of class and class interests" (2007, 11). If the charismatic CEO's vitality is rooted in his or her personality, inequality becomes an issue of self-improvement achieved or not achieved. Political analyses and programs that might use the lens of class to address growing inequality and skyrocketing CEO compensation have become spectators to the more important race to self-improvement in the pursuit of "prosperity" or "abundance." After a 2000 presidential debate between George W. Bush and Al Gore in which the latter had brought up these subjects, one woman in a televised focus group cheerily said, "We all want to be in that top one percent!" Such fantastical social arithmetic is only possible in the absence of any notion of class interest, inequality, or conflict.

Performance and Class

If the figure of the charismatic CEO has elided the realities of class in the neoliberal United States, it has also represented a claim to class power. Despite its inherent personalization, it is dependent on the recognition of others. In this, the charismatic CEO is no different from any other person wielding charismatic authority. Weber points out that it is only "through 'proving' himself," rather than by pointing to tradition, laws, rules, or expertise as a source of legitimacy, that such an individual can wield authority (1958, 246). Therefore, "it is recognition on the part of those subject to authority which is decisive for the validity of charisma" (Weber 1947, 359). Despite its individualistic appearance, charismatic authority is in fact social, relational, and political. It entails claims to power and wealth and the granting or withholding of approval for those claims by a variety of audiences. For the charismatic CEO, this translates into a need to prove himself or herself by taking decisive action to improve the economic position of the company he or she heads and to ensure that this is properly represented to a wider audience. The legitimacy of the charismatic CEO's claims to power and wealth has relied on performance, meant both as the "general success of [an] activity in light of some standard of achievement" and as the "display . . . of a recognized and culturally coded pattern of behavior" (Carlson 1996, 4–5).[4]

Their purported ability to enhance the economic position of corporations has been central to justifying the hiring and high pay of charismatic CEOs to stockholders, corporate board members, stock analysts, and the business press (Khurana 2002, 109–111; McKenzie 2001, 55–94). Two things are notable about this development. The first is the fact that this audience "attach[es] great value to observable performance metrics" (Khurana 2002, 109). This reliance on quantitative and ostensibly objective measurements was an important element of the broader practice of "benchmarking" that became ubiquitous in corporate America in the last several decades of the twentieth century. This practice was a result of both increasing international competition, which squeezed corporate profits and forced American corporations to take strides to increase their competitiveness, and efforts by shareholders to hold corporate management accountable (Larner and Le Heron 2004; Sklair 2001, 115–148). The rise of the charismatic CEO and the practice of benchmarking were linked from the beginning, both rooted in the changes in corporate governance that aimed to enhance corporate performance in response to the 1960s decline in profits. The second aspect of note is the assumed causal link between the presence of a certain CEO and overall organizational success. It is widely believed, not least among CEOs themselves, that corporate performance directly correlates with the leadership abilities of charismatic CEOs, notwithstanding evidence to the contrary (Khurana 2002, 21; Malmendier and Tate 2005). This is another aspect of the reduction of the corporation to its CEO, one that calls to mind what Marc Bousquet describes as "a 'management theory of value,' in which the labor of 'decision makers' . . . and not the strenuous efforts of a vast workforce, appears to be responsible" for organizational success (2008, 77). The charismatic CEO is the prime mover in corporate performance, the primary bearer of responsibility for success (or failure) and, thus, the rightful recipient of reward.

Thus, the charismatic CEO's claim to power relies on a notion of organizational performance that assumes the possibility and adequacy of objective measures of corporate success and a direct causal relationship between the actions of the CEO and such success. This claim is especially important in the context of intraclass politics within the corporate arena, as it justifies the fact that an increasing portion of profits have flowed to CEOs in the form of enormous salaries rather than to shareholders (Piketty and Saez 2004). Nevertheless, it also appeals to a broader audience, assuring the public at large that CEOs deserve what they earn.

The representational aspect of performance described above is ultimately more important to this broader appeal. The figure of the charismatic CEO is in large part constructed via the public self-representation of the ostensible characteristics of individual CEOs — their "uniqueness," "vision," "lateral thinking," "courage," "ability to see things, not the way they were but how they might be," and their responsibility for not just increased shareholder value but also "social value" (through both philanthropy and the contributions their firms' products make to consumers' quality of life), to use the words of two prominent CEOs quoted by journalist Louis Uchitelle (2007). The key outlet for such self-representations has been the CEO biography.

While it might seem odd to conceive of the publication of a biography as a political-economic event, the 1984 publication of Chrysler CEO Lee Iacocca's autobiography marked not just the emergence of a new literary genre but an important milestone in the development of contemporary American capitalism (Surowiecki 2002). Iacocca had engineered the turnaround of the American automobile company in the early 1980s. He was lionized in the press as a tough-talking, patriotic corporate savior. Along with this media buzz, Iacocca's best-selling autobiography was seminal to the development of this mythological narrative of the CEO. In it, he made the case that it was his personal qualities as a leader that had led to Chrysler's comeback, downplaying the importance of action by the federal government, which provided both loan guarantees and protection against imported automobiles.

Iacocca's autobiography was followed by scores of similar tomes that, aided by the emergence of a fawning popular business media, propelled the new image of the CEO as heroic savior into public culture (Guthey 1997; Guthey 2001; Schoenberger 2001). Biography — as a literary genre and in a more general sense — has served as the perfect vehicle for the construction of the figure of the charismatic CEO. The individualistic nature of the genre corresponds perfectly with the personalization of complex social phenomena in the figure of the charismatic CEO. CEO biographies also often serve a pedagogic function, providing lessons in leadership that anyone can ostensibly use. This has reinforced the identification of average people with CEOs as well as the depoliticizing notion that individuals are responsible for their own destiny. Finally, as Schoenberger has argued, while CEO biographies studiously avoid any mention of class, they constitute claims to class power:

> To publish the corporate autobiography is to make the claim that you have the right to the power that it represents you as wielding. Because of the discursive requirements of the genre and the ideology of capitalism this claim must be made on an individual basis: *I* have the right to this power because of who *I* am. But . . . the legitimacy of the claim to power cannot be established for the individual apart from his social and organizational position. It is in this sense that the individual claim of the autobiography necessarily rests on an implicit class foundation. Whatever the intentions of the people who wrote them . . . the larger importance of the genre is that it is part of this project of establishing and maintaining a ruling class. . . . (2001, 296)

The CEO biography provides a clear window onto the seemingly paradoxical class politics of the charismatic CEO: it represents a collective claim to class power made in the form of an individualized claim to extraordinariness. Class is elided even as claims to class power are made.

On "Giving Back"

One final element of the figure of the charismatic CEO already noted is worth explicating here: the importance of "giving back," as it is often phrased. This consists of traditional philanthropic activity in some cases, and the support of a particular cause in others, as with Bill Gates's focus on education and global health or Richard Branson's efforts to fight global warming. It can also involve "public service": while some high-level executives ran for political office, many others have served in various governmental positions that have been in essence "reserved" for ex-CEOs, such as the position of U.S secretary of the treasury.

This is clearly related to the recent shift toward "corporate responsibility" as an alternative to and preemption of state-based regulation or redistribution (Sklair 2001, 149–197). Slavoj Žižek writes of CEOs involved in charity:

> Their work of charity—their immense donations to public welfare—is not just a personal idiosyncrasy. . . . [It is] necessary from the strictly economic standpoint, since it allows the capitalist system to postpone its crisis. It re-establishes balance—a kind of redistribution of wealth to the truly needy—without falling into a fateful trap: the destructive logic of resentment and enforced statist redistribution of wealth. . . . Today's capitalism cannot reproduce itself on its own. It needs extra-economic charity to sustain the cycle of social reproduction. (2008, 23–24)

Understood from this point of view, such CEO charity is clearly a class project. It is an attempt to address the very inequalities and poverty in whose production their firms' actions are implicated in a way that does not fundamentally change the rules of the game. Or perhaps more accurately, it changes the rules in a way that is amenable to CEO philanthropists, as their own priorities and practices shape those of the institutions to which they give.[5] Moreover, philanthropic activity helps link CEOs in social networks, facilitating processes of class formation, as well as linking them with other elites to increase their influence (Rothkopf 2008).[6]

However, it is important not to dismiss the personal aspects of "giving back" too quickly, as Žižek does. This "conspicuous conscience," in David Rothkopf's perspicacious phrase (2008, 17), is targeted not just to other CEOs but also to the public at large, and has contributed to the constitution of the figure of the charismatic CEO. The idiosyncratic nature of the causes and institutions benefiting from this largesse helps humanize the charismatic CEO. Many CEOs cite personal connections to the causes they support. Such connections help flesh out their all-important biographies and accentuate their ability to overcome personal issues. Thus charismatic CEOs have been able to come across both as everyday people, who care about the world and want to see a better future for all, and as super-persons able to address the world's most intractable problems through their beneficence. Once again, we see the legitimization of class, power, and wealth via personalized qualities, in this case of generosity and social concern.

The figure of the charismatic CEO in the neoliberalizing United States has served to further the class project of restoring power and wealth to economic elites in a manner that elides class. As a cultural formation operating on a national scale, it has drawn on deep, if contradictory, currents in American society — individualism, the valorization of freedom and private property, egalitarianism, cultural populism, class inequality, the economic dominance of corporations, and a general aversion to class politics. However, it has done so in a new national context, marked by new forms of corporate organization and governance, cultural norms, political ideologies, and economic circumstances. Moreover, it has operated differently in different arenas — serving to placate intraclass conflicts in a corporate setting and interclass ones in a broader social setting.

ELECTING A CEO MAYOR

The election of Michael Bloomberg in 2001 was made possible by the application of the figure of the charismatic CEO in yet another context, that of urban governance. This might seem to be an obvious connection; after all, it was Bloomberg's enormous wealth that made his election a possibility, if not a foregone conclusion. But in fact, Bloomberg's wealth in itself owed relatively little to the figure of the charismatic CEO and transformations in corporate governance. As of 2001, Bloomberg LP was privately held, with Michael Bloomberg owning a 72 percent stake (Smith 2005). Putting aside the large portion of his wealth that was realizable only upon the sale of his portion of Bloomberg LP, Bloomberg's wealth was derived from his portion of the company's earnings and his outside investments rather than from the corporate board–approved salary and stock options packages that had enriched the charismatic CEOs of public corporations (Bloomberg and Winkler 2001, 199). But if the figure of the charismatic CEO had not been crucial to Bloomberg's fortune, its broader cultural appeal underwrote his political ascension. Bloomberg himself invoked it when he vowed that he would govern as a "CEO Mayor" (Lowry 2001b), and he was explicitly labeled as a charismatic CEO in the press at the time (Wolff 2001b).

As the personalization inherent in the figure of the charismatic CEO might suggest, Bloomberg's 2001 campaign for the New York City mayoralty rested on an intensely biographical premise. While Bloomberg assembled a capable team of policy experts and put forward a respectable platform, his policy positions were ultimately incidental. It was his own experience and characteristics that justified his run for mayor. As the *New York Times* noted at the time, "other than his business successes, Mr. Bloomberg . . . offered little during the campaign" (2001). Before turning to the role of the figure of the charismatic CEO in

Bloomberg's election, a brief discussion of his public biography is warranted, as this was the material upon which his campaign drew in appealing to the public.[7]

Born in 1942, Bloomberg was raised in a lower-middle-class household in Medford, Massachusetts, and went on to attend Johns Hopkins University and Harvard Business School.[8] After receiving his MBA, Bloomberg went to work for Salomon Brothers, an investment bank specializing in bond trading. Thanks to hard work and a knack for self-promotion, Bloomberg was a quick success and became a partner before turning thirty. In 1981, he was forced out of the firm, though hardly empty handed: he received a $10 million severance package. Striking out on his own, Bloomberg founded Innovative Market Systems (renamed Bloomberg LP in 1986) as a five-person, $300,000 start-up located in a stuffy room on Madison Avenue. The company aimed to satisfy the unmet need for a centralized source for information on bonds. Thanks to its cornering of the market in bond-pricing data and Bloomberg's skill and tenacity as a salesman, the Bloomberg "box," the computer terminal that was the conduit for the company's proprietary financial information, was soon ubiquitous in financial firms. In the 1990s the company successfully moved into media, giving it a fortuitous position at the intersection of the growing information and media industries. By 2000, it had grown into a global corporation with almost $3 billion in annual sales and a staff of 8,000 spread over 108 offices worldwide. Bloomberg LP was known for its unorthodox business model, only feasible because it was a private company and thus subject to relatively little oversight. The company focused more on growth of revenues than profits; it paid close attention to customer service and constant improvement in its product; it was organized in a relatively nonhierarchical and open manner, perhaps best symbolized by the open "bullpen" layout of its offices, in which no one, not even the CEO, had a private office; and it was noted for treating and paying its employees well, with intense loyalty and hard work expected in return.

As Michael Bloomberg's profile rose, he became a prominent philanthropist. By the late 1990s, he had given his alma mater Johns Hopkins over $100 million and made substantial contributions to a number of other institutions and causes. He also garnered a reputation as a socializer, holding dinner parties at his well-turned-out townhouse on East Seventy-ninth Street on Manhattan's Upper East Side that were known for their eclectic mixes of people and their self-consciously low-brow fare (fried chicken and coleslaw was typical). The divorced Bloomberg gained a reputation as something of a womanizer, dating singer Diana Ross among many others. He also became notorious for making abrasive, and at times sexist, remarks: his firm was sued three times in the 1990s for sexual harassment.

The less-than-savory aspects of Bloomberg's life actually contributed to his image as a straight-talking, political-correctness-bucking nonconformist. Indeed, one of the crucial elements of the Bloomberg myth was that he had been expelled from the elitist, white-shoe world of Wall Street only to triumphantly reemerge as head of a company whose products became indispensable to the very financial industry that had spurned him. This image as an "entrepreneurial David outsmarting bureaucratic, ossified, corporate Goliaths" (Spiro 1997), along with his less-than-angelic personal life and demeanor, helped cement Bloomberg's image as a man of the people despite his enormous wealth and lavish lifestyle.

Besides the general focus on biography, Michael Bloomberg's enactment of the figure of the charismatic CEO underwrote his 2001 campaign in a number of specific ways. Moreover, this enactment only had the power it did because of its articulation with a number of key aspects of the post–fiscal crisis neoliberalization of New York City.

Personalization and Performance in the Bloomberg Campaign

By 2001, Michael Bloomberg was identified with his eponymous company and its success. This was the sine qua non of Bloomberg's run for mayor. This identification attributed the company's success not to a unique set of historical and social circumstances but to abstract qualities such as leadership, vision, and management skill that could as easily be drawn upon in the governing of the city as they had been in the running of Bloomberg LP. Bloomberg's campaign appeal was pithily summed up by journalist Michael Wolff, who wrote a series of trenchant pieces on Bloomberg's campaign: "I'm a good manager; therefore, I should run the city" (2001a).

Drawing on the image of the charismatic CEO as efficacy personified, Bloomberg's campaign touted him as a "doer" and someone "who cares about performance" (Tierney 2001): "I'm somebody that gets things done," Bloomberg averred in one debate (Saul 2001). Bloomberg drew a sharp contrast between his own qualities and those of his Democratic opponent Mark Green, who he derided as "someone whose only purpose in life is to criticize and stop things" (Katz and Saul 2001) and as lacking experience in "managing a large organization, in leading a large number of people, in setting large budgets, and in actually doing things" (Nagourney 2001). The public claim that Bloomberg had performed as CEO was in a sense more important than its truth. In fact, relatively little was known about the actual profitability of the privately held Bloomberg LP (Wolff 2001a). The CEO biography and the development of the figure of the charismatic CEO permitted individual CEOs to reap huge financial rewards despite a lack of evidence that their companies' economic position justified such compensation. In a similar manner, Michael Bloomberg's biographical 2001 campaign was able to enact the figure of the potent, efficacious CEO and thus override any questions about his company's actual profitability.

This focus on performance resonated in New York City, as managerialism had become a nostrum of post–fiscal crisis governance. In fact, one of the greatest perceived successes of the Giuliani administration, the so-called CompStat system, which used information technology and statistics to measure the efficacy of the New York City Police Department (Vitale 2008), was a paradigmatic example of Clarke's "performance–evaluation nexus" (2004, 133). However, this sort of managerialism did not characterize Giuliani's mayoralty overall. In most other regards, by 2001 Giuliani had come to be seen as a run-of-the-mill politician, with his personal ambition for higher office apparent, his personal life a mess, and his administration tarred by patronage and corruption. In contrast, by promising to be a CEO mayor and to run the city like a corporation, Bloomberg not only made performance the central tenet of his campaign but did so in a way that resonated with post–fiscal crisis privatist ideology.

One particular thing that Bloomberg "had actually done" was given special emphasis in the campaign: he had created jobs and generated profits (Murphy and Archibold 2001). Bloomberg argued that his experience in starting and growing a successful business gave him particular insight into economic development policy, especially given the neoliberal emphasis on the stimulation of private investment (Murphy 2001b). How exactly this would work was somewhat vague, and the details supplied were relatively conventional, though there were some hints in the campaign that Bloomberg's particular experience in the private sector would impact his approach to economic development (Murphy 2001a). Nevertheless, Bloomberg's central argument was clear: his entrepreneurial and managerial experience would give him the ability to place the city on a sounder economic and fiscal footing. Bloomberg's focus on performance and on economic development, a focus that flowed from his enactment of the figure of the charismatic CEO, merged with longstanding trends in urban governance in the city. Taken together, these factors gave his campaign a resonance that otherwise it might have lacked.

"He Doesn't Owe Anybody"

Bloomberg stressed other important differences with traditional politicians in his 2001 campaign. He and his advocates argued that the fact that Bloomberg was financing his own campaign, which many criticized as a blatant attempt to buy the mayoralty, was in fact a public benefit: it ensured that Bloomberg would come into office unencumbered by obligations to campaign contributors. His enormous wealth meant that personal corruption would not be an issue. A lifelong Democrat who ran as a Republican in 2001, Bloomberg touted his independence from political parties as well as so-called special interests — his focus would be on getting things done, not on hewing to the line of party ideology or pleasing party bosses. Finally, Bloomberg portrayed his campaign as an extension of his previous philanthropic activity, describing it as a way to "give back" by putting his skills and experience to work for the good of the city he loved (Bumiller 2001b), driven by beneficence rather than fealty to any particular interests or ideology. While this left Bloomberg open to accusations of self-aggrandizement, it bolstered the notion that his campaign was rooted in his biography and personal idiosyncrasies.

All these things created an image of Bloomberg as radically independent of any sort of compromising political entanglements. His campaign ads, speeches, and advocates repeatedly made the claim that, as one supporter put it, "Bloomberg has so much money that he doesn't owe anybody" (Ojito 2001). Bloomberg's wealth and dearth of political experience functioned to portray him as a political monad, unattached and unencumbered by personal, political, ideological, or economic obligations — and thus uniquely qualified to work in the interests of New York City as a whole. This image of Bloomberg as politically sui generis was rooted in the figure of the charismatic CEO. As we have seen, one of the crucial functions of the inherent personalization of this figure is to lay claim to the prerogatives of class power even as both class and politics are elided. This elision allowed Bloomberg to emerge from his migration from the corporate to the political sphere as a political innocent. Even as he brought personal qualities of leadership and vision, he brought none of the normal and necessary, if at times distasteful, ties that politicians normally have.

Moreover, the portrayal of Bloomberg as a political innocent helped place him in the tradition of private-sector elite intervention in the city's governance that was reactivated after the fiscal crisis. The legitimacy of such intervention had always depended on the idea that such elites would be better able to determine the good of the city as a whole than politicians. Indeed, Bloomberg argued that his willingness to step out of a lucrative career demonstrated his commit-ment to New York City. He explicitly positioned himself in the tradition of business elites, like David Rockefeller and Felix Rohatyn, who had engaged in the city's governance (Murphy and Archibold 2001). Unlike those elites, how-ever, Bloomberg sought to demonstrate this commitment not through obscure state boards or private–public partnerships but in the seat of political power in New York City: the mayoralty.

Bloomberg's Constituency: The Postindustrial Elite

Bloomberg's individual ascendancy rested on processes of class transformation, including those linked not just to the rise of the figure of the charismatic CEO but also to the development of New York City's postindustrial elite. As we have seen, though New York City had become the home of a substantial and grow-ing fraction of the TCC, as of 2001 their power and wealth only had a limited impact on the city's governance. It was that wealth that formed the condition for TCC entrée into electoral politics, as it provided Bloomberg the ability to substitute massive campaign spending for the constituency building and politi-cal groundwork usually necessary to win a mayoral election. Bloomberg spent $74 million of his own money, a new high for a municipal campaign and more than three times the amount spent by Mark Green. This came to $98 per vote; in contrast, in 1997 Rudy Giuliani spent only $15 per vote in trouncing his Democratic challenger. As large as this amount seems, it was a relatively small portion of Bloomberg's wealth, valued at $4 billion in 2001 (Forbes 2001). In this most obvious of ways, the political rise of Michael Bloomberg and his ap-proach to urban governance was made possible by his portion of the enormous financial power of New York's TCC.

Bloomberg's political rise was also rooted in TCC place-making practices de-scribed previously, as his social, cultural, and economic connections among his class peers served as an important early source of support. Among the earliest supporters of his candidacy were his fellow TCC members, who "loved the idea of their energetic friend running City Hall and watching out for their interests" (Purnick 2009, 81–82). Likewise, his social connections with TCC members ac-tive in Democratic Party fundraising in some cases led the latter to moderate their activity on behalf of Bloomberg's Democratic opponents.

While the TCC was the social formation out of which Bloomberg emerged, his electoral success depended on appealing to a much broader swath of the city's voters. The city's PMC served as an indispensable constituency for Bloomberg. In contrast to other post–fiscal crisis mayors, Michael Bloomberg was extraordinarily attuned to the values, cultural preferences, urban imagi-naries, and practices of the PMC, putting forth a vision of the city as urbane, cosmopolitan, cultured, amenity filled, and well serviced that was deeply appealing to its members.

Steven Brint has identified two "political cultures" that have roots in the upper strata of the New York City's PMC: a "business culture" among higher-income professionals and corporate managers and a "liberal professional culture" oriented to humanistic values rooted in nonprofits, universities, cultural organizations, and government (1992, 172–173). In 2001, Michael Bloomberg managed to articulate a campaign message that appealed to both of these professional political cultures.

First, Bloomberg effortlessly tapped into business culture. His mythical rise from a middle-class background to the heights of the TCC on the basis of his own hard work, talent, and intelligence served to ratify the meritocratic aspirations of upper professionals, especially those in finance and business services. Indeed, Bloomberg — skilled manager, generous philanthropist, and cultural sophisticate — embodied the best of professional corporate culture. Moreover, Bloomberg often spoke of New York's status as a hub for the "best and the brightest" (Murphy 2001a), stoking business professionals' notion that their own "smartness" legitimized their high salaries and social power (see Ho 2005, 75). Finally, his emphasis on fiscal discipline and governmental efficiency appealed to corporate managers, financiers, and other professionals, especially after 9/11 intensified the city's already-growing fiscal woes.

For professionals in the liberal, humanistic camp, there was Bloomberg's social liberalism and tolerance, especially in terms of race. Likewise, Bloomberg's generous support of culture and the arts, his nonpartisanship, and his embrace of good government appealed to these professionals, especially those in the cultural and nonprofit sectors. Indeed, Bloomberg garnered the endorsement of a number of prominent civic and good government organizations. His faith in measurement and respect for expertise appealed to those whose primary economic asset was their own specialized knowledge and educational credentials, and this appeal was reinforced by his hiring of a number of well-regarded academics and policy experts to aid his campaign's policy development process.

This multidimensional appeal drew many members of the city's PMC into Bloomberg's 2001 electoral coalition (and eventually, as we will see, into his administration). Bloomberg did remarkably well in neighborhoods largely populated by white, Democratic, and well-off members of the PMC. In areas like Park Slope, Greenwich Village, and the Upper West Side, which as John Mollenkopf points out "should have been Green's natural base," the Republican

Bloomberg won about 40 percent of the vote, as compared to the 10 percent of these votes won by Republican George W. Bush in 2000 (2003, 126). In the end, a shift of 18,000 votes would have meant a Green victory (Mollenkopf 2003, 135). Thus, Bloomberg's ability to appeal to PMC voters despite being a Republican was crucial to his electoral victory.

Crisis, Leadership, and Contingency

The neoliberalization of New York City's governance and the rise of the charismatic CEO articulated in 2001 paved the way for the political rise of Michael Bloomberg. However, it would be wrong to see the election of a CEO mayor as preordained by these processes and forces. If not for specific events and developments, the notion of a CEO mayor would not have had the appeal that it did and Michael Bloomberg likely would have lost the election to Mark Green — and the trajectory of neoliberalization in New York City would have been very different. For, as of September 10, 2001, Michael Bloomberg's electoral prospects seemed dim. The "CEO mayor" platform seemed enough to make Bloomberg a viable candidate but not enough to make him a victorious one, as he consistently trailed Mark Green in the polls. However, two intervening events in the months between September 10 and the November 6 general election changed this.

The first of these was the terrorist attack of September 11. While the critique of the idea of the CEO mayor did not disappear after 9/11, Bloomberg's claims to decisive leadership and nonpartisanship resonated with a rattled citizenry more than ever. The calls for unity and an end to "politics as usual," along with the necessity to rebuild the World Trade Center site, steady the nerves of jittery corporations, and support the city's sagging economy, all dovetailed with Bloomberg's campaign message. The October endorsement of Mayor Giuliani, whose free-falling legacy was rescued by his post-9/11 political rebirth, cemented the notion that Bloomberg had what it would take to get the city back on its feet.

The second pivotal event of the 2001 campaign season was Mark Green's closely contested Democratic primary runoff defeat of Fernando Ferrer, who would have been the city's first Latino mayor. The bitter and divisive campaign left Latino voters disenchanted. They were joined in their disenchantment by African Americans, who had been angered by racist campaign tactics, aimed at largely white and Jewish neighborhoods, that raised prospects that the controversial African American activist, Reverend Al Sharpton, would have undue influence on a Ferrer administration. The already tenuous Democratic Party alliance of mutually suspicious Jews (and other white ethnics) and African Americans was torn asunder (Mollenkopf 2003, 2005). After tepidly endorsing Green, Ferrer was largely invisible during the general election; Sharpton went as far as calling for a boycott. As a result, Bloomberg received an unprecedented level of Latino and African American support, essentially throwing the election his way.[9]

So, while Bloomberg resolutely avoided the divisive racial politicking that past mayors like Giuliani and Ed Koch had engaged in, he nonetheless profited from racial division. This was true in an even deeper sense, as Bloomberg benefited from a long-term reluctance on the part of conservative white Democrats to vote for a mayoral candidate of their own party, which was committed to construction of a multiethnic progressive coalition (Mollenkopf 2003, 2005). In addition, the appeal of Bloomberg's nonpartisanship, his leadership experience as a CEO, and his managerial competence, all of which clearly could be interpreted racially even if not offered as such, was only heightened by intra–Democratic Party racial conflict.[10]

So if not for 9/11 and for an episode of racialized campaigning that activated long-running racial divides among the city's electorate, Bloomberg's autobiographical campaign appeal would have found far less purchase. These unhappy accidents, for Bloomberg at least, had the happiest of consequences, as his evocation of the figure of the charismatic CEO was given special salience by these contingencies. Without them, the remaking of neoliberal urban governance that the Bloomberg Way represented would not have emerged.

FROM THE CEO MAYOR TO THE BLOOMBERG WAY

Bloomberg's electoral campaign drew heavily on various currents and contradictions inherent in post–fiscal crisis neoliberalization, as well as the city's longer history, including privatism, managerialism, the legitimization of involvement of business elites in governance, and the need for a revitalized economic development policy. Moreover, the growth of the city's postindustrial elite gave Bloomberg a crucial social and electoral base.

While bolstered by these factors, the election of a bona fide charismatic CEO as mayor also drew on the class-inflected cultural politics inherent in the figure of the charismatic CEO. The personalized nature of Bloomberg's campaign was, in a seeming paradox, the key to understanding this class politics. As the personalization of both the corporation and the capacity of capital to transform the world, the figure of the charismatic CEO attributed to ostensibly extraordinary individuals the power they derived from their class position, thereby eliding class even as it justified the reality of class inequality. Moreover, this personalization permitted the kind of domain-crossing move that Bloomberg's run for mayor represented: If the unique qualities of the charismatic CEO were indeed rooted in the individual personality, why couldn't they be as efficacious in the realm of governance as they had been in business, as well as in philanthropy? And if they were, wouldn't this ability to use their talents to solve the problems of cities and nations and, indeed, of the world be the ultimate legitimization of the wealth and power of men like Michael Bloomberg?

In the case of Bloomberg himself, the key to providing such solutions would be applying the qualities inherent in the figure of the charismatic CEO to the workings of New York City government. And as the following chapters demonstrate, doing so involved the elaboration of a strategy of government that flowed naturally from the starting point of the CEO mayor: one that conceived of the city government as a corporation, business and residents as clients and customers, and the city itself as a product to be branded and marketed.

CHAPTER THREE

Running Government
like a Business

In their seminal how-to guide to entrepreneurial governance, David Osborne and Ted Gaebler flatly state that "government cannot be run like business" (1993, 21). While urging public administrators and politicians to pursue market-based reforms, they make it clear that there are fundamental differences in the functions, internal incentives, missions, and norms of government and business. Gaebler and Osborne go so far as to warn that "democracy would be the first casualty" of conflating making government more entrepreneurial with actually running government like a business (ibid., 22).

Osborne and Gaebler's pleas aside, conflating government and business has become a nostrum of neoliberal governance, particularly within cities (Clarke 2004, 119; Hackworth 2007, 10; Hall and Hubbard 1998a, 2). However, this concept has often been associated with policies that might better be characterized as running government *for* business, thus conflating business as an exemplar with business as a beneficiary. This notion also has been associated with a series of rather marginal and incoherent policy interventions, rather than the development and implementation of a coherent governmental strategy (Box 1999; Jessop 1998).

After his election, Mayor Bloomberg quickly demonstrated not only that he would act as a CEO mayor but also that the city would be run as a corporation. Valued businesses and residents would be treated as clients and customers, and the city itself was conceived of as a product to be branded and marketed. This chapter analyzes the early construction of the Bloomberg administration, with particular focus on the first three elements of the Bloomberg Way. In my discussion, I demonstrate that Bloomberg's corporatized approach to urban governance entailed not just increasing the city's friendliness to business or implementing a few corporate-inspired policies here and there but a more thorough reconceptualization and reformation of the concrete practices of local governance, particularly those in the sphere of development policy.

Moreover, I also show how class permeated this process. Class influenced both the staffing of the administration and the various organizational steps taken to ensure that Mayor Bloomberg would be able to "perform" in office, thus making good on broader claims to leadership on the part of the city's postindustrial elite. To begin, I discuss what was at stake in the administration's efforts to "run government like a business," then turn to the sorts of leadership, staffing, and bureaucratic reorganizations involved in this process.

PERFORMANCE, CLASS, AND RUNNING THE CITY LIKE A BUSINESS

One cannot understand what it meant for the Bloomberg administration to "run government like a business," or how doing so related to class, without taking into account the concept of performance. In chapter 2, I noted that performance, understood as both the successful accomplishment of a task and communication of this success, was crucial to the figure of the charismatic CEO, and in turn to Bloomberg's 2001 election as mayor. Once elected, Bloomberg had to make good on his claims of efficacy inherent in his enactment of the class-bound figure of the charismatic CEO. He also had to make sure that such efficacy was communicated to the electorate to which he would be accountable. He would have to rely less on the cultural power inherent in the figure of the charismatic CEO and more on tangible governmental results. Thus, translating Bloomberg's private-sector management experience and skill into concrete strategies of leadership, staffing, and bureaucratic organization — in other words, running the city like a business — was imperative. Doing so would create the governmental capacity to fulfill Bloomberg's campaign promises to reform the schools, strengthen the city's economy, and address its chronic budget problems. In addition, Bloomberg's prodigious skills as a salesman would be useful in conveying those results to the city's public.

But achieving "results" by running the government like a business was not just crucial to Bloomberg's personal political fortunes. The notion that city government would now be run like a business intensified the process of class mobilization that had begun with Daniel Doctoroff's founding of NYC2012 and reached a new level with Bloomberg's election. Linking class identity to urban governance, à la Geertz (1973), "deepened" the latter. What was at stake involved more than the standard political consequences — such as low poll ratings, unsuccessful reelection campaigns, and the like — but also the claim that the skills, desires, interests, and leadership of the city's postindustrial elite, and TCC in particular, were indispensable to the good of the city as a whole.

This claim was premised on the idea, as some postindustrial elites would declare, that the city "needed them." But they also needed the city, or at least certain actual or potential aspects of it. This brings us to a final reason why the performance promised by running the government like a business was crucial to the Bloomberg administration. Effective governance would transform the city as a place to do business and as a social milieu, in keeping with the interests and desires of the postindustrial elites who now were ensconced in city hall. Performance would thus fuse the self-interest of the postindustrial elite with that of the city as a whole. In other words, what was at stake in the seemingly banal staffing decisions and bureaucratic reorganizations that went on in the first year of the Bloomberg administration was the achievement of a new class hegemony in the city.

JUDGING THE CEO MAYOR: ACCOUNTABILITY, AUTONOMY, AND TRANSPARENCY

The sine qua non for achieving this goal was strong, decisive, and unconstrained leadership — the kind of leadership Mayor Bloomberg had promised to provide as a CEO mayor. But this leadership had specific qualities and implied a specific notion of accountability. Michael Bloomberg portrayed the CEO as the ultimate locus of responsibility and decision-making, and he asked to be judged on his accomplishments rather than on the basis of partisanship or political ideology. "In the end, it's one person's decision, one person's responsibility," Bloomberg writes in his autobiography. "A major part of the CEO's responsibilities is to be the ultimate risk taker and decision maker" (Bloomberg and Winkler 2001, 182). In return, employees must trust the CEO's judgment and fall in line with his decisions: "Either they believe in me, trust me, and are willing to take the risk that I will deliver success, or they don't. It's that simple. There's no haggling. I don't negotiate" (Bloomberg and Winkler 2001, 46–47). The CEO's acceptance of ultimate responsibility creates an obligation: leadership implies deference and loyalty on the part of those being led. This relationship between the leader and the led hinges on the notion of performance: It is the CEO's performance in the face of competition that generates the obligation to follow and that legitimizes his power.

As a CEO of a privately held company, Bloomberg in fact enjoyed a relative lack of accountability. In his autobiography he discusses the possibility of converting his company to public ownership: "Go Public? And have to answer to more partners, stockholders, and securities analysts? . . . For the moment, *answering to no one is the ultimate situation*" (Bloomberg and Winkler 2001, 187, emphasis added). As mayor, Bloomberg was now directly accountable to the voters of New York in a way he had never been accountable to anyone in his business career. However, aside from electoral "accountability moments," to borrow George W. Bush's term, Bloomberg's vision of mayoral leadership very much reflected his private-sector experience. He demanded of the city's citizenry — including city council members, members of community boards, and others — the kind of deference to his decisions that he had once demanded from his company's employees. As the CEO mayor, he needed unconstrained freedom to make decisions based on his own judgments of the best interests of the city.

But if the CEO mayor needed such autonomy, he also had to ensure that his achievements were visible to the public. At Bloomberg LP, Bloomberg had stressed transparency and openness. The most obvious example of this was the company's "bullpen" office layout, in which all employees, including the CEO, sat in an open arrangement of desks separated only by waist-high dividers. According to Bloomberg, this configuration served to facilitate teamwork, but more pertinently it allowed the monitoring of employees by management, by each other, and by office visitors, preventing bad work habits and undercutting intraoffice politics. "As is true with markets," he writes, "transparency produces fairness" (Bloomberg and Winkler 2001, 163). This physical layout symbolized a broader approach: as Bloomberg told one interviewer, "My whole business life has been out in the open" (Gimein 2002). In fact, Bloomberg took great care to manage and limit scrutiny of many aspects of his business life, made possible by his firm's private ownership. But the appearance of transparency was indispensable to Bloomberg's status as a charismatic CEO, as it allowed him to cultivate his image as an individual of extraordinary capabilities and potency.

In short, the dual notion of performance central to the notion of the CEO mayor translated into twin imperatives of autonomy and transparency. In fact, Bloomberg faced significant constraints on his autonomy as mayor. Most land use decisions and planning projects would be subject to ULURP. The New York City Council, while weak in many regards, had the power to pass local laws, vote yes or no on land use changes, and override mayoral vetoes. There were also a number of intergovernmental constraints on the city government's autonomy, such as New York State's control of its education system, the various State authorities that had significant power over land use decisions (especially in regards to state-owned land), the various financing and subsidy programs related to economic development policy, and the strings attached to various federal funding streams. An additional factor was the vulnerability of the city's economy to broader economic trends.

Nevertheless, the mayor was resolute in his belief that, as he said during his

2001 campaign with reference to the process of rebuilding the World Trade Center site, "the city should be responsible for its own destiny" (Nagourney 2001). He demanded and received control of the city's schools. The administration acted to circumvent the federal government's often incompetent and underfunded efforts to protect the city against further terrorist attacks after 9/11, as Police Commissioner Raymond Kelly built up an antiterrorism unit in the city's police department whose capabilities were extremely well regarded among counterterrorism experts worldwide (Finnegan 2005). Other attempts to assert the financial and political autonomy of the city were less successful, including efforts to have the state legislature allow the city to reinstate a commuter tax, to have the federal government change its formulas for terrorism funding to the city's benefit, and to have the state legislature reduce the city's portion of its Medicaid bill.

The new mayor vowed that his administration would be transparent and open. On a symbolic level, the bullpen layout was introduced into city hall. More substantively, a series of steps were taken to make available data that would allow for the evaluation of mayoral performance by both the public and the administration itself. Drawing on "best practices" in governmental management and on the corporate experience of its members, the administration developed a comprehensive system of measurement and reporting aimed at supplying different "audiences" — the public, agency managers, and "senior executives" (that is, the mayor and his deputy mayors) — with data of appropriate detail and frequency. The great majority of these data, in keeping with the private-sector faith in ostensibly objective "benchmarks," were quantitative in form. This system included the Citywide Accountability Program, an internal program founded in 2001 to provide detailed and frequently updated information that agency managers could use to "monitor and improve performance" (City of New York 2002b). In addition, it included the new 311 telephone system, which provided citizens with an easy way to report complaints and also served as a new source of data about public services. Later, in keeping with Bloomberg's long-held commitment to customer service, the administration sought to create "a comprehensive citywide customer satisfaction survey" to gauge how city residents judged the responsiveness and performance of city employees and agencies (Gardiner 2007). Finally, the administration revamped the *Mayor's Management Report*. Introduced as a 150-page tool of managerial efficiency and transparency after the 1970s fiscal crisis, this report had by 2001 degenerated into an unusable three-volume, 1,000-page grab bag of over 4,000 statistical indicators. In September 2002, the administration released its first version of the revised report, which was now conceptualized as a "Public Report

Card." The number of statistical indicators was reduced and the mix of indicators reoriented "toward reporting on 'outcome' or results-oriented statistics that demonstrate success or failure" (City of New York 2002b, 4). Indicators were made available on the city's Web site, with an easy-to-use mapping function that allowed citizens to evaluate city services in their neighborhoods. Finally, "based on best practices in performance reporting," the 2002 report contained a series of goals and targets against which important indicators could be measured. These "provide[d] a clear frame of reference for assessing performance and may take several forms . . . including . . . nationally recognized standards and the benchmarking of performance against other large cities" (City of New York 2002b, 4). While some criticized particular measurements or absences in the report (McIntyre 2004; Pasanen 2004), the *Mayor's Management Report* cannot be easily dismissed. Indicators in the 2002 and subsequent reports were often unflattering to the administration, and the mayor publicly acknowledged the areas in which the city's performance could improve. Whatever its flaws, the *Mayor's Management Report*, along with other publicly available forms of evaluation, were important steps toward the fulfillment of the CEO mayor's promise of transparency.

Besides the autonomy to make decisions and the transparency necessary for the public to judge his achievements, a third element was necessary for the CEO mayor's political success: governmental capacity. He needed a well-structured organization, staffed by capable people, that could get things done. And in the early months of Bloomberg's first term, the administration was taking steps to transform city government into just such an organization.

HIRING THE "RIGHT PEOPLE"

A few months after entering office, Mayor Bloomberg discussed how he had approached staffing his administration. "I'm a big believer in picking good people, giving them the tools, removing barriers to cooperation, promoting, and protecting them, and letting the professionals go and do what they do well," he said, before concluding: "I think I put exactly the right people in place" (2002a). Indeed, in his biography, Bloomberg had made it clear that while the CEO was "the ultimate risk taker and decision maker," it was crucial that he surround himself with creative, intelligent, and skilled employees and give them the freedom to think and act freely in pursuit of the goals he had established (Bloomberg and Winkler 2001, 182, 163–167). At Bloomberg LP, loyalty to the CEO was paired with respect for employees and their expertise and a stress on meritocracy. The company was perceived as a rewarding, if demanding, place to work, and it was known for low rates of employee turnover (Loomis 2007; Mnookin 2008). This ethos of meritocracy and loyalty shaped the staffing of Bloomberg's campaign and administration.

Even early on in his campaign Bloomberg took a different approach to hiring than had successful New York City mayoral candidates, at least since John Lindsay, whose administration had a deep technocratic and meritocratic streak. Mayors Abe Beame, Ed Koch, and David Dinkins all were politicians' politicians, with deep roots in Democratic Party politics, and they staffed key positions in their campaigns and administrations with government insiders and party players. The key positions in Rudy Giuliani's campaign and admin-istration were filled largely on the basis of personal and political loyalty. In contrast, Bloomberg's campaign — and later his administration — drew heav-ily on political outsiders, particularly, but not solely, from the private sector. Bloomberg's two key campaign advisors came from Bloomberg LP: Patricia Harris, who after an early stint in government had directed the company's phil-anthropic activity; and Kevin Sheekey, who after working as the chief of staff for New York Senator Daniel Patrick Moynihan had directed Bloomberg LP's government relations office. This reliance on individuals with private-sector experience and close personal connections to Bloomberg was paired with a reliance on urban experts of various sorts. Early on, the campaign asked a wide array of such experts for background policy papers for the candidate's edification; later, important positions in Bloomberg's campaign policy team were filled by a small but eclectic group of well-respected academics and other political novices, as well as a few experienced government insiders. In sum, the 2001 Bloomberg campaign relied on corporate networks for its top-level decision makers while demonstrating a respect for professional expertise in developing policy specifics.

Once elected, Bloomberg's stated priority was finding "good people" and the "right people" (2002a). Looking back on his first 100 days in office, Bloomberg said:

> I think . . . I have put together a great team. . . . It's a diverse group of people, with lots of ideas, a mixture of government experience and private-sector experi-ence. . . . I tried to have a balance, a lot of people who had been in government before, some of whom had gone off to the private sector and were coming back, and some absolute new faces who never had to deal with the problems and re-strictions the government places on you. I think that kind of a dynamic and that

kind of interaction — some people saying, "Why can't we do it," and others saying "here's why you can't" — having them fight it out in the road is a very good
thing. (2002a)

The new mayor's deputy mayors, policy advisors, and commissioners were
drawn from diverse backgrounds and sectors, and all had strong professional
experience and expertise relevant to their new positions. Nevertheless, the
staffing of his administration displayed the same pattern as his campaign, as
individuals with private-sector experience, and often with social or business
connections to Bloomberg, tended to fill the high-level positions closest to the
mayor. Along with the aforementioned Patricia Harris, who was appointed to
serve as deputy mayor for administration, and Kevin Sheekey, who served as
the mayor's key political advisor, a number of other Bloomberg LP executives
joined the administration. Bloomberg also tapped Joel Klein, who had served
as the corporate counsel to Bertelsmann AG after serving in the Clinton administration in various positions, to be chancellor of the city's school system.
However, the most important corporate executives who entered the administration filled key positions related to economic and urban development.

Assembling an Elite Development Team

Mayor Bloomberg inherited a city economy radically destabilized by 9/11, the
end of the 1990s stock market boom, and the onset of a national recession.
The brewing fiscal crisis facing the city in the wake of these three events led
many policy and business elites to argue that the city's economic base needed
to be diversified and its reliance on the financial industry lessened, even as
they called for steps to reassure financial firms considering leaving the city
in the wake of the terrorist attacks. Besides the rebuilding of the World Trade
Center site, there were a series of stalled or lagging development projects that
elites insisted were crucial to the city's economic future. All this, along with
the fact that Bloomberg had indicated during the 2001 campaign that if elected
he would bring his corporate experience to bear on strengthening the city's
economy, made it inevitable that economic and urban development would be
a key policy area for the new administration and that the new mayor would
pay special attention to the staffing of key economic development and planning
positions.

The most important economic development position to be filled would be
that of the deputy mayor for economic development and rebuilding, who would
be charged not only with leading the city government's role in the redevelopment

of Ground Zero but also with reinvigorating a stagnant city economy. While a number of candidates campaigned for the position — ex–deputy mayors, real estate developers, experienced development officials, and well-connected business executives — one man enjoyed broad support for the job among the city's elite, even if he was unknown to the vast majority of New Yorkers: NYC2012's Daniel Doctoroff. One corporate executive expressed Doctoroff's popularity among city elites well, saying, "When Mike Bloomberg became Mayor, I think Dan was everybody's choice to be deputy mayor" (Tagliabue 2002). He certainly was the first person Nat Leventhal, head of Bloomberg's personnel search committee (and a board member of NYC2012), thought of: "I knew what the job required. It was self-starting initiative and creativity and a quality of not being confined by the regular bureaucratic way of thinking. I never had anyone else in my mind" (Golson 2004).

Doctoroff had spent the past seven years developing a plan for the Olympics that would have major impacts on the entire city under the aegis of a completely private organization funded by donations from wealthy individuals and large corporations and accountable to no one. Like Bloomberg, he was unaccustomed to the strictures of public decision-making and the give-and-take of the city's normal political processes, let alone its highly contentious development politics. While Doctoroff had united the city's elite behind the Olympics bid, he had never implemented a single development project, large or small, or negotiated with an angry neighborhood organization, a critical good government group, or a truculent union. Peter Solomon, Doctoroff's mentor at Lehman Brothers in the early 1980s, discussed these issues with Doctoroff after he was asked to take the position. "I told him it was a great opportunity to use the Olympics to harness the political will to move dozens of projects that some of us have been interested in for years," said Solomon. "Of course, one of the challenges is that you're constantly balancing everybody's interests and your own interests" (Robbins and McIntyre 2004).

In fact, Doctoroff twice declined the position, reluctant to give up day-to-day control of NYC2012 (as well as for personal reasons). However, a late 2001 meeting with Mayor-elect Bloomberg ended with Doctoroff accepting the position and walking away with Bloomberg's admiration and trust. This mutually satisfactory agreement was generated from biographical similarity: both men were enormously ambitious, successful, wealthy, and motivated by a personal desire to "give back" to the city they loved via public service. Both believed deeply that their success in the private sector could be replicated in government. "I don't think in any previous government . . . they ever had somebody who was a real banker, who knew how to put together things, who knew what drives the private sector economy," Bloomberg said of Doctoroff. "He's got the attitude, 'I'm going to get it done. I'll find a way to do it'" (Robbins and McIntyre 2004).

Doctoroff's appointment signaled several things: that the Bloomberg administration was on board with NYC2012's development agenda; that land use, urban development, and the physical shape of the city would be an important element of the administration's economic development policy; and that corporate success, financial and managerial acumen, and an understanding of the needs of business, particularly the high-end financial services sector, were more important to Bloomberg than experience negotiating the treacherous waters of New York City development politics.

Doctoroff's position did not come with a large staff, though what it lacked in head count it made up for in access to the mayor. The most important site of organizational capacity for economic development policy was the EDC. Besides Doctoroff, Bloomberg's choice for EDC president would be the most important development-related appointment he would make. The conflict over this appointment, and the way it was resolved, demonstrated that the EDC would henceforth be run efficiently, transparently, and professionally as a true economic development agency focused on serving the needs of business, rather than, as in the past, as a patronage mill, a deal maker, a conduit for the privatization of city assets, or a vehicle for mayoral pet projects.

Prior to the Bloomberg administration, EDC presidents had generally been creatures of the murky world lying at the intersection of government and the private sector. As of Bloomberg's election, just such an individual held the position: Michael Carey, the well-connected son of former New York Governor Hugh Carey. The third EDC president in six years, Carey inherited the agency from former Republican councilmember Charles Millard, whose tenure was marked by ineffectiveness and corruption. Though Carey had made significant improvements at the agency, Bloomberg declined to keep him on. This perceived snub angered Carey's father, who had endorsed Bloomberg: the elder Carey reportedly complained to Bloomberg's aides, threatened to boycott his inauguration (he did, in fact, end up attending), and rallied a number of prominent Bloomberg supporters to his son's cause.

However, the mayor refused to cave in, and asked Andrew Alper, a political neophyte, to take the position. Alper had received his MBA from the University of Chicago before working for two decades at Goldman Sachs, where he served most recently as chief operating officer of its investment banking division. In a 2007 interview, I asked Alper about this offer and his eventual decision to accept it. Alper's explanation of his decision to join the administration, along with the justification Mayor Bloomberg gave for hiring Alper, is indicative of the ways in which meritocratic considerations, the desire to "give back," and social and business connections merged to establish the Bloomberg administration as a site of class mobilization.

In November 2001, shortly after Doctoroff had agreed to become deputy mayor, he asked Alper to take the position. Alper was initially reluctant to do so, but a number of things changed his mind. Among them was the commitment that Alper felt toward the city in its post-9/11 time of need and the promise that the Bloomberg administration would be different. "It was a pretty scary time. The city clearly needed help getting back on its feet. The World Trade Center was smoldering. Businesses [were] fleeing," Alper told me. "Doctoroff convinced me that (a) the city needed us, and (b) this would be a different kind of administration. We would have the opportunity to transcend politics and really have an impact on a city, which I felt I owe a lot to." He went on to cite the confluence between the city's post-9/11 situation and his own experience and skills in the corporate sector:

> We're in a very competitive business, the city. People don't think of it that way, but people make choices: Where do you want to live? Where you want to work? Where do you want to send your kids to school? Where do you want to visit as a tourist? We're in a competitive business, we're not low-cost producers, people can live many other places. Quality of life, in many cases, is better elsewhere in terms of the hassle factor. We're in the . . . position of being a high-cost producer in a competitive business and not knowing our clients. That struck me as really odd, and really fixable. It became clear to me that my background as somebody who [had tried] to cultivate clients [could help build the] relationship between the public sector and the private sector.

Mayor Bloomberg also emphasized Alper's skills in building relationships with business when he announced the appointment, saying that this "global . . . businessman" was "exactly the right kind of guy to bring in companies to the city and to keep companies here" (2002b, 2002a).

The analysis of why the "city needed" Alper, of why his particular experience and skills made him well qualified for this position, depended on a particular imagining of the city and an interpretation of the crisis that it faced after 9/11. Imagining the city in corporate terms and construing New York's post-9/11 crisis as one of business confidence, competitive advantage, and client relations created a compelling logic for Alper's decision as a policy novice to agree to head the city's primary economic development agency. As someone who had successfully cultivated clients in the highly competitive investment-banking world, Alper had the skills and the experience that the situation called for.

Such logic was widespread within the Bloomberg administration. Another example was Bloomberg's citation of Doctoroff's reputation as a hard-driving negotiator and tough dealmaker when naming him as deputy mayor. By reinterpreting areas of particular policy using the language and concepts of business and by positing that those areas of policy were crucial to resolving the city's post-9/11 crisis, corporate executives like Michael Bloomberg, Andrew Alper, and Dan Doctoroff, who had no government experience but did have abundant success in New York City's postindustrial economy, cast their entrée into city government as an obligation, a chance to "give back." But as I argue above, "giving back" through the application of corporate conceptions and practices to urban government also represented an opportunity to prove the legitimacy of corporate executives' claims to wealth and power, as well as to shape the city and its governance in line with the interests and desires of its members.

The staffing of the Bloomberg administration drew on class in other ways. As well as discussing the role of 9/11 and the skills he brought to the job, in our 2007 interview Alper described a set of preexisting personal and professional relationships, starting with his relationship with Daniel Doctoroff, as crucial to his decision to enter city hall:

> In business school, I was roommates with Dan Doctoroff's partner, Steve Gruber. Dan, coincidentally, was my wife's law school classmate [at the University of] Chicago Law School. Dan and Steve went to Lehman Brothers after they graduated. I got to know Dan through Steve. In the 1990s, I was running Goldman Sachs' Financial Institutions Group, which was advising the insurance companies. Dan and Steve set up a partnership to do private equity transactions in the insurance industry. So Dan and I negotiated against each other for two years in two pretty tough deals. In the course of that, [we] developed a lot of respect for each other. He then became a client. He asked us to represent him in signing portfolio companies. Through this, Dan and I became close friends.

As Mark Guthey (1997, 2001) points out, skill in negotiation is a fundamental building block of identity for high-level corporate executives.[1] Returning to Alper's views, we see that personal relationships and shared interests were crucial in his hiring:

When [Dan] first requested that I think about leaving Goldman for a city job, I said highly unlikely. I don't like politics very much. Never thought about public service. He said, well, keep an open mind. I said fine, whatever. He then called me when he had been named deputy mayor, and said would I consider running EDC. My first reaction was no, what is it? He said I'm not really entirely sure what it is but I know it's economic development. Just meet with the mayor. So, I go up and meet with the mayor. It's Dan, the mayor, and me. My resume has that I'm vice chairman of the board of the University of Chicago, [and] that I used to fly airplanes. The mayor talked about everything on my resume *except* economic development. We talked about universities [Alper had dedicated large amounts of money to his alma mater, the University of Chicago, just as Bloomberg had to Johns Hopkins University]. We talked about flying. I leave figuring I'm off the hook. He clearly has no interest in me as economic development head. The next morning, [Bloomberg] calls me [and] offers me a job in his administration. But for 9/11, but for my deep respect for Dan . . . .

This was not the only case in which these kinds of personal and professional connections affected hiring in the administration. We have already discussed the fact that Bloomberg hired a number of high-level executives from Bloomberg LP. We saw how the mutual identification between Bloomberg and Doctoroff helped cement Doctoroff's place in city hall; clearly, something similar took place in Alper's case, as indicated by the fact that mutual interests in university-oriented philanthropy and flying, rather than the nuts and bolts of economic development policy, dominated his conversation with the new mayor.[2]

The hiring of Andrew Alper clearly indicated how class relationships and identities shaped the highest levels of the administration. But it demonstrated a number of other things as well. Alper's political inexperience and self-effacing personality, along with the fact that he was Doctoroff's choice for the position, indicated that the hard-driving Doctoroff would be the key figure in the formulation and implementation of economic development policy. Alper's role would be to serve as a trusted liaison to his former compatriots in the private sector, particularly in the financial and business services sectors. Indeed, one of Alper's first initiatives demonstrated that the administration would work to meet even the most prosaic needs of business (and to provide for the convenience of corporate executives), as EDC worked to change parking regulations to ensure that "black cars," the corporate transportation of choice, would have better access to the entrances of Manhattan office buildings.

The final key economic development position Bloomberg needed to fill was one that had not even been considered as an economic development position in the previous administration. Under Mayor Giuliani, the DCP was not under the control of the deputy mayor for economic development, but rather the deputy mayor for planning and community relations, along with a grab bag of other city agencies in which Giuliani had little interest, such as the human rights commission and the department of community relations. In contrast, Mayor Bloomberg placed the DCP under the deputy mayor for economic development and rebuilding, which, along with Doctoroff's appointment to that position, indicated that urban planning and development would be taken seriously in the new administration. A final sign of this was the slate of candidates to become chair of the CPC, which in New York City also entails directing the DCP. All three candidates — Sherida Paulsen, chair of the City Landmarks Preservation Commission, NYC2012's Alexander Garvin, and Amanda Burden, a planner currently on the CPC — were experienced and well-regarded planners. Garvin was reputedly Doctoroff's pick for the position, but Bloomberg appointed Burden instead.

In part, this was due to social connections between Burden and Bloomberg. Burden, a wealthy heiress and socialite with deep connections in the city's old-line elite, was a neighbor of the mayor's on tony East Seventy-ninth Street (apparently they often saw each other on the street when Burden was walking her dog, a highly pedigreed pug). Her boyfriend, the television host Charlie Rose, filmed his television programs in Bloomberg LP's studios and both Rose and Burden had socialized with the mayor. At the press conference announcing Burden's appointment, Bloomberg jokingly said of the youthful fifty-seven-year-old: "She's not an old friend, she's a friend of long standing" (Cooper 2002).

As well as being a social acquaintance of Bloomberg, Burden was also a well-qualified and well-respected planner. Trained at Columbia University, her early professional mentor had been William "Holly" Whyte, who, along with Jane Jacobs, was the most prominent critic of the modernist urban renewal schemes that gutted the downtowns of so many postwar American cities (Jacobs 1992; Whyte 1980). Both Whyte and Jacobs championed a human-scale urbanism centered on lively street life, mixed uses, twenty-four-hour activity, and high-quality public spaces. Whyte's Project for Public Spaces, where Burden gained her first exposure to issues of urban design and public space in the early 1970s, was known for its exhaustively detailed studies of the ways in which people used public spaces throughout the city, from which it drew conclusions about the type of public spaces the city should be encouraging in its zoning laws. In the 1980s, Burden was in charge of the public spaces at Battery Park City, the planned development along the Hudson River in Lower Manhattan that many urban planners, designers, and architects consider a model of good urban design and planning.

"My relationships with Holly Whyte [are] at the core of everything that I believe in and that we're doing," Burden said in a 2004 speech. "Even though we are planning at a very broad level down, everything really comes down to how it affects the vibrancy and street life of communities. Last but not least, I believe . . . that good design is economic development" (2004). Though the relation between good urban design (and planning) and economic development would prove far more problematic than Burden anticipated, her commitment to the principles of post-urban-renewal urban planning was well established. As a member of the Giuliani-era CPC, she had often been a lone voice insisting on the importance of urban planning and design at a time when that body did little more than rubber-stamp zoning changes providing windfall profits for landowners. For many of the long-suffering planners at the DCP — and for those previously reluctant to enter DCP — Burden's appointment was a breath of fresh air, as it promised that high-quality planning reflecting professional best practice would be the new standard. However, the DCP would not be autonomous. Policy involving the nexus between urban planning and economic development would remain under Deputy Mayor Doctoroff's close control, especially since Burden's professional strengths and interests were geared more toward urban design than economic issues.

The hiring of Doctoroff, Alper, and Burden — all undoubtedly intelligent, skilled, and experienced — reflected Mayor Bloomberg's stated goal to hire "good people" who could work together to get things done. It also provided the basis for a newly coherent and comprehensive economic and urban development policy. The backgrounds, expertise, and experience of the members of this development team complemented each other well. Doctoroff was the hard-driving deal-maker with bold visions and a keen understanding of both urban development issues and what made the private sector tick; Alper was the diplomat who could reach out to businesses in the city and across the globe; and Burden was the "aesthetic watchdog" (Pogrebin 2004) who could temper attention to the bottom line with care for the city's urbanism and urbanity, so important to the "quality of life" sought by well-educated and highly skilled professionals. But these hires also demonstrated that the construction of the Bloomberg administration was becoming an exercise in class mobilization: by drawing on elite social and business networks and identification, and by legitimizing certain forms of expertise and experience, not just as relevant but as *necessary* to urban governance given the situation the city faced. This wasn't just about Michael Bloomberg anymore.

"New Professional Opportunities" in City Hall

It wasn't just about investment bankers, media moguls, and heiresses either: the Bloomberg administration drew on the city's upper professionals to staff positions at a variety of levels. Bloomberg's cross-class appeal, which was so important to his 2001 election, also served to pull many professionals who might have not otherwise considered government service into city hall — and into alliance with the members of the city's TCC also joining the administration.

Both Bloomberg's biography and his approach to governance provided the basis for this cross-class appeal. Bloomberg's public biography not only represented an enactment of the figure of the charismatic CEO but also was testimony to ideals of meritocracy and professional expertise. Through education, hard work, and talent, he had been able to transcend modest beginnings and achieve enormous levels of wealth and success. His upward path into and then out of the PMC clearly left an imprint. Before becoming mayor, he consistently displayed a respect for expertise and professional knowledge. For example, in his autobiography, Bloomberg wrote that the appeal that his first employer, Salomon Brothers, had for him as a young MBA was the investment bank's meritocratic ethos: its leaders rewarded "go-getters" rather than Ivy League legacies with "distinguished lineages, manners, [and] accents" (Bloomberg and Winkler 2001, 19). Another example was the faith he expressed in the judgment of public health and emergency management professionals during the post-9/11 anthrax attacks that occurred during the 2001 campaign. "You have professionals there to assess the risks and make decisions," he said. "That's what you have experts for. And if all of us think that we have the detailed knowledge, you're just wrong" (Murphy 2001b).

After Bloomberg was elected, he stayed true to these words in his high-level appointments, supplementing ultra-elites like Burden, Alper, Doctoroff, and Klein with well-respected and well-qualified professionals from a variety of backgrounds. In a number of cases, he appointed experienced government hands to key administration positions. However, they were not the kind of "serial" commissioners or deputy commissioners seen in previous administrations — politically well-connected but inexpert individuals who hopped among high-level positions at various agencies. Rather, many had risen through the ranks of city government and were chosen on the basis of their deep expertise in particular policy domains. Bloomberg also drew heavily on the city's not-for-profit and academic sectors, both hotbeds of professionalism and policy expertise.

By casting such a wide net, and by refusing to allow nakedly political or partisan considerations to govern his appointments in staffing the upper reaches of his administration, Bloomberg changed the way many highly skilled and well-educated professionals with promising or well-established careers perceived government employment.[3] Previously, if even considered at all, such work had not been seen as particularly rewarding, whether in terms of prestige, job satisfaction, or remuneration. But Bloomberg's actions signaled that the expertise and experience of professionals would be respected if they were to join his administration. Senior and junior city hall staffers told me that Bloomberg's meritocratic and professional ethic was a key factor in their decision to join the administration as well as in the decisions of their colleagues to do so. For instance, when I asked one young administration official, with an Ivy League MBA and a promising corporate career, about her decision to move from the private sector to government service, she said, "There are no political appointees in this administration. . . . The commissioners are a really talented bunch. Nobody's here because they volunteered for the mayor's campaign and certainly nobody's here because they gave money. It's very much a meritocracy." The notion that the hiring both of corporate executives like Doctoroff and Alper and of upper professionals was driven by meritocratic and professional, rather than political, considerations served to bind together the members of these groups that were moving into city hall.

Along with this embrace of meritocracy and professionalism came another characteristic of Mayor Bloomberg's corporate approach to governance that appealed to upper professionals. This approach was, as one ex-academic enthusiastically indicated to me, "more than good government, almost technocratic in some ways," or "administration by technocrats" as an ex–corporate employee told me. Bloomberg's so-called pragmatism redefined complex urban issues as a set of "problems" to be "solved" via the application of technical knowledge and evaluated via quantitative measurement. The administration's technocratic approach legitimized the expertise central to the class identity of upper professionals and lured them into public service, just as its corporate approach had legitimized the corporate experience of Alper and Doctoroff and their private-sector compatriots and pulled them into public service. Further, the *combination* of corporatism and technocracy that marked the Bloomberg Way served to create cross-class bonds.

Finally, upper professionals were also drawn into the administration by the allure of the charismatic CEO, as demonstrated in the words of this ex–corporate employee:

I am convinced this is the best job I'll ever have. Start with the fact that it's in New York, and it's in city hall, but it's for a guy who doesn't really owe anybody anything, who's obviously extraordinarily capable, who really wants to do the right thing. I've been in some meetings with the mayor, but not a lot, but you can't help but, you know, you can read the articles and know that this must be a smart guy. I've seen him at work. He's smart; he's sort of provocative. He likes to throw bombshells in meetings at you: why can't we do it this way, or why can't we do it that, you know. It's like a chief executive needling his people to be more creative. He's said this before, that his plan B is a lot better than most people's plan A. If he doesn't get reelected, he goes back to being a billionaire chief executive, or billionaire philanthropist, or a billionaire retiree, whatever the heck it is he wants to do. And that's a very liberating thing. You do meet politicians where their need to hold on to their job is palpable, because what else do you do, when this is all you've known, or this is what you've known for a long time?

Staffers of many different backgrounds expressed this sort of admiration to me, citing Bloomberg's managerial skills, vision, and intelligence. Others stressed the kind of CEO populism I discussed in the previous chapter; one person I spoke with called Bloomberg a believer in "entrepreneurship" whose "heart was with small business and not the Fortune 500."

The notion that Bloomberg was radically different from most politicians was ultimately the key to his appeal to upper professionals. That Bloomberg — as well as Doctoroff, Alper, and other corporate executives in the administration — had forsaken extremely attractive alternatives to enter public service, and had done so because of their dedication to the city rather than political ambition or ideology, made his a "different kind of administration," in the words of one of my city hall informants. "Bloomberg regenerated interest in government among younger people and professionals," one of Bloomberg's senior advisors said to me. "Many came from the private sector, [seeing] new professional opportunities and opportunities to create change by bringing their professional skills to bear on city issues. There's a different attitude — they won't be frustrated and bored. Bloomberg opened up a space for these people in city government and created a new excitement about public service." This notion, that working in the Bloomberg administration offered professionals a chance to "give back" to their city in a way that both drew upon their particular skills and promised to be professionally meaningful, was an important shared reference in city hall and served to bind together the professionals and corporate executives in the administration. As one young professional staffer said to me, "I wanted to work not just for city government, I wanted to work for New York City, and in particular I wanted to work for the Bloomberg administration."

Analysts have noted the tendency of professionals, whether in academia or in the corporate sector, to "identify upward," identifying with employers and those above them in the class structure (Brint 1994, 86; Dumenil and Levy 2004b, 132–133). This dynamic was clearly at work in the Bloomberg administration. The emphases on meritocracy, professionalism, and technocracy, the appeal of the figure of the charismatic CEO, and the shared interest in "giving back" in a professionally meaningful way served not only to draw upper professionals into the administration but to establish important cross-class solidarities within it. Upper professionals could only aspire to membership in the rarified business and social circles that the mayor, Burden, Alper, and Doctoroff moved in, to say nothing of the wealthy lifestyles they enjoyed. But they could rub shoulders with them in the corridors and conference rooms of city hall, if not as equals exactly, then with a high degree of mutual respect and regard. While Mayor Bloomberg and Deputy Mayor Doctoroff were clearly calling the shots, they were also willing to listen to their professional staff members and to defer to their expertise when appropriate.

This did not mean that there were not potential conflicts. There was a huge gap in material wealth between an investment banker like Doctoroff or Alper and even the best-paid academic or management consultant. This not only created the potential for resentment but also clouded the issue of motivation. Whereas for the very wealthy members of the administration, working for the city government was in fact a form of charity (for legal reasons, they had to accept a nominal annual salary of one dollar), the professionals who worked for the administration often found doing so financially rewarding, receiving unusually high salaries for government work (Cardwell and McGinty 2007). In combination with the fact that aides who temporarily left city hall to work on his reelection in 2005 received five- and even six-figure bonuses after Bloomberg won reelection, this led to concerns that staffers' loyalty would be to Bloomberg rather than to the government or the city as a whole (Roberts 2006). There were disagreements, generally subterranean, about standards of qualification: more than one policy expert or long-time government hand grumbled to me privately about the imperialistic attitudes of their former corporate compatriots. Bloomberg's top-down management style did not always sit well with academics or ex–nonprofit employees used to more collegial and consensual decision-making practices. Lastly was the potential conflict between the corporate technocracy embraced by the mayor and the professional technocracy that professionals in the administration were more comfortable with. Under the former, ends are determined by CEO fiat; the role of technical expertise is to develop the most efficient means to reach those ends and to measure whether or not they have been met. In the latter, the ends themselves — or the "public interest," to use the phrase applicable to government — can themselves be judged according to professional standards (Marcuse 2002, 159–161). As we shall see in the case of the Hudson Yards, this tension between corporate and professional technocracies would have very real consequences for the administration's development agenda.

Despite these potential tensions, the Bloomberg administration provided an unprecedented opportunity for the city's "best and brightest" to apply their expertise to the various problems and issues it faced. Professionalism, capability, creativity, problem solving, expertise, and performance were the new keywords in city hall. For Mayor Bloomberg, "running the city like a business" meant hiring the best-qualified people — not just, as one might expect, from the private sector but from wherever they were to be found — and respecting their skills and capabilities, even as he bore the final right of, and responsibility for, decision-making. Upper professionals and corporate executives reciprocated this respect by entering the administration in numbers not seen in decades, if ever. While their public service was motivated by a sense of desire to use their expertise and skill to serve their city, especially after 9/11, this commitment to "give back" was undergirded by a sense of collective identity founded upon social and personal connections, professional networks, commitments to meritocracy and technocracy, and a shared sense of self-regard. This process of class mobilization was justified by the idea, as Andrew Alper put it, that "the city needed us." The staffing of the Bloomberg administration itself represented a bid for class hegemony, with the rule of the postindustrial elite equated with the good of the city as a whole.

MAKING PERFORMANCE POSSIBLE: INCREASING ORGANIZATIONAL CAPACITY

With "exactly the right people in place," the task now was to achieve the economic and fiscal goals Bloomberg had set out in his campaign. In the expansive area of economic and urban development policy, this required the organizational capacity to develop and implement a coherent and comprehensive strategy. The effort to increase the capacity of the city government's development apparatus demonstrated in concrete terms what the idea of "running the city like a business" meant to ex–corporate executives like Bloomberg, Doctoroff, and Alper, as it entailed the importing of a number of corporate management practices directly into city government.

The best publicized of these corporate practices was the physical rearrangement of the mayor's offices in city hall to resemble the "bullpen" layout used in Bloomberg LP. However, this was just the tip of the iceberg: such practices were implemented in a far more thoroughgoing manner, especially in agencies headed by Deputy Mayor Doctoroff.[4] Weeks into Mayor Bloomberg's first term, and shortly after he hired Daniel Doctoroff, an important — if largely unnoticed — bureaucratic reshuffling took place: all city agencies relating to economic and urban development would now be under the control of the new deputy mayor for economic development and rebuilding. In previous administrations, these agencies — including the EDC, the DCP, the Department of Business Services (soon to be renamed the "Department of Small Business Services"), and the department of housing preservation and development — had reported to a variety of deputy mayors. Now one man, Daniel Doctoroff, would exercise a degree of bureaucratic control over development policies and projects unprecedented since the days of Robert Moses. Everything from the tiniest infractions of the city's signage regulations by small businesses to multimillion-dollar incentive deals for the city's biggest corporations, from the smallest neighborhood rezoning to redevelopment of the former World Trade Center site — all would be under Doctoroff's purview.

With the mayor's backing, Doctoroff quickly acted to ensure that these agencies would work in tandem by creating the Economic Development Agency Council. In the council's reportedly well-attended, engaging, and lively weekly or biweekly meetings, commissioners and other executives of agencies reporting to the deputy mayor met to discuss agency activities and interagency issues. EDAC, in combination with occasional corporate-style retreats, was apparently effective in "removing barriers to cooperation." In interviews with me and in other venues, commissioners and other city officials repeatedly highlighted increased interagency cooperation and its benefits. As CPC Chair Amanda Burden said of the interagency cooperation that the council helped bring about, "That's how you get things done, and that's what the Mayor is all about. It's about executive decisions and performance" (2004).

The establishment of the council also provided a forum for Doctoroff to assert bureaucratic control over the agencies under his command. He required each to develop a strategic plan in PowerPoint, the presentation software de rigueur in the private sector. These strategic plans included the agency's mission, agency-specific goals and initiatives to meet them, quarterly targets for progress, and so on. They served as both a comprehensive policy development tool used to coordinate the goals of each agency and a technique to encourage efficient management and to hold commissioners accountable for their agencies' performance. In the words of EDC President Alper, no stranger to such corporate management techniques, they provided "a road map to how to spend our time and our capital" and "a mechanism to ensure and measure success" with "metrics built into it to make sure that we're in fact doing what we say we're going to do" (2003b).

Such practices were not altogether novel at the EDC, which had long had close connections to the private sector and something of a corporate ethos. Nevertheless, the administration's explicitly corporate approach led to drastic changes in management and policy there, as EDC President Alper "set out to restructure EDC and instill a private sector focus [by] applying what he learned running Goldman's Investment Banking Division" (University of Chicago Graduate School of Business 2004). One example of this was the introduction of strict cost-benefit analysis to judge the worthiness of various subsidy programs and development projects. Another, more important, example was the agency's "reorganiz[ation] with a new 'client-centered' approach to retain and attract companies," as Bloomberg put it in his 2002 State of the Union address (2002c).

In April 2002, Alper announced an internal restructuring of his agency, which would "enable EDC to function more efficiently, empower decision-making at all levels, encourage horizontal collaboration and establish short- and long-term strategic goals" (New York City Economic Development Corporation 2002). The agency's structure was simplified and certain functions, including strategic planning and long-term infrastructure maintenance and development, were strengthened. As well as facilitating internal efficiency, the reorganization enhanced the EDC's capacity to approach economic and urban development in a comprehensive and proactive way, a real change at an agency that, as one long-time EDC official told me, "always had a short-term transaction culture — sell the land, get construction going, get a new factory, get new jobs."

The centerpiece of this reorganization was the creation of the Client Coverage Operating Division. This new division would be organized on the basis of, as one of Doctoroff's aides told me, a "client coverage model, obvious to any investment bank, but less obvious to a lot of city governments." In the private sector, this model consists of a series of "desks" staffed by experts responsible for a number of industry-specific tasks: monitoring events and developments, serving as the identifiable and trusted face of the company, and maintaining open communication. The consolidation of responsibility for expertise and outreach in one employee or group of employees allows the company to cull information that permits it to better serve current clients and target potential clients. The EDC's Client Coverage Operating Division reflected this, as indicated by the words of Doctoroff's aide:

> There is a person who is the media desk, whose job it is to understand what's going on with media companies [and] to keep tabs on who might be relocating, who's looking for space. When we get a call from a major media company saying we're thinking about relocating this guy at the media desk [can give] us information in terms of here's how much space they have, how many employees they have, here's what we've done for them, here's what we hear. We want [him] to understand not just real estate, but the peculiarities of the real estate needs facing a media company. Do they need large floor plate? How much are they willing to pay? Where are their employees located?

Serving as a source of expertise and a point of contact with a particular sector, the desk staff would be able to better understand the strengths and weaknesses of New York City as a place for business and, in EDC President Alper's words, "to make sure that we have proactive relationships and dialogues with companies and industries big and small throughout the five boroughs to make sure that we're being responsive" (2002b). To ensure that the division remained true to its private-sector origins, Alper hired a former Goldman Sachs colleague to oversee the industry desks.

The EDC adopted not just organizational aspects of the client coverage model but conceptual ones as well. Businesses were conceived of as "clients," as expressed succinctly by Deputy Mayor Doctoroff in a 2004 speech describing the creation of the Client Coverage Operating Division: "We began to think about covering our clients — the companies in this city who pay taxes and generate jobs — the way an investment bank or a commercial bank would" (2004a). Another of the division's aims was to understand how city government, and the city itself, could "add value" for these clients, just as a private-sector firm might do in providing a service or product. "We need to develop expertise and relationships in those industries that are growing," EDC President Alper told the city council in 2002, "to understand how we, as a City, can add value to their businesses and make sure we are a better host . . . for them" (2002a).

These various practices and conceptions, all "reminiscent of a private sector mentality," as one informant put it to me, were crucial to the development and implementation of a coherent and comprehensive development strategy. CPC Chair Burden expressed this in a 2004 speech. "Early on, in January 2002, Deputy Mayor Doctoroff instructed one of his agencies to develop a Strategic

Plan in PowerPoint," she said. "City Planning didn't know what a PowerPoint was! But we learned fast. He wanted strategic planning benchmarks — month-to-month benchmarks for two years about what we were going to achieve and when we were going to achieve it. And he held us to those benchmarks and we got judged by those plans all the time and those benchmarks, and we've kept to them" (2004). DCP's benchmarks consisted of a series of rezonings of an ambition and quantity unimaginable under previous administrations, which in fact were in large part successfully implemented over the next few years. Likewise, the EDC's corporate-inflected reorganization would permit it to effectively understand the city's "value proposition" and use this as a guide for economic development policy. Finally, the centralization of Doctoroff's control would allow for coordination and cooperation between agencies necessary for both the construction of a broad development agenda and the successful implementation of complex and multifaceted projects that were a part of it.

It was not just the development and implementation of this agenda that were important here but its communication as well. While seemingly a small detail, the use of PowerPoint, with its (at times deceptive) ability to present information neatly and simply, was in fact quite important. Administration officials used the PowerPoint presentations, embellished with attractive graphics and illustrations, as crucial public relations tools in speeches and presentations to various groups across the city. The presentations allowed officials to clearly and concisely communicate the tenets and goals of the administration's economic development policy, the ways in which their agencies' initiatives related to these goals, and progress toward them. Once again, we see the importance of the double notion of performance to the Bloomberg Way — the necessity to make good on the proposition that the skills and experience of the postindustrial elites moving into city hall would push the city toward economic growth and prosperity and the imperative of demonstrating this to the broader public.

RUNNING GOVERNMENT LIKE A BUSINESS: FROM THEORY TO PRACTICE

The early months of the Bloomberg administration provided a unique illustration of what "running government like a business" might mean to those who had actually done so. Unlike the typical neoliberal case, in which entrepreneurial or managerial logics are applied to particular and isolated policy realms, or what is called "businesslike governance" actually comprises enhancing the business climate, in the Bloomberg administration "running the city like a business" had profound impacts on concrete practices of urban governance such as hiring, bureaucratic organization, and evaluation.

However, this was not merely a dispassionate application of managerial expertise toward the ends of efficiency and good government. In fact, the importation of private-sector conceptions and practices into municipal government constituted a claim of legitimacy for the wealth and power — and now state power — wielded by members of the city's postindustrial elite. Various forms of expertise, experience, and skill were brought into city government, and the successful application of these forms to the city's problems would be the ultimate vindicator of such claims to class power. But these claims had to be recognized by New Yorkers at large. Successful governance had to be performed and communicated via a plethora of means: 311, the *Mayor's Management Report*, a redesigned city government Web site, customer service surveys, PowerPoint presentations, and the like.

But if "running the government like a business" constituted a class project in and of itself, it also was a means to an end. Bob Jessop argues that cities can only be held to be truly entrepreneurial in certain cases: "From a strategic viewpoint [an 'entrepreneurial city'] would be one that has achieved the capacity to act entrepreneurially. It may then itself directly act as an economic entrepreneur, targeting one or more . . . facets of the urban 'product'" (1998, 87). "Running the city like a business" created the capacity for the city government to act entrepreneurially by developing and implementing an aggressive and ambitious development agenda that approached the city as a product to be branded and marketed. It is to the details of this agenda that we now turn.

CHAPTER FOUR

The Luxury City

By summer 2002, the elements were in place for the administration to prepare "all of New York to compete, and win" (Bloomberg 2004). The CEO mayor had put the "right people" in place, drawing on the best offered by the private, public, and nonprofit sectors. He had established clear benchmarks and methods of measurement that would allow for the evaluation of performance. Bloomberg and his ex–private sector compatriots were applying their corporate management experience and deep knowledge of the private sector to create the organizational capacity necessary to achieve results. Agencies were being reorganized, core missions redefined, strategic plans written, and PowerPoint presentations prepared. Only one thing was missing: a strategy for competitive success.

In June 2002, EDC President Andrew Alper told the city council how the administration was going about developing such a strategy:

> We are, with a lot of people's help, trying to make sure that we do a better job of marketing and positioning New York City *as a brand*. McKinsey & Co. [has] interviewed companies . . . to help us think about what are our competitive advantages and disadvantages. . . . We are thinking about what companies we should target. . . . We want to put together a high impact road show, talk about the benefits of New York City, why it is a good place to live and to do business, and convince companies they should be here. . . . In the past, I think, we relied on the fact that New York is the crossroads of the world, it is the business capital of the world. We sort of let people come to us. Well, you know what? We need to go to them now. It is time for us to get on the road and tell our story. It is a very compelling story. Yes, it is expensive. Yes, it is crowded, but there is a reason it is crowded. It is a great place to live and to work . . . we have to get that story out. (2002a, emphasis added)

For the administration, competitive success required nothing less than the rebranding of New York City.

URBAN BRANDING AND ITS POTENTIAL

Since the mid-1960s, urban political elites have been faced with the difficult tasks of countering images of urban crisis and attracting investment, jobs, and desirable residents in a context of fiscal austerity and increasing inter-urban competition. In the United States, one of the responses has been to strengthen the "boosterist city marketing . . . deeply entrenched as a part of the North American agenda for the city" (Ward 1998a, 34).[1] However, these place-marketing practices quickly developed into something new. Contemporary place marketing, "while rooted in a long tradition, is distinguished both quali-tatively and quantitatively from the past" (Holcomb 1994, 120). First, contem-porary place marketing is a constitutive element of the dominant entrepreneur-ial model of urban governance; earlier place marketing did not rise to such importance (Brenner and Theodore 2002; Hall and Hubbard 1998a; Harvey 2001). Second, place marketing was boosted by the growth of the "modern 'institutional matrix' of media and marketing" in postindustrial cities in the last decades of the twentieth century (Greenberg 2008, 21). Innovations in market-ing, along with the expansion of the mass media and the growing importance of tourism to city economies, helped provide a supply-side impetus for the intensification of place marketing brought on by increased interurban competi-tion (Ashworth and Voogt 1994, 39–42; Greenberg 2008, 20–24). Most impor-tant for our discussion here was the emergence of "branding" as a corporate practice and professional field (Ashworth and Voogt 1994, 41–42; Greenberg 2008, 31–34).

Branding is centered on the notion that images or meanings can be mar-keted "even as the products to which they relate remain vaguely delineated or even non-existent" (Ashworth and Voogt 1994, 42). If traditional marketing was dependent on the fetishization of the commodity, that is, the attribution of qualities to a product in and of itself and the concomitant obscuring of the process of production, branding "promote[s] a fetishizing of the fetish: that is, the commodification of the reified image of the commodity itself" (Greenberg 2008, 31). Many corporations have become convinced that the images and meanings attributed to products not only have quantifiable value in and of themselves but are more important than the products. From the 1970s to the 1990s, many corporations "shifted their resources away from production and human resources via outsourcing and downsizing while concentrating the bulk of their capital on building powerful global brands" (Greenberg 2008, 32). As "weightless" corporations got out of the business of making things, products and the production process became subordinated to branding (Klein 2000). Through the last decades of the twentieth century, the notion of branding became ubiquitous, coming "into its own as a political, economic, and cultural strategy, packaging everything from soft drinks, cigarettes, and the corporations that sell them to cities, nations, political parties, and the individual self" (Greenberg 2008, 31–32).

Urban branding entails the development of a desired set of images and meanings — a brand — for the city, which can then guide efforts to, first, influence the perceptions of the city held by key individuals and groups — businesses, tourists, potential residents, actual residents, and other "target markets" — who might invest in, move to, or otherwise contribute to the city's well-being and, second, to reshape the city itself to bring it more in line with the brand. Urban branding departs from previous place marketing in that, like product branding, it subordinates the "product" to the brand: "A city must first decide on what kind of brand it wants to become, [and then] how it can create the mental, psychological, and emotional ties that are necessary for the city to really become this brand and what are the functional, physical attributes that the city needs to create, improve, highlight, and promote in order to support this brand," writes one urban branding expert (Kavaratzis 2007, 704). Urban branding comprises a sophisticated endeavor to understand the current and potential relationships among the images and meanings attributed to cities by "target markets," the characteristics of the city itself, and the broader field of competition, and to use this knowledge to guide interventions into the perceptions, workings, and landscape of the city. Thus urban branding has the potential to tie together knowledge of the city, urban imaginaries, the "real" material urban landscape, and urban governance.

Prior to the Bloomberg administration, this potential was largely unmet. Urban branding had typically taken two, more limited forms. The first is place-specific theming, entailing the development of distinctive urban districts aimed to reinforce or establish a particular image of the city via geographic synecdoche whereby the district is intended to represent the city as a whole (Gottdeiner 1997; Lukas 2007; Sorkin 1992). The second is the use of special events and other transitory spectacles to develop and reinforce a city's brand, the paradigmatic example being the Olympic Games (Andranovich, Burbank, and Heying 2001; Burbank, Andranovich, and Heying 2001; Gold and Gold 2007; Rutheiser 1996; Shoval 2002; Ward 2007b). Both forms of branding involve not just the development and communication of a desired image of the city but interventions into the processes and physical environments constituting urban life. Nevertheless, their delimitation in time and space has tended to diminish their impacts.

There is a third way in which branding can shape urban governance, one that has generally been observed more in theory than in practice. This is urban branding as "place management": here, the city's brand operates as the lodestar of urban governance, providing strategic coordination to a broad array of policy domains. The apotheosis of urban branding is reached when the brand drives coherence across policy domains, when "the city brand [is] not . . . distinguished from the content of the policies" (Kavaratzis and Ashworth 2007, 23). While branding is usually held to represent an effort to enhance urban competitiveness toward the end of economic development, urban branding's most dedicated advocates see it as having the potential to meet other goals, such as "achieving community development, reinforcing local identity and identification of the citizens with their city and activating all social forces to avoid social exclusion" (Kavaratzis 2004, 70). Urban branding as place management entails not just the coordination of policy but an attempt to fix a single urban imaginary in the minds of most, if not all, of the city's residents and users. This use of branding dramatically raises the political stakes, as it makes the claim that benefits of branding will be inclusive, generating economic benefits and a renewed sense of belonging and mutual commitment throughout the city's populace.

We are now far from logos and slogans. This furthest extension of the logic of branding represents a comprehensive and totalizing model of urban governance. It relates a variety of policy domains such as infrastructure, service provision, and urban development to processes of urban identification. Moreover, the advocates of urban branding as place management explicitly posit the importance of branding the city *as a whole*. According to its advocates, the central question of urban branding is whether it can "create in the minds of all people who encounter the city the feeling that they are dealing with an entity, with one thing, which they could have a relationship with" (Kavaratzis 2004, 71). Urban branding as place management requires the imaginative reification of the city.

As its advocates ruefully note, urban branding as place management is far less common than other, less ambitious forms of the practice. The integration of branding into the highest levels of urban governance has been hamstrung by two key problems. The first is the fact that such integration requires collaboration between two distinct groups: private-sector marketers and government officials. The latter tend to have a limited understanding of what branding entails, confusing it with more traditional place-marketing techniques, which can lead to problems of coordination and conflict (Hankinson 2001; Kavaratzis and Ashworth 2007; Ward 2000; Ward and Gold 1994, 11). The second and related problem is that, from the perspective of branding "science," cities tend to put the horse before the cart. They allow existing priorities and projects to drive the brand, rather than developing the brand first and then organizing a governance strategy around it (Kavaratzis and Ashworth 2007; Trueman, Klemm, and Giroud 2004).

BRANDING IN NEW YORK CITY BEFORE BLOOMBERG

New York City has been one of a handful of cities in the United States in which urban branding has approximated place management, if briefly and in limited ways.[2] As Miriam Greenberg has ably documented (2000; 2003; 2008), the campaign to transform the image of New York from that of a cesspool of disorder, dirt, crime, and racial unrest to that of a modern, cosmopolitan, orderly, business- and tourist-friendly city was integral to the post–fiscal crisis struggle of city elites to remake the city's political economy and landscape. Various marketing efforts — the most famous being the seminal "I ♥ NY" campaign of the late 1970s — were coordinated with changes in state policy in order to strengthen the city's image-sensitive postindustrial and real-estate sectors; appeal to tourists, investors, and white-collar workers; and render invisible poverty, crime, and the city's working classes (Greenberg 2008, 7–12). However, this coordination waned in the early 1990s as recession, a stock market crash, and the resultant shrinking of public budgets led to the privatization of the marketing of the city (Greenberg 2003, 405). While the Giuliani administration's quality of life campaign and its embrace of corporate retailers and offices, along with the fruition of the highly symbolic redevelopment of Times Square (Chesluk 2008; Reichl 1999; Sagalyn 2001), reinforced the independent branding of the city by the corporate sector, the two efforts were parallel, rather than integrated. Moreover, this image and the transformation it drove were tightly circumscribed in space, generally limited to Manhattan below Ninety-sixth Street and a few close-by neighborhoods in Brooklyn and Queens (Angotti 2008, 46–50; Greenberg 2003, 402; Sorkin 2002, 203).

The terrorist attacks of September 11, 2001, catalyzed a new round of rebranding in New York City, as alarmed city elites sought to stem the flow of residents, businesses, and tourist dollars from the city. While noting that this was a "descendant of the marketing-led approach that was used during the 1970s," Greenberg argues that the Bloomberg administration "normalized and institutionalized the branding approach to an unprecedented extent" (2008, 13). In the remainder of this chapter, I explore the institutionalization of urban branding as place management under the Bloomberg administration, which represented the final, crucial element of the Bloomberg Way — the treatment of the city as a product. First, I describe the administration's campaign to understand the city's image, its competitive strengths and weaknesses, and its potential target markets. Second, I discuss the designation of a new brand for the city. Third, I examine the administration's communication of the brand and its efforts to reshape "the product" in accordance with its new brand. Finally, I discuss the ways in which branding New York City reinforced the linking of class and governance endemic to the Bloomberg administration.

UNDERSTANDING NEW YORK AS A BRAND

Marketing and selling products has always been a knowledge-intensive enterprise. However, branding's subordination of product to image has magnified the importance of knowledge in marketing. "'Brands are made in the mind,'" Naomi Klein points out, "thus requiring a new level of creative and scientific expertise" (Greenberg 2008, 33). In particular, branding requires "identifying the target market and the nature of competition. . . . It is necessary to decide (1) who the target consumer is, (2) who the main competitors are, (3) how the brand is similar to these competitors, and (4) how the brand is different from these competitors" (Keller 1997, 95). It should be noted that branding is a highly focused and selective form of knowledge production. The determination of the "target market" is the key step; once this is accomplished it becomes the focus of "brand positioning," the process of "finding the proper location in the minds of a *group of consumers or market segment* so that they think about the product in the right or desired way" (Keller 1997, 95, emphasis added).

Once the target market is determined, the brand faces the challenge of competition to secure its loyalty. Once competitor products are identified, the role of the brand is to "differentiate products that appear similar in features, attributes, and possibly even benefits" (Davis 2002, 4). Such differentiation "may be rational and tangible — related to product performance of the brand — or more symbolic, emotional, and intangible — related to what the brand represents" (Keller 1997, 39). The "rational and tangible" points of differentiation involve the ability of the branded product to "add value" to a greater extent than other products (Hankinson 2004, 111). In urban branding, this is especially true when the target market is comprised of businesses rather than potential residents or tourists (Hankinson 2004, 114). However, in product branding, these economic points of differentiation are not favored over, or even seen as necessarily distinct from, "symbolic, emotional, and intangible" ones. Thus, branding often

entails the production of knowledge of products as *cultural objects*: as constitutive of consumer identity, as endowed with identities of their own, and as
repositories of meaning (Clark 2004; Gobe 2001; Holt 2004).

As key economic development officials and agencies of the Bloomberg administration embarked on an effort to generate knowledge of New York City as
a brand between January 2002 and January 2003, they followed the nostrums
of branding science to a significant degree. Drawing on everything from consultations with experts and corporate executives to brand surveys, they first
identified a target market and then explored how New York City could be made
distinct — in ways both tangible and intangible — from its competitors in the
minds of those in that target market.

One thing was absolutely clear at the outset: a new strategy was needed.
Andrew Alper, referring to the ongoing flight of office jobs to New Jersey, told
the city council in mid-2002 that "they are killing us" (2002a). The office towers standing on the western shore of the Hudson River were a galling reminder
of the exodus of jobs and businesses from the city over the past three decades.
During the 1990s, company after company — including lynchpins of the city's
financial sector like Goldman Sachs, Merrill Lynch, JPMorgan Chase, and
Morgan Stanley — had moved tens of thousands of back-office and high-end
employees to Jersey City, Hoboken, and the rest of Hudson County. Alper expressed the belief, widely shared among city policy elites, that the extended
stock market boom of the 1980s and 1990s had masked an erosion of the city's
long-term ability to compete for jobs, revenue, and the highly educated workers demanded by high-margin, high-value-added corporations.[3] Many of these
experts also shared a negative judgment of the Giuliani administration's economic development strategies. Though Mayor Giuliani's law and order campaign had played a crucial role in reestablishing New York's image as a safe
place to do business, his economic development policy had been reactive, limited to often overgenerous or unnecessary tax incentive deals, neglectful of
long-term investment in infrastructure, overly focused on the financial and
media industries in Manhattan, and, worst of all, ineffective.

New Jersey's job-poaching success was largely due to its notoriously generous business incentive programs. However, by late 2001 the consensus among
city economic development experts was that a reliance on tax incentives was
not only futile but actually harmful. During the 1980s and 1990s, billions of
dollars of tax revenues had been forgone. The indiscriminate use of subsidy
deals led to a situation where competitors of subsidized companies demanded
(and often received) equal treatment, even if they had no intentions of leaving
the city. In fact, many economic development experts concluded that there was

a flaw in the very premise of an economic development policy based on tax incentives. Given New York's real estate market and the costs of providing public service, the city would never be able to compete on the basis of cost alone.

However, there was no consensus on the best way to move forward. Planning groups stressed the importance of maintenance and enhancement of the city's transportation infrastructure and development of its waterfronts. Labor, liberal academics, and community groups pushed for job training, wage floors, and the protection and strengthening of manufacturing and other heavily unionized sectors. Policy organizations and experts with a neoliberal bent, along with the Partnership for New York City, called for support for the biotechnology industry and the cultivation of links between the city's universities and high-tech sectors. Finally, real estate elites were calling for steps to stimulate office construction. While the Bloomberg administration paid attention to these groups and drew on their ideas, it listened most carefully to the city's current and prospective "clients" — that is, private-sector corporations.

Faced with a failed competitive strategy and uncertainty about how to move forward, Mayor Bloomberg, Deputy Mayor Doctoroff, and EDC President Alper did what any smart executive would do: they brought in the consultants. In spring 2002, the administration asked management consulting firm McKinsey & Company to do its part to aid the city's post-9/11 recovery by conducting a pro bono study of the city's market position. Centered on a survey of corporate executives, the study aimed to measure perceptions of the city as a place to do business, to evaluate its competitive strengths and weaknesses, and ultimately to formulate a strategy to enhance the city's ability to attract and retain business.[4]

Competitive strengths identified by McKinsey consultants included the size of the city's market; the "depth of the talent pool" (economic development officials were fond of pointing out that the number of New Yorkers with college degrees exceeded the total population of San Francisco); cosmopolitanism; cultural amenities and dynamism; the city's reputation as a place that attracted the ambitious and well educated; transportation infrastructure; and the quality and number of the city's educational, medical, and scientific institutions. Competitive weaknesses included perceptions that the city was unsafe and environmentally unfriendly; the inadequacy of public schools; and, unsurprisingly, the high costs of housing, commercial space, energy, and taxes.

The report concluded with a series of recommendations concerning how the city should target economic development policy. The study identified, in the words of EDC President Alper, "high impact industries and functions within industries that we should be trying to attract into New York" (2003b). The idea

was to refine city efforts to attract and retain businesses by identifying companies, industries, and economic functions with internal characteristics and locational needs that made them likely to consider New York City. By pinpointing
what Alper called "disconnect[s] between competitive strength and commercial activity" (Temple-Raston 2004b), McKinsey provided a list of companies,
industries, and economic functions that the city would be most likely to attract. Such focused targeting was new to public-sector economic development
policy in New York, but it was old hat for the ex–private sector members of
the Bloomberg administration's economic development team: "Just like an investment bank would," Alper said, "we want to actually have a list of targets,
of companies that should be here that are not" (2002a). Highest on this list,
according to one administration official with whom I spoke, were companies
who valued the city's competitive strengths more than its competitive weaknesses and thus were ripe for the picking: "[It's] about understanding which
companies are worthy of extending incentives to and which are not; which are
the industries we're never going to win; which are the companies that won't
survive here without extensive government incentives, maybe it makes sense
to cut them loose; which are the companies that are never leaving no matter
what; and which are the companies that are in the sweet spot, which are the
industries that we are going to win fairly easily." The administration hoped this
approach would make the practice of business attraction and retention more
rational and efficient. By understanding what the city had to offer to which
companies, they could calibrate their efforts to attract, retain, or convince companies to expand in the city; in other words, they would focus intently on the
target market.

The administration used other means to understand the city's strengths and
weaknesses as a place to do business. In a 2004 interview, Patricia Noonan, the
vice president for economic development at the Partnership for New York City,
told me, "Our guys know those guys. There's a personal thing there. Someone
with a business background recognizes that business people have good
ideas. . . . There have been more opportunities for sharing and [discussing] best
practices in areas where there is business expertise than there was previously."
By "our guys," Noonan was referring to the CEOs who formed the Partnership's
core membership. By "those guys," she was referring to Mayor Bloomberg and
Deputy Mayor Doctoroff, both of whom had been members of the Partnership
before entering city government. As Bloomberg's economic development team
developed its understanding of the city's competitive strengths and weaknesses,
it was natural for them to turn to the Partnership,, whose members made decisions concerning the location of their companies' various functions. From

very early in Mayor Bloomberg's first term, administration officials engaged with the Partnership's staff and member CEOs in both formal task forces and informal brainstorming sessions. Indeed, the relationship between EDC and the Partnership was institutionalized in 2002, when in order "to help really create that bond between the public and private sector in New York City" (Alper 2003b), Andrew Alper invited Partnership President Kathryn Wylde to join the EDC's Board of Directors.

In our interview, Patricia Noonan laid out the general principles of economic development strategy that emerged from consultations between the Partnership and the Bloomberg administration. First, she argued that the near impossibility of lowering real estate costs, along with the fact that major tax cutting would gut crucial public services, made high costs inevitable in New York City. "Any company that is here has made the decision that cost is not the most important thing," she told me; "otherwise they wouldn't be here." Given this, city officials needed to be clearly focused on companies able to afford doing business in the city and take advantage of its competitive strengths, the most notable of which was the quality of the labor force. "Talent is what drives it," Noonan said; "that's our absolute top asset. . . . Every businessperson will tell you that." However, this factor alone could not ensure the city's competitive edge, as companies could access a comparable labor pool in metropolitan locations with lower costs, like Connecticut or New Jersey. Other "assets," such as the quality of the city's public services and transportation infrastructure, also needed to be developed. Noonan identified intangibles as vitally important as well. "If we're going to cost more, and we *are* going to cost more, we'd better have other things to make up for it," she said. "Part of it is, New York is New York. It's the skyline, the excitement. It's all these things, and companies value that. It's the stuff we know intrinsically, but is harder to count, that makes New York a viable location." In other words, urbanism itself — the city's culture, diversity, density, and cosmopolitanism — was a selling point. Indeed, Noonan's words echoed those of the ex–management consultant discussed in chapter 3, who highlighted the appeal of New York's urbanism to executives in global firms: "It's a prestige value. It's important in terms of international flavor and [the] sense that this is a place where if you're an up-and-coming executive anywhere around the world, you have to spend some time here."

Given the difficulty of quantifying these types of phenomena, attracting firms was a matter of determining the best way to communicate these advantages. "How do you articulate that?" Noonan asked. "I think EDC is going to be able to [communicate] New York's value proposition. We're never going to be the cheapest, but here are the things we have. Those of us engaged in economic development, those of us who have an interest in making sure New York remains competitive, have to do a better job, to keep trying to improve the way we market the stuff you can't count." In other words, economic development needed to take meaning, identity, and symbolism into account.

IDENTIFYING THE NEW BRAND: THE LUXURY CITY

Bloomberg's own business background at the intersection of the media, information technology, and financial industries — all high-margin and high-value-added industries — had shaped his own ideas about the relative importance of cost. As a CEO, Bloomberg had been notable for emphasizing high-quality customer service, generosity to employees (in exchange for expectations of absolute loyalty), and the creation of a comfortable, even luxurious, work environment. "We always have our offices in the best and most expensive parts of town while our competitors look for bargain space in the low-rent districts. It gets back to who you think is more important, your people or outsiders," Bloomberg writes in his autobiography. "I believe [in] the best for *us*. This is true not only at 'headquarters,' but everyplace. Our offices around the globe all work and look the same. The best locations and décor money can buy" (2001, 163). He stuck to this strategy even during tough times, avoiding the usual corporate practice of paring back expenses or eliminating jobs. As Partnership President Wylde put it: "He is not a guy out of corporate. . . . He is an entrepreneurial growth guy. He believes service is the way to build a business, and to build a brand" (Steinhauer 2002b).

As any newly minted MBA would be aware, the choice between cost-based competition and value-based competition (which allows for premium pricing) is one of the fundamental choices any corporate manager must make. And there is little doubt which path branding experts see as more beneficial. For example, one such expert decries "destructive price competition," writing that "the customer's loyalty needs to be based not on prices, but on points of differentiation, including brand personality, intangibles, emotional benefits and self-expressive benefits" (Aaker 2002). Management super-guru Tom Peters puts it even more starkly: "In an increasingly crowded marketplace, fools will compete on price. Winners will find a way to create lasting value in the customer's mind" (Aaker and Joachimsthaler 2000, 16).

If Bloomberg, Doctoroff, and Alper had been anything in their private careers, they had certainly been winners. Both their own experience and state-of-the-art branding theory emphasized value over cost; these ideas were now being reinforced by the consensus of economic development experts, the McKinsey report, and the administration's brainstorming sessions with the Partnership for New York City. Lowering the costs of doing business could never be the key to enhancing the city's competitiveness. Rather, it was the city's labor pool and its intangibles — the particular *value* that a city location offered businesses — that gave it a unique competitive advantage.

Early in January 2003, nearly a hundred of the city's top businesspeople and civic leaders attended an economic development summit cosponsored by the Partnership and EDC. Closed to the press, the summit included three roundtable discussions, one focused on ways in which the "private sector can strengthen New York City's fundamental competitive advantages and strategies to retain and attract private sector investment and jobs"; another on "marketing New York City domestically and abroad to encourage investment, job attraction and expanded tourism"; and still another on enhancing efforts to lobby the federal government on behalf of New York City's interests (City of New York 2003b). Robert Rubin, former secretary of the treasury and chairman of Citigroup, moderated the roundtables, and Mayor Bloomberg took part in all three. Issues addressed included risk management and security issues in the wake of 9/11, the need for viable office districts in the boroughs outside of Manhattan, strengthening the city's "first-class talent pool," and the need to "collaborate in branding and presenting the City's attributes to non-resident companies to stimulate economic growth and diversification" (City of New York 2003b).

In his remarks during and after the summit, Mayor Bloomberg indicated that his experience as a CEO had shaped his approach to economic and urban development policy. "I've spent my career thinking about the strategies that institutions in the private sector should pursue," he said, "and the more I learn about this institution called New York City, the more I see the ways in which it needs to think like a private company" (Cardwell 2003). And what was the mayor's conclusion in thinking about the city like a private company? "New York City is never going to be the lowest-priced place to do business; it is just the most efficient place to do business," Bloomberg told reporters after the summit. "You have to get value for the moneys that you're going to spend" (Cardwell 2003). However, only certain companies would be able to spend this amount of money and take advantage of the value offered in return. Thus, New York City would not compete for those companies for which cost was an overriding concern in locational decision-making. Instead, it would target a more upscale market segment. Mayor Bloomberg used remarkable language to make this point: "If New York City is a business, it isn't Wal-Mart — it isn't trying to be the lowest-priced product in the market. It's a high-end product, maybe even a luxury product" (Cardwell 2003).

The Bloomberg administration's importation of private-sector conceptions into the public-sector practice of economic development had reached its logical conclusion. The mayor could operate as a CEO, corporate management techniques such as strategic planning could be deployed in city agencies, businesses could be treated as valued clients, and the EDC could be restructured using a client coverage model. Then why not conceptualize the city as a product? This product could have a certain position in the marketplace and a specific value to add in the production process, and it could be effectively branded and marketed, just like any other product. The particular market for this product was the very high-end corporate market from which Bloomberg and his ex–private sector compatriots had emerged, and which the Partnership represented. "When you . . . get to the higher value-added businesses," Robert Rubin said at the summit, "the advantage of being here is so enormous that [the city's] going to continue to hold and attract businesses" (Cardwell 2003). A number of other summit participants agreed that a New York City location had enormous value, despite its high costs, for this subset of companies.

The upshot of the summit was clear. Out was the old "one size fits all" approach, where a lower-cost environment, achieved through tax cuts and tax incentives, was the be-all and end-all of economic development policy. In was an approach that focused on attracting those firms for which cost was not the paramount concern in locational decision-making. Economic development was no longer a matter of bribing companies to stay but rather of, first, identifying and informing firms with appropriate needs of the advantages New York had to offer and, second, building on those advantages.

REBRANDING NEW YORK CITY

In his 2003 State of the City address, given two weeks after the economic development summit, Mayor Bloomberg publicly presented a comprehensive and coherent economic development strategy driven by the city's brand as a luxury product. After arguing that only a growing economy could solve the city's long-term fiscal and economic problems, the mayor neatly summed up the premises and principles of his administration's economic development strategy: "New York is in a fierce, worldwide competition; our strategy must be to hone our competitive advantages. We must offer the best product — and sell it, forcefully" (2003b). Just as he had done as the CEO of Bloomberg LP, the mayor would implement a branding-led entrepreneurial strategy that would ensure the city's future growth and prosperity.

Mayor Bloomberg went on to present the city's competitive strengths and weaknesses in his address. Reflecting his administration's consultations with the Partnership and McKinsey, he presented the city's labor pool as its greatest economic asset. "Our unique value added is our diverse eight million citizens and workforce," Bloomberg said. "It's what makes us the best city to live in and do business." He indicated which of the city's citizens and workers actually constituted this "value added": "the best, the brightest," "the most talented," that is, the well-educated professionals who staffed the postindustrial sectors.

Finally, Mayor Bloomberg laid out a multipronged strategy for "offering and selling the best product." Some of the elements of this strategy were predictable — an aggressive urban marketing campaign, for instance. Less predictable was a shift in tax policy, both in terms of citywide taxes and in specific tax-incentive deals aimed at particular corporations. And most remarkable was the notion that urban development could be treated as product development.

Brand Communication

In his 2003 State of the City address, Mayor Bloomberg proposed a major marketing campaign involving direct media, road shows, corporate outreach, and advertising. Though such campaigns were nothing new in New York, this one was novel in both coherence and comprehensiveness, a result of the integrating role played by New York City's luxury city brand. This campaign had two distinct, but mutually reinforcing parts.

The first was a targeted and proactive effort to attract new companies and events to the city, to stir up new business, as it were. In mid-2003, EDC President Alper told the city council that "Senior EDC staff and City officials regularly meet with companies to present the case for doing business in New York. We call it our value proposition discussion" (Alper 2003a). Specifically targeted were the executives of companies that, according to the city's target market research, "aren't here but should be," as well as the executives of companies that might be convinced to expand extant New York City operations. Along with the use of common tools of corporate attraction like direct mailings and media advertising, high-level city officials, including Mayor Bloomberg, traveled through the city, the nation, and the globe to make the case for New York. As one economic development official pointed out to me, their presence added a unique element to these "road shows": "They lend a sense of sort of comfort and reassurance, when these guys hit the road to meet with international companies and say come to New York. . . . They have credibility [and] have run significant operations. They speak the language." Or, as Partnership for New York City President Wylde put it, "unlike Ed Koch and David Dinkins, Bloomberg doesn't need to lead a parade of New York business leaders [around the world]. He alone has the relationships and the international credibility. He's the whole show" (Sargent 2003b).

Indeed, Mayor Bloomberg, Deputy Mayor Doctoroff, and EDC President Alper understood their potential clients intimately—their values, tastes, and psychology—and used this knowledge during these trips. For example, in March 2003, Alper and Doctoroff led a two-day trip to London during which they met with executives of over twenty of the largest companies in the United Kingdom. The trip included one-on-one meetings with CEOs and a reception for both executives and what Alper called "influencers"—key business and media figures with a great deal of sway in London business circles (Levy 2003b). The capstone of the trip was an exclusive dinner party for a select group of corporate executives held at Mayor Bloomberg's Victorian townhouse, an elegant redbrick structure located on tony Cadogan Square. The use of the mayor's luxurious London home was of a piece with the idea that New York was a luxury product: the accoutrements of wealth were as much a part of marketing the city's new brand as the presentations and the videos and were intended to reinforce the prestige value of a New York City location. This sensibility was evident in other stops on the international road show over the next couple of years, including trips to global corporate hubs like Lille, Beijing, Munich, and Seoul. Perhaps most notable was a breakfast hosted by Deputy Mayor Doctoroff at the 2004 World Economic Forum in Davos, Switzerland.

As gratifying as these international trips may have been to the cosmopolitan self-regard of economic development officials and their corporate brethren, they were not the only, or even the most important, element of the administration's business outreach campaign. Despite the proclivities of some city officials toward "global city" rhetoric that stressed competition with cities like London, Berlin, and Singapore, economic development officials were well aware that to a significant degree the city's competition was domestic, or even regional, and focused their efforts accordingly. The staff of EDC's new Client Coverage Operating Division paid close attention to developments in their assigned industries. When a merger, new venture, or expansion was announced, they lost no time in contacting executives of the companies involved to pitch the value of a New York City location. While this type of work is the bread and butter of economic development agencies throughout the country, the Bloomberg administration's outreach efforts were notable for their proactive quality, facilitated by the client coverage model implemented at EDC, and for the mobilization of the personal connections of officials like Alper and Doctoroff.

These pitches were geared toward specific economic sectors. The city's rebranding campaign generated a list of specific industries held to be well suited to take advantage of the city's "value proposition," including biotechnology, pharmaceuticals, tourism, and television and film production.[5] This "sectoral development" approach was aimed at diversifying the city's economy and reducing its reliance on the unstable and highly cyclical financial, business services, and real estate industries.[6] So, the administration aimed to boost the biotechnology industry by providing suitable space and aiding universities' efforts to commercialize their research. Likewise, it attempted to strengthen the tourism industry by developing facilities for cruise ships in Brooklyn, expanding the Jacob Javits Convention Center, stimulating hotel construction, and stepping up city tourism advertising campaigns.

As part of its efforts to expand tourism, the Bloomberg administration focused considerable attention on attracting mega-events to the city. The EDC, in conjunction with the city's official tourism board, NYC & Co., formed the Permanent Host Committee, charged with coordinating the city's efforts to draw large events like national political conventions, Super Bowls, and so on.[7] And, of course, the administration threw itself behind the ongoing effort to bring the most mega of mega-events, the Summer Olympics, to the city in 2012. While these efforts were aimed at bolstering the tourism industry and generating tax revenue for the city, they also raised the city's international profile and provided publicity for its brand.

In his 2003 State of the City address, the mayor described the second element of his administration's brand communication strategy:

> We'll take advantage of our brand. New York is the best-known city on the planet. Our skyline is recognized worldwide. News from our streets reaches homes around the globe. At last count, more than 340 songs have been written about New York. Yet, as a city, we've never taken direct, coordinated custody of our image. By changing that, we can realize additional city revenues immediately. Many companies are interested in sponsorship agreements, similar to their sponsorship of major sporting and charitable events. We'll do this in a way that protects the integrity of our services and that creates financial returns benefiting all New Yorkers. (2003b)

In April 2003, Mayor Bloomberg created the position of chief marketing officer (CMO) for the City of New York, hiring Joseph Perello, a marketing executive, to fill the position. Mayor Bloomberg charged Perello and his team with marketing the city in the most literal sense:

> [The CMO] will establish a centralized marketing strategy for the City that will enable us to effectively leverage the world's affection and admiration for New York City and the unique assets that we possess. . . . The primary objectives of . . . the Officer include identifying the core marketing assets of the City and each City agency and tastefully centraliz[ing] them into a comprehensive value proposition to corporate sponsors much the same way any successful sports franchise or museum develops corporate support. Simultaneously, the CMO will develop proprietary City trademarks to license and distribute much the same way the NFL or the NBA develops, licenses and distributes their team and league marks. (City of New York 2003a)

The CMO was also to work with city agencies charged with drawing megaevents and film and television production to the city to ensure that the city's image was protected and enhanced.

Under Perello's guidance, the city did indeed aggressively "take custody" of its brand. There were crackdowns on the sale of unlicensed goods adorned with city logos. The city also arranged sponsorship deals with the soft-drink company Snapple, which was given a monopoly on vending machines in the city's public schools, and the History Channel, which was given free advertising on city-owned property in exchange for featuring the city in programming and advertising.[8] While sponsorship deals with credit card companies were considered and rejected — the city did not want to compete with good corporate citizens like the city's financial companies — deals were pursued that would put city-related logos and images on pajamas, toys, sports bras, golf balls, earmuffs, hair accessories, and more, all of which could be purchased on a new city merchandise Web site. However, sensitive to the possibility of undermining the city's brand and to accusations of crass commercialism, officials vowed to avoid deals that were not "tasteful" (no shot glasses, for instance). To counter critics who objected to the commercialization of the city's image and the privatization of rights to its use, the administration portrayed these deals as an alternative to cutting services or raising taxes.

From Cost to Value

The Bloomberg administration's brand-driven outreach and marketing campaigns were remarkable for their coherence and coordination. However, the real potential for the integration of branding into urban governance would only be met when branding guided basic fiscal decisions regarding taxation, spending, and service provision. Prior to Mayor Bloomberg's election, tax policy had been the economic development tool of choice in post–fiscal crisis New York City. Under Mayor Giuliani, the centrality of tax policy only increased. A subscriber to conservative tax-cutting orthodoxy, Giuliani slashed a number of city taxes in an effort to stimulate the city's economy, in addition to engaging in an unprecedented corporate-retention subsidy spree that drastically reduced the tax burdens of many of the city's largest and wealthiest companies.

Mayor Bloomberg was certainly not cavalier toward taxes, as demonstrated by his insistence during the 2001 campaign that he would not raise taxes and by his administration's attempts to find alternative sources of revenue through sponsorship and merchandising deals. Nevertheless, he downplayed taxes' negative impact on business. For instance, after his election Bloomberg publicly scoffed at companies for which tax rates were decisive in locational decision-making, saying that "any company that makes a decision as to where they are going to be based on the tax rate is a company that won't be around very long. . . . If you're down to that incremental margin, you don't have a business" (Tierney 2001). Deemphasizing tax cutting was of a piece with the notion that the city needed to compete on the basis of value rather than cost.

This approach was translated into policy early in the administration's first term, as it acted to end so-called corporate welfare. Among the Bloomberg administration's first actions upon taking office was to scuttle one of its predecessor's most publicized and controversial incentive deals, a proposed $1.1 billion subsidy to the New York Stock Exchange. If implemented, this would have represented the largest subsidy ever given a private entity in the history of New York State — all the more alarming given the fact that there was little evidence that such a move was ever seriously considered or was even feasible. In May 2002, Mayor Bloomberg called the threatened move "inconceivable," and he went on to say, "Come on, this is the Big Apple. This is the financial center of the world and that isn't going anyplace and the [Exchange] understands that" (Williams 2002).

The belief in the city's intrinsic attractiveness to business (or to certain businesses, anyway) regardless of cost played an important role in the development of the administration's policy toward the use of discretionary tax incentives to retain companies.[9] By mid-2002, EDC President Alper had outlined a transparent process and a stringent set of criteria for discretionary corporate retention deals, bringing an increased degree of skepticism and scrutiny to companies' claims that they were considering a move out of the city. He also elaborated clear guidelines for the size and structure of any deal that was offered, which included the use of "clawback" provisions imposing penalties on firms who violated the terms of their deals. The industry desks of the EDC's Client Coverage Operating Division played an important role here, acting to head off prospective demands for tax subsidies by tracking upcoming lease terminations and other developments, sizing up the likelihood of a company's move out of the city, proactively contacting companies and encouraging them to stay without the use of tax incentives, and evaluating the importance of companies that did threaten to leave to the city's economic base.

The killing of the New York Stock Exchange proposal provided initial evidence that there would be a new standard for retention deals, but its outrageously generous terms and the fact that virtually no one outside of the Giuliani administration thought it necessary made it a relatively easy target. A more important test came later in 2002, when the securities firm Bear Stearns made a play for its third job-retention incentive package in just over a decade. Despite earlier commitments to keep jobs in the city, it threatened to move 1,500 jobs to New Jersey when the lease for its downtown Brooklyn location ended in 2004 unless it was granted a subsidy to move the jobs to Lower Manhattan. Administration officials accused the firm of trying to renege on its commitments, and by the end of 2002 negotiations were at an impasse. Ultimately, the administration refused to grant any new incentives — and Bear Stearns did not move any employees to New Jersey.[10] Though the administration would go on to grant some tax deals to existing New York City companies, they typically met the criteria that Alper had laid out and were nowhere as frequent as in the past.

In addition, the administration shifted the focus of tax incentive deals away from retaining companies and jobs already in the city. Instead, it emphasized the use of tax incentives to achieve job and revenue growth by encouraging existing city companies to expand their operations or by attracting new firms. For example, in 2002 the city granted subsidies to two New York firms, the Hearst Corporation and the Bank of America, in exchange for expansions that both promised to create jobs and involved the construction of new Manhattan office buildings. Subsidies were also used to lure new firms into the city, though they usually were a minor element of intensive campaigns to woo these firms' executives, often with the personal involvement of high-level city officials. For instance, in 2004 Virgin Atlantic was granted a small, $11 million subsidy for locating the headquarters of its new low-fare airline in New York City. City officials and Virgin executives indicated that the subsidy was less important in this decision than the city's deep and talented labor pool and the intensive, apparently successful efforts on the part of EDC President Alper and others to argue that the city's cultural dynamism was a perfect fit with Virgin's "hip" image (Kim 2004; Magill 2004).

"We've essentially ended corporate welfare as we know it," Mayor Bloomberg told an audience of corporate executives in late 2003, "by no longer paying companies — who wouldn't have left anyway — to stay in our great city" (Bloomberg 2003a). This statement must be taken with a grain of salt, as the administration's definition of "corporate welfare" was narrow, excluding a host of other forms of corporate subsidization besides retention subsidies (Moody 2007, 170–172).[11] Nevertheless, the policy it described represented an important shift away from the idea that cost reduction for particular companies was the be-all and end-all of economic development policy and indicated that the administration's embrace of an economic development policy based on the value the city could offer was more than rhetoric alone.

A second way in which the administration privileged value over cost was captured by the headline of a 2002 *New York Times* article discussing Bloomberg's plans to address the city's budget deficit: "What Kind of Businessman Raises Your Taxes?" (Steinhauer 2002b). Since the fiscal crisis of the 1970s, New York City's mayors had primarily relied on slashing city spending rather than raising taxes to close the city's recurring budget gaps. In contrast, faced with huge budget deficits in late 2002, Bloomberg put forward a plan including $3 in tax increases for every $2 in budget cuts, most of which resulted from one-time savings rather than service cuts or layoffs. The mayor's plan included an increased commuter tax (which required, and never received, the approval of the state legislature) and a whopping 25 percent increase in the city's property tax, which could be enacted without state government approval and which was passed by the city council, though after being reduced to 18.5 percent.

Mayor Bloomberg repeatedly defended the tax hikes by evoking the memory of the fiscal crisis of the 1970s. For Bloomberg, the lesson of that crisis was the foolishness of rashly cutting services in the name of fiscal responsibility and economic recovery. In his 2003 State of the City address, he stressed the importance of high-quality public services for the city's economic success:

> [D]uring the fiscal crisis of the 1970s, services were cut so much that crime gripped whole neighborhoods, fires gutted whole blocks, and garbage littered the streets. . . . I won't permit that history to repeat itself. . . . Last month, we took the difficult but necessary step of raising the property tax rate. . . . No one likes the imposition of taxes. . . . But devastating the very services that make this the world's second home is far worse than paying more. . . . Taxes and frugality are far better than crime, filth and abandonment. (2003b)

According to the mayor, the central choice faced in balancing the budget was between "paying more" and "devastating the very services that make this the world's second home" (a slogan describing New York that was a product of the city's branding campaign). Higher taxes, while clearly undesirable, would not undermine the city's economic position; in contrast, gutting the services that taxes provided would do far more to undermine the city's desirability as a place to live and do business. Despite predictable and sustained critiques from anti-tax conservatives and some business groups (McMahon 2005; New York Post 2002; New York Sun 2003), Bloomberg stuck to this position throughout his first term in office. Even as his 2005 reelection campaign geared up, he refused to rule out further tax increases if reelected. "My objective would be to bring taxes down, but when you say, 'taxes are too high' you're talking about a number out of context. The real issue is after you pay your taxes, what kind of a life do you have?" Bloomberg said. "If you think taxes are too high, I would argue you're probably a little bit out of step with businesses that are coming here, businesses that are expanding here, people who are driving residential real estate prices up. . . . Nobody wants to pay taxes, [but] would you really like to go back up to 2,200 murders a year?" (Saul 2005c; Seifman 2005). The answer then to the question posed by the *New York Times*? The kind of businessman who raised taxes was one who believed that quality city services created more value for business than lower taxes.[12]

Urban Development as Product Development

In the Bloomberg administration's urban marketing campaign and in its prioritization of city services over lower taxes, we can see how the city's brand as a luxury product well worth its high cost provided a guide to two important aspects of urban governance. But as remarkable as this was, it was not the whole story. For the city's brand as a luxury product also guided urban development strategy and linked it to these other areas of policy. Indeed, it was in the arena of urban development that the Bloomberg Way reached its apotheosis, subjecting the very urbanism of the city itself to its corporate logic.

As has been discussed, the practice of branding is centered on the notion that products are subordinate to brands: the brand should shape the product, rather than merely reflect its qualities. In the context of urban branding this translates into the fact that "cities are rebuilt to reflect their marketing imagery" (Holcomb 1994, 117). As Greenberg puts it in her discussion of early branding campaigns in New York, "the 'real' material city was altered as much as possible to conform to the idealized image of the brand" (Greenberg 2008,

34). Going further, we might say that the aim of urban branding is not just to narrow the gap between the desired image of the city and its reality but to eliminate it altogether. In the evocative language of one urban branding expert, urban branding "demands associating the place with 'stories' about the place not by simply adding them next to the name or trying to imply them by isolating beautiful images of the place. The 'stories' need to be built in the place, not least by planning and design interventions" (Kavaratzis 2005, 336). While urban development has always been a cultural process, shaped by the exigencies of meaning and imagination (Low 2000; McDonogh 1999; Rotenberg and McDonogh 1993), under urban branding such factors not only impinge upon development but are central to it: development becomes cultural all the way down.

Since urban branding has typically been associated with the promotion of tourism and entertainment, the cultural aspects of development under urban branding are usually intended to act as a spur to *consumption* (Hannigan 2003). This was true of the Bloomberg administration's strategy to build the luxury city. However, this strategy went one step further: efforts to "build stories into the place" were also intended to strengthen the city's role in *production*. For the postindustrial sectors that comprised the target market of the administration's branding efforts, the city itself—both the built environment and the urban culture that animated it—served as an economic input. Thus, the city was branded not just as a product to be consumed but as one that would serve as an element of postindustrial production in both direct and indirect ways.

Nearly three decades ago, Henri Lefebvre predicted that urbanism would soon supplant industrialization as the central "problematic" of capitalist society. In the course of making this sweeping claim Lefebvre made the observation that "urban reality modifies the relations of production. . . . It becomes a productive force, like science" (Lefebvre 2003, 15). In the branding-inspired development strategy that was crucial to the Bloomberg Way, we can see a realization of this prediction—the city was imagined and reshaped as a value-adding product, an input into the postindustrial production process itself.[13]

In his 2003 State of the City address, Mayor Bloomberg argued that exploiting the city's competitive advantages required nothing less than an aggressive transformation of its physical form in order to produce an environment appropriate to the needs and desires of well-educated professionals and those businesses in the financial, media, and business services sectors that employed them. "To capitalize on [our] strength[s], we'll continue to transform New York physically . . . to make it even more attractive to the world's most talented people. . . . New York is the city where the world's best and brightest want to live and work," Bloomberg said. "That gives us an unmatched competitive edge, one we'll sharpen with investments in neighborhoods, parks and housing. . . . We'll invest in neighborhood livability, cultural organizations, education, research and medicine [and we'll] expand and develop business districts in all five boroughs" (2003b). Bloomberg went on to outline an aggressive and comprehensive program of urban development that was followed faithfully over the next few years by the agencies under Deputy Mayor Doctoroff's control.

This program had two central elements, each aimed to enhance the city's brand. The first was the creation of a high-quality residential and recreation environment. This included the facilitation of housing development, primarily luxury housing, throughout the city but especially in Williamsburg/Greenpoint, West Chelsea, Harlem, and downtown Brooklyn. This housing, along with other development, was to be built according to high architectural and design standards, as the DCP sought to increase the city's profile as a center of cutting-edge architecture. The result was a number of luxury housing developments that provided not only all the expected amenities but also the distinction of living in a building designed by a globally renowned architect like Richard Meier or Bernard Tschumi. The administration's residential strategy also included curtailing "inappropriate" residential development to protect "neighborhood character" in suburban-style, single-family-home neighborhoods in the outer boroughs. Together, these two initiatives served several upscale market segments: young single professionals, retired empty nesters, and families seeking to stay in the city.

Also emphasized was the development of parks and open space, especially along waterfront areas. The former site of the Fresh Kills landfill in Staten Island was slated to become a massive new park with everything from mountain bike trails to equestrian facilities; the city's network of bike paths was to be lengthened and strengthened, especially on the waterfront; sidewalk cafes were to be encouraged; and specific waterfront sites in West Harlem, Williamsburg/Greenpoint, and the far west side of Manhattan were to be developed with a mix of uses. Indeed, mixed-use plans aimed at creating "unique spaces" were proposed for areas throughout the city, from Lower Manhattan to Morrisania in the Bronx. This residential and recreational strategy was intended to create a luxurious urban environment, a set of "unequaled amenities" attractive to well-educated professionals, including lush parks, extensive leisure opportunities, and aesthetically pleasing residential options.

The second major element of the administration's urban development agenda was the creation and enhancement of diverse office districts throughout the city. After the January 2003 economic development summit, Deputy Mayor

Doctoroff remarked that "we must find creative ways to build on and improve the City's unique competitive advantages to attract companies and spur private investment. We . . . need to develop areas outside the traditional central business districts of Midtown and Lower Manhattan so that companies that need to diversify or need lower cost alternatives can be accommodated within the five boroughs" (City of New York 2003b). Even more clearly conceptualizing urban development as product development, in 2004 Doctoroff spoke of the need to "offer different products for different corporate customers. Lots of the people who want to be in New York want to be in Midtown Manhattan, and Midtown Manhattan is pretty much at capacity. So we're trying to [expand that district]. We're trying to do it all over the city. . . . We recognize we've got to offer different things to different people" (DeDapper 2004). The administration formulated plans for commercial development in a number of different areas, each aimed at a particular segment of the office market. Downtown Brooklyn and Long Island City, for example, were intended to compete with New Jersey for lower-cost office space housing back-office functions that did not need to be situated in Lower or Midtown Manhattan but still needed to be relatively close by. Jamaica, in Queens near the JFK airport, was conceived of as "an airport corporate park environment" (Alper 2004). Other districts — Harlem, the Hub in the Bronx, and Flushing in Queens — were to be developed as commercial centers geared toward industries that served local markets, like government services and health care, and supplemented with a mix of retail, entertainment, and tourism-related development.

While all the elements of this two-pronged "five-borough development strategy," as the mayor repeatedly called it, were important, one project was given priority: the Hudson Yards plan, which by 2002 — as I detail in chapter 6 — had developed into one of the most ambitious planning ventures in city history. Despite some early hesitancy on Mayor Bloomberg's part to have the city fund an Olympic stadium in the context of a harsh fiscal crisis, he quickly committed to the project, a commitment assured by the appointment of Doctoroff as deputy mayor. By early 2003 the importance of the plan was apparent. In his State of the City address, Bloomberg called the plan "our first priority" and devoted several minutes to discussing the plan, while barely mentioning plans for World Trade Center site redevelopment (2003b).

The Hudson Yards plan served as both the capstone of the Bloomberg administration's urban and economic development strategy and a microcosm of the strategy itself. It would create the city's next great high-end office district, an extension of Midtown Manhattan, which was rapidly running out of space to grow and which was clearly viewed by the mayor and the deputy mayor as the city's premier CBD.[14] Its eighty-story office buildings would provide suitable homes for the high-margin companies that administration officials had indicated were best suited to capitalize on a New York City location. Moreover, the Hudson Yards plan included luxury housing, waterfront development, and new open spaces, not to mention a convention center expansion that would stimulate the tourism industry. Finally, the stadium was the most important element of NYC2012's plan for the Olympics, the biggest mega-event of them all, one that reinforced the ideas of competition, ambition, cosmopolitanism, and diversity so crucial to the administration's efforts to market the city.[15]

Deputy Mayor Daniel Doctoroff brought into city government a strong belief in the importance of urban development to economic development. This approach had grown in the hothouse of NYC2012, as Doctoroff, NYC2012 Chief Planner Alexander Garvin, and others developed an Olympic plan that reflected the agenda of the city's real estate elite, aimed above all at stimulating an array of stalled or wished-for urban development projects that had as their raison d'être the increase of property values in certain areas of the city. This agenda consisted of a real estate development strategy legitimized as a jobs strategy (Fitch 1993, 49). It was a "supply side" approach in which the subsidized construction of high-end office and residential space would ostensibly lead to the expansion of jobs and economic activity in the city's postindustrial sectors. Moreover, this real-estate-centered strategy was narrow in terms of both scope and content. It focused on particular projects rather than on the city as a whole, and on the construction of high-end office space and luxury housing to the exclusion of open space, infrastructure, urban design, and so on.

Doctoroff's appointment ensured that the NYC2012 plan and its component parts, the most important of which was the Hudson Yards plan, would remain significant. However, the Olympic plan was now embedded in a development strategy very different than the one in which it had originated. Urban development now had to do much more than guarantee that real estate values and profits rose. In the name of squarely facing interurban competition, it had to advance the city's brand as a luxury product through the provision of a multidimensional urban environment conducive to employees and employers in the high-value-added postindustrial sectors that comprised the city's target market. This included not just office towers and high-end housing but the construction of open and recreational space and the cultivation of culture, aesthetics, leisure, consumption, and neighborhood quality of life. As I discuss in subsequent chapters, this new rationality of development would shift the justification and function of the Olympic plan, and of the Hudson Yards plan, in subtle but important ways.

THE CLASS POLITICS OF URBAN BRANDING

New York City's brand as a luxury product — the idea that, at least for the target market of high-valued-added companies in the media, finance, and business services sectors, the value inherent in a city location outweighed its high cost — provided a coherent strategic framework for a host of policy areas. While there were precedents for much of what was included under the rubric of the city's brand — marketing of city merchandise, plans for the development of themed districts like the far west side, and the bid for the Summer Olympics, for instance — this brand linked these interventions with policy domains not typically included in past branding campaigns: basic fiscal policy, service provision, proactive outreach to business, and policies governing the use of tax subsidies to attract, grow, or retain business. One could also include the administration's education policy reforms, aimed at enhancing the quality of the labor pool so important to the city's target market (Moody 2007, 187), as well as the invigoration of cultural policy aimed to support the cultural institutions and activities that were an important element of the city's appeal to postindustrial elites (Currid 2007, 165–166). The city's brand as a luxury city both shaped the details of particular policy areas and bound these policy areas into a coherent competitive strategy.

Thus, the Bloomberg administration's use of branding seemed to fulfill the potential for branding as place management to provide a coherent approach to urban governance. In large part this was due to the fact that the individuals immersed in the practice, conceptions, and language of branding were now governing: the gap between city officials and branders that had been a primary obstacle to urban branding achieving its potential as a form of urban governance was now closed. But if the unity of branders and government officials permitted the drastically increased coherence, scope, and role of branding in urban governance, it also demonstrated the contradictions both of branding in general and its use by the Bloomberg administration.

Like the Bloomberg Way in general, branding, due to its corporate and at least pseudoscientific nature, is often represented as providing a means to overcome politics as usual, to "depoliticiz[e] previous cleavages [like] race, class, and party identification" (Pasotti 2010, 5), in order to fulfill the interests of the city as a whole. It holds at least the promise of inclusiveness, of generating what we might call "urban patriotism" among a wide array of groups. Moreover, it does this in a way that permits urban political elites to avoid confronting fundamental issues in urban governance, such as national urban policy (or a lack thereof); the lack of resources for infrastructure, public works, and municipal services; the persistence of urban inequality, racial conflict, and poverty; and the reality of zero-sum interurban competition. In other words, urban branding promises a cheap and relatively painless way for urban political elites to at least appear to be doing something to enhance urban competitiveness in a manner that accepts, rather than challenges, existing political and economic arrangements (Greenberg 2008; Ruben 2001; Short 1999). But what the fusion of branders and governmental officials in the Bloomberg administration demonstrates is that branding's antipolitics are undermined by not only its inability to overcome existing political cleavages but also its engendering of new forms of political conflict. In this case, these conflicts, far from depoliticizing the cleavage of class, actually intensified it, as both the selection of a target market for the city's brand and the urban imaginary that animated it were deeply influenced by the class identity of the branders now ensconced in city hall.

The determinative role of selecting a target market for a city's brand, which necessitates the privileging of the desires and interests of certain groups over others, gives it major political ramifications. Despite the portrayal of urban branding as having the potential to achieve the inclusion of a wide array of groups, it is in fact premised on an original exclusion, that of the interests of those outside the target market. Bloomberg acknowledged this: in the same speech in which he described the city as a "luxury product," he also remarked that "New York offers tremendous value, *but only for those companies able to capitalize on it*" (Cardwell 2003, emphasis added). But what was not acknowledged was that this conclusion was deeply affected by the particular experiences and interests of key officials and administration allies. The twist in this case was that those selecting the target market chose to target themselves and those like them: executives and upper professionals in high-value-added, postindustrial sectors. The move away from cost as the basis of competitive strategy certainly made sense to those who had been instrumental in the rebranding of the city, given the sectors from which they had emerged. Furthermore, the heavy emphasis on the city's urbanism and labor force as its most important competitive strengths reflected the experience, outlook, and self-regard of a well-educated, professionalized, cosmopolitan postindustrial elite.

These individuals and groups represented a severely limited, if dominant, point of view, one that excluded the experiences of low-wage service workers or middle-income professionals squeezed by the high costs of living in the city. Indeed, it did not represent the views of much of the city's business community, including many real estate elites, small business owners, and owners of manu-facturing and other industrial businesses. By early 2003, a split was emerging in the city's business community, with small business owners, industrial and manufacturing interests, and real estate elites on one side and the Partnership on the other. This conflict had erupted with Mayor Bloomberg's 2002 propos-als to raise taxes to close the city's budget deficits, as the Partnership refrained from opposing the tax hikes, much to the consternation of representatives of real estate and small business and of the business press. This controversy sig-naled a deeper divergence, as a new calculus of cost and value represented by the idea of the luxury city had very different economic and political implica-tions for various industries and sectors. Most notable was the unfamiliar spot in which it placed the real estate industry. Real estate was now outside the innermost circle of power, along with beleaguered manufacturing firms and small businesses. As one developer complained after Bloomberg announced his tax hike, "He's not seeking our counsel. He didn't talk to us. He just said it" (Bagli 2002). Thus, the city's rebranding had implications for the balance of power among the city's elites.

The conflicts and tensions generated by the selection of the target market for the city's rebranding strategy were not just about economic interest alone, but were linked to highly charged issues of meaning, representation, and identity. The Bloomberg administration's urban branding campaign, like all such cam-paigns, not only tried to fix a target market but also, in its selection of a new brand for the city, to fix a particular urban imaginary as official, dominant, and consensual. Urban branding is premised on the idea that the branding process can discover and construct "a unique . . . identity" that can become broadly shared across a city's population (Kavaratzis and Ashworth 2005, 510). But confidence in the branding process to determine and strengthen a single city identity that can become broadly shared is belied by the fact that "repre-sentations of the city are not politically neutral" and thus branding constitutes "a struggle for the meaning of the city" (Short 1999, 53).[16] Just as the selection of the target market is political, so too is the selection of the specific identity that will become the basis for branding the city.

The branding of New York as a luxury city was thus loaded with political significance. For those who contributed to the development of this brand, the city was a place of not just luxury but also cosmopolitanism, globality, elite sociality and leisure, competition, innovation, and ambition. All these things made it a magnet for "the best and brightest," as Bloomberg called the highly educated professionals and executives who circulated in the city's postindus-trial sectors — and who were now ensconced in city hall. This imagined New

York City served as the symbolic undergirding for the administration's branding campaign to the exclusion of other extant and possible imaginings of the city. It was clearly, once again, a product of the particular class position and experience widespread among the administration's top officials, as well as among the participants in its branding research, including the executives surveyed by McKinsey & Company and the CEO members of the Partnership for New York City. Indeed, the concept of luxury itself is linked to class. In her insightful ethnography of luxury hotels, Rachel Sherman notes that the consumption of luxury products and services not only reflects structural inequality but actually constitutes it: "Through the consumption of luxury service, the guest is constituted not just as a legitimate customer, but also as a privileged subject," she writes. "What appears as a recognition of the individual's needs and desires, is in fact a recognition of class prerogatives. Like schools, social clubs, and other upper-class institutions, the hotel helps guests to gain . . . 'a sense of one's place.' . . . Guests emerge from the hotel with higher expectations and a new sense of entitlement" (2007, 225). Using the luxury hotel as an analogy, we can see that the effort to enhance New York City as a luxury product does more than just reflect the ostensible importance of certain types of businesses and residents to its economic future; rather it suggests that the city would become an incubator of elite identity, with the best and the brightest "emerging" from the city with a stronger sense of class identification and entitlement.

However, the analogy has its limits. In luxury hotels class inequalities are visible and class privileges legitimate; both are fundamental to the very mission of the establishment. In New York City, and in cities in general, such inequalities and privileges are contested, and the concept of luxury itself is a highly charged one, with by no means unambiguously positive connotations. For many New Yorkers struggling with the high costs of housing, food, and other necessities, the city's luxuriousness was exactly the problem. Moreover, for many New Yorkers the decidedly nonluxurious qualities of the city — its grittiness, embrace of radical difference, and status as a fount of alternatives to the cultural mainstream — constituted its appeal.

The particular ways in which these conflicts over the imagining of the city played out in the context of debates over the administration's luxury city–inspired urban development strategy, and the Hudson Yards project in particular, are discussed in detail in the following chapters. While these issues are always present in debates over urban development, the administration's institutionalization of branding served to inject issues of urban meaning and identity directly into the heart of development politics. What would be at issue in these debates was not just the shape of particular plans or neighborhoods, but what New York represented and what being a New Yorker meant: urban development politics were about to become intensely personal.

CLASS, POLITICS, AND THE LUXURY CITY

This chapter has described the completion of the corporate analogy that constituted the Bloomberg Way. Just as the mayor was a CEO, the city government a corporation, and businesses and residents clients and customers, the city itself was now a product to be branded, marketed, and developed. This branding entailed the application of specific techniques of knowledge production, the linkage and substantiation of several domains of urban governance by the city's luxury city brand, the deployment of urban imaginaries, and plans for the transformation of the city's landscape. Class played a crucial role in all of this: for the Bloomberg administration and its allies, rebranding New York City was a class project. Through the application of particular forms of knowledge and expertise, the Bloomberg administration sought to make the city more attractive to a certain class grouping, which was also the source of many of the authors of this branding campaign. Moreover, it proposed to do so by constructing an urban development and marketing agenda guided by a brand derived from a particular urban imaginary itself reflective of a particular class identity.

Nothing captures the role of class in this rebranding process as powerfully as does the London road show that took place in March 2003. The luxurious lifestyle represented by Bloomberg's mansion in London and the mobilization of networks of TCC members and other elites at the social events during that visit themselves served as testaments to the bona fides of the luxury city, to the status of New York as both a good place to do business and a good place to be a businessperson. As a crucial constitutive element of the Bloomberg Way, the rebranding of New York City injected politics directly into this explicitly antipolitical approach to urban governance.

CHAPTER FIVE

The Bloomberg Way

This, then, was the Bloomberg Way: the mayor as CEO, the city government as a corporation, valued businesses as clients, citizens as customers, and the city itself as a product. While corporate language and management practices in government have become more common in recent decades, the Bloomberg administration was more than inflected or influenced by the corporate experience of the mayor and his key economic development officials. Instead, corporate rationality was pervasive and foundational, the DNA of the Bloomberg Way. This gave economic and urban development policy a coherence and comprehensiveness lacking in the past. There were integration and coordination of processes of producing knowledge of the city, managerial techniques and a strategy for physically remaking the city.

The corporate rationality of the Bloomberg Way, and the development agenda that emerged from it, clearly reflected the experience, underwrote the power, and furthered the interests and desires of the city's postindustrial elite. Yet the Bloomberg Way was represented as serving the interests of the city as a whole, as providing a path to shared prosperity, as "preparing *all* of New York to compete, and to win, in the future" (Bloomberg 2004, emphasis added). Inherent in this approach to urban governance was an insistence that a single, overarching interest of the city could be not only identified but also achieved if the right policies were pursued. These results could be obtained, the mayor promised, if New Yorkers kept "the good of our whole city ahead of any narrow ideological or political interests" (2003b). Thus the Bloomberg Way constituted a denial of the legitimacy of "groups and their struggles" (Isin 1998, 55) even as it was itself a product of such struggles. It was simultaneously deeply antipolitical and deeply political. This was the crucial and constitutive contradiction of the Bloomberg Way.

THE ANTIPOLITICS OF THE BLOOMBERG WAY

Bloomberg's refusal to participate in the glad-handing, back-slapping, baby-kissing theater so often described as "politics" received much attention. But the Bloomberg Way attempted a more profound submergence of politics, a denial of the inevitability, let alone the desirability, of conflict in a city teeming with diversity and inequality. This approach was aligned with a broader shift in American society since the mid-1970s. The period of neoliberalization has been marked by a "national ethos of . . . antipolitics" (Boggs 2000, 12), characterized by the withdrawal of many citizens from political and even electoral participation as well as the denigration of the political sphere as inauthentic, ineffectual, corrupt, and divorced from the needs and desires of the citizenry (Boggs 2000; Frank 2000). This shift has been bolstered by the valorization of "the market" and all things corporate, as the ineptitude of the state and the political system are contrasted with the private sector's ability to get things done — to "perform." This corporate-inflected antipolitics is both linked to and reinforced by a concomitant technocratization of public policy, as the ostensibly apolitical application of expertise toward the solutions of clearly defined problems has become more and more influential in a number of policy realms, including those of "development" and antipoverty policy (Ferguson 1990), environmental policy (McAvoy 1999), and welfare reform (Lyon-Callo and Hyatt 2003), as well as entrepreneurial urban policy (Gough 2002). In its intermingling of corporate and technocratic antipolitics, the Bloomberg Way provides a unique example of this antipolitical ethos; it also demonstrates its spatial dimension.

Corporate Antipolitics

The antipolitics of the Bloomberg Way were deeply rooted in its corporate nature. By casting the city government as a corporation, businesses as clients, and the city as a product, the administration made the implicit claim that the fundamental aim of economic and urban development policy was as clear and well defined as the fundamental aim of a firm.[1] Whereas competitiveness in the name of profit is the overriding objective of corporate management, the Bloomberg Way posited urban competitiveness toward the end of economic growth as the overriding objective of urban management. Such growth would supply increased tax revenues that the mayor argued represented the only long-term solution to the city's recurrent budget crises and the only way in which high-quality city services could be maintained (Bloomberg 2003b). Economic growth would also provide more jobs, which Bloomberg was wont to call "the most effective social policy" (Bloomberg 2003a).[2]

This transposition of corporate logic into urban governance, and the antipolitics it represented, had two important implications. The first was the radical reduction of the possible standards of urban development policy to one:

the ability to attract and retain targeted businesses and individuals, that is, to enhance the city's competitiveness. Even a cursory glance at New York City history, to say nothing of urban history in general, indicates that economic and urban development policies and projects are inherently divisive and conflictive, marked by racial and class tension, community opposition, litigiousness, cross-industry dispute, real estate manipulation, intergovernmental conflict, clashes of ego, and deep divergences in types of claims on and values attributed to particular places by their different users. But the overwhelming focus on competitiveness marginalized questions of distribution, whether of jobs, income, tax burdens, state largesse, or economic benefits. What became the key metrics of policy were the quantitative outcomes of enhanced competitiveness — the growth of jobs, aggregate city income, and overall tax revenue.

The second was the model of accountability intrinsic to the Bloomberg Way. Mayor Bloomberg, armed with his own business expertise and that of his economic development officials, claimed the prerogative to determine the most efficient and effective strategy to enhance the city's competitiveness, while asking to be judged on the basis of the success of this strategy. Just as the mayor had expected his employees at Bloomberg LP to defer to his decisions and judge him by the firm's bottom line, so New York City's citizenry was expected to defer to the CEO mayor's decisions and reserve their judgment until the "accountability moments" provided by elections. This translated into a prioritization of outcome-based accountability over the sort of procedural accountability that might ensure public participation and input into governmental decision-making.

It was not at all a given that such a model of accountability could survive the transposition from corporate to urban governance. The fact that Bloomberg LP was a private company had meant that Michael Bloomberg had not been subject to the kind of accountability expected of a CEO of a publicly held company, to say nothing of an elected official. The arbiter of accountability for Bloomberg as a CEO had been the market for his company's products. In such a situation, Bloomberg's outcome-based model of accountability might have been tenable. However, accountability worked very differently in the realm of urban governance, certainly in New York City. Even given the long-term erosion of public participation and input that has accompanied the move toward often exclusive, ad hoc, and opaque "stakeholder" models of participation in urban governance in entrepreneurial cities in general (Swyngedouw, Moulaert, and Rodriguez 2002) and New York in particular (Marcuse 2002, 157–159), process-based measures of accountability that ensure some level of public participation in and scrutiny of governmental decision-making did exist in New York. This was especially true in the area of urban development, as the centralization of power under Robert Moses and the massive displacement of poor people and industry under the city's urban renewal program (Schwartz 1993) had led to a number of important efforts to decentralize control and ensure citizen participation in planning and development decisions (Angotti 1997). While often ineffective, these still had the potential to subject the process of governmental decision-making to procedural forms of accountability foreign to the corporate world. These procedural mechanisms were in direct conflict with the Bloomberg Way; one of the two would have to give.

Technocratic Antipolitics

The corporate nature of the Bloomberg Way foreclosed the legitimate expression of conflicting interests, values, or desires in the formulation of the means and the ends of urban policy and sought to radically diminish the space of politics in New York City. Moreover, one particular characteristic of the corporate model that was being imported from the private to the public sector reinforced this antipolitical thrust: a deep technocratic streak. As one high-level aide hedgingly acknowledged to me, the administration's approach was "more than good government, [but] almost technocratic in some ways." It is the nexus between technocracy and corporate management practice that defined the particular business culture from which Bloomberg, Alper, and Doctoroff emerged: that of the TCC, centered on the professional and meritocratic figure of the "global executive," dedicated to the pursuit of expert-determined "best practices" and quantitatively measured "benchmarking" (Sklair 2001).

I have discussed the mayor's respect for professionalism and expertise, as well as the ways in which his campaign promise to deliver "performance" was translated into an emphasis on the necessity of evaluation — within the administration and of the administration by the public — through the use of quantitative measurement (which of course dovetailed with the quantitative approach to economic growth just discussed). Indeed, Mayor Bloomberg's demand that he be judged on the basis of performance was premised on the existence of adequate and unambiguous metrics of this performance. Moreover, the idea of performance implies a strict separation between ends and means, treating questions of policy as a matter of finding the "best," most efficient and effective, means to achieve a particular, predetermined end, thus reducing complex and contentious interventions with profound political implications to straightforward applications of technical expertise. The high-level and low-level staff that Mayor Bloomberg had hired based on professional qualifications and relevant expertise would be responsible for developing the best means to the ends the mayor had declared paramount. This technocratic ethos suited many of these professionals, whose expressed rejection of "politics as usual" and admiration for the mayor for being "above politics" echoed the distaste for politics often displayed by professionals (Marcuse 2002, 160–161). In doing so, they, like the administration they were a part of, made the implicit — and incorrect — claim that the ends of the policies and interventions embodied by the Bloomberg Way were broadly shared and not subject to political challenge.

Spatial Antipolitics

Finally, inherent in both the synoptic quality of the Bloomberg Way and its premise of the pervasive importance of interurban competition was a particular antipolitical spatial ideology: New York City was conceived of as a bounded and socially unified economic unit in competition with other such units. This emerged most clearly in the administration's rebranding campaign. In the previous chapter, I briefly noted that branding implies a reified understanding of the spatiality of the city. As James DeFilippis (2004, 24) points out, the notion that the city is a "thing" has been crucial to both entrepreneurial urban governance and the arguments of its advocates. Indeed, the idea that a place can be understood as an entity has been a cornerstone of economistic reasoning about cities since Paul Peterson (1981), the Milton Friedman of urban neoliberalism, influentially applied the principles of neoclassical economics to urban governance. Such reasoning and the derivative notions that city government can be run like a corporation and the city itself branded like a product rely on a particular spatial ideology, whereby cities are understood as bounded, coherent entities in competition with other such entities.

On the one hand, there is some truth in this. As local governments have become more concerned with increasing the attractiveness of that which lies within their jurisdiction, they have become, despite the market-centric rhetoric of neoliberalism, more actively involved in direct interventions into local economies and landscapes (Brenner and Theodore 2002; Gough 2002). Thus, there is a sense in which "the city" as a spatial phenomenon can, to some degree, be conflated with its political boundaries.[3] However, this ignores the fact not only that, as urban scholars have long pointed out, cities are embedded in and affected by broader social, economic, and political relations but also that cities and these extralocal factors are engaged in a mutually constitutive relationship, albeit one structured by struggle and power (Harvey 1989; Leeds 1994, 209–246). This spatial reification of the city has three practical implications, each of which can be seen in the context of the Bloomberg Way.

The first is an overestimation of the degree to which cities (via their governments) can act to increase their own competitiveness and thus create benefits for its citizens (DeFilippis 2004, 17–36). This faith in local autonomy is glaringly apparent in the practical literature on branding, which contains virtually no acknowledgment of constraints that extralocal processes and powers place on local governments, with the exception of interurban competition itself. The result is a high degree of optimism concerning not just the efficacy of branding as a method to transform the governance and shape of the city but also the ability of these transformations to create meaningful benefits for those within the city. Moreover, as Peck (2005, 765) points out, the notion that cities *can* act on their own to improve their circumstances often transmutes into the notion that cities *must* do so, usually via the adoption of one or another nostrum of neoliberal orthodoxy.

In fact, the Bloomberg administration acted quickly to assert the city's self-determination in a variety of ways, a step consonant with the autonomy Mayor Bloomberg viewed as key to achieving performance as a CEO mayor. Despite the success of some of these efforts, particularly those seeking to diminish the city's reliance on higher levels of governance, the autonomy of city government — a legal creation of the New York State government, subject to state and federal oversight, and dependent on state and federal funds — was limited in important ways by these relationships. And this is to say nothing of other factors that impinged upon the city's ability to conduct its own affairs, such as the global financial crisis, the impact of federal immigration policy on the city's labor markets, and the antiurban bias in the structure of the constitutions of New York State and the United States. Despite Bloomberg's wish that "the city should be responsible for its own destiny" (Nagourney 2001), city government did not and could not operate as an autonomous and self-contained unit.

Second, the notion of the city as a bounded entity implies the inevitability of current patterns of interurban competition. There is no acknowledgment that such patterns might be changed, or that cities' pursuit of entrepreneurial strategies reinforces and exacerbates the pressure of interurban competition (Harvey 2001; Peck and Tickell 2002). Somewhat paradoxically given the ascription of autonomy to cities, interurban competition leads to a dramatic narrowing of the alternatives that cities can consider, as any policy that might potentially undermine competitiveness is *verboten* and policies implemented successfully elsewhere are dutifully aped (Peck 2005; Ward 2006). Moreover, the notion that the competitive field exists prior to and regardless of the action of cities acting individually or collectively results in "fast policy transfer" (Peck 2002) — the quick circulation of urban policy innovations that occurs as cities imitate each other, which degrades the ability of any particular urban intervention to actually achieve a sustainable competitive advantage (Peck and Tickell 2002; Tabb 1982). It also forecloses the possibility that more beneficial results might be achieved via interurban *cooperation* aimed at taking steps to lessen the destructive effects of interurban competition (DeFilippis 2004, 30; Harvey 2001, 368).

As we have seen, the Bloomberg administration, to an extraordinary degree and to the exclusion of virtually all other governmental ends, placed enhancing competitiveness at the center of urban governance. When it did go beyond focusing on increasing the city's competitiveness, it focused on reshaping various competitive fields to the city's advantage — for instance, by coordinating lobbying efforts in Washington, D.C., or Albany or by pushing to change federal formulas for the distribution of antiterrorism aid — rather than reducing interurban competition or allaying its negative consequences. This was in part a product of the Bloomberg Way's corporate nature and class constitution, as the highest members of the administration saw competition as a beneficial force for all involved (Brash 2006b). However, this acceptance of the "extralocal rule systems to which [cities] are . . . subjected" (Peck and Tickell 2002, 393) was also a product of the spatial ideology inherent in the Bloomberg Way.

Finally, the idea that the city is an entity implies that there is an interest of the city as a whole, despite the multiple and conflicting interests of the individuals and social groups that populate it. Peterson was seminal in reconciling these two seemingly irreconcilable points; he did so by proposing that the social role of individuals and groups as residents of a particular locality could be abstracted from their other social roles (1981, 21). This proceeds from a spatial premise: the notion that residency in a territory *in itself* comprises a "role" can only be sensible if one imbues the territoriality — and thus the boundedness — of the city with its own social efficacy. Thus, if we reject the notion that the city is a bounded entity, we must also reject the notion that there can be an identifiable "interest of the city as a whole." Or to put it another way, while there may in fact be an identifiable role — or more accurately, an identity — that derives from commitment to place, it does not operate distinct from other, nonlocal ones, such as race, class, gender, and so on.

Furthermore, Peterson assumes the singularity and homogeneity of this "role," a dangerous assumption given that urban identity is a subject of debate and conflict. Rather than thinking of this as a "role," we might instead think about this as what Michel-Rolph Trouillot (2001, 132) has called the "identification effect," consisting of the not-always-realized "capacity to develop a shared conviction that 'we are all in the same boat' and therefore to interpellate subjects as homogenous members of various imagined communities." Here, this identification effect was formed on an urban rather than a national scale and aimed to delegitimize or elide conflict internal to New York City. Thus, it was essential to the antipolitics of the Bloomberg Way. While it would be a mistake to view this "urban patriotism," as we might call it, as a fait accompli or, even more problematically, as an a priori form of consciousness waiting to be discovered, it would also be a mistake to underestimate its power, especially in the environment of post-9/11 New York City.

Despite the challenges posed by both theory and, as the persistence and exacerbation of inequality in cities pursuing entrepreneurial policies demonstrate, empirical evidence (Fainstein 2001b), the straightforward position that "policies which enhance the desirability or attractiveness of the territory are in the city's interest because they benefit all residents — in their role as residents of the community" (Peterson 1981, 21) is a bedrock principle of both urban neoliberalism in general and the Bloomberg Way in particular.[4] While this is reflected in the notion that "preparing all of New York to compete, and win" would redound to the benefit of all New Yorkers, it was also present in the way in which the administration's branding campaign sought to fix the notion that New York was a luxury city as an official, singular, and consensual urban imaginary. Furthermore, as we shall see in chapter 9, the Bloomberg administration's deployment of "urban patriotism" played a crucial role in its endeavors to win support for the Hudson Yards plan.

These three consequences of the antipolitical spatial ideology inherent in the Bloomberg Way — that there is a unitary interest of the city as a whole, that the city's only alternative is to pursue this interest via enhancing competitiveness, and that the success of such a strategy is within the power of the cities acting alone — constitute what Peck (2005, 765) has called an "insidious scalar narrative," whereby cities are not only things but also things endowed with agency, a unified interest, and ultimate responsibility for their own fate. Under the Bloomberg Way, this reifying logic was linked to a corporate and technocratic ethos, intensifying its antipolitical qualities and leading to the specific reification of the city as a product. Having discussed the explicit antipolitical ethos of the Bloomberg Way, let us now turn to its implicit political nature.

THE (CLASS) POLITICS OF THE BLOOMBERG WAY

As Richard Shearmur has noted, the analogizing of business and government, a fundamental tenet of all entrepreneurial urban governance and one taken to its logical conclusion by the Bloomberg Way, is deeply flawed:

> A city does not produce a single item nor have a simple finality: it is a site of production for many different things, but also a place where people live and die, where social conflicts occur, and where many groups and coalitions express widely differing needs, aims, and ambitions. In a city, there can be no consensus on what the purpose of competition should be, or on who should benefit. Thus when a claim is made that a city should become more competitive, the first question should be "Who is making the claim?," and the second one "Who would benefit"? (2008, 613)

Claims that a city must become more competitive underwrite the interests of a specific set of actors, rather than the unitary and shared interest of the city as a whole: they are political. In the case of the Bloomberg Way, this was exacerbated by the fact that both of Shearmur's questions had but a single answer — the city's postindustrial elite, composed of both members of the city's TCC and upper professionals. The Bloomberg Way was a class project, an effort to legitimize the power and wealth of the members of this class alliance and to reshape the city in line with its interests and desires.

Moreover, this class project was now working directly through the mechanism of state power. Drawing on a variety of existing governmental practices and norms incubated in the post–fiscal crisis neoliberalization of the city's governance — elite intervention, privatism, privatization, the centrality of competitiveness, the need for business-friendliness, and so on — the Bloomberg Way represented a reworked neoliberalism, a new articulated ensemble of governmental practices, processes, and conceptions. But whereas previously the neoliberalization of the city's governance had been a somewhat incoherent, inconsistent, and ineffective affair, the Bloomberg Way represented a much more coherent and focused approach to governance, one that had the potential, at least, to avoid some of the pitfalls of this post–fiscal crisis neoliberalization and put the city on a sustainable political-economic footing.

This revitalization of the capacity for action of the local state is worthy of comment for two reasons. First, it distinguishes the Bloomberg Way from the patterns of state practices so often found in anthropological analyses of the state, which typically highlight the contradictions, disjunctures, instabilities, disaggregations, contestations, and decentralizations of the state (Das and

Poole 2004; Gupta 1995; Trouillot 2001). And indeed, the Bloomberg Way was not exempt from this; the remainder of this book focuses on the ways in which the controversy over the Hudson Yards plan exposed and exacerbated its inherent contradictions and tensions. Nevertheless, the Bloomberg Way's coherence reminds us of the broader point of anthropological work on the state, and of the tradition of critical state theory that it draws upon: while the coherency, stability, and fixity of the state must not be assumed a priori, neither can they be precluded.[5] The point, as Akhil Gupta has put it, is "leav[ing] open the theoretical question as to the conditions under which the state *does* operate as a cohesive and unitary whole" (1995, 392).

Philip Abrams provides a clue as to where to look for the source of such conditions. He notes that typically "political institutions conspicuously fail to display a unity of practice. . . . They are divided against one another, volatile and confused . . . with no sustained consistency of purpose." There are exceptions to this, however: "Such enduring unity of practice as the ensemble of political institutions achieve is palpably imposed on them by 'external' economic, fiscal and military organizations and interests" (Abrams 2006, 124).[6] To the (not insignificant) degree that the Bloomberg Way did display such a "unity of practice" it was indeed imposed by an external interest, that of class. Thus it was the marriage of class to state power that distinguished it from the typical pattern of disjuncture and incoherence.

But if this marriage of class to state power provided coherence to state practice, it also created new forms of political division and conflict. As the postindustrial elite first reworked the institutions of the local state and then, through those institutions, attempted to reshape New York City as a place to live and do business in a way conducive to its interests and desires, a number of fundamental issues concerning the relationships among the state, social groups, and the economy arose, all of which had important, and often novel, political implications.

In a general sense, the application of the skills, concepts, language, and experience of the postindustrial elites who entered city government represented a claim to the legitimacy of their class power and wealth. Their willingness and ability to take on the problems of the city served as evidence of both their extraordinariness (and thus the rightness of their enrichment and empowerment over the past decades) and their commitment to the common good (which served to elide divisions of class altogether in the name of social, or urban, solidarity). This was true of the claims to efficacy and managerial expertise inherent in the notion of the CEO mayor, as well as the technocratic assertion that the city's "problems" could be addressed by the proper application of the expert knowledge of the upper professionals who for the first time in thirty years found themselves welcomed in city hall. What the postindustrial elites that populated the highest levels of the administration described using the humble language of "public service" and "giving back" was in fact an assertion of their rightful place as the rulers of the city, an audacious and deeply political act that other elite groups at the pinnacle of city politics were sure to notice — and respond to. This play for class hegemony worked through grounded state practice in a number of ways, and in so doing generated a number of new political conflicts.

A number of policies proposed by the administration, especially in the area of urban development, were the product of the class-inflected imagining of New York as a place of competition, innovation, and cosmopolitanism that drew the "best and the brightest" from around the globe. This inspired the city's campaign to rebrand the city as a luxury product, which in turn guided policy-making in areas from taxes to urban development. The attempt to "fix" a single urban imaginary and have it serve as a basis for policy opened up a cultural front in the city's development politics. Now, the meaning of the city and the symbolic value of various groups within it were as much at stake as the shape of certain neighborhoods or the uses of certain parcels of land.

In addition, it had enormous implications for the material concerns that are the nitty-gritty of urban governance and that often dominate debates over economic and urban development: land use, real estate value, the distribution of tax burdens, the provision of services, and so on. The luxury city strategy privileged the needs of high-value-added companies (and their elite employees) for which the value of a New York location outweighed the cost, to the detriment of more cost-sensitive industries and residents. It proposed to restructure the city as not just a space of residence and identification but an economic field — to the benefit of certain interests (such as the media, finance, business services, and information technology sectors in which the postindustrial elites had incubated) and the detriment of others.

While the adverse implications the luxury city strategy had for small businesses and industrial and manufacturing interests (to say nothing of the millions of individual New Yorkers for whom the city's high costs of living posed a daily challenge) were important, it was its implications for the city's heretofore-dominant real estate interests that were especially noteworthy. The details of the administration's development agenda, as well as the revival of coherent, state-led development itself, augured a major restructuring of the relationship between the local state (now in the hands of the postindustrial elite) and the real estate interests that had been the prime beneficiary of the fragmented and privatized approach to development so long seen in New York City. This development agenda was structured by a different rationality than that of strict real estate profitability. Deputy Mayor Doctoroff captured this in early 2005 when speaking of the administration's desire to substitute luxury housing for office space at the World Trade Center redevelopment site over the wishes of Larry Silverstein, the site's owner and a prominent developer. He said that "there is an inherent conflict between someone who is market-driven and the city's interests, which should be rationally discussed" (Magnet 2005). For decades, the interest of the city and the interest of "market-driven" real estate investment had been conflated: what was good for real estate was good for New York. But no longer. The logic of "market-driven" real estate development and that of the "rationally" determined "city's interest" often were in accord, as demonstrated by the dedication shared by real estate interests and the administration to stimulate commercial and residential construction throughout the city and bring the 2012 Olympic Games to New York. But they were not identical. For the first time in decades, state action in the development arena did not have the provision of nearly unconditional support for real estate interests as its raison d'être, instead focusing on a broader strategy of interurban competitiveness that at times worked directly against the interests of real estate.

The postindustrial elite, particularly its TCC members in city hall, asserted that it was their interests rather than those of real estate that hewed closest to the interest of the city as a whole and that, via their control of the local state, they were best suited to lead the city toward that interest. Thus, the postindustrial elite's effort to establish its class hegemony in the city demanded a concomitant strengthening of the organizational capacities of the local state. The reorganization of the institutions of city government in line with managerial practices imported into city hall from the private sector was the bureaucratic prerequisite for the formulation and implementation of a coherent set of policies — as well as for bringing wayward interests into line. The centralization of all the city agencies related to economic and urban development, under the command of Deputy Mayor Doctoroff, was especially important in this regard, as it gave him control of what one reporter aptly called "an awesome arsenal of city development agencies" with power over almost every aspect of the city economic and urban development policy (Golson 2004).

Using this control, Doctoroff and other key members of the administration's development team, as well as the mayor himself, dangled a number of carrots to acquire the consent of key actors, and they brandished a number of sticks when coercion was deemed necessary, all in order to implement, generate support for, and vitiate opposition to the development agenda that was so crucial to their reworking of the city as an economic field and, ultimately, to the postindustrial elite's play for class hegemony in the city. The willingness of the administration, most crucially via Andrew Alper's new "client-centered" EDC, to reach out to and support certain businesses comprised the more solicitous side of this strategy. Through a variety of means — such as making it easier for executives' black cars to get around the city, the judicious use of tax incentives, and enhancing the appeal of the city as an urban environment to well-educated members of the labor force — the administration channeled benefits toward high-valued-added companies that in their view belonged in the luxury city.

But as one administration policy advisor told me, being "client-centered" was not the same as "pander[ing] to business." The Bloomberg administration was willing to deploy state power against the interests of certain businesses, even those in the postindustrial sectors, when they did not, as that advisor described it, "hold up [their] end." This was evident in the willingness of the administration not only to call the bluff of companies like Bear Stearns and the New York Stock Exchange when they made hollow threats to leave the city unless subsidized but also to publicly label them as desirous of "corporate welfare," as well as in Mayor Bloomberg's frequent public admonishment of fellow corporate executives he perceived as acting badly.

The administration's ability and willingness to employ state power to both induce and coerce was particularly important in its disciplining of the real estate industry. Doctoroff's centralized control over the city government's development apparatus gave him the ability to mete out rewards to real estate developers and others who chose to follow the administration's dictates and punishments to those who did not. While the administration steadfastly rejected the notion that the deputy mayor took advantage of this ability, it was effective nonetheless as many in the real estate industry certainly saw the fate of their projects as dependent on staying in the good graces of the deputy mayor.

This newly assertive and coherent stance on the part of the local state was widely noted — at times in praise and at times in condemnation. While liberals and good-government types cautiously praised the Bloomberg Way's assertion that "the city's interests" should guide development policy rather than "the market," many real estate elites and conservative advocates of small governments interpreted it as a sudden and jarring incursion of the state into the private sector. This led to the labeling of Mayor Bloomberg as, depending on one's political stripes, either a "left-leaning progressive" (Barbaro 2009b) or a typical big-government, urban liberal (Peck 2006a, 691–692). This might have been in keeping with the orthodox dualism that dominates American political discourse. But it missed the crucial fact that the newly invigorated ability of the local state to act in a coherent and forceful manner, its newfound "unity of purpose," was supplied by shared class interests, experiences, desires, and practices. What was at issue was not the shifting boundary between the state and society but the way in which a certain social grouping — the postindustrial elite — had, through its mobilization and participation in governance, transformed the local state into a vehicle for class politics and thus rendered this boundary largely irrelevant.

A POLITICIZED ASSAULT ON POLITICS

The Bloomberg Way, to use John Clarke's fortuitous words, represented a "politicized assault on 'politics'" (2004, 90), and in so doing was a continuation of the broader class war from above raging in New York City and the United States for the better part of four decades. Clearly, this seemingly paradoxical political formation has important strengths, as it has been for the most part successful in obscuring or justifying the restoration of power to economic elites central to neoliberalism. Yet it is vulnerable to contradiction, as its political nature threatens to undermine its antipolitical facade. In the case of the Bloomberg Way this vulnerability was heightened by the fact that the administration had centered its development strategy on the Hudson Yards plan, which was profoundly shaped by political considerations and interests. Moreover, the area the plan addressed, the far west side of Manhattan, had been the site of some of the most contentious battles over the shape of the city's built environment. If the Bloomberg administration wanted a rigorous test of the efficacy of its corporate, technocratic, and antipolitical urban governance strategy, it could not have picked a better place, or a better plan.

CHAPTER SIX

Far West Side Stories

If Lower Manhattan is haunted by office towers that once were, the far west side of Manhattan is haunted by office towers that are yet to be. The area west of Eighth Avenue between roughly Thirtieth and Fifty-ninth streets has long been targeted by New York City elites as a site for the expansion of the midtown Manhattan CBD. From the 1920s onward, the city's most powerful real estate developers and brilliant planners have churned out proposals for the commercial development of an area once labeled by prominent real estate family scion and Giuliani-era CPC Chair Joseph Rose as "our birthright . . . our future, our growth potential" (2000). As of the mid-1990s, these visions remained unfulfilled. The westward expansion of the midtown Manhattan CBD reached Ninth Avenue only after a long and halting process that left the far west side littered with the corpses of failed commercial development plans. However, during the late 1990s a number of elite planning efforts came together to make the long-heralded redevelopment of the area once again seem imminent. Of these, NYC2012's was the most important, associating the development agenda of the city's real estate elite with the internationalism, cosmopolitanism, and celebration of competition represented by the Olympics movement. This effort, it was hoped, would vitiate the political opposition that had scuttled other efforts to redevelop the far west side.

By making the redevelopment of the far west side of Manhattan its "first priority" (Bloomberg 2003b), the Bloomberg administration was entering dangerous territory. The far west side had been the site of both the most grandiose plans and the bitterest defeats of the real estate elite. For any number of developers and planners, NYC2012's push for far west side development, now taken up by the administration, represented an opportunity to fulfill the decades-old vision of a bustling, contemporary, and profitable midtown Manhattan CBD stretching all the way to the Hudson River. For local community groups, housing activists, and residents, this push represented the latest in a series of incursions into their neighborhood. Former efforts swathed the area with transportation infrastructure and left the prospect of high-end commercial and residential development looming, literally, in the shape of new skyscrapers on the eastern edge of Times Square. To better understand the situation inherited by the corporate, antipolitical Bloomberg Way, this chapter outlines the history of far west side development and its discontents. It also describes in some detail the overlapping plans produced by NYC2012 and the DCP that together formed the basis for the Bloomberg administration's Hudson Yards plan.

THE LONG DEVELOPMENT OF THE HUDSON YARDS PLAN

Midtown was originally centered on the east side of Manhattan along Madison and Park avenues from roughly Fortieth to Sixtieth streets. It moved westward in three great bursts of office construction during the late 1920s, the late 1960s and early 1970s, and the 1980s. With the aid of a mid-eighties downzoning of the east side that forced commercial development westward, along with the richly subsidized redevelopment of Times Square and its environs, the last of these booms resulted in office towers appearing for the first time west of Seventh Avenue.[1] The last of these booms left in its wake a copious amount of unoccupied office space that was not absorbed until the late 1990s when construction began again and development reached what had long been considered the eastern boundary of the far west side, Eighth Avenue.[2]

This halting and difficult colonization of speakeasies, porn shops, low-scale residential buildings, industrial lofts, and low-rent entertainment districts belied the long-made claims that the development of the far west side was imminent. It took decades of plans, foundation studies, relocations, condemnations, developers' machinations, and public subsidization to achieve what had been treated for decades as a fait accompli: the expansion of the CBD westward to Eighth Avenue. This history began with the RPA's seminal 1929 plan and continued into the 1960s, when both the RPA and the Lindsay administration targeted the far west side for development.[3]

The Lindsay administration's 1969 plan was the most fleshed out and ambitious of these — and indeed of any plan for the far west side until the development of the Hudson Yards plan three decades later. It proposed the intensive commercial and residential development of the far west side, particularly the area west of Eighth Avenue between Forty-second and Fifty-ninth streets. It included plans for 30 million square feet (msf) of office space, new hotels, and housing, most of it strung along Forty-eighth Street; parks and other civic facilities; a new subway line; and development of the Hudson River waterfront, where a new convention center and ocean-liner terminal would be built. It was conceived of as self-financing: the tax revenue generated by the development was expected to cover the costs of planned public improvements.

The 1969 plan left a number of legacies, generally not of the kind envisioned by its authors. One was the Jacob K. Javits Convention Center — and it was finished seventeen years after the plan was released. Even then, the center was situated far from the location that was originally proposed and never sparked the kind of peripheral development its planners anticipated.

A second legacy of the 1969 plan was even more disheartening to those who envisioned a far west side of skyscrapers and luxury housing. It can be traced to the injudicious decision of Lindsay administration planners to target the northern, residential portion of the far west side for commercial redevelopment. Long known as "Hell's Kitchen," a name whose origins lay in the area's nineteenth-century reputation for criminality and violence, this residential neighborhood had once extended southward to Thirty-fourth Street. However, by the 1960s the southern portion of the area was dominated by transportation infrastructure: the elevated West Side Highway, which cut the neighborhood off from the river; an elaborate network of roads and ramps serving the Lincoln Tunnel and the Port Authority Bus Terminal; and rail cuts and yards servicing Pennsylvania Station. Previous decades had seen hundreds of tenement buildings demolished and thousands of residents displaced in the name of transportation efficiency (Conard and Smiley 2002). Only the portion of Hell's Kitchen lying north of Forty-second Street was relatively untouched by the bulldozer and wrecking ball.

Unsurprisingly, the proposed extension of the Midtown CBD into this area generated much rancor among residents. Drawing on deep wellsprings of political activism and awareness generated by past and current development fights, as well as the neighborhood's history as a union haven, residents successfully opposed most elements of the Lindsay plan.[4] In exchange for accepting the convention center, they won major neighborhood protections in the form of the Clinton Special District, which contained zoning, preservation, and antitenant harassment provisions that protected the area's low-rise, residential, and affordable character. Ironically, the only success for those who dreamed of a midtown Manhattan CBD running from river to river, the Javits Center, came at the cost of removing almost two-thirds of the far west side from the development slate. The only realistic location for remaining commercial development on the far west side was the portion lying between Thirty-fourth and Forty-second streets.

A third important legacy of the 1969 plan was found not on the streets of Hell's Kitchen but in the offices of the city's planning and development organizations. The failure of the 1969 plan and the subsequent post–fiscal crisis fragmentation of planning left a number of frustrated planners in its wake. While ex-Lindsay officials like Alexander Garvin, Jay Kriegel, Alexander Cooper, and Jacquelin Robertson all continued on to successful careers, it was not until the mid-1990s that they again had the opportunity to engage in the sort of ambitious, comprehensive planning the Lindsay administration had embraced. That opportunity was provided by NYC2012. These ex-Lindsay officials, along with a handful of others, assumed important roles in the development of the bid and its most important element, the Hudson Yards plan.[5] This continuity in personnel between the 1969 plan and the Hudson Yards plan was reflected in a continuity of form: the later plan contained many of the same elements as the earlier one.

In light of the fiscal crisis of the 1970s and its aftermath, the predictions of massive postindustrial job growth upon which the plans of the RPA and the Lindsay administration were premised seemed like a cruel joke. However, as the city emerged from the fiscal and economic depths in the 1980s, visions of west side office towers once again danced in the heads of city planners. While the commercial redevelopment of Times Square that began in the late 1980s slowly pushed the edge of the CBD westward, plans to further expand Midtown proposed by both the Koch and Dinkins administrations ultimately amounted to naught. Mayor Giuliani, elected in 1993, was happy to push Times Square redevelopment along; however, his ideological rejection of urban planning made a more ambitious push for CBD expansion unlikely.

However, the late 1980s and early 1990s did see a good deal of activity around one key far west side development site, the Caemmerer Hudson Rail Yards, or the Hudson rail yards as the site is commonly known.[6] These twenty-six acres of railroad tracks lie well below the grade of the street and are constituted by two megablocks, bordered on the east and west by Tenth and Twelfth avenues, on the south and north by Thirtieth and Thirty-third streets, and bisected by Eleventh Avenue. Owned by the MTA, they have long served as storage space for Long Island Rail Road commuter trains after they drop off their cargo of suburban commuters at Penn Station, two blocks to the east. Their close proximity to Midtown Manhattan, Penn Station, the Hudson River, and the Javits Center, as well as their ownership by a state agency, which exempts plans for their use from the normal city review process, has long made the rail yards a tantalizing, if impractical, development site. Driven by comparisons to the New York Central rail yards lying to the north of Grand Central Station under what is now Park Avenue, which in the early twentieth century were decked and developed with luxurious apartment and office buildings to form the then-core

The Hudson rail yards, facing west. (Used with permission of New York City Economic Development Corporation)

of Manhattan's Midtown CBD, real estate developers and planners have long sought to transform this literal hole in the ground into a profitable development project.

The yards became a viable development site in the late 1970s, when Richard Ravitch, head of the MTA and west side real estate developer, oversaw the construction, in the yards, of support columns that would be able to support a deck. Once it was possible to build over the yards without disrupting their transportation functions, development proposals quickly emerged. In 1986, the Canadian development company Olympia and York, famous for their development of London's Docklands, announced a plan to raze Madison Square Garden, the arena that lies atop Penn Station at Thirty-third Street and Seventh Avenue, replace it with twin office towers and a retail complex, and erect office buildings and a new arena over the rail yards. A year later, the company was about to finalize a deal with the MTA and the owners of the Garden when the stock market and real estate market crashed, scuttling the plan. Soon after, the MTA developed its own plan to build a new arena and office buildings over the rail yards, but it was done in by the same forces that doomed Olympia and York's plan.

In the early 1990s, George Steinbrenner, the owner of the New York Yankees baseball franchise, tormented by years of losing teams and declining attendance at Yankee Stadium, located in the down-at-the-heels South Bronx, began to agitate for a new stadium, eyeing New Jersey as a potential location. In early 1993, New York Governor Mario Cuomo proposed the Hudson rail yards as a site for a new Yankee Stadium along with an adjoining commercial and entertainment complex. Mayor Dinkins opposed the plan, instead offering Steinbrenner a $150 million Yankee Stadium renovation. In 1994, with Giuliani, a vocal and lifelong Yankees fan, installed in city hall, the team's attendance continuing to sag, and Steinbrenner's stadium desire stoked by new, publicly subsidized ballparks being built for his team's competitors in Baltimore, Chicago, and elsewhere, the plan to move the Yankees to the Hudson rail yards was revived. For the next five years, Mayor Giuliani led a forceful campaign to bring his beloved Yankees to the far west side of Manhattan. However, by 1999 the plan was dead, done in by widespread condemnation from planners, economic development professionals, community groups, liberals, government officials, and real estate developers (who desired the site for their own, more profitable, uses). This outcome was also the result of the Yankees' remarkable late-1990s run, which saw them win a handful of championships and their attendance, payroll, and profits shoot through the roof, thus rendering incredible claims that the team could not compete in the South Bronx.

While plans for a Yankee Stadium on the rail yards were moribund by 1999, plans for another stadium there — an Olympic Stadium — were very much alive. By mid-1996, with the idea of a New York City Olympic Games gaining momentum, Mayor Giuliani formed a task force to study the possibility of submitting a bid for the 2008 Games. While the mayor and members of NYC2008 warned against interpreting this as a marriage of convenience, their words of caution rang false: NYC2012 needed government support, and Giuliani needed the political cover that an Olympic bid would provide for his unpopular campaign for a west side stadium. Plans for a west side Olympic Stadium came into the world baptized by intra-elite politics.

Daniel Doctoroff's recruitment of Alexander Garvin as NYC2012's lead planner gave both the development agenda behind the bid and the bid itself the stamp of professional approval. Coming from such a prominent and well-respected planner, the idea of using the bid as a vehicle to push urban development projects was more politically palatable than if it had come from real estate developers or the Giuliani administration. Other urban planners quickly got on board, lured by the notion, as one planner put it, that "the Olympics would be the 21st-century equivalent of Robert Moses, the one way you can mobilize support for massive public investment" (Applebome 1996). By early 1997, the Olympics bid had garnered support from a broad range of real estate elites, and preliminary planning efforts had begun. However, in May 1997, the United States Olympic Committee (USOC) told NYC2012 that it was deferring all American bids for the Summer Games until 2012, and its plans gathered dust for almost two years.[7]

When NYC2012 went on hiatus in 1997, the commercial redevelopment of the far west side had not yet resurfaced as a central concern of the city's real estate elite. By 1999, things were different. Deregulation and a skyrocketing stock market had supercharged the city's financial sector. A new high-tech sector was growing in a "Silicon Alley" running along Broadway from SoHo to Chelsea. The glittering new theaters and retail stores of a sanitized Times Square were packed with well-heeled suburbanites and tourists from all over the world pumping their money into a newly revived tourist economy.

All this economic activity generated some office development, particularly in Times Square, where several large firms built new headquarters. But it was not enough: office rents shot upward and commercial vacancy rates plummeted. As had been the case in the late 1920s and again in the late 1960s, members of the city's real estate elite began agitating for a major expansion of the city's CBD, especially on Manhattan's west side. In addition, the city's tourism boosters lamented the shoddy state of the Javits Center and pointed to the convention business being lost to cities across the country, where new and refurbished convention centers were coming on line at an unprecedented rate.[8] CBD and convention center expansion on the far west side were back on the table.

Renewed interest in stimulating office development and the demise of his proposal for a west side Yankee Stadium led Mayor Giuliani to change his approach to far west side development. While acknowledging that the Yankees would not be coming to the Hudson rail yards, in his 1999 State of the City address Giuliani proposed an expanded "convention and sports corridor" running down Eleventh Avenue and across Thirty-third Street. This proposal included a renovated Javits Center connected to a new domed stadium on the western Hudson rail yards, which would serve as a home to the New York Jets football franchise (whose involvement is discussed below) and as auxiliary space for the Javits Center. It would be complemented on the eastern part of the rail yards by a new Madison Square Garden replacing the old arena above Penn Station, which would be torn down and replaced with office towers. All of this would be served by an extension of the Number 7 subway line, which at the time terminated at Eighth Avenue and Forty-second Street in Times Square. Giuliani's proposal was met with some skepticism, given his inability to start any other major development project or to coexist peacefully with Governor Pataki, whose support would be necessary. In addition, it did not provide for the large-scale expansion of the Midtown CBD increasingly in vogue among members of the city's real estate elite. However, the proposal did add to the momentum of the broader movement for far west side redevelopment.

This momentum was now centered on NYC2012. Its leaders were working closely with city and state officials, prominent real estate developers, and other real estate elites to formulate plans for CBD expansion. Alexander Garvin and his team developed a number of options for the location of Olympics facilities, including the use of existing or temporary facilities. Generating the most enthusiasm, however, was the possibility of locating these facilities on Manhattan's far west side as part of a larger commercial redevelopment plan. Faced with the need for Olympic facilities, the need for more office space, Giuliani's proposal for a sports and convention corridor, and potential controversy about a west side stadium, NYC2012's planners made a bold choice, as *New Yorker* magazine architecture critic Paul Goldberger described:

> Garvin thought about all the proposals that had been made for the site, and he wondered if the solution was not to just say yes to everything. There was enough land to build a stadium, construct a few skyscrapers and a new Madison Square Garden, have some open space, and put in a station for subway and commuter trains. All these pieces would have to be somewhat jammed together, and there wouldn't be room for the sea of parked cars that surrounds every other football stadium, but wasn't that the point? To figure out how to make the most un–New York thing imaginable — a huge venue for sporting events — in a New York way? (2000)

It was also the point to figure out how to satisfy the interests of all the elites who had joined forces behind NYC2012. Garvin's gambit was not just a planning decision driven by principles of urbanism, but a *political* decision: to sell the Olympics to real estate and corporate elites as CBD and convention center expansion; to sell the Olympics to the mayor as a way to finally get a stadium on the west side; to sell the stadium to the governor as a Javits Center expansion, a pet project of Pataki's for years; and to sell CBD expansion and the stadium to planning advocates and potential stadium opponents as an urbanistically sound plan for open space and transit expansion. This was at once an efficient planning solution, an audacious mega-project proposal, and an intricate political balancing act.

As the Olympic plan neared completion in early 2000, its far west side elements became more solid and more expansive, now including proposals not just for the Hudson rail yards but for the thirty-nine square blocks west of Ninth Avenue between Twenty-eighth and Forty-first streets. In fact, commercial redevelopment became more and more central in public justifications of the entire endeavor, with the stadium and Olympics facilities presented as a means to that end. NYC2012 planners thus enthusiastically hooked the organization's own agenda — the planning of a 2012 Olympic bid — into the broader agenda for CBD expansion emerging from the Giuliani administration and from the city's real estate elite.

Bearing out the skeptical reaction to the proposals made in Mayor Giuliani's 1999 State of the City address, the administration had done little to advance his "convention and sports corridor" during that year. But when the mayor took to the dais a year later for his 2000 State of the City speech, it was apparent that one thing *had* advanced since: the ambition of his proposals for the far west side. Late in this speech, after retreating from an earlier threat to "blow up" the Board of Education building in Brooklyn (now he was just proposing to sell it), the mayor outlined a proposal for what he called "Midtown West." Alongside the elements outlined a year earlier — a subway extension, a stadium, an arena, and a convention center expansion — was now a proposal for large-scale commercial development. Giuliani also publicly threw his support behind NYC2012's formative plan. Indeed, the Giuliani administration, and the DCP in particular, had been actively working with NYC2012 to coordinate the two emerging plans.

A third group joined the city government and NYC2012 in pushing the commercial redevelopment of the far west side. One week after Mayor Giuliani's 2000 address, U.S. Senator Charles Schumer announced the creation of a high-powered commission, the Group of 35, to develop a plan to spark and guide future office development. Cochaired by Schumer and former U.S. Treasury Secretary Robert Rubin, the commission was dominated by real estate elites and corporate executives, though it included a handful of labor leaders, policy professionals, and planners.[9] Several of its members were directly involved in NYC2012's planning process, and many others would donate money to the bid or serve on its board of directors or one of its committees. The Group of 35 quickly joined NYC2012 and the DCP in identifying the far west side as a key location for office development. In a report issued in June 2001, it essentially used the NYC2012's plan for the area as a prototype for such development on the far west side (though the Group of 35's report did not propose a stadium). For the first time in three decades, the city's political, corporate, and real estate elites were all united behind the project of redeveloping the far west side. The political will, it seemed, was there; only the details were missing.

That would change in short order. Though the physical elements of NYC2012's proposals for the Hudson Yards area (discussed below) were in place by early 2000, the issues of financing the development and selling the proposal to a public that had rejected a far west side stadium for the Yankees remained. By spring of 2000, NYC2012's planners were discussing the possibility of having the plan finance itself rather than drawing on the funding streams typically used in large capital projects.[10] This was expected to be a political selling point: the project, in theory at least, would not draw funding away from other development projects financed through traditional means. However, it also meant that its funding would not be subject to the politically unpredictable legislative approval process, a fact that made it vulnerable to accusations that the avoidance of legislative review violated norms of accountability, public process, and democratic decision-making.

As 2000 progressed, there was one piece of external financing that NYC2012's planners would be able to count on, as it became clear that the New York Jets were willing to invest a large chunk of private capital in the construction of a west side stadium. After the May 1999 death of Leon Hess, the long-time owner of the Jets, Johnson & Johnson heir Robert Wood "Woody" Johnson IV bought the team. He quickly announced his interest in moving the Jets out of New Jersey as of the 2008 expiration date of the team's lease at the dumpy Giants Stadium, shared with the region's other football team, the New York Giants (and the site of Doctoroff's 1994 Olympic revelation). Preferably, the team would move to the west side of Manhattan, where it would no longer have to share a stadium or revenues from the exorbitant prices that the team could charge for luxury suites, season tickets, and personal seat licenses.

NYC2012's planners expected the Jets to pick up the majority of the cost of a new stadium, estimated at the time at between $100 and $300 million, with the city funding the balance. Without this private funding for a far west side stadium, an existing facility—most likely Shea Stadium in Queens—would have to be used for the Olympics. While this would not undermine the bid, it would undermine the plans for far west side redevelopment: without an Olympic stadium, these plans would not benefit from the rosy glow of the Games. With the involvement of the Jets, NYC2012's planners could now drop alternative sites for the Olympic stadium from consideration and focus on the west side alone.

The hopes that the city would do its financial part to construct a Jets/Olympic stadium were bolstered when Mayor Giuliani playfully reached out to Woody Johnson during his 2000 State of the City address, saying, "We could make a naming rights deal. We'd get a lot of money for that. . . . We could come up with a name like . . . 'Johnson and Johnson Stadium.' . . . I just picked one out. We could have the Jets play there" (Giuliani 2000). Giuliani, Johnson, the National Football League, and NYC2012 were soon in intense discussions about moving the Jets to Manhattan. In mid-2000, the Jets hired Jay Cross, a deceptively soft-spoken Canadian who had guided successful stadium-building campaigns in Toronto and Miami, to head its team of experienced and high-powered lobbyists. Not long afterward, the Jets floated their first design plans for the stadium, which would be linked to the Javits Convention Center. However, Javits's officials, who deemed such a southward extension only a marginal improvement, rejected these plans. About a year later, after hiring the architectural firm of Kohn Pedersen Fox, the Jets released a plan that added a northward expansion of the Javits Center. In the meantime, the team raised the stakes by hinting that they would consider a move to Los Angeles if the stadium were not built.

With the Jets providing the investment that made a west side stadium financially viable, NYC2012 was able to finalize both its citywide Olympic plan and its Hudson Yards plan. In September 2000, NYC2012 released its "Olympic X" plan, which strung various Olympic venues along two transit axes forming a giant "X" centered on the Olympic Village in Long Island City, Queens. Though the details of particular venues were still sketchy, NYC2012 was clearly making progress on all fronts.

In contrast, the stadium had received the bulk of the Giuliani administration's attention since the mayor had made his Midtown West proposal in January. The renewed prospects of a west side stadium even pushed Giuliani to take steps to repair his relationship with Governor Pataki, whose control of both the Javits Center, built on state land and run by a state authority, and the MTA, which owned the Hudson rail yards and which would have say over any Number 7 subway line extension, gave him ultimate power over the project.[11] That Giuliani seemed more interested in meeting with Jets and NFL executives than in pushing the DCP to produce a rezoning plan for the area did not go unnoticed in elite circles. By September 2000, planners, corporate executives, and real estate developers were publicly expressing concern that the administration was focused too much on the stadium and not enough on CBD expansion (Bagli 2000). *Crain's New York Business*, the city's leading business paper, expressed this frustration, editorializing that far west side development "in truth . . . doesn't have much to do with whether to build a sports stadium for the football Jets or the baseball Yankees, or . . . a dome to accommodate conventions. What's at stake is whether the city can muster the resolve to allow the central business district to expand to an area now occupied by train yards, abandoned warehouses and a few thousand people. It is not an exaggeration to say that the economic future of the city is at stake" (2000). The administration heeded this concern, and as of January 2001, DCP staff, working with NYC2012's planners, had made the formulation of a rezoning plan for the area their top priority. By the end of 2001, both the city's and NYC2012's planning processes had borne fruit.

TWO PLANS, ONE VISION

NYC2012 released its plan in August (NYC2012 2001). In November, just weeks before Giuliani left city hall, the DCP took the first official step in the public process of rezoning the far west side by issuing *Far West Midtown: A Framework for Development* (the Framework) (New York City Department of City Planning 2001). These plans overlapped and complemented each other in ways that made clear that while the two planning processes that had produced them were nominally separate, they were for all intents and purposes one. However, there were some important differences between the two.

Both plans were premised on the idea that the city was facing a critical office space shortage that jeopardized its economic future, and pointed to the far west side as the best location for much-needed CBD expansion. In broad terms, the Framework and the NYC2012 plan made very similar proposals for land use in the area. Both called for a northward expansion of the Javits Center; an extension of the Number 7 subway line to Eleventh Avenue and Thirty-third Street; a network of open space; and the rezoning of the area to permit increased commercial and residential development. Both plans recognized low-scale residential uses east of Tenth Avenue, especially to the north of the area, and, while not proposing any major land-use changes for this area, did propose significant increases in residential density.

The two plans' proposals for the Hudson rail yards complemented each other nicely. The Framework made a gesture toward flexibility, laying out two development scenarios for the entirety of the Hudson rail yards. The first was an "office use" alternative, similar to the MTA's 1989 plans for the rail yards. The second was a "multiuse facility" alternative "consistent with the plans put forward by NYC2012 for . . . this location" (New York City Department of City Planning 2001, 34). Any real doubt that the multiuse facility alternative was viewed by the Framework's authors as a fait accompli was dispelled by the rough sketch of the alternative included in that plan: it was not only "consistent with" but virtually identical to NYC2012's detailed proposals for the Hudson rail yards.

The NYC2012 plan included detailed proposals for both the eastern and western rail yards, both of which would be decked to permit development.

The Javits Center would expand southward, connecting with a new 72,000-seat stadium sitting on the western rail yards. The eastern rail yards would hold two large hotels to house conventioneers and, during the Olympic Games, journalists. Also located there would be a new Madison Square Garden and an International Broadcast Center serving as the media's home base during the Games. Afterward, this 1.2 msf tower would become a "signature office building" anchoring commercial development on the rail yards (NYC2012 2001, 49). These new buildings on the eastern rail yards would be complemented by an eight-and-a-half-acre square with a large green space, shopping arcades, pedestrian pathways, and cafes; the square would serve as the main gathering place for the 2012 Olympics. Extending northward from the eastern rail yards, bifurcating the long blocks between Tenth and Eleventh avenues and terminating at Thirty-ninth Street, would be a new boulevard serving as an inviting conduit to the rail yards from the north. It would also provide more lots with avenue frontage — a valued real estate commodity — and "distinctive new addresses for corporate offices and shops" (ibid., 34).

If the Framework only briefly considered the programming of the Hudson rail yards, it did contain technical analyses and in-depth proposals for the rezoning and urban design of the entire area, as might be expected given that DCP would be responsible for ushering the necessary changes to the city's zoning code through ULURP. Its authors proposed a physical division of the far west side into several areas characterized by specific land uses. The most important of these was an axis centered on Thirty-third Street, where proposed commercial development would stretch east to Seventh Avenue, encompassing the current sites of Penn Station, Madison Square Garden, and the James Farley Post Office, all of which were the subject of extant redevelopment plans of various degrees of specificity and advancement. A "second leg of a high-density commercial office core" would be provided in the area between Tenth and Eleventh avenues, separated from the midtown CBD by several blocks of residential development (New York City Department of City Planning 2001, IV).

Echoing earlier plans, the Framework and the NYC2012 plans were proposed to be largely, if not completely, self-financing. In both cases, revenues generated by new commercial development would play a crucial role in financing the multi-billion-dollar cost of extending transportation lines, decking the rail yards, expanding the Javits Center, and building open space. The NYC2012 plan claimed, "[B]y using only new revenues that would not have existed but for the investment in the infrastructure itself, the Hudson Yards plan can in effect be 'self-financed.' In fact, the financing structure proposed for the Hudson Yards district would fund more than two billion dollars worth of new infrastructure without government subsidies" (NYC2012 2001, 79).

According to NYC2012, the plan's funding would have four sources, all but one of which would be self-generated. First, new development in the area would provide incremental tax revenue. Second, the entirety of the rail yards would be upzoned to allow for density in excess of what was actually proposed to be built there, creating unused commercial development rights that could be sold to developers building nearby.[12] Third, the right to develop portions of the newly decked eastern rail yards would be sold to developers, who would build the proposed media center and two hotels. It was assumed that the MTA, which owned the development rights to both rail yards, would relinquish them in exchange for not having to pay for the Number 7 subway line extension (NYC2012 2001, 83). Finally, NYC2012's plan indicated that additional sources of public funds would be necessary, as the state and city governments, along with the New York Jets, were expected to make "contributions," unspecified in amount, to fund the stadium and a portion of the Javits Center expansion (ibid., 81).

The Framework spelled out some of the mechanisms that would permit this self-financing plan to work. After considering the possibility of using normal capital budget processes to fund the plan and conceding that they would probably be sufficient, the Framework ultimately advised against their use, since "the capital improvements for Far West Midtown would be placed in direct competition with all other City and State capital priorities, decreasing the likelihood that these improvements . . . would be implemented in a coordinated and timely manner" (New York City Department of City Planning 2001, 61). In other words, self-financing provided insurance that the plans for the far west side would be shielded from competition with other, more politically popular, projects for capital funding. To accomplish this, the Framework proposed the use of tax increment financing (TIF) and/or the use of a zoning mechanism that would allow developers to build additional space in exchange for direct payments to a fund dedicated to repaying the bonds floated to cover the plan's costs.[13] Though both would permit the project to be self-financing, the Framework's authors favored the zoning bonus mechanism. They noted that TIF would preclude the use of tax subsidies to encourage development, since such subsidies would reduce tax payments and thus the revenue available to pay back bonds (an odd concern considering claims that the city's office space crunch had office developers salivating at the chance to build office buildings on the far west side should the area be rezoned and supplied with adequate transportation). The zoning bonus mechanism, on the other hand, had several advantages, not least of which was that, unlike TIF, it could be written directly into the city's zoning code and thus would not require state legislation.

Since the implementation of the Hudson Yards plan, if it was adopted and if New York was named as the host of the 2012 Summer Games, would be subject to a strict deadline, the authors of NYC2012's plan paid a good amount of attention to governance and implementation. The plan outlined a detailed development timeline and proposed the creation of a powerful new Hudson Yards Development Authority: "a single entity that can coordinate and execute all of the aspects of the plan . . . able to acquire necessary land, hold and sell development rights, and sell bonds backed solely by revenues generated by the project itself, thereby eliminating any potential conflict with existing public resources" (NYC2012 2001, 77). Like self-financing, this would reduce public accountability and legislative oversight, as the new authority would displace the public agencies normally charged with these activities. The plan did gesture in the direction of public accountability, but only faintly, indicating that the new authority would include "representatives from both the City and the State," though their identity and method of appointment were unspecified (ibid., 77). The Framework's authors, on the other hand, proposed that the plan be carried out by existing governmental entities. The Framework ends by providing a target date for the completion of the Number 7 subway line extension, which would take the most time to construct. By now, the reader can probably guess this date: 2012.

The greatest difference between these plans was one of tone and purpose. The Framework was primarily technical, featuring copious amounts of data, arcane planning terminology, and in-depth technical analyses. NYC2012's plan reflected a different aim: to persuade. In contrast to the Framework's technical maps and rough hand-drawn renderings, the illustrations in NYC2012's plan were bright, colorful, and often rendered digitally. The language in NYC2012's plan was aimed to inspire, calling for "a grand vision for New York City's future" and emphasizing urbanism and aesthetics rather than economics (NYC2012 2001, 7). Where the Framework began by addressing the city's office space shortage, NYC2012's plan began with a discussion of the city's history of grand planning and place-making: Lincoln Center, the United Nations, Park Avenue, and Central Park were all invoked as historical precedents for the redevelopment of the far west side. Given the lingering hostility toward the notion of a west side stadium, NYC2012's planners foregrounded the economic impact that the multiuse facility on the western Hudson rail yards would have in its role as a "Great Hall" for the Javits Center. They also highlighted its planning function as a "catalyst necessary to transform the Hudson Yards into a 24-hour neighborhood" and deemphasized its role as a sports stadium (ibid., 51, 53). While the Framework concluded by listing the governmental approvals necessary to carry out the redevelopment of the far west side, NYC2012's plan ended with an uplifting discussion of the role the Olympic bid would play in unifying the city. "Here at last," read the final sentence of the plan's text, "a plan where everybody wins" (ibid., 94).

This final section touted the political efficacy of the Olympic bid itself, arguing that this project, self-financing (almost) and self-governing, would be well-positioned to avoid the dangers that had scuttled previous efforts to develop the far west side. It is worth quoting at some length:

> Proposals for building over the Hudson Yards and improving the surrounding area date back to at least the 1920s. None of these proposals succeeded, despite considerable support, because they failed to fully address all the competing goals for the district's development. Today, the Javits Center desperately needs to expand. The Department of City Planning, Senator Schumer's Group of 35, and other civic leaders believe that action is needed to spur development of the area to ease the shortage of office and residential space. The community is calling for more parks, better transit, and relief from traffic congestion. And the New York Jets are seeking to return to New York City. . . . How then can the 2012 Olympic bid possibly contribute to this crowded field of players? The answer lies in the unique ability of the Olympic Games to act as a catalyst for change on a broad scale, and to satisfy often competing objectives. Nearly every host city, from Tokyo in 1964 to Sydney in 2000, has capitalized on the enormous public enthusiasm for the Olympic Games, the worldwide scrutiny, and the fact the event occurs on a deadline, to undertake major infrastructure projects that would otherwise never have been possible. (NYC2012 2001, 89)

Let me make two observations about this passage.

First, plans for the area had failed to materialize not merely because "they failed to fully address all the competing goals for the district's development," which seems to be a euphemism for "political conflict." Though politics undoubtedly had played a role, failure had been at least as much a result of ideology and economics, as planners and other development elites had consistently envisioned uses for the area that, while in line with long-held postindustrial visions of a Midtown CBD running from river to river, were not economically feasible given the state of the city's real estate market. This was especially true of the western edge of the area, where NYC2012 proposed the most intensive commercial development. The large real estate developers who would actually build the office building that would populate this district had, as of yet, never displayed a keen desire to make the leap from the contiguous Midtown CBD over Ninth and Tenth avenues to the waterfront — residential developers may have been interested, perhaps, but not commercial developers. Historically, office development had tended to creep, not leap, and to heat up only after increased office employment had generated sufficient demand. Thus, rising office employment in the 1990s only generated additional demand for office space *after* the glut of office space built during the 1980s was absorbed; even then, new commercial development took place primarily in the areas to the immediate west and south of the existing Midtown CBD.

NYC2012's planners described a quite different real estate dynamic, one often articulated by past advocates of postindustrialism in New York City (Fitch 1993). They seemed to believe that the supply of office space would generate demand, that building office space would somehow generate the workers that would fill that space, or, alternatively, that the "ideas economy," the "information economy," or "globalization" generated a never-ending supply of office jobs that could be "captured" merely by supplying an adequate stock of office space. Moreover, they seemed to believe that this office space could be plunked down in any underdeveloped district located anywhere near the existing CBD. The economic placelessness implicit in the various theories of postindustrialism espoused in the past had a local corollary in the idea that office development *within* the city was only loosely governed by the old-fashioned logic of spatial contiguity.

Second, when discussing political matters the plan enunciated an odd mix of naive optimism and hardened cynicism. On one hand, while placing much of the blame for the failure of far west side development on political conflict, the plan ultimately underplayed its depth and intractability. It argued that the same political conflict that, despite "considerable support," had doomed eighty years of development proposals for the far west side would be neatly defused by a bid for a two-week event more than a decade in the future. On the other hand, NYC2012 was not above hedging its bets by shielding the plan from the vagaries of the public approval process. Despite the assertion that "public enthusiasm" for the Olympic Games would make a new era of far west side development possible, NYC2012 actually showed little faith that the people of New York and their elected representatives would cooperate. They proposed doing everything possible to ensure that the financing and governance of the Hudson Yards project would be exempt from normal public review and participation or, to put it in the euphemistic language of NYC2012, that it could be implemented "without conflicting with other . . . budget priorities" (NYC2012 2001, 11). In fact, the avoidance of public review belies a worry on the part of

NYC2012's leadership that the project would not fare well in such conflict; the self-contained quality of the Hudson Yards plan provided insurance against the shortsightedness of the public and its elected representatives, who might not understand the benefits of the Olympics and the development it would catalyze.

EMBRACING PRIVATIZED PLANNING, REJECTING COMMUNITY PLANNING

The DCP's Framework and NYC2012's Hudson Yards plan proposed virtually identical land uses, physical plans, and financing strategies. While some of the similarities between the Framework and the NYC2012 plan resulted from the physical constraints of the far west side, many others were the result of cooperation between the planners at the private NYC2012 and their counterparts at the public DCP. DCP staff at all levels worked to ensure that the Framework, while remaining workable if the Olympic bid was not successful, accommodated as many of the elements of NYC2012's plan as possible.

Indeed, NYC2012's relation to city government went beyond consultation. NYC2012's Executive Director Jay Kriegel, testifying before the city council in late 2002, said that the bid, while "independent of government," was able to act "on behalf of the government" since it had been "authorized by the Mayor and the city council by a 1998 resolution to bid on behalf of New York City before the United States Olympic Committee and then the [International Olympic Committee (IOC)] to get the games" (Kriegel 2002b). City officials and NYC2012's leaders and planners saw nothing wrong with this, since the Olympic bid was a large undertaking that would necessarily involve many aspects of city government, and because it represented an extension of the postindustrial agenda that had dominated development in New York City for decades. Moreover, the kind of privatized planning represented by the Olympic bid, as we have seen, was also a recurring feature of this development history. Nonetheless, this exercise in privatized planning is noteworthy for two reasons.

The first relates to the specific form this instance of privatized planning took: a bid for the Summer Olympic Games. NYC2012, unlike most Olympic bid organizations, was *entirely* privately funded and run, even if it had received a public imprimatur. Prior to 1984 most Olympic bids were guided by national governments, though public–private partnerships have always had a greater role in U.S. bids. Since then, bidding for the Olympics has become more city guided, typically involving local public–private partnerships even in cities outside the United States (Shoval 2002). Nevertheless, even bids in U.S. cities have often involved some sort of direct public control over the bid, even if public accountability was often evaded (Andranovich, Burbank, and Heying 2001, 121–124).

While the bid's private status was touted as a great boon for New York, making the expenditure of scarce public funds on the bid unnecessary, it also allowed NYC2012 to hold meetings and develop its plan behind closed doors, without the participation of elected officials, community members, or the public at large. Though NYC2012 did conduct a public outreach campaign, speaking with community, business, and civic groups, there was no institutionalized forum for public participation in its planning process. Certain pieces of the Olympic plan would eventually be subject to public review, but the overall plan submitted to the USOC and later to the IOC was not. Major decisions fundamental to the bid's physical plan — locating the Olympic stadium on the far west side rather than in Queens, for example — were made privately, and then publicly presented as a fait accompli. The public's enthusiasm for the Olympic Games was welcome; their ideas and opinions about how it might impact their city were not.

DCP's endorsement and duplication of a private plan that would result in the transformation of a significant area of Manhattan, one developed without any public input by a small group of elites, were noteworthy — and questionable — for a second reason: members of the far west side community had their own ideas about the area's development, ideas that received little attention from NYC2012 or city hall. Years of opposing a west side Yankee stadium had kept many locals engaged and angry, and despite the hopes of NYC2012's planners to the contrary, they were no more willing to accept a Jets/Olympics stadium than a Yankee stadium. In addition, a protracted though ultimately unsuccessful battle against the Giuliani administration's plan to allow the transfer of development rights over theaters in and around Times Square to Eighth Avenue, which formed the border of the Clinton Special District, had only recently ended, leaving in place a local organizational infrastructure and a host of politicized neighborhood activists (Chesluk 2008, 165–187). Many had been associated with the Clinton Special District Coalition, an umbrella group of affordable housing advocates, block associations, and other community groups. These neighborhood activists and residents eyed the activities of NYC2012, city hall, the Jets, and DCP with great suspicion. As John Fisher, a leader of the Coalition, put it, "They want to pave over the neighborhood and make an office park. . . . When you get the Olympics and the NFL and the mayor and the entire real estate industry up against you, you've got problems" (Demause 2000).

One prominent neighborhood group associated with the Clinton Special District Coalition was the Hell's Kitchen Neighborhood Association (HKNA). In 1998, HKNA had approached the Design Trust for Public Space, a non-profit organization dedicated to improving public space in the city, proposing that the organizations collaborate in a community planning process for "Hell's Kitchen South," as the area was called by many local residents, who in rejecting new monikers like "Hudson Yards" and "Midtown West" sought to emphasize continuity with the area's gritty, residential, and low-scale past. This led to a yearlong series of meetings that included residents, local business people, and landowners, culminating in a June 1999 conference held, appropriately enough, at the Javits Center. The aim was to preempt plans for development coming from city hall and NYC2012 by presenting a concrete alternative that reflected the interests and desires of neighborhood residents, landowners, and businesses even as it acknowledged the inevitability of development in the area. As Meta Brunzema, a local architect who was one of the leaders of this planning process, told me several years later, "We all realized there would be development, and we didn't want to have to lie down in front of bulldozers" (2004).

Out of these meetings came a series of planning principles used to formulate a November 2001 study elaborating proposals for the commercial and residential development of Hell's Kitchen South that fit its existing character and precluded wholesale displacement or gentrification (Conard and Smiley 2002). While rejecting a stadium, the study took steps to accommodate commercial development, including the expansion of the Javits Center and office buildings on the neighborhood's margins. For the heart of the area, it envisioned a contemporary version of its historical mix of residential and industrial uses: a good number of moderate-scale new residences as well as low-scale buildings for light industry, design, and small-scale and craft production. The study emphasized the need for affordable housing, and called for open space, enhanced waterfront access, community services, high environmental and design standards, and the mitigation of the impacts of local traffic congestion produced by the Lincoln Tunnel and the Port Authority Bus Station. Though the proposals in this report would evolve over time, the plan set forth planning principles that would continue to serve as an important counterpoint to the Hudson Yards plan. Moreover, when it was adopted in 2003 by the Manhattan Community Board Four (CB4), the local planning board representing the far west side, the HKNA plan gained the imprimatur of the body with the strongest claim of representing the wishes of the community.

Like the plans of NYC2012 and DCP, the HKNA plan was professional, detailed, and responsive to the purported need for commercial development on the far west side. Unlike those plans, it was the product of a participatory planning process. The fact that such a plan existed cast into doubt not only the legitimacy of the incipient and unequal partnership between NYC2012 and DCP but also the ease with which it might achieve its ends.

"THE BATTLE FOR THE WEST SIDE IS UNDERWAY"

By the turn of the new century, the commercial development of the far west side was, for the first time since the city's 1969 plan, the focus of New York City's development politics. The interest of the Jets in a new stadium; NYC2012's focus on the far west side as a key site for Olympic venues; the city administration's evolving plans for a far west side stadium and an expansion of the Javits Center; and the concern of the city's real estate elite that the city was rapidly running out of office space: all these agendas had converged on the Hudson rail yards and the surrounding area. It was apparent that these sixty or so square blocks would be the focus of sustained attention in the next few years. It was also apparent that the emergent plans for the far west side would also be the subject of intense political conflict. As of 2000, as *Crain's New York Business* put it, "the battle for the west side is underway" (2000).

The DCP, NYC2012, and the Jets were targeting a neighborhood that was politicized, organized, focused on planning issues, and long opposed to mega-development schemes. It was also a neighborhood with a tradition of affordable housing production and activism rooted in the city's progressive mid-twentieth-century labor movement, which had provided not only good wages and workplace protections but a whole range of benefits, from health care to public and cultural amenities (Freeman 2000). The area's union-built housing was home to many older union members who had been active in that movement, and who would bring its values and tactics to the conflict over the Hudson Yards plan. The neighborhood was also home to a number of politically progressive and professionally independent architects, lawyers, and urban planners, who would bring their own expertise and status to bear in that conflict.

Intimations of future conflict were not only coming from far west side locals; there were also rumblings of discord among elites. In late 2000 several executives, real estate developers, and planners signaled their displeasure with a mayor more concerned with building stadiums than office buildings. However, for other elites, the concern was not with the administration's priorities but with the notion of a west side stadium itself. In December 2000, a number of business executives, real estate developers, union leaders, and other elites formed the Hudson Yards Coalition to advocate for the redevelopment of the far west side. The organization's inaugural meeting was far from peaceful. While the fifty members in attendance were unanimous in their support for rezoning the far west side for commercial development and for expanding the Javits Center, the stadium drew a mixed response. Real estate elites in particular expressed concern that the benefits of a stadium were not worth the political controversy that came with it. Douglas Durst, scion of a major real estate family owning many midtown office buildings, remarked that "there is a need to develop that area [but] throwing in a stadium makes it that much more difficult" (Bagli 2001). Six months later, Mayor Giuliani and Daniel Doctoroff pitched their far west side redevelopment plans to the Hudson Yards Coalition. They received a warm reception, as the organization's members were pleased that CBD expansion was once again high on the development agenda. However, many continued to express fears that the stadium would place the entire plan at risk, while others wondered if a stadium was the best use of such a prime development site.[14] At this point, real estate elites were still willing to publicly argue that a far west side stadium was acceptable *only* if it did not jeopardize the area's commercial development. As we shall see, this would not always be the case.

So, when the newly elected Michael Bloomberg hired Daniel Doctoroff, he got more than a deputy mayor for economic development and rebuilding. Now the Olympic bid and the Hudson Yards plan were irreversibly tied to the new administration. Mayor Bloomberg was on a collision course with the contentious realities of New York City development politics: well-organized community opposition; entrenched real estate interests; messy and complex intergovernmental relations; a complex land-use review process; a city council attempting to balance governing, fundraising, and the demands of the city's many political constituencies; an affordable housing crisis; an affordable office space crisis; and last, but not least, the legacy of post–World War II liberalism.

But Michael Bloomberg had inherited not just the politics around the Hudson Yards plan but the politics embedded within it. By "saying yes to everything," as Paul Goldberger put it, NYC2012 had united a broad array of elites behind its quest for the 2012 Summer Games. The Javits Center was the pet of the tourism, hospitality, entertainment, and retail industries; the proposed office and residential development, along with the extension of the subway, thrilled the city's real estate elites; and the opportunity to plan and design an entirely new district, encompassing a wide mix of uses, waterfront development, and development of an open space network, awoke the Moses lying in the hearts of elite urban planners. But this political balancing act left little flexibility: changing the plan itself threatened the elite coalition that had formed around it. Would the antipolitical Bloomberg Way be capable of building support and gaining approval for a plan soaked in politics? Would the formidable salesmanship of Daniel Doctoroff and Michael Bloomberg be up to such a task? These are the questions that the next three chapters seek to answer. Each chapter addresses one of three strategies used by the Bloomberg administration to construct and gain support for the plan. These strategies all drew on the Bloomberg Way and sought to shape the Hudson Yards plan and its marketing in a distinct — and antipolitical — way.

CHAPTER SEVEN

Why the RPA Mattered

On the warm summer evening of August 4, 2004, I walked down Ninth Avenue with Anthony Borelli, the district manager of CB4, whose leaders were at the forefront of the opposition to the Hudson Yards plan. It was almost 10 p.m., and we were looking for a spot to grab a hamburger and a beer after spending several hours in a small conference room with most of the CB4's leadership, several staff members from DCP, and a smattering of lawyers and planners as they discussed the plan. The previous day, CB4 had held a raucous public hearing at which DCP staffers presented the plan, CB4's leadership outlined their official response, and the plan's supporters and critics volubly expressed their opinions of the plan (and of each other). The meeting Anthony and I had attended that evening was an opportunity for CB4's Land Use Committee to incorporate comments made at the public hearing and to hammer out the details of its written response to the Hudson Yards plan before submitting it to the DCP.

As Anthony and I walked, the conversation shifted away from the mind-numbing planning minutiae that had been the focus of that evening's meeting. I asked Anthony if he would be attending an event, entitled "Envisioning the West Side" and sponsored by state senator and plan opponent Tom Duane, scheduled for the next night. The forum promised to be contentious, as it would include several of the key players, pro and con, in the debate over the plan: Christine Quinn, the far west side's city councilwoman and a harsh critic of the plan; Vishaan Chakrabarti, the director of DCP's Manhattan office and its leading public advocate of the plan; Deputy Mayor Daniel Doctoroff; and Robert Yaro, president of the RPA. I mentioned that I was especially interested in seeing Chakrabarti, Doctoroff, and Yaro in the same room in light of an important report on the Hudson Yards plan the RPA had recently issued. While supportive of the notion of redeveloping the far west side as a mixed use district providing high-density residential and commercial development, the report had criticized many particulars of the plan, most notably the proposed stadium. This was a blow to the Bloomberg administration, which had taken the unusual step of intensely lobbying the RPA's board of directors earlier in the year when rumors began to circulate that the organization would not endorse the plan.

In the midst of our conversation, Anthony asked a simple, but penetrating, question. Why, he asked, did the administration care what the RPA thought at all? After all, the organization had been a politically irrelevant proponent of mainstream urban planning for three decades. Yet, here was Doctoroff, along with CPC Chair Amanda Burden, NYC2012's President Jay Kriegel, and Real Estate Board of New York President Steven Spinola, intensely — and in the opinion of some RPA board members, heavy-handedly — lobbying for the organization's approval. What had changed? What was going on?

In the following discussion I provide an answer to Borelli's question. In doing so, I argue that one aspect of the Bloomberg Way — its technocratic embrace of professionalism and expertise — both inspired and undermined the administration's efforts to gain support for the plan. However, I also maintain that, by focusing and constraining the debate over the plan in certain ways, this tactic shaped the broader terrain of urban development politics in a manner that actually strengthened the Bloomberg Way. I begin by outlining the arguments made by administration officials and their allies that the plan was an example of best planning practice, both in terms of the ostensibly participatory process used to develop the plan and in terms of its substance. Next, I describe the difficult task of selling the far west side stadium as consistent with these practices. I then outline the largely negative response, as the plan was soundly rejected by both professional planning groups and CB4 on the basis of the same principles the plan claimed to represent. I also describe a series of alternative plans for the far west side that at times better advanced the administration's purported planning goals for the district than did its own Hudson Yards plan. The chapter concludes with a discussion of the political ramifications of the technocratic aspects of the Bloomberg Way.

COMMUNITY PARTICIPATION AND ITS LIMITS

Since the early 1970s, community participation has been viewed as an important element in urban planning for reasons of both efficacy and democratic principle (Forester 1999; Hanna 2000; Healy 1993; Innes 1996). Though "participatory planning" is not without serious limitations (Angotti 2008, 29; Arnstein 1969), it has become widespread practice in the United States, providing a modicum of opportunity for citizens to voice their interests and desires concerning urban development. Thus, the claim that the administration was committed to a participatory planning process was an important element of the broader claim that the Hudson Yards plan was an exercise in best planning practice.

The night after my conversation with Borelli, I attended Duane's "Envisioning" session. Facing a skeptical, if not outright hostile, crowd, Deputy Mayor Doctoroff and the DCP's Chakrabarti expressed their commitment to soliciting input from far west side residents, elected officials, and business and property owners. Doctoroff (2004b) touted the "two hundred meetings that we have attended with community . . . and civic groups," arguing that "the plan ha[d] changed [and] evolved" as a result of these meetings and describing the administration as still "amenable to changes." Councilwoman Quinn, despite her opposition to much of the Hudson Yards plan, acknowledged the administration's willingness to make such presentations, saying that "Mayor Bloomberg has never shut us out or locked us out, or sent no representation to neighborhood events, like Mayor Giuliani did. . . . I think your voices are being heard and this is an important thing to know as we move forward through the process" (2004).

Whether the administration's commitment to soliciting input or the fact that the voices of the far west side were "being heard" would lead to substantive changes in the plan was another matter entirely. The administration did make certain changes to the Hudson Yards plan, at least early in the process. But after a certain point such changes ceased as the demands of the far west side community, as represented by CB4, began to conflict with the financial and political exigencies embodied in the plan.

Reason for Hope

The late 1990s saw far west side community groups and leaders taking a proactive approach to the seemingly inevitable redevelopment of the area, resulting in the 2001 HKNA planning study, which was later adopted by CB4. While that study rejected the stadium, it did embrace new development, including the expansion of the Javits Center, substantial residential development, and some commercial development. In part, this was done as a result of political calculation in order to avoid appearing overly obstructionist. However, it also reflected the makeup of CB4's leadership, which comprised a number of professionals, including lawyers, architects, planners, and affordable housing developers, who were well versed in best planning practices and the technical details of planning in New York City. While not averse to taking political stands when necessary, CB4's leaders tended toward engagement and compromise. As of 2002, there were reasons to expect that approach would ensure that the community's concerns about the Hudson Yards plan would be incorporated as the plan developed.

First, the west side development boom of the late 1990s led to close working relationships, and a sense of cooperation and mutual respect, between DCP staff and CB4's leadership. Anna Hayes Levin, the chair of CB4's land use committee, had left her position as corporate counsel for the French conglomerate LVMH Moët Hennessy Louis Vuitton SA to become more active in local planning issues. Levin brought to the job an ethos of professionalism, civic-mindedness, and lawyerly attention to detail, and in a 2004 interview, as well as in subsequent informal conversations, she had nothing but good things to say about DCP staff she had worked with. She described them to me as "engaged, committed, serious public servants" (2004a). These staffers made several productive and friendly community presentations of the DCP's Framework throughout 2002, and even in the later, more contentious, period of the planning process, they maintained amicable relationships with the leadership of CB4.

The appointment of Amanda Burden as CPC chair was also a promising sign. As Levin told me:

> Burden made it clear as soon as she was appointed that she had a totally different vision for how this was going to unfold and a real commitment to community involvement. She hauled in . . . a small group of us . . . for initial presentations of the work they were doing. She hired Cooper Robertson to do [urban design work], and we went off to meetings with Robertson for discussion before their plan came out. . . . We had a whole series of check-in conversations in those very early days. (2004a)

Given that the principles set out in the HKNA planning study—the importance of mixed uses, the preservation of neighborhood character, and modesty of scale—meshed with Burden's vision of planning, there seemed to be every reason to believe that her appointment not only would open up space for community participation in the development of the Hudson Yards plan but that this participation would actually affect the shape of the plan.

The first year of Bloomberg's mayoralty seemed to bear out these hopes, as through 2002 planners from DCP engaged in fruitful discussions with CB4. In early 2003, the DCP along with Burden and her staff presented a revised version of the plan, dubbed the "Hudson Yards Master Plan: Preferred Direction" (also referred to as the Preferred Direction) to far west side community leaders and residents. Though the Preferred Direction generally followed the outlines of the Framework, there were some changes. While some countered the wishes of far west side locals—for example, the office development alternative for the development of the Western Hudson rail yards was gone, with only the "multi-use facility" (the stadium) alternative remaining — others did not. Among them were a network of green space, which included a full-block park just south of the stadium, and moves to protect and even expand the relatively low-scale residential parts of the far west side. Referring to the 2002 consultations that led to these elements of the Preferred Direction, Levin told me, "It was out of those discussions that City Planning began talking about Ninth Avenue as 'Main Street.' We made it clear to them that they absolutely needed to recognize the existing character of Ninth Avenue. I think initially the Framework would [have accomplished] a totally different Ninth Avenue and we wiped the whole thing out" (2004a). Early discussions between DCP, CB4, and other far west side community leaders seemed to have borne fruit.

The Requirements of Self-Financing and the Limits of Participation

Despite these changes, CB4's leadership still had serious concerns about several elements of the evolving Hudson Yards plan. Among them was the emerging relationship between the financing of the plan and the high densities of commercial development it proposed. The Preferred Direction, though short on details, reiterated the notion that the project could be "self-financing" and, importantly, demonstrated that this necessitated very high levels of density (New York City Department of City Planning 2003, 10). As we have seen, self-financing served an important political purpose, shielding the plan from public review and legislative approval. However, it also had important planning implications, as a certain amount of value had to be created (and thus density built) in order for the costs of the plan to be covered. This curtailed the ability of the DCP's staff to accommodate community demands for decreased density, if they were so inclined.

In its official response to the Preferred Direction, CB4 expressed trepidation concerning this crucial linkage between commercial density and self-financing, opposing self-financing and proposing that the overall level of development in the plan be reduced and the focus shifted to the western Hudson rail yards (Sindin and Levin 2003a). This of course could only be achieved if the administration, as CB4's leadership insisted it should, dropped plans for a stadium and instead developed the western rail yards as an extension of the Thirty-third Street commercial corridor. Finally, CB4's response to the Preferred Direction called for an "affordable housing plan that is an integral part of the overall plan" (ibid.). Though CB4, HKNA, and other community groups had long identified affordable housing as a top development priority for the residents of the far west side, neither the Framework nor the Preferred Direction made any mention of affordable housing.

Far west side community leaders continued engaging in cooperative and generally friendly communication with DCP staff as the Hudson Yards plan moved forward through the spring of 2003. This time period was crucial, as the next official step in the plan's development, its entry into the environmental review process required by state and city law, would solidify the plan and make it more difficult to change. The first step in this process was to develop and hold hearings on a "Draft Scoping Document" (DSD) that would delineate the state actions necessary to implement the project and would provide direction for the writing of an Environmental Impact Statement (EIS) outlining its predicted impacts on everything from natural resources to socioeconomic conditions as well as measures to mitigate these impacts.

The DSD was released by the MTA and the DCP in April 2003 (New York City Department of City Planning and Metropolitan Transportation Authority 2003). It included details of the mechanisms that would be used to finance the project. In each of the "sub-districts" into which the Hudson Yards area was divided, a base and a maximum level of density would be established.[1] Commercial building at a density above the base level would require payment into a "District Improvement Fund," while residential development above this level would have to include a certain amount of affordable housing (a practice known as "inclusionary zoning"). In addition, the creation of development rights on the Eastern Hudson rail yards and their transfer to the Eleventh Avenue corridor, first proposed by NYC2012, would be used to generate revenue.[2] The ability to meet the enormous costs — now estimated at $3 billion, twice NYC2012's original estimates — of extending the Number 7 subway line, constructing the open space network, and decking the rail yards would depend, to a significant degree, on the level of commercial development in the Hudson Yards area. The exigencies of self-financing, as much as projected demand for office space, were driving the level of density included in the Hudson Yards plan.

A second noteworthy element of the DSD was its outline of goals for the Hudson Yards plan, which would serve as criteria against which the plan and the alternatives included in the EIS would be measured. As well as broad goals like "provid[ing] opportunities for significant new office development" and "encourag[ing] new housing," the DSD included quite specific goals such as "develop[ing] a new Multi-Use Facility to provide a venue to host a variety of large-scale sports, exhibition and entertainment events and to serve as a home facility for the New York Jets" (New York City Department of City Planning and Metropolitan Transportation Authority 2003, 9–10). Thus the DSD pre-ordained the outcome of the environmental review process, which ostensibly served to provide an early mechanism for public input. Its failure to consider alternatives to the major goals of the redevelopment of the far west side created a circular logic whereby alternative plans would be rejected for not meeting the goals enumerated in the DSD, which were themselves clearly derived from the administration's Hudson Yards plan. It was unsurprising, then, that the EIS, upon its 2004 release, concluded that all the plans without a stadium were deficient, and only the Bloomberg administration's version would satisfy all the goals laid out in the DSD. As Eric Goldstein of the National Resources Defense Council noted at that time, the EIS was set up "not to analyze alternatives or stimulate debate, but rather to justify a public policy decision that had already been made" (2004).

By mid-2003, it was apparent that demands for reduced density could only be met by scrapping self-financing, significantly reducing the cost of the plan by eliminating the Number 7 line subway extension or replacing it with a less costly alternative, or gaining land-use flexibility through the elimination of the stadium. However, from their inception in the offices of NYC2012, these were the elements of the plan that were absolutely nonnegotiable; indeed, they were its political raison d'être. The demands imposed on the plan by community participation were in irreconcilable conflict with the plan's political function, which was to unify the city's elite behind the Olympic bid and ultimately behind the effort to redevelop the far west side of Manhattan.

This did not mean that CB4, encouraged by its early victories, did not keep trying. In a June 2003 letter sent to the DCP and the MTA, CB4's leaders outlined a series of objections to the DSD, decrying the continued inclusion of the stadium; its lack of a solid, affordable housing plan; and the fact that the level of density proposed was "driven by self-financing requirements rather than actual shown need" (Sindin and Levin 2003b). These suggestions were rebuffed, as they impinged upon elements of the plan that could not be altered, no matter how committed DCP Chair Burden and her staffers might be to community participation.

Some minor changes to the plan were made in late 2004 and early 2005 as it moved through ULURP and toward the city council floor. But by mid-2003, despite the Bloomberg administration's avowed commitment to community participation, opportunities for significant community involvement in shaping the fundamentals of the Hudson Yards plan had ended. "Looking back, I think we've had very cordial and open relations with City Planning," Anna Hayes Levin said to me in September 2004. "But there came a time about a year ago, when Doctoroff told them to stop making changes to the plan. So, while we kept talking nothing much happened. . . . That is not the inclination of Burden or her department. That is the direction from Doctoroff, who with his background as a hedge-fund guy, has a hold-no-prisoners, make-no-negotiations, screw-'em-all, I'm-gonna-win attitude."

Splitting the Plan, Avoiding Public Review

If mid-2003 marked the de facto demise of community participation in the formulation of the Hudson Yards plan, the official announcement of its end came in early 2004, when the administration decided to legally divide the Hudson Yards plan in two, splitting it down Eleventh Avenue. The portions of the plan addressing the area to the east of the avenue — the rezoning, the extension of the Number 7 subway line, and the construction of the midblock boulevard and open space on the Eastern Hudson rail yards — would go through ULURP, which gave CB4, the Manhattan borough president, and the Manhattan borough board advisory votes and the CPC and the city council binding up-or-down votes. However, the portions of the plan for the New York State–owned area to the west of Eleventh Avenue, including the stadium, were not subject to ULURP and would require no legislative approval whatsoever.

While some members of the city council seemed relieved to avoid this political hot potato, critics of the plan, and particularly of the stadium, were infuriated. Despite all the talk of participation and transparency, the administration was not only ignoring the wishes of the far west side community but also using the technicalities of state and city law to evade legislative approval for the most controversial portion of the plan. Mayor Bloomberg claimed that "nobody is trying to cut anyone out" of the stadium approval process (Temple-Raston 2004a), but this was exactly what was happening. The desire to avoid public review had trumped effective community participation, an important element of best planning practice.

INVOKING PLANNING ORTHODOXY

The Hudson Yards plan issued by NYC2012 in 2001 invoked many of the buzzwords and principles of best planning practice. It argued that the plan would create a vibrant new mixed-use district, characterized by high-quality public space and vital street life. Waterfront access would be enhanced, and the extension of mass transit, commuter rail, and ferry service to the area, along with roadway improvements, would have the environmentally beneficial effect of reducing traffic congestion. Indeed, individuals associated with NYC2012 and the city's real estate elite consistently touted the developing Hudson Yards plan as an example of exceptional planning. Real Estate Board of New York President Steven Spinola called it "probably the best planning work in decades" (Rayman and Robin 2004). Richard Anderson, the president of the New York City Building Congress, wrote editorials calling the plan "good regional planning" (2004b), and at a September 2004 hearing he touted his own planning credentials in justifying his support. "I've been President of the Regional Plan Association, also the American Planning Association. And I've been chairman of the American Planning Association College of Fellows. I think my planning credentials are fairly strong," Anderson said. "And in my judgment from a planning standpoint the Department of City Planning has served this Commission exceptionally well with this rezoning proposal. It is well thought through. It is balanced. And it compliments so many other very important planning initiatives that you have before you in the City of New York right now. In fact, I would call this the era of good planning in New York City" (2004a). At that same hearing, Donald Elliott, who had been CPC chair during the Lindsay administration and was intimately involved in the 1969 plan for the far west side, called the Hudson Yards plan "an extraordinary act of sensible, careful planning" (2004).

While the Hudson Yards plan had always been touted as an example of good planning, the argument that it represented best planning practice became especially important and prominent once the Bloomberg administration's DCP, now headed by Amanda Burden, took custody of the plan. The deployment of terms associated with best planning practices began in earnest with the issuing of the Preferred Direction and the DSD, the first planning documents the administration produced, and continued as the plan moved into ULURP in mid-2004. In hearings and presentations held as part of that process, DCP staff and other city officials took pains to justify the Hudson Yards plan using the terms of best planning practice.

One DCP staffer, Vishaan Chakrabarti, was especially prominent in doing so. Chakrabarti had been hired with Doctoroff's blessing in the fall of 2002 to head DCP's Manhattan office and quickly became the main public proponent of the plan. Chakrabarti had been trained as an architect and a planner and had eventually become an associate partner at Skidmore, Owings, and Merrill, a renowned corporate architecture firm. Chakrabarti was a rising star in the city's real estate elite, drawing the attention of both the Partnership for New York City, which granted him a prestigious fellowship, and *Crain's New York Business*, which included him in their 2001 "40 under 40" list of up-and-coming New

Yorkers. While many DCP staff and administration members would use terms and ideas associated with best planning practice to justify the Hudson Yards plan, Chakrabarti provided the most forceful defense of its status as an example of best planning practice.

The Bloomberg administration's defense of the Hudson Yards plan as a piece of cutting-edge planning can be divided into three broad claims, each of which was challenged by the plan's opponents. First, the plan was advertised as an example of comprehensive planning. Second, the plan was touted as an exercise in "urban placemaking" that would create the city's "next great place." Finally, the plan's defenders attempted to justify the stadium in planning terms, arguing that unlike most urban stadiums, typically viewed as planning disasters, this one would be a key element in the eventual success of the Hudson Yards plan.

The Hudson Yards Plan as Comprehensive and Environmentally Sound Planning

On September 23, 2004, the MTA and DCP held a joint public hearing on the Hudson Yards plan. William Wheeler, an MTA executive, introduced the plan, saying, "We decided that from the very beginning we would combine land use and transportation planning. . . . This is best practice planning. It's something that many of you who will speak today have urged us to do and we are pleased to give you a single, comprehensive picture of how land use and transportation will interact and be mutually supportive" (2004). The decision to combine transportation and land-use planning, made years ago in the offices of NYC2012, was undoubtedly eminently sensible. Without better access to the area, commercial development at the scale being proposed would be difficult to implement (a cautionary tale cited by the plan's proponents was the example of London's Canary Wharf, a riverside commercial development that lagged until mass transit was extended to the area). While planning groups endorsed this as an obvious if praiseworthy move, the plan's defenders portrayed it as bold and innovative.

Chakrabarti was especially vocal on this point, arguing again and again for the significance of combining transportation and land use planning. He insisted that by rezoning the area and extending the transportation network at the same time, the administration was not just expanding midtown Manhattan CBD but actually fighting urban sprawl by ensuring that commercial development would flow into the city rather than into suburban or exurban areas. "[Manhattan] has to have the room to grow for our environment," Chakrabarti said in August 2004, "because if we allow regional sprawl, we will be like so many other cities in America, traffic-choked and environmentally damaging" (2004b).

Chakrabarti did more than make the rather banal point that development in the center city rather than in the suburbs would mitigate urban sprawl. A few weeks earlier, Chakrabarti had used the term "transit-based development" to describe the Hudson Yards plan in a presentation to CB4 (2004a). The more prevalent synonym for this term, "transit-oriented development," started appearing in DCP presentations and documents (New York City Department of City Planning and Metropolitan Transportation Authority 2003, 1) soon after Chakrabarti was hired in October 2002 and continued to be used by DCP staff throughout 2003 and 2004. Such terms became planning buzzwords in the 1990s, associated with the "New Urbanism," a school of planning thought aimed at counteracting urban sprawl and perceived suburban anomie through higher densities, more and better public space, and residential diversity (Katz 1994). Planners like Peter Calthorpe added an environmental component to this mix, insisting that such development be centered on mass transit (1993).

The use of such language in defense of the Hudson Yards plan was an odd twist, given the fact that actually constructed transit-oriented developments have generally been located outside of city centers. In fact, as the RPA pointed out, virtually any project or rezoning proposed for Manhattan could be considered transit-oriented development, since "almost any activity located in the Manhattan CBD will have a higher share of transit use than a similar facility located elsewhere" (Regional Plan Association 2004, 24). The phrase, along with other urban planning jargon, was being used as a post hoc justification by DCP staff for a plan whose elements had been in place years before.

Rather than ameliorating opposition, the claims that the Hudson Yards plan was both comprehensive and environmentally sound became a point of contention. For example, when one advocate of the plan called it an example of "smart [and] environmentally friendly regional planning" (Sciame 2004) at a September 2004 hearing, the response was one of the loudest and most negative responses of the evening: the plan's opponents shouted "No! No!" and booed him soundly. During that hearing and many others, plan opponents decried its negative environmental effects, highlighting the EIS's warnings that the plan would have severe impacts on air quality and traffic congestion and that the sewage generated by the area's redevelopment might occasionally overwhelm the city's waste treatment system and spill into the Hudson River. They also pointed out that the plan's requirement that builders supply significant amounts of parking violated the city's own policy, in place for two decades, of limiting the provision of parking in Manhattan below 110th Street in order to reduce automobile congestion and pollution. The plan's critics also lamented that the plan represented an unfulfilled opportunity to promote environmentally friendly development, or "green building." They argued that it was imperative to include requirements for green building in a redevelopment of this size, not just because of the development's direct impacts on the environment but also because of its potential to spur similar building around the city, thus enhancing the competitiveness of New York's construction and design sectors.

Critics also argued that the plan was far from comprehensive and actually neglected fundamental issues of basic infrastructure and service provision. In September 2004, Manhattan Borough President C. Virginia Fields pointed out that since the amount of office space included in the plan was comparable to the amount that existed in the entirety of cities like Pittsburgh or Detroit, it was crucial to "ask what you need when developing a new city" (2004). Many politicians and community members argued that the plan did not adequately account for the provision of basic fire, police, electrical, medical, education, and social services and facilities, leading to concerns that already overburdened city services would be further eroded. Invoking the events of September 11, 2001, some plan opponents argued that the EIS should have discussed the ramifications of terrorism, specifically the wisdom of building eighty-story potential targets. They also questioned the impact of this new development on the city's ability to respond to a future attack.

The efforts of the Bloomberg administration to sell the plan as comprehensive and environmentally sound were rebuffed in their very own terms. For every argument that plan proponents made using the language of environmental and comprehensive planning, its opponents made a counterargument in the same language. But the administration had other claims to make concerning the Hudson Yards plan's bona fides.

The Hudson Yards Plan as Urban Place-Making

The phrase "transit-oriented development" was not the only piece of planning jargon to appear in the DSD. The proposal also claimed that the redevelopment of the far west side would result in a "vital 24-hour neighborhood containing a mix of commercial, residential, retail, open space, and recreational uses contributing significantly to the vitality of the City as a whole" (New York City Department of City Planning and Metropolitan Transportation Authority 2003, 4). This claim clearly invoked Jane Jacobs's critique (1992) of modernist, mono-use urban renewal planning, which by the 1990s had hardened into a new planning orthodoxy. It stressed street life, a broad mix of land uses, and well-maintained and well-ordered public space in the pursuit of an urban sense of place. NYC2012 planners, who argued from the beginning that the entire Hudson Yards plan had to be an exercise in "placemaking," were the first to use such rhetoric. Later, Mayor Bloomberg described the plan as creating "a vibrant, mixed-use community" (Bagli 2004a). Deputy Mayor Doctoroff vowed it would create a "pulsating, 24-hour neighborhood" (Edozien 2003) and called it "an opportunity to turn the area into one of New York's great places . . . a worthy successor to Rockefeller Center and Lincoln Center" (Horowitz 2004).

However, it was Amanda Burden and her compatriots at DCP who had the most invested in promoting the Hudson Yards plan as an example of first-class urban place-making; professional identities and careers were at stake here. The result was an onslaught of Jacobs-esque planning jargon in defense of the plan. This began very early in DCP's stewardship of the plan; such language was not only included in the DSD but also used in DCP presentations of the Preferred Direction in early 2003. Burden said at one such presentation that "we want to create a unique and special place where people want to live, work, visit and spend time" (Colangelo 2003). Such rhetoric continued throughout ULURP. For example, Chakrabarti told the CPC in October 2004 that the goal of the plan was to create a "mixed use, 24/7 neighborhood," rather than a "deserted office park environment" (2004a).

In addition to using language to sell the plan as an exercise in urban place-making, the DCP staff also employed visual aids. First appearing in the Preferred Direction, and then in both subsequent planning documents and the PowerPoint presentations that were by 2003 de rigueur in administration presentations of the plan, were a variety of colorful renderings. In keeping with the conventions of the rendering trade (Dunlap 2003), they portrayed the plan's outcome in (literally) the best light possible, with the sun always shining brightly over all the elements of a successful mixed-use, 24/7 neighborhood: active street life, well-designed and inviting public and open space, a human scale, and a diverse population presumably drawn by the district's retail, residential, and commercial mix. In an April 2004 speech, as she displayed a series of such renderings, Burden stressed their importance in DCP presentations: "[They] help the community understand . . . urban design goals that they might want to achieve [and] the physical manifestations of the site," she said. "[By] illustrating these master plans . . . we can engage in a productive dialogue with . . . both the residential community and the development community" (2004).

In fact, the renderings did little to advance the city's case for the Hudson Yards plan. In large part this was due to what the drawings did *not* depict. As

Rendering of the Hudson Yards plan, facing west. (Used with permission of New York City Economic Development Corporation)

opponents of the plan noted, there was no sign of the increased traffic predicted by the EIS. Conspicuously absent was the effect of the eighty-story office buildings that were the crux of the plan. Their proposed height and bulk was minimized by either depicting only the first few floors of such buildings or by using aerial perspectives obscuring their scale in relation to the street. These omissions led the intended targets of these renderings to view them with skepticism, if not outright hostility.

Indeed, opponents of the plan often used these renderings in ironic or creative ways. Some used them in testimony against the plan to great rhetorical effect, contrasting their rosy portrayal of the future with the plan's harsh potential consequences. One far west side resident, testifying before CB4 in August 2004, noted of her building: "On that beautiful artist's rendering of this construction project, we are right underneath an 80 story building!" One CB4 member, testifying before the CPC, said:

> We have all seen the City's images of a completed Hudson Yards project that includes sweeping vistas from broad promenades and open plazas and parks, all lightly populated by people walking, sitting on the grass or eating in outdoor cafes. In stark contrast, the text of the EIS talks of requiring sealed and double-glazed windows because of unacceptable noise levels, windows that can't be opened because of the air pollution outside, quote, unavoidable pedestrian contact, unquote, on overcrowded sidewalks, long lines at stair and elevator entrances to subways, and more than five minutes for a car to cross an intersection.

Instead of the idyllic outdoor experience depicted by the City, the EIS calls up images of sidewalk skirmishes conducted with breathing masks and earplugs. (Compton 2004)

The HKNA plan included its own rendering of the development permitted by the Hudson Yards plan, which visually countered arguments that the Hudson Yards plan was on a human scale and that the commercial development proposed by the city would be in context with the area's character. It also made the point that the development of the HKNA plan would better mesh with that character.

Finally, an episode during a September 2004 CPC hearing demonstrated the futility of using visual aids to sell the plan, given the actuality of what was proposed. At the beginning of the hearing, a DCP staffer had the unenviable task of presenting the plan to an audience of several hundred people, evenly split between rowdy construction-union members supportive of the plan and angry community members opposed to it. As the staffer discussed the details of the commercial development proposed for the Eleventh Avenue corridor, an image of typical buildings that might rise there flashed on the screen behind the dais. While a few construction workers cheered, they were drowned out by vehement booing lasting almost an entire minute. The opposition to the Hudson

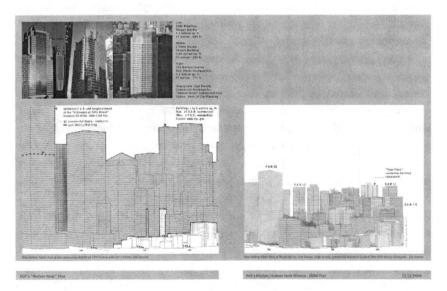

HKNA's comparison of the density of its plan with that of the Hudson Yards plan. (Meta Brunzema Architect P.C.)

DCP photograph of typical office buildings permitted in the Hudson Yards plan.
(Metropolitan Transportation Authority/New York City Department of City Planning)

Yards plan was not due to a lack of communication, as assumed by Burden's
rationale for the use of renderings, which was consistent with the planning
canard that "conflicts of interest . . . are only matters of inadequate technical
understanding that professionals should try to convert to consensus" (Marcuse
2002, 160–161). For opponents, the problem with the plan as a piece of urban
place-making was the kind of place it proposed to make.

Indeed, this was true of not just the renderings themselves but the broader
claims that the plan embodied Jacobs-esque urbanism. CPC Chair Burden and
her staff did all they could to make these claims plausible, devising a series of
guidelines intended to create a more urbanistically sound, pedestrian friendly,
and human-scaled environment as part of the rezoning plan for the area, efforts
generally well received by critics of the plan. And while in broad terms the plan
would create a mixed-use district with an active street life and a network of
public space, in its particulars it failed to jibe with the kind of place envisioned
by Jane Jacobs, William Whyte, and other advocates of the new planning orthodoxy. While it did contain a mix of uses, they were generally cordoned off from
each other, with each "sub-district" dominated by a single use. The fine-grained
mix of uses advocated by Jane Jacobs was largely absent, except in the "Hell's
Kitchen Main Street" area to the northeast, where such a pattern was well established. Claiming that the plan would create a "24/7 neighborhood" chafed
against its primary economic raison d'être, which was to fashion an extension
of the (essentially mono-use) midtown Manhattan CBD. Tellingly, the adminis-

tration had to be pushed by the CB4's leadership to include more housing that would enhance the area's status as a mixed-use, 24/7 neighborhood. While the plan would create a "vibrant street life" of sorts, the kind of congestion seen in the midtown Manhattan CBD was a far cry from the cafes, sidewalk vendors, engaging and unique ground-level uses, unpredictability, and opportunity for slow-paced strolling and people watching that such rhetoric calls to mind. Finally, while the open space network clearly would provide a much-needed dose of green to the far west side, much of it consisted of grandiose parks and promenades geared toward the geographical nexus of Thirty-third Street and Eleventh Avenue, where the commercial district, the stadium, and the Olympic square would converge. This contrasted with the kind of small, user-friendly parks advocated by the CB4's leadership as well as Burden's mentor, William H. Whyte (1980, 172–173).

The mobilization of Jacobs-esque language to describe a plan that would place a row of eighty-story office buildings across from a monolithic convention center and stadium stretched credibility: after all, Jacobs's model of vital urbanism was the West Village, not midtown Manhattan. Try as they might, Amanda Burden and her staff at DCP could not get around the fundamental contradiction between the reality of what was being proposed and the rhetoric of urban place-making. Indeed, when Burden would say things like "you have to have density to get vibrancy, we believe that deeply, deeply, deeply," she only called attention to this contradiction (Dunlap 2005).

This contradiction was noted and exploited by plan opponents. Architectural critic Nicholas Ouroussoff, in a scathing review, wrote that the plan "mistakenly assume[d] that all urban density is good, regardless of its quality," adding that it would "enrich developers, while adding nothing of value to the public realm. If this is our vision of humane urban planning," he concluded, "we should fear for the future" (Ouroussoff 2004). CB4 President Walter Mankoff pled for the respect for place that the Hudson Yards plan supposedly embraced:

> We see the rail yards and the surrounding underutilized land as part of a much broader historic Hell's Kitchen area. We cherish its diversity. Its buildings are old and new, large and small. Its residents come from all walks of life and reflect many income levels and ethnic backgrounds. Its businesses, large and small, play an important part in our city's economy. A rational Hudson Yards rezoning plan would build on the best of today while providing for the commercial and residential needs of the future. . . . The Administration, in contrast, has put on blinders to all alternatives and only sees the wasteland in our area. It's doubly unfortunate. The plan damages the present while offering a future that is so unsound that it

has been widely criticized by some of the most respected planners and civic organizations of our day. (2004)

And in an extraordinary moment at a September 2004 CPC hearing, an opponent of the plan managed in one fell rhetorical swoop to discredit it as a piece of "humane urban planning" by invoking the words of a planner close to Amanda Burden's heart:

> OPPONENT: A great urbanist thinker taught us to [reading from a book] "see cities as habitats for people rather than simply as economic machines, transportation modes or grandiose architectural stage sets." Do you know who that was, Ms. Burden?
>
> AMANDA BURDEN: I don't know.
>
> OPPONENT: That was William H. Whyte.
>
> AMANDA BURDEN: Oh.
>
> OPPONENT: Thank you.

SELLING THE STADIUM

Promoting eighty-story office buildings as an exercise in urban place-making was difficult. But this paled in comparison to selling a stadium as best planning practice. There was near unanimity among planners that stadiums, and especially football stadiums, had negative effects on surrounding areas and were physically ill-suited for construction near dense, residential locations like those abutting the Hudson rail yards to the northeast and south. Nevertheless, the Bloomberg administration and its allies, particularly the management of the New York Jets, conducted a vigorous campaign to justify the stadium in planning terms. This campaign focused on the role of the stadium in the context of the overall Hudson Yards plan and the design of the stadium itself.

The New York Sports and Convention Center

On June 3, 2004, hundreds of construction union members and other stadium supporters in green T-shirts proclaiming "Build It!" descended on city hall. They were countered by hundreds of anti-stadium activists, many of whom were far west side residents, wearing their own anti-stadium T-shirts. All had gathered to voice their opinions at a city council hearing on the stadium.

After a rowdy rally at which pro-stadium supporters cheered a succession of speakers — politicians, labor leaders, and retired Jets like Greg Buttle and Dave Herman, who drew the loudest response — and a press conference on the city hall steps that saw politicians like Councilwoman Quinn and Assemblyman Richard Gottfried excoriate the stadium plan, everyone poured into the ornate city hall chamber. During the rally, the anti-stadium crowd had taken most of the floor seats, leaving the pro-stadium forces only the balcony seats, from which they booed and taunted their opponents below.

After a few introductory words — and pleas for civility — from Council Speaker Gifford Miller and Councilman James Sanders, who chaired the hearing, testimony began. After representatives of the state and the Jets voiced enthusiastic support for the stadium, the man whom everyone was waiting to hear from — Deputy Mayor Doctoroff — took his place at the mike to a mix of boos and cheers. Doctoroff launched into an impassioned defense of the planning rationale for the stadium. "I think it's fair to say that over the past several months, as debate on this topic has intensified, there has been a vast amount of misinformation that's been spread," he said. He then went on to argue for a crucial semantic distinction. "Let me repeat what I think is the most significant myth; and that is, that the New York Sports and Convention Center will just be a stadium. It's not just a stadium." Later, Doctoroff was even blunter, scolding a councilmember who had used the word "stadium," saying, "I refuse to acknowledge that it's just [a] stadium" (2004d).

For Doctoroff and the other proponents of the Hudson Yards plan, rejecting the "myth" that the building in question was merely a stadium entailed labeling it as a "multi-use facility" and later as "the New York Sports and Convention Center" (NYSCC). This semantic distinction was crucial in countering the well-established perception of football stadiums and their surroundings as urban black holes devoid of all activity on nongame days. Stadium proponents conceded that this might be the case with a stand-alone stadium but insisted that the building's convention center functions, as well as its ability to host concerts and sporting events, would make it different. Stadium defenders even commissioned a report on other stadium projects that either doubled as convention centers or were part of larger, multiuse developments that brought together commercial, retail, and residential uses, and therefore had created new, dynamic neighborhoods (Alschuler 2004).

It was also argued that the location of the stadium over the western rail yards was important. The stadium, along with the development proposed for the eastern rail yards, would "fill a gaping hole" in the fabric of the far west side that had long served to retard development. Mayor Bloomberg himself, though failing to toe Doctoroff's semantic line, made this argument. "The truth of the matter is nobody will build over there unless there are people there already," he said in late 2004. "The great thing about the stadium is it will get people there . . . it will be a magnet" (Saul 2004). In December 2004, a DCP official told me that the stadium was a kind of planning loss leader: "Putting something [on the western rail yards] that's going to be animated, that's the whole thing. It's like the sale item, putting milk on sale for 39 cents a gallon instead of four dollars a gallon . . . to get people into the store," he told me. "You're putting this thing here, and you're animating it on the sides that need to be animated, so that there will be people coming. . . . Once it's up and running it's like a self-fulfilling prophecy. The hard part is getting the first guy to come here." The Jets would be that "first guy," filling the void of the western rail yards, so that commercial and residential developers would follow. Indeed, stadium proponents used April 2004 reports that the Guggenheim Museum was considering building a satellite museum on the eastern rail yards to further this argument (an actual plan for a far west side Guggenheim never materialized).

This argument seemed plausible, at least on first glance. However, when I relayed it to another DCP staffer, she pointed out its fundamental flaw, saying dubiously, "That's the argument anyway . . . but what would fill that hole was already determined." No one denied that two three-city-block rail yards were an impediment to development. The larger issue for opponents of the plan, and certainly for the planners that opposed it, was not the necessity to develop the rail yards, but the wisdom of the particular use being proposed for them. Did it make sense to put a stadium, or even a "multi-use facility," on a waterfront property located in the heart of the city?

The RPA answered with an emphatic "no" in its 2004 report on the Hudson Yards plan, stating, "There is no compelling need to place [the NYSCC] in a part of the city that should be devoted to high-value, high-density office and residential development. . . . Fortunately, the alternative is not simply a choice between the NYSCC or an open rail yard" (Regional Plan Association 2004, 5). The report went on to lay out in excruciating detail the planning arguments against the stadium, concluding that the stadium would generate congestion that would conflict with other proposed uses, block access to the waterfront, and "create an unpleasant pedestrian experience in its vicinity" (ibid., 25). Taking direct aim at the central planning argument for the stadium, the RPA maintained that it was highly unlikely to spur development, given that stadiums are typically designed to retain patrons and their money, not to disperse them into the surrounding neighborhood, and given the fact that the city's own analysis projected that the facility would be used only 136 days per year.

Once the RPA released its report, several other civic and planning organizations joined it in condemning the stadium, citing similar concerns.

"One of the Revolutionary and Iconic Buildings in the World"

This was the phrase used by Deputy Mayor Doctoroff to describe the NYSCC in a September 2004 speech (2004a). In the effort to market the stadium to a skeptical public, its form had been a selling point from the beginning, as Jets executives drew on the power of design to move the stadium forward. In doing so, they were drawing on common practice among stadium planners and architects, a fact revealed to me when I attended a July 2004 panel at which prominent architect Peter Eisenman stated flatly that stadium architecture was first and foremost "geared towards media promotion. . . . We spend less energy on designing than on mediating what we design. . . . Normally architects don't talk about this, but this is where the action is. Our client displays other media portraying the stadium, not the design itself" (2004). Echoing this point, the planner Raymond Gastil, who would succeed Chakrabarti as the head of DCP's Manhattan office in January 2005, wrote that "the Jets knew that to build their stadium, they would have to push very hard in the arena of public opinion and they decided to pump up the architectural vision of the type of building their stadium would be, demanding an icon" (2002, 104). Selling the NYSCC

The Jets stadium. (New York Jets)

to the public was largely a media-driven project, as renderings of the stadium became ubiquitous both at presentations and hearings and in print and television media.

These renderings were produced by the New York architectural firm of Kohn Pedersen Fox Associates. The Jets had insisted upon an architect from New York City, who would be able to integrate the stadium into the complex mix of uses, scales, and infrastructure surrounding the western rail yards. William Pedersen, one of the firm's principals, described the stadium's design as driven by three objectives: first, the building should connect the inland community to the river; second, it should be an integrated part of the urban context; and third, the building should constitute both "a retrospective gesture" by drawing on historic Hudson River piers and the "muscularity" of the George Washington Bridge and "a prophetic gesture in the form of sustainability" (2004). Each of these elements was meant to fit with the overall effort to sell the Hudson Yards plan as an exercise in the best planning practice.

In fact, the design of the stadium incorporated retail space, restaurants, and cultural institutions, as well as pedestrian links to the river. Also, the stadium was integrated with a project especially dear to Amanda Burden and other advocates of human-scale urban development: the High Line, a long-abandoned elevated train trestle running north from the Meatpacking District to West Thirty-fourth Street, which was slated for redevelopment as an elevated pedestrian way. Moreover, the stadium itself was designed as a cutting-edge green building, including wind turbines and solar paneling that would permit it to generate enough energy to meet, if not exceed, its needs and including a rooftop retention pond that would supply much of the water used in the building. All this was intended to enhance the stadium's status as an exemplar of sustainability and Jacobs-esque urbanism.

Many of these flourishes were the result of pressure from CPC Chair Burden and other DCP staff. The inclusion of a stadium in the plans for the far west side was hard to square with Burden's commitment to small-scale, fine-grained urban development.[3] Indeed, there were rumors of discord within the administration, specifically between Burden and Doctoroff, concerning the location of the stadium. Apparently, though, Burden had accepted the inevitability of a stadium and had chosen to push for elements that would soften its edges and ameliorate its negative consequences rather than oppose it outright. She insisted that her efforts had been effective, pointing to the inclusion of parks on all four sides of the stadium and retail and other street-level activity on its edges. Burden said that "we've been pushing the Jets very, very hard to improve the design — I am very intent on doing that" (Pogrebin 2004).

In fact, Burden, along with staff from the DCP and the Municipal Arts Society, a prominent civic group dedicated to urban design (and one of the only such groups not to reject the stadium outright), had been drafted to assist in improving the stadium's design. In February 2005, the Jets released a new design that attempted to address some of the concerns about the stadium. The height of the stadium was reduced, at the cost of the wind turbines (power would come from an upstate wind farm), and it was now wrapped in a transparent glass veil to give it a lighter, less massive appearance and make it less of a visual barrier to the waterfront. There was also more public and retail space, as well as a new broadcast studio.

The effort to sell the stadium on the basis of urbanism, design, and sustainability reached an apogee just after these changes were made. Alexander Cooper and Jacquelin Robertson, the two ex–Lindsay administration officials whose urban design firm had created the Hudson Yards urban design master plan, lent their considerable prestige to the stadium in an extraordinary editorial that laid out the case for the stadium as an "an icon of urbanism":

> From a planning and design perspective, the [NYSCC] fits perfectly with New York tradition and history. . . . From the beginning this city has flourished because of its waterfront connection to the Old and New Worlds. . . . Recent design modifications and a height reduction . . . connect the enterprise even more powerfully and viscerally to the urban fabric. . . . It is . . . urban through and through. . . . Its design is a daring expression of 21st-century architectural possibilities. The architects . . . have intuitively deferred to the majesty of [Manhattan's street] grid to define the building's dimensions and volume. . . . The stadium's pioneering design, which is reflective of the glitter of Times Square, with its super graphics and dramatic signs, will become a contemporary iconography. . . . Brilliant and — even without its wind turbines — still green, the design incorporates a network of sustainable technologies both to delight and to conserve. . . . It is a triumph of design and civic responsibility — rooted in history and embracing the future. It is architecturally bold, environmentally forward-looking and urbanistically engaged. . . . Decades from today we want the public to look back and celebrate what has been achieved, rather than lament a failure of imagination. The gift of our waterfront, as envisioned more than 350 years ago, is ours once again to seize. (Cooper and Robertson 2005)

I quote at length here because this editorial is perhaps the most striking, concentrated, and rhetorically ornate example of the use of the language of urbanism, design, and sustainability in the campaign to sell what was, in essence, a football stadium.

What is also striking was the almost complete failure of this effort. CB4 Chair Mankoff's response to the much-ballyhooed unveiling of the new stadium design in February 2005 encapsulated the attitude of stadium opponents to the efforts to deploy the stadium's design to garner support for the stadium: "It's a minor cosmetic change. It doesn't offset the environmental impact of the stadium, the crowding and traffic issues. It's so trivial" (Bagli 2005a). Despite the effort to use semantics, design, planning rhetoric, and environmentalism to make it appear otherwise, the NYSCC remained what it had always been since its conception in the offices of NYC2012 in the late 1990s. It was large, bulky, and blocky; it generated congestion and traffic; and it was in use less than 40 percent of the time. In other words, it was a stadium.

THE HUDSON YARDS PLAN REJECTED

Despite the Bloomberg administration's purported dedication to best planning practices, the Hudson Yards plan was rejected by both CB4 and a number of civic and planning organizations that had the ability to impart the imprimatur of best planning practice. The RPA was the most important of these, as its professionalism, technical expertise, and lack of partisanship, in the context of a Bloomberg administration that openly embraced these qualities, gave it a level of public authority it had not enjoyed in decades. Its report on the plan, released in July 2004, represented a stunning rebuke to the Bloomberg administration and its claims that the Hudson Yards plan was "a planning *tour de force*," as one of its advocates put it (Levin 2004b). As well as challenging the rationale for a far west side stadium, the report called for a delay in building the expensive Number 7 line extension until after development in the area had picked up; a rebalancing of the mix of uses in the plan toward residential, retail, and cultural uses and away from commercial development; additional efforts to creatively use open space in order to cover up unattractive traffic infrastructure; and stronger connections to the waterfront and more waterfront green space.

The RPA's criticisms were especially potent because they operated using the same set of assumptions and conceptions that the Hudson Yards plan's proponents claimed as their own. The report alleged the necessity of a "new, 21st Century business district on the Far West Side of Midtown Manhattan" (Regional Plan Association 2004, 3); explicitly endorsed the plan's goals "to provide office space that will allow the City's economy to expand, to improve the City's competitiveness in the convention and tourism industries, and to bring the Olympics to New York in 2012" (ibid., 14); and reflected reigning

planning orthodoxy in its stress on waterfront access, mixed-use development, vital street life, and open space. As RPA President Robert Yaro, sitting
on a dais with Daniel Doctoroff and Vishaan Chakrabarti at the August 2004
"Envisioning Session," stated, "Our differences with the city over the . . . plan
have nothing to do with the overall goal [of] finding ways that the west side can
accommodate a significant part of the city's economic and population growth"
(2004). From the RPA's perspective, this was a disagreement about the means
to a shared end, a technical dispute rather than a political one. But given its
devotion to these ends, and its status as the city's premier guardian of planning
doxa, the RPA's rejection of the plan was in fact a political setback.

A second blow came in August 2004, when CB4 issued its official response
to the Hudson Yards plan. While CB4's rejection of the plan was neither un-
expected nor particularly damaging in and of itself, the way the rejection was
framed, in the context of the administration's avowed commitment to good
planning, did have a deleterious effect. Crucially, CB4's response did not reject
all of the plan's premises outright; instead it managed to negotiate a tricky path
between the stated goals of the HKNA plan (which CB4 had endorsed in 2003)
and those of the Hudson Yards plan. The response was based on a fundamental
insight that struck CB4's Anna Hayes Levin months earlier:

> I realized as I was studying the Environmental Impact Statement and reading the
> alternatives that there's a low-density alternative that the city has included which
> is just the base rezoning. And that's when the light bulb went on. . . . That's the
> way for us to present our response! We can say we like this alternative, and it's
> the city's own alternative. It's the base zoning. Do that part. All the nasty stuff is
> in the text, the district improvement bonus; all the development rights transfers;
> all the things that create the density that we oppose are in the text. So that's why
> we set up our response the way we did. And it's interesting to watch now how it's
> playing out through the process because other people are picking up on that. You
> can have your doubts about the base rezoning; there are some problems with it.
> But it still becomes a very useful framework in which to think of this. (2004a)

By embracing the base rezoning, and rejecting the zoning text, which contained
the mechanisms that allowed for the increased density that would in turn produce the revenues that allowed the plan to be self-financing, CB4 created a
middle path between wholesale endorsement and flat-out rejection. West side
politicians could draw on this to express their disapproval of certain parts of
the plan (and thus side with their constituents, who overwhelmingly opposed
the plan) without taking the political risks that would be incurred (such as
the antipathy of the real estate industry, the administration, and construction

unions) by rejecting the plan outright. As the plan worked its way through ULURP, this gambit shaped both the response of politicians and negotiations between the Bloomberg administration and the city council.

As well as providing this middle path, CB4's response laid out convincing arguments proving that many elements of the administration's plan were in violation of best planning practices. Many of these echoed previous objections CB4 had made to the plan, such as the emphasis on large parks serving commercial areas rather than small neighborhood parks, the lack of connections to the waterfront, the risk inherent in the self-financing plan, the excessive commercial density that flowed from it, and the absence of an affordable housing plan. The response also expressed concern that the Hudson Yards plan did not respect its context, enumerating the threats it posed to numerous architectural and historical landmarks in the area (this was targeted at Amanda Burden, a strong advocate of historic preservation). It identified a number of breaks with New York City planning precedent, including the lack of limits on density in certain locations and the inclusion of more parking than had previously been standard practice. Invoking the history of urban renewal that catalyzed Jane Jacobs's work, it objected to the condemnation and displacement of a number of residences and businesses. Finally, challenging the administration's commitment to community participation, it drew attention to elements in the plan that would preclude public review of certain future city actions in the Hudson Yards area. All of this was laid out in clear, well-reasoned prose.

CB4's response impressed even proponents of the plan. DCP staff that had worked with CB4's leadership gave it praise, even as they disagreed with its conclusions. Several members of the CPC praised CB4, even as they voted in favor of the plan. One commissioner, despite his vote for the Hudson Yards rezoning plan, went as far as saying that he had "never seen a more well-thought-out presentation of community response" at the November 2004 CPC meeting at which that plan was passed (Cantor 2004).

While CB4's response did not prevent the rezoning portions of the plan that went through ULURP from gaining the approval of the CPC, and eventually the city council, it played a crucial role in providing planning arguments against the plan. Especially notable was the fact that community leaders were able to understand, explain, and repackage for public consumption the complexities and details of the zoning code; the various financing plans for different elements of the Hudson Yards plan; stadium, convention center, and real estate economics; and the project's mammoth EIS. Just as the CB4's analysis of the Hudson Yards rezoning plan provided politicians a middle way between wholesale acceptance and complete rejection, their ability to penetrate the technical intricacies of planning practice and to master the language of both planning technicality and best planning practice provided busy politicians and other public figures with concise and accurate arguments that they could use in justifying their opposition to the plan and/or its elements. Also, CB4's steadfast position that the Hudson Yards plan had to include a comprehensive and concrete affordable housing plan provided the basis for a broader coalition pushing for such a plan in the second half of 2004. Finally, as the focus moved in 2005 to the process of approving the stadium, CB4's arguments played a crucial role in articulating the citywide opposition to the stadium. After the stadium was voted down by an obscure state board consisting of representatives of State Senate Majority Leader Joe Bruno, State Assembly Speaker Sheldon Silver, and Governor George Pataki in June 2005, Anna Hayes Levin observed that "the stuff you heard coming out of [Silver's and Bruno's] mouths were arguments we helped develop that went up through the food chain . . . and in the end won the day. . . . We've learned how to take our own parochial interests and connect them up with the broader interests that other New Yorkers might have because we knew we weren't going to kill this if it was just a 'not in my backyard' argument" (Murphy 2005). CB4 did not, to the degree that the RPA did, share a commitment to the ends of the Hudson Yards plan, though its members were emphatic that this did not mean they were opposed to development per se. However, by taking full advantage of the changing political matrix created by the Bloomberg administration's embrace of technocratic principles of urban planning, CB4 was able to fend off or alter some of the elements of the Hudson Yards plan it found most objectionable, most importantly the far west side stadium. The ability of CB4 leaders to command the language and substance of mainstream planning orthodoxy was made politically effective by the Bloomberg Way itself.

PLANNING UNBOUND

Anna Hayes Levin put her finger on something very important when she noted the need to avoid the NIMBY label. Despite the fact that moderate and well-educated professionals like the Natural Resource Defense Council's Eric Goldstein, the RPA's Robert Yaro, and Levin herself shared many of the dispositions and attitudes held by DCP planners and administration officials, they were still vulnerable to being portrayed as knee-jerk opponents of development. And in fact, opponents of the Hudson Yards plan were subject to a barrage of abuse from local media outlets, many of which held staunchly prodevelopment stances. One pundit wrote that "the arguments against the stadium from self-styled community activists, shortsighted Luddites, and reflexive NIMBY advocates all boil down to a Bartleby-esque 'I would prefer not to' [driven by] nostalgia for the present" (Avlon 2004). *Crain's New York Business* labeled plan opponents as "reflexively anti-development" (2005). *Crain's* also dismissed the RPA as "an organization that prefers no growth to growth it can't channel as it deems best" (2004a); the *Daily News* condemned the organization and other stadium opponents as "misguided do-gooders . . . [with their] heads in the clouds" (2004). As we shall see in chapter 9, the Bloomberg administration would itself deploy similar rhetoric, though inflected by the class identity of its key members.

These slurs, while still impacting the way CB4 and others shaped their negative responses to the plan, lost some of their purchase when juxtaposed with the fact that the rejections of the Hudson Yards plan by the far west side community and planning groups were accompanied by positive proposals for far west side development. Indeed, as the debate over the Hudson Yards plan ramped up through 2003 and into late 2004, no fewer than four alternative plans for the area emerged. These included two plans for the Hudson rail yards alone, both of which were intended to be compatible with the administration's plans for the rest of the area: one by the RPA and a second by the Cablevision corporation, which vehemently opposed the stadium, viewing it as a potential competitor with its Madison Square Garden arena. The other two plans addressed a larger swath of the far west side: the HKNA plan mentioned above, and a plan released by Baruch College's Steven L. Newman Real Estate Institute.

Each of these four plans accepted the premise that the redevelopment of the far west side was necessary, including levels of density comparable to that in the administration's plan. With the exception of Cablevision's plan, the plans contained proposals to expand the Javits Center, and all four contained proposals for significant amounts of new office space. Again with the exception of Cablevision's plan, these schemes, like the ostensibly "comprehensive" Hudson Yards plan, considered transportation and land use together. All these plans sought to facilitate private real estate development investment, at times more so than the administration's plan, which actually forbade residential development in much of the area, even if the market called for it and, as will be discussed in the next chapter, placed the city government in the role of a developer. This was particularly true of Cablevision's plan, which was to be funded by its own private capital, and the Newman plan, which, by making several waterfront blocks available for private high-end residential development, would, in one of its advocates' words, "unleash $3 billion worth of real estate value" (Wollman 2004). Finally, all these plans laid claim to the mantles of post-Jacobs urbanism and best planning practice.[4]

Yet these plans departed from the official Hudson Yards plan in significant ways. Most obviously, these plans all dismissed the need for a stadium; indeed, all four explicitly argued that devoting the western Hudson rail yards to a stadium precluded the sensible planning and development of the area.[5] All four plans shifted the balance of density proposed away from commercial and toward residential uses, and they all were either less costly or easier to finance than the Hudson Yards plan. This was achieved by using conventional means of financing, by replacing the costly extension of the Number 7 subway with cheaper alternatives, or by delaying the subway construction until development was underway. Finally, because of their provenance, the RPA and HKNA plans both belied the claims that the Hudson Yards plan represented best planning practice and participatory planning; after all, the local steward of planning orthodoxy and the community itself laid out plans that in many ways improved upon the purported aims of the Hudson Yards plan.

While not without problems — which Vishaan Chakrabarti and Daniel Doctoroff in particular seemed to take delight in pointing out in great detail — these plans challenged, and often outdid, the Hudson Yards plan on its own terms. Moreover, they did so without necessarily including a stadium. The array of alternatives that could be imagined once the stadium was removed illustrated that this element of the Hudson Yards plan, by occupying a large piece of land that could otherwise absorb huge amounts of density, and by cutting off the waterfront, far from being the key to far west side development, was *the* fundamental hindrance to sound planning for the area.

In the same conversation I describe at the beginning of this chapter, CB4's Anthony Borelli noted the one result of the willingness of the Bloomberg administration to engage in ambitious, large-scale planning. "The RPA, the Newman Institute — now everyone can think big. It has unleashed the pent up floodgates of planners' desire to do big planning," he said. "It created the opportunity for planning organizations to be heard." In an ironic twist, the Bloomberg administration's own explicit endorsement of comprehensive, sustainable, and technically sound planning unleashed a torrent of planning energy that resulted in a plethora of competing visions for the far west side and for the western rail yards, visions that helped undermine the Hudson Yards plan's professional bona fides.

WHY THE RPA MATTERED

By early 2005, it would not have been surprising to learn that Mayor Bloomberg and Deputy Mayor Doctoroff regretted ever opening this particular can of worms. By hiring Amanda Burden and by attempting to legitimize the Hudson Yards plan using the language of best planning practice, the administration opened the plan up to an avenue of critique that otherwise might not have been available. It had sparked a burst of planning creativity that led to the production of a number of plans that were more efficient and effective in meeting the planning goals of the Hudson Yards plan. However, the omission of the stadium from all these plans ensured that they could not meet the political goals that the Hudson Yards plan had been constructed to meet years ago by NYC2012, as did their dismissal of self-financing, which from the beginning served the highly political function of shielding the Hudson Yards plan from public review and governance.

When the legitimacy of the use of these planning terms to describe the Hudson Yards plan was challenged either directly or indirectly by the alternative plans that emerged throughout 2004 and 2005, the plan's proponents could, and did, engage critics in substantive, professional debate. The August 3, 2004, panel discussion described above, which included Doctoroff, RPA President Yaro, and the DCP's Vishaan Chakrabarti, saw Chakrabarti and Doctoroff engage in a spirited defense of the Hudson Yards plan and lay out a planning critique of the RPA's position on the project. Doctoroff sent a lengthy (and respectful) letter to the RPA's board before it released, in July 2004, its report, which laid out in detail the city's case for the Hudson Yards plan. But what they could not do was change the plan in any significant way. Doing so would require the removal of the stadium, whose inclusion on the western Hudson rail yards doubled as the political lynchpin of the plan and the central obstacle to the sound planning of the far west side. So while there were alterations to the Hudson Yards plan — a small reduction in the amount of commercial space, a slight shift of density to the Thirty-third Street corridor, and some new green spaces — there was never any possibility that the stadium would be removed or that the amount of commercial density would be significantly reduced.

The administration was caught in a fundamental contradiction that arose out of the Bloomberg Way itself. On one hand, Mayor Bloomberg was a dedicated advocate of an antipolitical ethos of technocratic professionalism, willing to defer to the bearers of technical expertise. On the other hand, the plan that was being sold using the language of technocratic best planning practice was itself deeply political, an amalgam of elements — the most crucial of which was the stadium — that had been strung together by NYC2012's planners in an effort to produce a plan that satisfied a number of elite constituencies and thus was politically, as well as technically, workable. Even if the new mayor wished to radically alter the plan (which he did not), doing so would have threatened the political coalition that supported the Olympic bid (which he enthusiastically endorsed). Thus, the plan was amenable to marketing — the product was designed and ready to be sold — but it was far less amenable to alteration in line with technical planning or community critique. This gave many of the planning arguments for the overall plan, and for the stadium in particular, a distinctly post hoc feel. Its proponents attempted to pin a litany of ill-suited planning terms onto the plan: transit-oriented development, mixed-use development, street life, 24/7 neighborhood, sustainability, green building, place-making, and so on.

However, the news for the Bloomberg administration here was not all bad. Even as technocratic critiques were brought to bear by the RPA and others, they left the deeper aspects of the plan, and the approach to governance it was a part of, untouched. While some progressive organizations criticized the Bloomberg administration's broad development agenda and the Hudson Yards plan from a specifically class-based point of view, arguing that it privileged the interests of wealthy New Yorkers over those of the middle class, the working class, and the poor, the professionals and mainstream planners opposed to the plan generally criticized it on technical grounds, focusing not so much on the ends it would serve but on the means to accomplish those ostensibly agreed-upon ends. They generally shared the Bloomberg Way's proposition of the existence of a unified city interest, which comprised enhancing competitiveness via postindustrial development. Indeed, many of the professionals I spoke to who opposed the plan, including those from the far west side, were quick to proclaim their admiration for the ambition of the administration's urban development agenda, even if they objected to its particulars. Some expressed support and admiration for Mayor Bloomberg even as he pushed the Hudson Yards plan forward. This contradictory disposition was true as well of the broader ranks of professional planners and urban experts, including those within the administration and the RPA. Their willingness to either continue working on the plan even as they had serious reservations about it or to continue to offer constructive critiques of the plan testified to the resonance of the Bloomberg Way for bearers of professional expertise. The mayor's respect for such professional expertise, rejection of "politics as usual," managerial competence, and refusal to play by the rules of politics as usual appealed to these professionals' technocratic and consensualist political outlook, as well as to their sense of themselves as bearers of expert knowledge.

If the line of critique that the administration opened up by its endorsement of best planning practice undermined its ability to bring the Hudson Yards plan to fruition, it also served to define the boundaries of political conflict. The

fact that the debate over the stadium, and the Hudson Yards plan more generally, was conducted in technocratic language, focusing on the ways in which
the scheme might or might not conform to best planning practice, meant that
other, more radical critiques of the plan and the administration's broader development strategy were marginalized. The strategy of HKNA and CB4, both of
which were caught between professionalism and class- or justice-based advocacy, reflected this. Both the HKNA's plan and CB4's response to the Hudson
Yards plan accepted the fact of far west side development and the basic outlines of such development that NYC2012 had produced in the 1990s as givens,
and sought to further their interests within this existing framework by arguing
for its technical inadequacy. This was a perfectly understandable strategy and,
given the eventual demise of the stadium, an effective one. It was entered into
in full awareness, as many of the leaders of the far west side opposition to the
stadium acknowledged — and at times expressed apprehension about — this
strategic choice. Nevertheless, by acceding to the terms of the debate set by the
Bloomberg Way, the opponents of the Hudson Yards plan helped solidify its
power to shape the terrain of political conflict over urban development in New
York City.

On the one hand, then, the contradiction between the technocratic and antipolitical embrace of best planning practice inherent in the Bloomberg Way and
the highly political construction of the Hudson Yards plan undercut the ability
of the administration to use best planning practice to gain support for its passage. On the other hand, these same technocratic and antipolitical aspects of
the Bloomberg Way, and the invigoration and legitimization of urban planning
that they engendered, served to focus and constrain the debate over the plan
in such a way that strengthened the ability of the Bloomberg Way to shape the
political terrain. The RPA mattered because the Bloomberg Way's technocratic
bent made it matter. And the fact that the RPA did matter was itself indicative
of the growing, if still tenuous, power of the Bloomberg Way.

CHAPTER EIGHT

The Logic of Investment

Though the Bloomberg administration spent a good deal of time, money, and energy on selling the Hudson Yards plan as an example of good planning, its primary justification for the plan was its economic impact. The Bloomberg administration incorporated the Hudson Yards plan into the luxury city strategy, constructing the plan and presenting its economic benefits in a way that reflected the administration's corporate and technocratic approach to governance. Specifically, the administration sought to construct and portray the Hudson Yards plan as a *profitable investment*. These efforts to sell the Hudson Yards plan as a profitable investment involved two separate tasks. The first was the administration's campaign to design and generate support for the rezoning portion of the plan (I refer to this as "the rezoning"). The second was the effort to finance the NYSCC, a.k.a. the stadium, and then sell it as an economic boon for the city (I refer to this portion of the plan, which also included the Javits Center expansion, as "the convention corridor").

These two tasks played out over slightly different time frames: the former started in early 2003 and ended in late 2004, while the latter occurred between early 2004 and mid-2005. They also ultimately had disparate outcomes, as they involved different governmental and political dynamics. Despite these differences, both were animated by an antipolitical and corporate logic of investment. But even as this logic of investment drove the administration's construction and marketing of the Hudson Yards plan, it manifested a number of contradictions that reduced this logic's political efficacy and ability to guide policy-making.

The chapter addresses these issues in several sections. The first describes the relationship between the administration's luxury city approach to development, in which the Hudson Yards plan played a key role, and the logic of investment. Here, the emphasis is on how the logic of investment operated as *a logic*, a set of suppositions underlying governmental practice, while subsequent discussion describes how this logic fared in the context of actual governmental and political practice. The second section describes the difficult process of developing the details of the financing plans for the rezoning and the convention corridor, as well as the contradictions in the Bloomberg Way in general and the logic of investment in particular that emerged during that process. In the third section, I examine three lines of debate these financing plans generated, each illustrating a different aspect of the antipolitical logic of investment and each describing new forms and sites of conflict generated by this logic. The fourth section details the successful efforts of allies of the administration to use more traditional and explicitly political means to gain support for the Hudson Yards plan. In the conclusion of the chapter, I discuss the political ramifications of deploying the logic of investment.

THE LUXURY CITY, THE HUDSON YARDS, AND THE LOGIC OF INVESTMENT

In chapter 4, I argued that the Hudson Yards plan served as both microcosm and capstone of the administration's luxury city urban and economic development strategy. Here, I want to focus on the goals that the plan and strategy were supposed to achieve and on the concrete mechanisms that would permit their realization. The administration and its allies claimed that the city's quantitative growth was absolutely crucial to its future economic and social health. Such growth could best be assured by the city government employing a logic of investment, whereby it would select and pursue investments (particular development projects) in "the product" (the city as an urban environment) that would ultimately lead to increased "profit" (incremental tax revenue). Thus, in early 2004 CPC Chair Amanda Burden described the basic premise of the Hudson Yards plan by saying, "New York City must grow" (2004). The Hudson Yards plan was vital to this aim, as it would allow the city to capture its rightful share of economic growth on regional, national, and global levels.

These claims had significant continuities with the past, echoing decades of argument that expanding the midtown Manhattan CBD to the Hudson River would generate massive amounts of postindustrial employment. These older arguments reflected the interests of the city's real estate elite and comprised, in Fitch's words, "a real estate strategy . . . disguised as a jobs strategy" (1993, 49). For real estate elites, the primary justification for the Hudson Yards plan was that it would expand the city's supply of office space (and, secondarily, luxury housing) and thus the city's postindustrial, office-based economy. This expansion in turn, it was argued, would lead to job growth. Of course, it would also lead to enormous profits as one of the last frontiers of Manhattan real estate was developed.

Bloomberg administration officials did not disagree with the notion that the growth of the city's office stock was required to secure its economic future.

However, the logic of the Bloomberg Way and the luxury city development strategy differed in important ways from the real estate profit–driven logic that had long governed development policy in the city. Most notably, Bloomberg administration officials explicitly placed the need for more office space, and thus the Hudson Yards plan, directly in the context of interurban competition. In August 2004, the DCP's Vishaan Chakrabarti pulled together the need for office towers (that is, "density"), global competition, and the compulsion of growth, saying, "We also need to grow. Density is good. Density is the reason we all live here. . . . I met my counterpart from the city of Paris a few months ago, who explained to me that 10 years ago the city of Paris passed a moratorium on building anything more than a five story building in the heart of Paris. In that ten years, they lost 150,000 jobs. We are going to grow or die in this competitive environment" (2004b). Such compulsion toward growth is inherent in capitalism (Marx 1990), as well as in capitalist urbanization (Logan and Molotch 1987). Nevertheless, the notion that New York must "grow or die," while in part a rhetorical exaggeration, was remarkable for its clarification of this compulsion, as well as its centrality to the Bloomberg Way. At the heart of the Bloomberg administration's case for the Hudson Yards plan as an economic development project was the argument that an increasingly competitive world required that the city grow just to stand still.

The notion that cities must make various sorts of entrepreneurial investments in order to enhance competitiveness has been a hallmark of urban neoliberalism. While such investments are typically "speculative in execution and design" (Harvey 2001, 353), they seldom tightly hew to a private-sector logic of investment, given both the tension between the economistic logic of investment and political considerations that urban policy makers must take into account, along with the varied ends of such investments (Jessop 1998, 82; Shearmur 2008). The Bloomberg administration's embrace of the logic of investment represented an extension of neoliberal practice and was driven by a number of pressures that all cities face in an environment of enhanced interurban competition. However, it also departed from previous practice in important ways.

The administration's embrace of the logic of investment was notable for its pervasiveness and literal-mindedness. For the administration such a logic of investment was not metaphorical window dressing but a deeply held principle of governance. At one point during the debate over the Hudson Yards plan, Deputy Mayor Doctoroff declared, "Our job . . . is to invest the City's money wisely so that the pie is ultimately bigger than it is today . . . to invest scarce dollars to earn more dollars that will enable us to pay for . . . important priorities — health care, housing, police and fire protection, the list goes on and on" (2004d). Thus, the Bloomberg administration's investment strategy did have a clear aim, one (ostensibly) uncontaminated by political considerations. Whereas for the city's real estate elite, office space had been an end disguised as a means, for the Bloomberg administration office space was a means to an end, or rather two ends: the expansion of city revenues and employment. Of these, it was the first that the Bloomberg administration prioritized. As one advocate of alternative economic development strategies aptly put it to me, the administration pursued "a revenue-based strategy, not a job-based strategy" (Damiani 2004). Speaking of the Hudson Yards plan in June 2004, Deputy Mayor Doctoroff said: "What we're trying to do is generate new incremental additional tax revenues. . . . It's what the investment in the west side is all about. . . . If you look at the west side plan as a whole, we contemplate a public sector investment of 4.5 billion dollars, but over a 30-year period of time, from 2005 to 2035, above and beyond the cost of interest and principal on the debt that we're going to incur to finance that four and a half billion, we foresee additional new tax revenue that would not have existed but for those investments of roughly $67 billion." That is to say, as Doctoroff concluded, it would generate a "substantial profit" (2004d). Moreover, this focus on investments generating "profits" in the form of incremental tax revenue contrasted with the more common situation whereby neoliberal interventions entailed either the direct subsidization of private-sector activity or "the public sector assum[ing] the risk and the private sector tak[ing] the benefit" (Harvey 2001, 353). In this case, both the rewards and the risks would be borne by city government.

All this was a direct consequence of the Bloomberg Way: seeing the city government as a corporation led to the notion that its purpose was to invest toward the generation of profit. This logic of investment was also in keeping with the administration's antipolitical and technocratic qualities. A strategy focused on job creation would raise difficult questions about the distribution and quality of jobs. Focusing on revenue lent itself not just to private-sector techniques and conceptions but also to the practices of measurement and quantification that were an important element of the Bloomberg Way. Claims that the Hudson Yards project would be a profitable investment were premised on the idea that economic and cost projections could be used to accurately and unproblematically measure the quantitative costs and benefits, and thus the profitability, of the project.

The emphasis on investing toward the end of profit, as well as the faith in quantitative measurement, led to a willingness to tolerate a level of financial risk well above that typically seen in state-funded development projects, even in the neoliberal era. This stemmed in part from the private-sector backgrounds of officials like Bloomberg and Doctoroff, who had made their fortunes and reputations through their ability to accurately make judgments about the balances of risks and rewards in potential investment given the proper data. Also important here was how the Bloomberg Way related to the broader context of intense interurban competition, in which cities' "capacity . . . to remain at the top of both world and national hierarchies is linked to their ability to remain at the forefront of economic and institutional innovation" (Jessop 1998, 86). This necessity to constantly "innovate," which the luxury city strategy defined as being able to provide services, infrastructure, and urban environments appealing to the city's "target market" of high-value-added corporations and their employees, demanded a level of revenue that only very profitable — and therefore more risky — investments could supply.

This all added up to a new, more active role for government in economic development. Instead of imposing austerity, supporting the profitable development of real estate, or creating a better business climate, government was to serve as an entrepreneurial investor, looking for opportunities, sometimes safe, sometimes risky, to invest taxpayer dollars that would both enhance the "product," that is, the city as an urban environment hospitable to high-end corporations and their employees, and generate "profit" that could be invested anew. This logic of investment shaped the Bloomberg administration's development and marketing of the Hudson Yards plan, and had important effects on the debate over the plan. Its most important immediate effect was that it placed the means of financing the various elements of the Hudson Yards plan front and center in the construction of and debate over the plan. After all, the details of the plan's financing were the key to ensuring its profitability. It is to those details that we now turn.

FINANCING (AND SPLITTING) THE HUDSON YARDS PLAN

The need for the Hudson Yards plan to be self-financing, first generated by NYC2012's wish to avoid public review and competition with other development priorities and reinforced by the Bloomberg Way's emphasis on the autonomy of the CEO mayor, was intensified by the logic of investment, which was premised on the notion that particular investments and thus their expected costs and benefits could be considered as discrete interventions. Along with the enormous cost of the project, this made the plans for financing the Hudson Yards both significant and complex.

Unsurprisingly, then, details of the Hudson Yards financing plan were slow to emerge. Through 2002 and early 2003, it was widely assumed that a version of TIF would be used. While TIF would have established a freestanding funding stream and governance structure, it presented problems. The most important was that the projected incremental gain in property taxes, the only source of revenue available to TIF districts under New York State law, would not be sufficient to cover the rapidly increasing estimates of the project's cost. So, in February 2003, a month after the Bloomberg administration said it would release a financing plan, it announced that it would not be using TIF, and Deputy Mayor Doctoroff promised that a reworked plan would be released in late spring.

Late spring passed, and then summer, and then fall — and no financing plan was issued. Administration officials urged patience, pointing to the complexity of the Hudson Yards plan, which Doctoroff aptly likened to "a Rubik's Cube" (Levy 2003a). The administration was struggling to align a number of factors, including the ever-rising costs of existing elements and pressure for the city to fund additional elements of the project, most importantly a portion of the Javits Center expansion. In December 2003, the administration submitted a request for proposals to the investment banks that did most of the underwriting of city bond offerings, asking that they develop detailed financing packages using various revenue streams already identified by the administration. While requesting that all financing options be considered, administration officials indicated in their public comments that they favored a self-financing plan.

However, if self-financing were to be used, it would no longer be used for the project in its entirety. The administration's decision to split the plan along Eleventh Avenue was codified in its request for proposals: the banks were asked to consider only the portions of the Hudson Yards plan lying east of Eleventh Avenue, that is, those associated with the rezoning portion of the plan. If the administration was going to backtrack on the years of claims by Doctoroff and NYC2012 that the Hudson Yards plan would be self-financing, this was the least damaging way to do it. The portion of the plan going through ULURP, and thus subject to legislative review, would be financially self-supporting, making it more appealing to the cost-conscious city council members who would ultimately vote on it. The funding of the western portion of the plan, comprising the convention corridor (that is, the stadium and the Javits Center expansion), would be shielded from legislative approval. This made the self-financing of this portion of the plan less critical, as the administration could attempt to squeeze funds from the region's complex and opaque network of state and city public authorities and development corporations, as well as the New York Jets.

In any case, two things were now apparent. First, major portions of the Hudson Yards plan would in fact *not* be able to finance themselves, a potential political peril the administration had been able to minimize but not eliminate. Second, the development of plans for the financing of the Hudson Yards plan would proceed on two distinct tracks, one addressing the still self-financing rezoning, and another addressing the no longer self-financing convention corridor.

Self-Financing the Rezoning

In February 2004, the administration released a financing plan, developed in partnership with Goldman Sachs, JPMorgan Chase, and Bear Stearns, who would act as senior underwriters for the bond offering that would fund the rezoning. The plan proposed $3.6 billion in borrowing to cover principal and interest, backed by $16 billion in revenues generated between 2005 and 2035 from Payments in Lieu of Taxes (PILOTs), Payments in Lieu of Sales Taxes, residential property taxes, District Improvement Fund payments, and proceeds from the transfer of development rights.[1] Three aspects of this financing plan were especially notable.

The first regarded the project's governance. The mayor would create the Hudson Yards Infrastructure Corporation (HYIC), a local development corporation that would serve as a financing conduit and coordinating entity, and appoint its three board members. The HYIC would sell its own bonds, backed only by the revenue streams described above, which would flow directly to the HYIC. Any remaining revenue would be passed on to the city. As a local development corporation, it would also have the right to exempt certain businesses from property and other taxes and then to negotiate PILOTs without legislative approval. The HYIC would thus make the Hudson Yards project operationally and financially independent of normal city agencies and legislative oversight.

The second noteworthy aspect of the self-financing plan was the manner in which the administration proposed to solve the problem of timing. Driven by the deadline of a (potential) 2012 Olympics and the need to spur commercial development as quickly as possible, $2.8 billion would have to be borrowed upfront for capital improvements, most notably the subway extension. This would generate $800 million in interest payments due between 2005 and 2012; only about $300 million in revenue was projected to be available during this time. This gap could have been closed by the HYIC selling more long-term bonds, putting the money in the bank, and using it to pay the debt service. However, this would have increased the already large upfront costs of the project. Instead, the administration chose to defer these costs — and thus increase them — by proposing to use so-called commercial paper, a form of low-cost, short-term borrowing typically used by private companies to bridge temporal gaps between investment and return. The city would borrow commercial paper and, when it became due at the end of the year, borrow more to pay back the principal and the interest owed. (This kind of rolling over of commercial paper is fairly common in private-sector credit markets.) In all, about a billion dollars in commercial paper would be borrowed by 2012, when project revenues were projected to be sufficient to begin to pay down the commercial paper debt.

The use of commercial paper was new to public finance in New York City. Also new, and potentially more problematic than the use of commercial paper in and of itself, was the method that the administration proposed to enhance the credit worthiness of the HYIC, which could not avail itself of the commercial credit insurance typically used by private companies. It proposed that the Transitional Finance Authority (TFA), created in 1997 by the state legislature as a mechanism to expand the city's borrowing capacity, back the debt. This meant that if the HYIC could not find lenders to finance the annual rollover of its commercial paper, the TFA would do so, using money otherwise destined for the normal city budget. Thus, the commercial paper portion of the financing plan put the city on the hook for hundreds of millions of dollars.

The third noteworthy aspect of the rezoning financing plan was that it placed the HYIC in the role of a real estate developer. Since the plan was self-financing, the HYIC would be dependent on commercial development in the area proceeding on pace with the optimistic projections of office space demand that served as the scaffolding of the financial plan. A downturn in demand for office space or a glutted office market could throw the whole project into financial disarray — with dire consequences for the HYIC, the TFA, and the city itself, which was unlikely to let the HYIC default on its bonds. The plan did contain provisions for subsidies to commercial developers intended to spark development should it lag. But since they took the form of reduced PILOTs, which were the largest sources of HYIC revenue, such subsidies would reduce the revenue flowing to the HYIC if used imprudently (that is, if not stimulating development that would have otherwise not occurred).

Like a private developer, then, the HYIC was dependent on its investment generating revenues to pay for the debt incurred in making that investment. Like a private developer, the HYIC would have to finesse the balance between reducing prices to spark demand and generating enough revenue to pay debt service. Like a private developer, the HYIC would be forced to compete for tenants with areas of development elsewhere in the city. Unlike a developer, however, the HYIC could not use revenues from other, more successful investments to cover shortfalls in the Hudson Yards area. The self-financing plan placed all the burdens borne by a private developer on the HYIC without conferring upon it any of the advantages.

Ghost-Financing the Convention Corridor

The plans for financing of the convention corridor should have been significantly less complex than those of the rezoning. This was due not just to the fact that splitting the Hudson Yards plan along Eleventh Avenue removed the necessity for the convention corridor to be self-financing and subject to legislative approval but also to the fact that state ownership of the land west of Eleventh meant that bonds issued by the state's main economic development agency, the Empire State Development Corporation (ESDC), or some other state authority could be used to fund the construction of the Javits Center expansion and a good portion of the stadium. However, while these state entities could issue the bonds, the Bloomberg administration had to find identifiable and adequate sources of funding to back them. This would prove to be a difficult task.

By late 2004, all of the pieces of the $1.4 billion in funding for the relatively uncontroversial Javits Center were falling into place — except one. Still uncertain was where the city would find the $350 million it had committed to the project in mid-2003, when advocates of the convention center expansion publicly expressed their worry that it was being overshadowed by the stadium and the rezoning plan. Initially, Mayor Bloomberg had proposed borrowing against money flowing to the city from the Battery Park City Authority, but this was quickly scuttled by the overwhelmingly negative reaction of civic groups and affordable housing activists, who had long complained that commitments made when the Battery Park City development was first built to use this money for affordable housing had not been met. In December 2004, when the state's portion of funding for the Javits Center expansion was approved, Daniel Doctoroff could only say that the city would use an unspecified stream of PILOTs, user fees, and other revenue controlled by the mayor, rather than the city's normal capital budget, to make its contribution to the project's funding.

As difficult as it was for the city to find money to finance its portion of the Javits Center expansion, that was nothing compared to the difficulty of raising money for the far more controversial stadium. In February 2004, it was agreed that the $1.4 billion cost of the NYSCC would be split: the city and the state each would be responsible for half the $600 million cost of decking the western Hudson rail yards, and the Jets would bear responsibility for all remaining costs, including cost overruns. In December, the Bloomberg administration announced a plan to meet its $300 billion commitment without having to receive any legislative approval: it would draw on the hundreds of millions of dollars generated by PILOTs from projects throughout the city, which (excluding the money generated by the Battery Park City Authority) amounted to just enough to cover the city's annual debt service for its contributions to both the Javits Center expansion and the NYSCC. This apparent solution was short-lived. City council Speaker Gifford Miller, a stadium opponent, and a candidate for mayor in the 2005 election, asserted that the use of PILOTs as a "mayoral slush fund" violated the council's power to appropriate funds and quickly pushed through legislation outlawing the practice (Hu and Bagli 2005). The administration in turn claimed that the legislation abrogated mayoral powers, and the issue headed to the courts, leaving this strategy for funding the stadium in limbo.[2]

In early 2005, the ESDC adopted and then approved a General Project Plan (GPP) for the NYSCC. It included proposals for $1 billion issuance of state bonds, which would fund much of the stadium's construction and which was subject to the unanimous approval of the Public Authorities Control Board (PACB). It also indicated that if the state legislature did not approve state funding for the NYSCC, the city would be responsible for the entire $600 million cost of decking the rail yards. Despite reassurances from ESDC President Charles Gargano that this additional obligation could be avoided by "shuffling money around" (Topousis 2004b), it was ironic that the city was being asked to potentially take on additional responsibility when it was unable to identify a revenue stream to back its own $300 million portion of the NYSCC. Even as the GPP for the stadium moved onto the agenda of PACB, which would determine its fate, in the spring of 2005, the source of the city's contribution to the stadium funding was undetermined. Apparently, for the Bloomberg administration, no funding source was better than one that required legislative approval.

Profitability, Autonomy, and Class

In the administration's efforts to design financing plans for the rezoning and the convention corridor, the emphasis on profitability prioritized through the logic of investment began to chafe against other concerns that were also derived from the Bloomberg Way. The most important of these was the principle of autonomy, which as we have seen was crucial to the notion of the CEO mayor. The Bloomberg administration sought to maximize not just profit but also its ability to assert control over the implementation and rewards of the plan by employing (or creating) governmental bodies that were under the control of the mayor, shielded from legislative power, or, better yet, both. It also sought to shift risk away from these autonomous bodies when possible, as demonstrated by the use of the TFA to back HYIC bonds. The result was a far more complex, and contradictory, situation than a straightforward logic of investment would seem to entail. The rough correlation between risk and reward that defines typical investment scenarios was now complicated by the exigencies of autonomy.

Indeed, when profitability's calculus of risk and reward conflicted with the imperative of autonomy, the administration actually chose to increase risk and decrease the potential of reward rather than relinquish control over a project's implementation and funding. This was demonstrated by its decision to have the HYIC issue its own bonds, rather than using cheaper, standard General Obligation bonds, which added hundreds of millions, if not billions, of dollars in interest costs to the plan (New York City Independent Budget Office 2004d, 6–7). It is also evident in the decision to carve out a sort of semiautonomous zone on the far west side, a zone in which development would be exempt from normal taxes and instead subject to PILOTs and other alternative levies, the proceeds of which would be captured by the HYIC. While this shielded the project and its financing from legislative approval, it also generated a good deal of risk, as the HYIC would be dependent on a spatially delimited set of revenues. Finally, it is illustrated by the administration's decision to use commercial paper (rather than additional borrowing, which might have given pause to investors in HYIC bonds) to bridge the gap between revenues and expenses in the early years of the project, a decision that minimized upfront costs while increasing costs in the long run. This was a tradeoff between two kinds of risks: the risk of reduced financial gain or even loss, and the risk that normal legislative and budgeting processes would kill or delay the project. Getting the project underway and completed quickly, without undue interference or delay, trumped democratic niceties and even profitability.

Some of the means that the administration was using to maximize its autonomy were actually very old. After all, the governmental netherworld of local development corporations, public authorities, alternative bond-issuing mechanisms, PILOTs, and development agencies was developed from the 1920s onward in order to evade "the tight democratic shackles [that] might undermine the . . . capacity to develop and act on coherent plans to meet complex regional problems" (Doig 1993, 41). The origin of this governmental complex was tightly linked to the Progressive-era development of the PMC and its claims to rule on the basis of its technocratic expertise (Isin 1998, 47). But its use by the Bloomberg administration, coupled with the employment of complex financial practices that typically were found only in the private sector, such as the use of commercial paper, was animated by a different class project. Specifically, this was the claim to class power inherent in the notion of the CEO as avatar of efficacy or, in Bloomberg's more colloquial terms, as "somebody that gets things done" (Saul 2001). Getting this thing — the Hudson Yards plan — done was critical both to the success of the luxury city strategy and to the assertion of class power that the Bloomberg Way represented. It was not just the logic of investment in itself that made the financing plans yet another instance in which this form of urban governance reflected class but also the Bloomberg administration's demand for the autonomy to make investment decisions in accordance with its own experience, expertise, and judgment.

The Hudson Yards financing plans comprised a new approach to funding public works, one that might reestablish costly and ambitious planning projects as feasible tools of economic and urban development. However, it was fraught with internal contradictions, as the imperatives of autonomy and those of profitability, both derived from the class politics of the Bloomberg Way, conflicted. Moreover, despite the administration's efforts to shield the Hudson Yards plan from public approval, there were still a certain number of governmental hurdles it had to overcome, including the city council's approval of the rezoning plan and the PACB's approval of the state bonds that would fund the convention center corridor. Some degree of public support would be required to accomplish these goals, especially in the case of the city council. And just as the details of the financing plan grew out of the Bloomberg Way, so too did the administration's efforts to gain this public support.

DEBATING THE FINANCING PLANS

The infusion of autonomy into the Hudson Yards plan was aimed at ensuring that Mayor Bloomberg would be, as he had been as a CEO, "the ultimate risk taker and decision maker" (Bloomberg and Winkler 2001, 182). However, the CEO's acting as such depended on the proper attitude of his employees: "Either they believe in me, trust me, and are willing to take the risk that I will deliver success, or they don't" (Bloomberg and Winkler 2001, 46–47). The question, as the public debate over the Hudson Yards plan began in earnest in early 2004, was whether or not the unruly and varied constituencies entailed in the debate over the Hudson Yards plan would in fact defer to Bloomberg's demand for the opportunity to deliver success — or, to put it in slightly different terms, to perform.

There were three central lines of debate over the financing of the Hudson Yards plan, each of which was shaped by the Bloomberg Way and the logic of investment. The first concerned the "profitability of the stadium," which could only be established if its costs and benefits could be exactly quantified. Second, the Hudson Yards rezoning plan was bedeviled by fundamental questions concerning the level of risk appropriate for a publicly funded project, especially in light of the city's 1970s fiscal crisis, which was in part caused by risky, off-budget techniques for financing urban development. The third line of debate, immediately pertaining to the rezoning but ultimately having consequences for the stadium, raised a divisive political issue that the Bloomberg administration's antipolitical and corporate approach was especially ill suited to deal with, the long-standing competition between Manhattan's two CBDs.

The NYSCC: Investment or Subsidy?

The Bloomberg administration deployed the logic of investment with special fervor in their justifications of the NYSCC. For instance, during a June 2004 hearing, Deputy Mayor Doctoroff told the city council that "the opposition will suggest that we're simply spending $600 million of public resources. . . . The reality, when we actually look at the numbers, is that the New York Sports and Convention Center . . . is a terrific investment that . . . will generate a substantial profit" (2004d). Portraying the stadium as a profitable investment that would generate revenue for other priorities might reduce the political fallout from the decision to fund the city's portion of the stadium using existing city resources, rather than via the revenue it would generate itself. Moreover, establishing the stadium's profitability might counter the conventional wisdom that public investments in stadiums were rarely, if ever, recouped (Noll and Zimbalist 1997). This contention was based on the familiar argument that the NYSCC was not just a stadium. Jets president Jay Cross, trying to preempt the arguments of the unanimously anti-stadium economists slated to testify later in that June 2004 hearing, said, "That's why the same tired economic analysis that might apply to fully subsidized stadium-only facilities in cities like Baltimore and Cincinnati does not apply to this model, the New York model. . . . The academics have to go back to first principles and completely comprehend two distinct industries, sports and conventions. They have not done that" (2004). Just as the NYSCC's function as a convention center would permit it to spark development on the far west side, so too would it permit the project to generate increased tax revenues.

Such claims of profitability gave particular salience to the projections of the project's costs and benefits. Stadium boosters had been armed with exact measures of this profitability by a March 2004 study of the economic benefits of the NYSCC conducted by the consulting firm Ernst & Young and paid for by the Jets (New York Jets 2004). The study indicated that the NYSCC would result in an annual profit of $33 million, generating $73 million in state and city taxes while only costing $40 million in annual debt service.

While the Jets-funded study of the NYSCC's economic impact provided the basis for claims of its profitability, its provenance generated much skepticism. Basing public policy and the expenditure of public funds on a study funded by a private, interested party raised major questions, questions that could not be easily laid to rest by the claims of state and city officials that they had subjected Ernst & Young's data to all manner of stress tests and alternative models. Indeed, both the origin of this study and the questionable record of economic impact studies in general raised the possibility that overly optimistic assumptions had led to overstatements of the NYSCC's benefits.[3] Opponents of the NYSCC raised this issue again and again, arguing that the use of this study by city and state officials demonstrated that the relationship between the administration and the Jets was overly cozy, and that the administration's commitment to the NYSCC was absolute.

A second economic impact study played a key role in the debate over the stadium's profitability. In June 2004, the Independent Budget Office (IBO), an independent, city-funded, nonpartisan policy analysis organization, issued its own appraisal of the stadium's economic impact (New York City Independent Budget Office 2004b). The IBO's analysis provided ammunition to both critics and proponents of the NYSCC, indicating that while the Ernst & Young study had overstated the economic impact of the stadium, it still would generate between $2.5 and $10 million in incremental tax revenue per year. On one hand, the NYSCC's proponents, despite their criticisms of the study as "pessimistic," "inexpert," and "ultraconservative," touted the fact that "even . . . the Independent Budget Office" acknowledged the stadium's profitability (Doctoroff 2004a). On the other hand, by explicitly emphasizing the inherent uncertainty involved in the kind of projections upon which the Bloomberg administration was making its claims that the NYSCC represented a profitable investment, the IBO study helped undermine such claims. The all-important numbers were getting fuzzy.

One number that the administration and its allies had insisted was absolutely clear was the $600 million the city and the state together had agreed to spend on the NYSCC. Since the Jets were responsible for all the stadium's remaining costs, including cost overruns, it was claimed that this figure provided a clear baseline to which costs could be compared in calculating the stadium's profitability. However, as time went on, evidence grew that there were a num-

ber of hidden costs that substantially increased the amount of public investment required by the NYSCC.

In July 2004, it was reported that the ESDC was considering granting the Jets
the ability to cover some $450 million of the NYSCC's costs using tax-exempt,
private activity bonds. While the Jets would have been responsible for paying
back these bonds, the tax-exempt status of the bonds reduced the interest rate
the team would have to pay in order to find buyers for them. The potential
use of such bonds to fund the NYSCC gave already suspicious stadium opponents even more of an incentive to keep their eyes peeled for hidden subsidies
and costs.

The GPP provided stadium opponents with a wealth of evidence that the
$600 million committed by the city and the state did not represent the outer
limit of public expenditure on the stadium. One red flag was a complex arrangement involving the Jets' payment, or nonpayment, of property taxes.
Since the western Hudson rail yards were owned by the state, the Jets would
make PILOTs instead of paying real estate taxes; these PILOTs, rather than flowing into state or city coffers, would be used to pay off the tax-exempt bonds
that ESDC would make available to the Jets. This, as critics delighted in pointing
out, was akin to private homeowners being permitted to use their property tax
payments to pay off their mortgages. Eventually it became clear that the Jets
were committed to avoiding taxes as they faced a ballooning price tag for the
NYSCC. While Jets and city officials came up with a variety of reasons why this
should not be considered a subsidy, to many stadium opponents it seemed just
that — and one that rang in at a whopping $450 million.

In addition, the GPP did not indicate funding sources for a number of pieces
of infrastructure associated with the NYSCC. Many of these elements were included in the renderings of the building and also served to provide the kind of
"seamless connections" to the surrounding areas that underwrote claims that
the NYSCC would be an "icon of urbanism." The Jets agreed to pick up some of
these costs, and there were indications (though no commitments) that NYC2012
would as well. Stadium opponents claimed that unless there were solid indications otherwise, it was likely that the bulk of these costs would ultimately be
borne by the city or the state, and thus represented an additional public subsidy
of at least $100 million.

Finally, as of November 2004, when the GPP was released, the Jets had offered the MTA, who owned the right to develop the yards, $100 million for those
rights. Many observers, including some who supported the stadium, were out-
raged, given the fact that the MTA itself placed the value of those development
rights at upward of $1 billion. Though the Jets later agreed to pay $280 million

for those rights, this offer was still viewed by many as an unconscionable give-away of public resources.

Taking all this into account, critics charged that the entire amount of public money that would be expended on the NYSCC was not $600 million but well over $1 billion. Despite the best efforts of stadium proponents, over time the accuracy of the base line against which the NYSCC's "profitability" could be measured began to come into question. These revelations that $600 million was only the tip of the public expenditure iceberg combined with the questioning of the projections provided in the Jets-funded economic impact study to radically destabilize the Bloomberg administration's claims that the stadium represented a profitable public investment. The involvement of the Jets, which originally provided a crucial injection of private capital, as well as an ongoing use for the stadium after 2012, led to accusations that the administration was engaged not in an innovative exercise in applying private-sector logic to urban development but in typical stadium subsidization. Ironically, it was an instance of public–private partnership, that mainstay of entrepreneurial governance, which made it more difficult to defend the stadium using the private-sector-derived logic of investment.

Risk, Faith, History, and Office Space Projections

A second debate over the Bloomberg administration's reliance on quantification to establish the profitability of a portion of the Hudson Yards plan centered on its proposed amount of office space. While the Framework had proposed roughly 30 million square feet (msf) of office space in the area, it contained no real justification for that number. Eventually, the administration commissioned a study to determine future demand for office space on the far west side.

The study, released in spring 2003, produced a range of estimates of the amount of office space that the far west side could absorb by 2025, each of which was dependent on a series of assumptions concerning technical matters. These assumptions included the number of office-based jobs projected to be created in the region as a whole, the rate at which different areas in the region and the city had historically "captured" this job growth, the amount of space necessary for each office worker, and the potential for commercial development on existing sites in Midtown Manhattan (Economic Research Associates and Cushman & Wakefield 2003). The report ultimately settled on a baseline estimate of a bit less than 20 msf of office space that could realistically be absorbed by the Hudson Yards area by 2025.

The uncertainty inherent in the construction of this estimate contrasted sharply with the confidence with which administration officials deployed it as proof of the need for large-scale office development in the far west side. Again and again in public and media presentations of the plan, officials like Deputy Mayor Doctoroff and the DCP's Vishaan Chakrabarti would run through a quick litany of numbers — 443,000 office jobs in the region would generate 110 msf of demand for office space, 68 msf of which would be in New York City, and only 49 msf of which could be built in other areas in the city or absorbed via turn-over. According to these officials, such figures established a 19 msf "office space gap" that if not filled by development in the Hudson Yards would lead to jobs being lost to other "global cities" like London or Shanghai (Chakrabarti 2004a; DeDapper 2004). Only if directly challenged — a rare occasion given their aura of solidity — would these officials acknowledge the uncertainty of the projections upon which their claims were based, and even then they would argue that these claims, far from being overly optimistic, were in fact quite conservative.

Nevertheless, the need for this amount of office space, let alone the 28 msf that was proposed as the Hudson Yards plan entered ULURP, came under serious scrutiny. Many worried that the level of commercial development that the city projected was overly optimistic. If commercial development did not materialize, the financial underpinnings of the plan would be threatened. In August 2004, the IBO released a report concluding that office job growth in the city between 2005 and 2035 would generate significantly less demand for office space than the Bloomberg administration was projecting (New York City Independent Budget Office 2004c). While this report took direct aim at the specific number touted by administration officials, it also foregrounded the fact that the projections of office job growth and office space demand were inherently uncertain and should be treated tentatively, especially when forecast so far into the future. Moreover, many supportive of the basic premises of the Hudson Yards plan publicly questioned the Bloomberg administration's projections of office space demand. In particular, the plan's concentration of office space at the western edge of the Hudson Yards, far from Midtown Manhattan, made the projected level of demand even more questionable. Even some prominent office developers publicly questioned the city's office space projections: Douglas Durst, the scion of a prominent real estate family whose holdings included a number of Midtown office buildings, and a proponent of the far west side development, said in early 2003, "I don't see how you project demand for 30 million square feet of office space" (Sargent 2003a).

Changes in the city's postindustrial economy and its relationship to the built environment made forecasts of increased demand for office space even more dubious. Many argued that the city's postindustrial economy was likely to shrink, given its declining share of the region's and the nation's financial and business services industries, as well as the decentralization of routine back office functions in those industries (Bowles and Kotkin 2003; Fiscal Policy Institute 2002a). Moreover, a number of urbanists involved in the debate over the Hudson Yards were predicting that existing postindustrial activity was likely to use space in a different way, with more emphasis on high-level functions and live-work space and a greater use of green buildings (Sagalyn 2004; Brunzema 2004). All this augured less demand in the future for the kind of large floor-plate office buildings that these industries typically used, and which the Hudson Yards plan was built around. These technical matters were a prominent feature in the public debate of the Hudson Yards plan, as critics of the plan voiced them in the media and in public hearings. CB4 used them in its critique of the rezoning plan, as did individual far west side community members and politicians who opposed the plan.

Far from ending the discussion, then, the administration's claim that there existed a cut-and-dried 19 msf office space gap that had to be filled by the Hudson Yards plan propelled the arcane details of office space projection directly into the political debate over the plan. Moreover, the administration had staked the future solvency of its self-financing plan for the rezoning of the Hudson Yards area on the accuracy of such office space demand projections. If they proved incorrect, the plan's (and the city's) finances would be in danger; if they proved correct, the city would enjoy a bonanza of new tax revenue. One's degree of faith in these office space projections thus became a proxy for the degree of risk one saw as appropriate for the city government to take on.

Unsurprisingly, community critics of the plan raised the issue of risk many times. They argued directly against the administration's claim that the additional risk of the Hudson Yards financing plan was worthwhile because it prevented competition with other projects funded through the city's normal capital budget. However, objections to the level of risk inherent in the self-financing plan also came from a less expected direction. A number of politicians, developers, and prodevelopment conservatives, who had strong connections to the city's real estate industry and endorsed the importance of CBD expansion, objected to the high-stakes gamble that the administration had made.

For these individuals, this gamble was all the more worrisome given the lessons of history. For example, in a December 2004 council hearing, Richard Ravitch, the former developer and head of the MTA, expressed sympathy with Doctoroff even as he challenged the wisdom of the course charted by the deputy mayor and his colleagues. Ravitch drew an explicit parallel between plans to have the ostensibly independent HYIC float bonds backed by future revenues with the 1965 decision on the part of the state legislature to permit a quasi-state organization, the Urban Development Corporation, to borrow against estimated future revenues, which occasioned a later state bailout that helped precipitate the city's 1970s fiscal crisis. Ravitch said:

> I have spent my life building things based on assumptions about what the future revenues will be, and I am not unsympathetic, but I know bonds cannot be sold just on the credit of the [HYIC]. When Mr. Doctoroff says that the City isn't obligated on that, he is absolutely correct, and I am sure he means it honestly. But to suggest it would not affect the credit of the City is silly, because the City in no way could ever permit a default of the [HYIC]. . . . The case in point is the one that I lived through . . . in 1975, when the bank said, if you let [the Urban Development Corporation] go broke, we acknowledge it is not a legally enforceable debt of the State of New York. But if you let it go under, we will not lend the State of New York a dime. (2004a)

Other developers, financiers, and politicians who had lived through the 1970s fiscal crisis — including none other than Felix Rohatyn (Bagli 2004c) — cautioned against the use of off-budget and risky financing schemes. Even the Financial Control Board, which had overseen city finances since the fiscal crisis, expressed concerns that using the TFA as a credit enhancer posed risks to the city's fiscal health (New York State Financial Control Board 2004, 37–38). These elites, otherwise supportive of the redevelopment of the far west side saw, in the administration's methods of financing of the Hudson Yards plan, "all of the things that had led to the crisis of the seventies," as Ravitch bluntly put it (Cassidy 2005).

Ultimately administration officials and proponents of the Hudson Yards plan had to acknowledge the additional risk inherent in the self-financing plan. Mayor Bloomberg himself called it "a more expensive, riskier way to finance" (Temple-Raston 2004c). Administration officials argued that the fact that resources for such large capital investments were so scarce, and the plan's potential payoff so huge, made the Hudson Yards plan "an investment we cannot afford not to make" (Doctoroff 2004c). If this meant more risk so be it. "What you really have to do from the city's point of view is to look at what the economic benefits are," Mayor Bloomberg said in reference to the Hudson Yards plan. "Everybody wants guarantees in everything. That's not the way the world works. You have to be willing to invest and run some risks and the city has the same obligation. If we don't do that we won't have a city for our kids and grandkids" (Bloomberg and Gambling 2004). Hyperbole aside, what was at stake here was not the sheer survival of the city but rather what kind of city would be bequeathed to those kids and grandkids: a city made prosperous by ancestors' willingness to take bold, risky action or one sliding into poverty and mediocrity as a result of inertia and fear of failure.

Indeed, even as the Bloomberg administration's case for the Hudson Yards plan depended on quantitative analyses — office space projections, cost/benefit analyses, and cost and revenue projections — it also depended on less rationalistic methods: it was "selling the future," as one official put it (Page 2004). The mayor, the deputy mayor, and other proponents of the plan argued that a prosperous future demanded what Goldman Sachs, in its response to the city's Request for Proposals for the Hudson Yards financing plan, called a "leap of faith" (Rayman 2004). While Goldman used this language in regard to potential investors, it applied to a much broader group as well. Just as Bloomberg the CEO had demanded faith from his investors and employees, Bloomberg the CEO mayor was now asking the entire citizenry of New York to take the leap of faith that the Hudson Yards self-financing required. Such a leap was justified by Bloomberg and Doctoroff's investment and entrepreneurial success, their private-sector experience, their knowledge of "how the world works." While quantitative rationales for the self-financing plan were important, they ultimately served to buttress a more fundamental demand: "trust us." Trust our management acumen; trust our judgment of the appropriate mix of risk, reward, and autonomy for public projects; trust our ability to recognize a good investment when we see it; trust our interpretation of the past and our understanding of the future. Yes, the Hudson Yards financing plan was risky, but it was a risk that the city, in the capable hands of the Bloomberg administration, should be willing to take. This demand for trust was intrinsic to the logic of investment, as even legitimate, nonspeculative capitalist investment, Žižek notes, "is, at its very core, a risky wager that a scheme will turn out to be profitable" (2009, 36).

Critics of the self-financing plan may have had confidence in Bloomberg's leadership, or optimism about the future of commercial development in the Hudson Yards. Nevertheless their understandings of history and their conceptions of fiscal prudence prevented them from abdicating their own judgment and endorsing the administration's "faith-based" plan, as Ravitch derisively labeled it (2004b). In the end, this debate gave rise to two irreconcilable approaches to public finance: one cautious, risk averse, and heedful of past mistakes; and another optimistic, much more tolerant of risk, and expressing confidence in its proponents' ability to shape the future. But whereas for critics of the self-financing plan this was a policy issue concerning the balance of risk, autonomy, and reward appropriate to public projects, for administration officials like Bloomberg and Doctoroff the key issue was class identity, as the plan called directly into question the unbridled faith that these TCC members held in their capacity to shape the future. As demonstrated by the scorn they expressed for those who did not share this faith, which is discussed in the next chapter, this was personal.

Competition with Downtown

These questions about the Hudson Yards self-financing plan were premised on the idea that the necessary demand for office space *would not* materialize as predicted. Others, however, feared that this office demand *would* arise, with dire consequences for another important commercial district, Lower Manhattan. Planning groups, city planning commissioners, members of the media, downtown politicians, real estate developers, and business interests all expressed concern that the development of the Hudson Yards would divert real estate development, commercial tenants, and public resources from Lower Manhattan and thus undermine the district's ability to recover from the destruction of the World Trade Center. This concern was made more acute by the fact that Midtown Manhattan had slowly been eclipsing Lower Manhattan as the city's premier business district since at least the mid-1980s (Boyer 2002, 113–114).

Although Mayor Bloomberg, along with Deputy Mayor Doctoroff and other prominent officials, often claimed that the redevelopment of Lower Manhattan was their first priority, their actions (and at times even their words) indicated otherwise. While downtown's advocates, most prominent among them State Assembly Speaker Sheldon Silver, whose district encompassed the former site of the World Trade Center, sought to reestablish downtown as a viable commercial center after 9/11, the mayor seemed to have other ideas. In December 2002, he proposed that the future of the area would be as a mixed-use district rather than a traditional CBD. The administration consistently argued that too much office space was being planned for the World Trade Center site. It successfully pushed for the use of Liberty Bonds, originally intended to provide federal aid to the effort to rebuild Lower Manhattan, in Midtown Manhattan. The Hudson Yards plan's financial structure would create enormous pressure on current and future administrations to stimulate development on the far west side, as the HYIC's (and indirectly, the city's) fiscal health would rely on projected office development materializing (indeed, the Bloomberg administration was already proposing to offer incentives to spur far west side commercial development). Finally, on a more personal note, both Mayor Bloomberg and Deputy Mayor Doctoroff had a history of investing in Midtown Manhattan property and businesses.

All this indicated the administration's clear belief that the future of the city's commercial development lay in an expanding Midtown. It raised fears that, as Silver put it, "the development of the West Side may be done to the detriment of downtown" (Rogers 2002). And in fact, throughout 2004 and early 2005, the Lower Manhattan redevelopment process moved forward very slowly, as the Bloomberg administration focused on far west side redevelopment.[4] The situation came to a head in May 2005, when Silver threatened to use his power as a PACB member to block state funding for the NYSCC if a "Marshall Plan" to spark downtown's commercial redevelopment was not forthcoming.

The administration responded to this critique in a number of ways: by defending its office space projections; by arguing that the redevelopment of Lower Manhattan would be well underway by the time commercial development in the Hudson Yards began in 2010; and, most importantly, by arguing, in keeping with the Bloomberg Way, that these two office districts were, as Doctoroff put it, "entirely different products" (see also Doctoroff 2004a; Robin and Rayman 2002).[5] While this argument was meant to defend the administration against accusations that it was prioritizing the west side over downtown, it was quickly picked up and repeated by defenders of the Hudson Yards plan and by Midtown interests in such a way that actually reinforced the fears of downtown interests. Exemplary was a 2004 editorial in *Crain's New York Business*, which had long proposed that the future of the city's economy lay in Midtown. "While everyone hopes downtown will continue to be a vital economic center, many of the biggest and most expansion-minded employers in the city see their choice as between midtown and some other town," it read. "Unless the West Side is developed, there will be no space for them when the economy rebounds, and they will move elsewhere" (*Crain's New York Business* 2004b). The idea that downtown and Midtown were competing for a different corporate clientele, coupled with the administration's claims that the Hudson Yards was crucial to New York's competitiveness as a global city, left downtown advocates with the uneasy impression that the administration was attempting, as Sheldon Silver would put it after blocking the NYSCC, "to shift the financial and business capital of the world out of Lower Manhattan and over to the West Side" (Bagli and Cooper 2005).

The Logic of Investment and Its (Anti)Politics

In the debate over the Hudson Yards plan as an economic development project, the Bloomberg Way opened up new political vulnerabilities even as it generated new forms of governmental practice. Most obviously, the administration's use of the logic of investment to construct and sell the plan gave the plan's financing, and the projections upon which it was based, a saliency it might not have otherwise had — with enormous implications. Few actually challenged Doctoroff's argument that "our job is to invest," but without a solid source of capital and solid projections of an investment's likely profitability, it was most difficult to close the deal. Indeed, two members of the PACB, State Majority Leader Joe Bruno and State Assembly Speaker Silver, pointed to unanswered questions about the NYSCC's costs and benefits when justifying their refusal to approve the project.

While the logic of investment opened up significant lines of critique, it also served to define the terrain of political struggle. Critics of the stadium often implicitly embraced this logic, challenging the administration's calculations of the relative level of costs and benefits that the stadium or rezoning would generate, or the relative level of risk inherent therein, rather than the logic of investment itself. For example, even as its reports called attention to the fallibility of the figures that the Bloomberg administration was using to make its case, the IBO also implicitly reproduced, and thus helped bolster, the logic of investment in its conclusion that the stadium would in fact generate a profit, if a small one. Likewise while eviscerating the administration's statements of its costs and benefits, the critique that the stadium was overly subsidized implied the possibility that it might have been a profitable investment if the numbers had worked out properly. Finally, to the degree that criticism of the rezoning focused on the details of self-financing rather than on the fact of self-financing itself (as it did when it reached the city council, as I discuss shortly), it reinforced the administration's logic of investment. After all, any self-financing scheme would by definition be isolated from other projects and expenditures, and thus more amenable to being conceived of as a discrete investment. In all these ways, critics of the administration's approach to the Hudson Yards plan, as much as the administration itself, were arguing in terms defined by the logic of investment.

However, it was not just the logic of investment in and of itself that was crucial here. Also important was the way in which that logic merged with the antipolitical tendencies of the Bloomberg Way, particularly the notion of a unitary city interest. As articulated by administration members in debates over the Hudson Yards plan, this interest was defined as the ability to generate profit. It was the job of the CEO mayor to determine the most efficient and effective way to achieve this, and the job of the citizenry to defer to Bloomberg's judgment to show faith in his ability to bring the future into conformity with his vision. The logic of investment entailed a denial of politics, of the fact that the ends of city policy are neither self-evident nor singular.

Such a denial of politics was also inherent in the notion that downtown and Midtown were different products with different target markets. Sheldon Silver and the downtown interests he represented interpreted the Hudson Yards plan in explicitly political terms, as an attempt to prioritize commercial development in one area of the city, thus favoring one group of real estate and business interests over another. The administration, on the other hand, sidestepped such thorny issues by arguing that the niche-market logic inherent in its development strategy vitiated the need for such political-geographic tradeoffs. But this antipolitical rhetoric disguised a deeper political reality: despite its denials of favoring Midtown over downtown, the Bloomberg administration had made just such a choice. Not only was Silver's constituency getting the short end of the stick, but the administration was denying that the stick even had a short end. This foreclosed the possibility of the kind of bargaining that typically is the grist of urban development politics. This particular denial of politics would prove to be momentous, as it would ultimately be the undoing of the NYSCC, the funding of which Sheldon Silver ultimately controlled by virtue of his seat on the PACB. After the PACB's rejection of the stadium's funding, Silver referred to the administration's refusal to bargain until late in the game, saying, "I just think that nobody's opinion counted until it counted. . . . They never talked to Senator Bruno, they never talked to me. They just proceeded ahead" (Steinhauer 2005).

POLITICS TO THE RESCUE

Happily for the Bloomberg administration, and for the fate of the rezoning portion of the Hudson Yards plan, these antipolitics were not broadly shared. For portions of the Hudson Yards plan were rescued — and others nearly rescued — by politics. In the case of the rezoning portion of the plan, this came in the form of preexisting support for the commercial development; in the case of the stadium, it was in the form of a campaign to woo specific constituencies.

The City Council Rescues the Rezoning Plan

By splitting the Hudson Yards plan down the middle, the administration had ensured that only one portion of the Hudson Yards plan — the rezoning of the area east of Eleventh Avenue — required city council approval. Once the CPC approved the Hudson Yards rezoning plan on November 21, 2005, the plan moved onto the agenda of the city council, which now had to approve or reject the plan within 50 days. This would be the council's only opportunity to weigh in on the Hudson Yards plan. And although it had no legal mandate to address the NYSCC, its ability to kill or fundamentally alter the rezoning plan gave it political leverage in regard to the NYSCC — should it choose to use it.

The two hearings on the Hudson Yards rezoning plan, held over three days in December 2005, made it clear that this would not happen, as council leaders dutifully followed the path the Bloomberg administration had laid out for them. Rather than discuss what one exasperated stadium opponent called "the elephant in the room" (Gottfried 2004), they maintained that the fact that the rezoning did not include the stadium gave them no choice but to rule any mention of the stadium out of order — despite the clear planning linkages between the two sides of the plan.

Without the stadium, the rezoning became a straightforward, if enormous, development plan, except for the matter of self-financing. Given the council's fealty to real estate interests, there was little likelihood that the council would vote it down. While council members made impassioned calls for more affordable housing, less density, and assurances that low-end office workers in Hudson Yards office buildings would receive decent wages, the central premise of the rezoning plan — the idea that the city's economic future hinged on the commercial redevelopment of the area — was never meaningfully debated, let alone challenged. The self-financing plan was another matter, as a number of council members expressed concern that it was unnecessarily costly and risky. However, rather than seeing this as a fatal flaw, they called for the council and administration to work together to improve the plan's financing. Despite their efforts to avoid its jurisdiction, in the city council the administration found not an obstinate opponent but a willing partner.

Just over a month after the two city council hearings on the plan, the council's zoning and franchising subcommittee, which had to approve the Hudson Yards rezoning plan for it to move onto the council floor, convened in a small room packed with onlookers. Earlier hearings had ended with tension and uncertainty in the air; the atmosphere now was friendly, relaxed, and full of bonhomie. Before the meeting devolved into an orgy of self-congratulation and before the subcommittee voted nearly unanimously to approve the plan, the committee's cochair, Tony Avella, outlined the agreement the council and the Bloomberg administration had reached: the number of affordable housing units included in the plan had been raised slightly; a number of tenant protection measures had been put in place; the commercial development had been reduced to about 24 msf; the administration had committed not to use any of the revenue generated east of Eleventh Avenue for costs relating to the NYSCC or the Javits Center expansion (which it had never actually proposed to do); and steps had been taken to broaden participation in the governance of the HYIC.

Perhaps most notable was the resolution of the issues concerning the self-financing plan. Normal capital-budgeting process would still not be used, and the rezoning remained self-financing, with one important exception. Instead of using commercial paper backed by the TFA, the council had agreed to appropriate nearly $1 billion from the city's operating budget to right the imbalance between costs and revenues that would emerge over the first decade of the plan's implementation. Ironically, a few weeks of engagement with the council had accomplished what years of work had not: the administration now had a financing plan with reduced risks and costs even as it ensured that the public expenditures did not have to compete with other projects for funding. This was clearly, as one west side community organizer who had led opposition to the Hudson Yards plan told me, "a victory for the [administration]."

Several days later, the entire council passed the Hudson Yards rezoning plan. Despite months of heated rhetoric, all but two council members rose in turn and voted to approve the rezoning plan, generally prefacing their votes with remarks celebrating the concessions that the council had won from the administration. While some aye voters expressed hesitancy about portions of the plan, none mentioned the possibility that too much office space was being planned for the area. Only one councilmember, Charles Barron, a former Black Panther from Brooklyn who voted against the plan, challenged the notion that the economic interest of the city as a whole would be served by large-scale office development on the far west side and by the office-based industries that would fill those buildings. He decried the provision of large property tax breaks for developers even as the city was raising property taxes for small homeowners and cutting services for poor and working-class people, saying, "We are mandating $900 million of cuts from other areas of the budget in the next 10 years, and committing $46 million this year [to the Hudson Yards project] before we even enter budget negotiations with the mayor. Last year we couldn't even get $10 million for youth programs" (2005).

The Bloomberg administration had severely overestimated the council's desire to block the Hudson Yards rezoning. The proposition that the office-based economy, and the construction of the buildings that housed it, was central to the city's economic future was apparently so self-evident to the vast majority of council members that it was not even worthy of debate. The ongoing power of the city's real estate elite and the commitment of the city's political class to postindustrial development had rescued the rezoning plan. The Bloomberg administration's efforts to ensure its autonomy via the rezoning financing plan had almost scuttled a redevelopment plan that, because it had an existing political constituency, was unlikely to fail in the first place.

Profit . . . or Jobs?

Though the stadium served a vital political role by binding various elite groups to the Hudson Yards plan, it did not have an existing political constituency in the way the postindustrial redevelopment of the far west side did. Indeed, after it became apparent that the rezoning and the Javits Center expansion were headed for approval, the strong support of real estate and tourist industries for the NYSCC might have been expected to flag, as the Olympic bid had already fulfilled its function as a "forcing mechanism" for the commercial redevelopment of the far west side of Manhattan. Moreover, as we have seen, the Bloomberg administration's antipolitical effort to sell the stadium to a dubious public on the basis of its ostensible profitability was foundering. In short, as 2004 wore on, it seemed like the NYSCC was in trouble.

However, while the administration was sidestepping politics, another proponent of the stadium was diving headlong into the messy business of scaring up support for the stadium using old-fashioned and tried-and-true methods. In early 2003, the New York Jets began a wide-ranging campaign to enlist grassroots support for the NYSCC, making barroom presentations, targeting specific constituencies in media campaigns, and, most effectively, ensuring specific groups' support by dangling the prospect of employment in the construction and operation of the NYSCC.

The easiest targets were the city's powerful construction and building trades unions. These unions had long served as a bedrock of working-class support for development. Years of relatively slow construction activity and the increasing use of nonunion labor made a citywide construction boom, fed by a 2012 New York Olympics and the redevelopment of the far west side, especially appealing. Accordingly, the city's construction and building trades unions were eager to support the NYSCC in exchange for a pledge by the Jets to use union construction labor. Moreover, in exchange for promises to use union labor in various aspects of the NYSCC, the Jets were able to secure broad enough union support that the stadium eventually won the endorsement of the New York City Central Labor Council, the governing body for all of the city's labor unions.

The Jets also targeted the city's minority leadership, a more difficult task since redevelopment projects in New York City had historically imposed heavy burdens on poor and working-class African Americans and Latinos, while providing few benefits in return (Schwartz 1993). Moreover, many black and Latino politicians were also deeply concerned about the diversion of public resources to private interests, especially in the context of the post-1970s fiscal crisis squeeze on New York City's social welfare programs, which had intensified under the Giuliani administration and seemed likely to continue as the city faced large budget deficits in the early years of Mayor Bloomberg's first term.

Despite these obstacles, the Jets campaign to enlist minority support for the NYSCC eventually bore fruit, as Jets officials patiently and persistently lobbied African American and Latino groups, newspapers, and legislators. A turning point was reached in mid-2004, when Jets officials announced the team would work with the Minority Business Leadership Council, an umbrella group of trade associations representing, among other groups, African Americans, women, Hispanics, and Caribbeans, to develop "the most inclusive and comprehensive MWBE [Minority- and Women-owned Business Enterprise] program seen to date" (Cross 2004). By spring 2005, the stadium had received the support of a number of high-profile minority leaders, including the Reverend Al Sharpton, probably the best-known black political figure in New York City.

This campaign would have been less effective if not for the dire economic circumstances facing many minority New Yorkers, especially African American men, and the increasingly limited set of options faced by their representatives and advocates. At the same time as the debate over the stadium was going forward, evidence that New York City's 1990s boom had done little to improve the economic standing of poor and working-class African Americans and Latinos was circulating (see, for example, Levitan 2004). Given the post–fiscal crisis erosion of liberalism, partnerships with the private sector seemed as likely to deliver concrete benefits as the local state. The real estate industry, whose well-paid union jobs had long been the dominion of white ethnic men, was a particularly ripe target in this regard. The construction of the NYSCC presented an opportunity for minority leaders to guide some of the employment and business associated with the project toward their constituencies, as well as an opportunity to spur public action by setting a precedent for other large development projects. This tactic was not without its detractors, including more radical African Americans like City Councilman Charles Barron and Harlem-based labor activist Jim Haughton, who argued that the MWBE program would do little to actually change discriminatory hiring and contracting practices in the construction industry and who decried the Jets for their unseemly capitalization on the economic distress of African Americans and other minorities.

The Jets' efforts to garner minority support also resulted in strongly pro-stadium legislative blocs. By May 2005, the stadium had the support of almost all of the city council's African American and Latino members. The Jets had also built a fair amount of support in the state assembly, as roughly a third of assembly Democrats (who held a 104–44 majority) endorsed the project despite the opposition of their leader, Speaker Sheldon Silver. This included most of the city's delegation and a majority of the black, Puerto Rican, and Hispanic caucus. However, this also presented dangers: Silver deeply resented the efforts of the Jets to directly woo assembly members, perceiving them as attempts to circumvent his authority.

These subterranean tensions and unpleasantries did not prevent the Jets from prominently touting minority and union support in their media, public relations, and political campaigns for the stadium. The Jets held well-publicized events around the development of their MWBE program; a typical example was a January 2005 event held at Harlem's historic Bethel AME Church, hosted by black performer Paul Mooney, featuring famous African American choirs, and attended by a broad array of African American reverends, politicians, civic leaders, and sports figures. After his March 2005 endorsement of the stadium, Al Sharpton was featured prominently in television commercials, declaring "the Jets have come to labor, have come to the black and Latino community and have made firm commitments, which sets a standard for doing business in this city" (Saul 2005e).

The Administration Comes on Board

On a warm summer day in late September 2004, thousands of union members gathered on West Thirty-third Street between Ninth and Tenth avenues. A large stage had been set up at the eastern end of the street; Madison Square Garden, whose owner, Cablevision, had emerged as the bête noire of pro-stadium advocates, loomed in the background. As I walked into the rally, a band played a version of the 1980s hit "We Built This City" in tribute to the gathered hard-hat- and work-boot-clad construction union members, many of whom held signs proclaiming "Jobs Now!" and wore T-shirts adorned with an image of the NYSCC along with the words "Build It!" Pro-stadium ads and videos promoting

Pro-stadium rally, September 29, 2004. (Julian Brash)

the Olympic bid played on a large video screen above the stage. As the rally progressed, a stream of union leaders, past and present New York Jets, and pro-stadium politicians touted the jobs the NYSCC would provide. One speaker led the crowd in a call-and-response chant, shouting, "What do we want?" to which the crowd answered with a rousing roar: "Jobs!" Then labor leader Ed Malloy derided Cablevision and other stadium opponents as "opponents of progress"; ex-mayor Ed Koch trumpeted his just-announced support for the NYSCC, claiming that its opponents were suffering from "NIMBY syndrome"; and ex-Jet Joe Klecko urged the crowd to "kick ass and take names" as had his successful teams of the 1980s. Following this, there was a lull of a few minutes as the crowd waited for the afternoon's last speaker to arrive and address the crowd.

Finally, that speaker emerged: Mayor Michael Bloomberg. A slender, small-statured, and restrained man, Mayor Bloomberg looked awkward and out of place among the beefy ex–football players, the working-class white ethnic union leaders, and the multiethnic mix of politicians surrounding him, though he had taken off his suit coat and rolled up his shirtsleeves in an apparent effort to fit in. When he stepped up to the podium, his first words were not about the profit that the stadium would generate or the Olympics; rather, he led the crowd in a chant of "Jobs! Jobs! Jobs!"

The union and minority support the Jets' promises of jobs had engendered made it increasingly difficult for stadium opponents to argue that the project was little more than a giveaway to a wealthy corporation. The stadium now had a mass constituency, a fact that lent credence to the claims of its advocates that it would deliver broad-based benefits. Accordingly, by the late fall of 2004, the administration's public justification for the stadium had begun to shift toward the jobs it would provide to various groups, a trend that grew more pronounced as the stadium headed for its date with the PACB in mid-2005. The NYSCC was portrayed as an example of urban Keynesianism, intended to put money in the pockets of the city's working people struggling to feed their families. "Don't spell it J-E-T-S," said Bloomberg in January 2005, referring to a chant popular among fans of the team, and implicitly shifting attention away from the wealthy football team that would call the stadium home: "spell it J-O-B-S " (Janison and Murphy 2005).

The numbers used to establish the NYSCC as a jobs generator were just as fuzzy as those used to establish the stadium's profitability. Moreover, it was a relatively inefficient means to create jobs (Demause 2004). But whereas fuzzy numbers and overly optimistic claims had stymied the administration's effort to sell the stadium as a profitable investment, this was not the case here. There was a simple reason for this. Unlike the profit the NYSCC would purportedly generate, the jobs that would be created would flow to identifiable, organized, and motivated political constituencies. The successful Jets-led effort to develop support for the stadium was an artful exercise in political bargaining, acknowledging and drawing upon, rather than ignoring or dismissing, important economic and racial differences in the city.

An Unusable Payoff

Once again the administration's antipolitical approach to building support for the stadium needed — and had received — a political bailout. However, the very success of the Jets' efforts to build political support points to one of the supreme ironies of the conflict over the redevelopment of the far west side. By wooing labor and minority constituencies, the Jets had won over a majority of the city council and a large plurality in the state assembly. While this political support provided important public relations benefits, in the end it was useless. This was the case because of the desire of NYC2012 and, later and more importantly, the Bloomberg administration to avoid legislative review of the financing for the

NYSCC. Both NYC2012 and the Bloomberg administration overestimated the degree and obduracy of opposition to the NYSCC and underestimated the possibility that support for the NYSCC could be won through political means. For this, the Bloomberg administration, NYC2012, and the Jets would pay dearly. Avoiding legislative review had placed the fate of the NYSCC in the hands of Sheldon Silver, one of the PACB's members, whose anger at the administration was stoked by its refusal to address competition between the Hudson Yards and Lower Manhattan, as well as the Jets' perceived meddling with his assembly caucus. Silver's ability and inclination to kill the stadium in June 2005 can be directly traced to the decision made years before to avoid the necessity of legislative approval of the project.

THE FUTILITY OF ANTIPOLITICS

In all the hearings, rallies, and press conferences that I attended in the course of the debate over the Hudson Yards plan, I never once heard a crowd chant "Profit! Profit! Profit!" I never once saw a stadium supporter wearing a T-shirt proclaiming "Tax Revenue Now!" But I did hear and see, again and again, expressions of support for the NYSCC based on the jobs it would create, often made by the very people who could anticipate getting those jobs. While Deputy Mayor Doctoroff was lamenting the inability of stadium opponents to understand how profitable it would be, what a brilliant investment it was, and how lucky New Yorkers were to have the opportunity to invest their tax dollars in such a groundbreaking building, the Jets were doing the painstaking work of building political support: attempting to understand the concerns of potential allies and making concessions and offering benefits to meet those concerns. This political legwork gave the arguments that the NYSCC would create jobs a heft and effectiveness never achieved by other arguments for the stadium. The jobs argument worked not because the numbers supporting it were convincing but because it was an argument backed up by the avowed support of a political constituency. Indeed, it seems likely that the Jets' efforts to woo union and minority support for the NYSCC would have resulted in the project receiving legislative approval, despite the questions raised about its effects on the far west side's development and its profitability — if only the Bloomberg administration, driven by its antipolitical and corporate approach to governance, had not worked so hard to avoid this procedural route.

Likewise, the Bloomberg administration's major contributions to construction of the Hudson Yards rezoning plan were all of limited effectiveness in generating political support. The self-financing plan, which took on higher costs and risks in exchange for giving the administration the autonomy it felt it needed to "get things done," was the aspect of the plan with which the city council expressed the most unease. The notion that downtown and Midtown CBDs were different products serving different clienteles only served to anger downtown interests. In tandem with the much-resented efforts on the part of the Jets to garner minority support among members of Silver's Democratic assembly caucus, this corporatized construction of the relationship between the two CBDs eventually led Assembly Speaker Sheldon Silver to use his power over state funding of the NYSCC to kill that project. The demand for faith in the administration's vision of the future clashed with the reality of the past, as many New Yorkers, including those supportive of west side development, saw in the Hudson Yards self-financing plan the danger of a repeat of the 1970s fiscal crisis. So rather than consolidating support for the rezoning plan, these arguments, all derived from the logic of investment, actually undermined it. The success the rezoning plan did have in the city council was due to the deep reservoirs of support for postindustrial development among the city's political elite and the real estate elites who provided much of their funding.

All this demonstrates the dangers posed by the Bloomberg Way's refusal to recognize the legitimacy, or even the existence, of political conflict. This refusal was doubly harmful, for even as the Bloomberg administration denied the existence and legitimacy of political conflict, it was engaged in it. For example, Deputy Mayor Doctoroff's summary dismissal of the possibility that there might be economic competition, and thus political conflict, between downtown and Midtown lay uncomfortably with the fact that the administration as a whole and its key members were firmly committed to Midtown Manhattan as the city's premier CBD. Likewise, the exchange of employment for political support sat uncomfortably with the Bloomberg Way, seemingly more appropriate to the political machines of Boss Tweed's nineteenth-century New York than the corporate technocracy of Michael Bloomberg's twenty-first-century version of the city. As we have seen, the Bloomberg Way was premised on the existence and identification of a unitary interest of the city as a whole, the delegitimization of particular interests, and the rejection of political conflict. However, the efforts of the Jets to build a political constituency supportive of the stadium, to which the administration was a willing party, explicitly relied on appeals to such interests. In doing so, these efforts actually facilitated and fomented political division, as opponents of the stadium were cast as inimical not just to the project, but to the economic well-being of minorities and union members. This undermined the Bloomberg administration's antipolitical approach and made it difficult to accept claims on the part of administration officials that they were concerned only with the greater good of the city and that this administration — and this urban development plan — was somehow "above politics."

However, it is important not to overemphasize the limits of the Bloomberg Way in this discussion. Even as the debates over the rezoning and stadium portions of the Hudson Yards plan revealed the tensions and weaknesses of this approach to urban governance, they also demonstrated its growing power. After all, the rezoning did pass. Though the HYIC board was made more inclusive and the project's financing more dependent on city council appropriations, a remarkable degree of mayoral control over the plan's future development was preserved. While the city's real estate elite provided a crucial boost here, the administration's ability to design a coherent and workable plan, and its ability to create the organizational capacity to forcefully guide it through the approval process, was in large part attributable to the Bloomberg Way. The fact that Mayor Bloomberg had presided over the rezoning of an area whose development had been frustrated for so long proved that he could deliver the goods to the city's real estate elite, even if he was to a substantial degree independent of its power and even if his luxury city strategy might not always conform with the logic of real estate profitability.

Indeed, one episode from the debate over the Hudson Yards plan demonstrates that the Bloomberg Way had become powerful enough not just to deliver these goods but also to allow the administration to directly impose its will on real estate elites. In early 2005, developers had a chance to translate their doubts about the stadium portion of the plan into action, when Cablevision's unsolicited bid for the rights to the western Hudson rail yards forced the MTA to open up bidding for the rights. Not a single major New York City developer bid for them, a remarkable turn of events given their desirability as a development site. The reasons for this were straightforward: developers were afraid to incur the wrath of the administration, especially given the centralization of control over economic and urban development agencies — and thus over the fate of many development and building projects — in the hands of Deputy Mayor Doctoroff. Developers expressed their displeasure at this situation and their interest in developing the rail yards, but only anonymously. For example, one prominent Midtown Manhattan developer, who had designs on the rail yard and provided financial support to stadium opponents, refrained from bidding on the rights to develop the yards and swore to secrecy the recipients of his aid. The rail yards are "clearly valuable," another major developer anonymously said, "but can anyone in my position say so on the record? Everyone, including me, is scared to cross [Doctoroff] on this. I've got too many things cooking in this town" (Bagli 2005b). Developers were "in the witness protection program," as Richard Ravitch memorably put it (Robbins 2005b). While this might have understated their still considerable power, it nonetheless demonstrated the Bloomberg Way had created significant and intimidating enough sources and avenues of power to win the deference of the city's real estate elite.

In addition, the Bloomberg Way largely succeeded in structuring the terrain of political conflict over the Hudson Yards plan. Though in part attributable to the hold of postindustrial common sense, the fact that much of the debate over the rezoning portion of the plan concerned not the end of postindustrial development on the far west side but rather the means of achieving these goals — in particular the relationships between office space projections and the self-financing plan — reflected the power of the Bloomberg administration to determine the parameters of the debate. This was also true of the debate over the stadium, as the numbers that the administration claimed to establish its profitability were a central focus. Even as it lost ground in this debate, the administration succeeded in forcing stadium opponents to spend time and energy debunking these numbers.

Finally, the administration seemed to learn an important lesson in the course of the debate over the Hudson Yards plan, signified by the emphasis it placed on jobs rather than profit in the latter portion of the debate over the stadium. The ability of the administration and its allies to use political means to generate support for the plan while sacrificing little in return indicated that the administration's antipolitical stance could be tempered without ceding a significant degree of the CEO mayor's autonomy. This did not mean that there were still not real threats to this autonomy — such as the PACB — but it did mean that they were rarer and less robust than the administration initially feared. Given thirty years of neoliberalization, the "politics as usual" that Mayor Bloomberg so often condemned was more hospitable than hostile to his approach to urban governance.

Despite this shift, the notion of a unitary city interest was still a crucial and unaltered element of the Bloomberg Way. While willing to negotiate to ensure that potentially recalcitrant factions would go along with the administration's notion of the best interests of the city, Mayor Bloomberg and his key aides from the private sector still demanded deference to their notion of the best interest of the city. As the next chapter demonstrates, this demand represented the final card for the administration to play in its effort to gain approval for the stadium. And it was one that went straight to the class character of the Bloomberg Way.

CHAPTER NINE

The Bloomberg Way and Its Others

Up to this point, I have made much of the rationalistic, technocratic, and calculative aspects of the Bloomberg Way. Whether celebrating technical expertise or avowing that the "facts are the facts," Mayor Bloomberg and his key aides presented themselves as hardheaded, realistic, and pragmatic. Yet this rationalism was leavened by seemingly incongruous elements — for example, the demand for faith inherent in the Hudson Yards plan's financing schemes or the celebration of New York City as a "luxury city" that underwrote the administration's economic and urban development strategy. In other words, we have seen glimmerings of how the Bloomberg Way was animated by a particular urban imaginary, which was itself linked to a particular class identity. In this chapter I address directly the relationships among governance, urban imaginaries, and class in the Bloomberg Way. I do so by focusing on the efforts of the Bloomberg administration and NYC2012 to use the city's bid for the 2012 Summer Olympic Games to generate public support for the NYSCC. In these efforts, they attempted to mobilize what I will call "urban patriotism" to discredit opponents of the stadium.

This mobilization of urban patriotism emerged directly out of the antipolitical Bloomberg Way. Specifically, the administration and its allies argued that the Olympic bid was in the interest of the city as a whole, that the NYSCC was absolutely necessary to the bid, and that to oppose a stadium on the far west side of Manhattan was to oppose the best interests of the city itself. But what became apparent as the administration and its allies made such claims was that what "the city itself" represented was the crux of this issue. For the content of the urban patriotism they mobilized — the particular urban imaginary and identity it drew upon — was a direct expression of the class politics that shaped the Bloomberg Way. This mobilization would be effective only if New York's broader citizenry shared this particular urban imaginary and identity — and they did not. Instead, critics and opponents of the NYSCC, the Hudson Yards plan, and the Olympic bid had their own notions of what the city represented and what it meant to be a New Yorker. These urban imaginaries and identities varied, as did the interests to which they were linked, thus preventing the emergence of a coherent and comprehensive opposition that might articulate an alternative to the Bloomberg Way. Nevertheless, they ensured that attempts to mobilize urban patriotism could not paper over deep questions about whose interests would be served by public policy. The denigration of those who dared oppose the NYSCC, and thus the Olympics, as insufficiently committed to the city, which was meant to quell dissent, instead raised a series of fundamental questions: Who was the city for? What kind of city would — and should — New York be? And who would decide?

BUILDING THE CHAIN: LINKING THE OLYMPICS AND THE NYSCC

Olympic boosters had long hoped that the public enthusiasm for the games would provide political cover for the various development projects that comprised the Olympic plan. This was particularly crucial in regards to the NYSCC, given the fate of previous stadium proposals for the far west side. Would the prospect of a New York City Olympics prove so seductive, so appealing, and so obviously beneficial to the city as a whole that New Yorkers otherwise inclined to oppose a far west side stadium would set aside their objections for the (ostensible) greater good of the city?

It took a fair amount of work to create the conditions under which the Olympic bid could be rendered politically effective vis-à-vis the redevelopment of the far west side. First, it had to be established that hosting the Olympics was unquestionably in the city's best interests. Second, the redevelopment of the far west side had to be made indispensable to the Olympic bid; this was accomplished by preempting consideration of alternative sites for the Olympic stadium. Thirdly, the administration and NYC2012 had to counter arguments that the vote of the PACB be delayed until *after* the IOC had made its decision on whether or not the 2012 Games would be held in New York. If the games went to another city (as was widely expected), the stadium would have to succeed on its own merits, without the boost that association with the bid was expected to supply. Thus, the administration and NYC2012 argued fiercely that the NYSCC needed to be approved well before the IOC's decision was to be made in July 2005, throwing up deadline after deadline by which the stadium absolutely *had* to be approved if the city's bid was not to be placed in serious jeopardy.

Establishing the Best Interests of the City

After the USOC selected New York to represent the United States in the competition for the 2012 Games in November 2002, the city council held a series of hearings on the potential impacts of NYC2012's Olympic plan. At the first of these hearings, held in December 2002, one council member noted that "what we begin to hear is what is good for the Olympics is good for New York," and asked if the bid (and the fact that Doctoroff, who had founded the bid, was now the city's main development official) "skew[ed] New York's priorities" (Gioia 2002). Doctoroff's answer was telling:

> You can agree or disagree about the specific components of [the effort to bring the Olympic Games to New York], but nobody benefits from it other than the people of the City of New York. . . . The priorities that we have as a City can be advanced as a result of the Olympics and not the other way around. . . . I really think they are one and the same. I don't think there's any inconsistencies. . . . We're not developing the west side to help the Olympics. The Olympics, in large part, are helping us do what we need to do on the far west side. (2002)

As the notion that the priorities "we" have as a city, among them the development of the far west side, were identical with the priorities of the Olympic bid makes clear, those active in and supportive of the bid portrayed themselves as representative of the interests of the city as a whole.

As time went on Olympic supporters publicly argued that New Yorkers had in fact been unified by the Olympic bid, and thus agreed that it was in the city's best interests. In June 2004, NYC2012 President Jay Kriegel declared that "all the research shows that the Olympics, more than any other issue, brings New Yorkers together. Across every economic, racial, ethnic line, [it has] tremendous popularity" (2004). In fact, the "diverse but united community," as Olympic proponent and New York University President John Sexton called it (Horowitz 2004), supporting the bid was in fact limited to a small and unrepresentative group of New Yorkers. The bid was developed in private, without the participation of the vast majority of individuals and groups involved in planning and development issues in the city, let alone the participation of the city's general citizenry. As a result, the development plan put forth by the bid reflected the priorities of the city's elites, particularly the city's real estate elites. As one member of this group, Doctoroff's mentor Peter Solomon, said, "The brilliance of the . . . plan is that it incorporates almost every idea we've been working on for 30 years" (Bagli 2004d). However, with a few exceptions, the Olympic plan largely excluded development projects and priorities favored by those outside of the circle of elites involved in its design, excluding, for example, the popular Second Avenue Subway or major provisions for affordable housing.

However sincere Doctoroff, Kriegel, Sexton, Solomon, and other NYC2012 officials and supporters were in their belief that the urban development priorities the bid channeled were in the best interests of the city as a whole, they did not seem confident that most New Yorkers would share their belief in the merits of the particular projects they proposed. This was demonstrated by the strategy of using the desirability of bringing the games to New York and the civic pride generated if the city was selected to counteract potential opposition to these projects; if that did not work, the avoidance of public review built into the plan from the beginning would. NYC2012 sought to defuse and evade politics, not to deny their existence altogether.

The Bloomberg administration at least implicitly endorsed the use of the bid as a "forcing mechanism" that would be valuable in furthering the development agenda animating the bid. But in incorporating the particular development projects included in the Olympic plan into its luxury city development strategy, it treated these projects not as profitable ends in themselves but as means to enhance the city's brand. Thus, the Hudson Yards plan, the Queens West housing development, and a number of athletic and leisure facilities throughout the city would serve both as Olympic venues and as new assets that would help communicate the city's brand as a luxury product to employees and employers in the high-value-added postindustrial sectors and aid in the creation of an urban environment appealing to that "target market."

The administration incorporated the games into its rebranding of New York in other ways. For instance, in his 2003 State of the City address, Mayor Bloomberg linked the games to the international road shows that the administration conducted to market the city:

> A road show organized by our Economic Development Corporation will promote our city worldwide. Their sales pitch in cities around the globe will be that New York is the world's second home — a place where people from literally anywhere, if they have a dream, and are willing to work — can succeed. That's the message that won us the right to represent the United States in the international competition for the 2012 Olympics. We're confident it will win us attention from businesses around the world that are looking for new markets and opportunities for growth. (Bloomberg 2003b)

Likewise, the administration portrayed the games as exemplary of the sorts of mega-events that the administration saw as burnishing its brand as well as generating jobs and, more importantly, tax revenues. In early 2005, Mayor Bloomberg described the benefits of the games. "Having the Summer Games here . . . would also pump nearly $12 billion into our local economy . . . [and] produce 135,000 new jobs," he said. "Big events in New York — like the Olympic Games and *The Gates* [a 2005 Central Park art installation] — will always be incredible opportunities to create jobs and boost our tax revenues" (2005). The Olympic bid was portrayed by the Bloomberg administration as consonant with its broader development strategy, itself depicted as faithfully and unproblematically reflecting the interest of the city as a whole. For NYC2012, the Olympics clearly served a political purpose; Mayor Bloomberg, on the other hand, portrayed the games as an apolitical economic development project indisputably in the best interest of the city.

NYC2012 and Mayor Bloomberg thus took different routes to arrive at the conclusion that the Olympic bid was in the best interest of the city as a whole. However, once they did so, they worked in tandem to create the conditions in which the political efficacy of this "fact" could be maximized. Two strategies, one spatial and the other temporal, were used to do so. First, it was argued that the stadium had to be *here*, that is, on the far west side of Manhattan. Second, it was argued that the stadium had to be approved *now*, that is, well before the IOC made its July 2005 decision selecting the host city of the 2012 Summer Games.

There Is No Alternative Location

In early 2002, the USOC requested that U.S. candidate cities prepare a fallback alternative to their original Olympic stadium proposals. In response, NYC2012 developed a plan that would permit Shea Stadium, located in northwestern Queens, to be used as an alternative to the NYSCC. In late 2002, Doctoroff acknowledged the Shea Stadium alternative in testimony to the city council, though he claimed that it would provide "an inferior result that would result in a much lower chance of winning [the competition for the 2012 Games]" (Doctoroff 2002).

This was the last time until the NYSCC was rejected by the PACB in June 2005 that Doctoroff or any other administration or NYC2012 official publicly acknowledged the Shea Stadium alternative. After the USOC selected New York as the nation's candidate city for the 2012 Summer Games in November 2002, NYC2012 and the Bloomberg administration not only dropped the Queens alternative from consideration but also refused to acknowledge that it had ever existed. In February 2005, Doctoroff insisted that "there is no alternate plan. There never has been an alternate plan" (Goldin 2005). Moreover, NYC2012 did not include an alternative location for the stadium in the versions of its bid subsequently submitted to the IOC.

As time progressed and opposition to the NYSCC grew, a number of politicians and planners opposed to the NYSCC but supportive of the Olympic bid revived the possibility of building a stadium in Queens as a less controversial, costly, and disruptive alternative. Bloomberg administration and NYC2012 officials reacted vehemently, arguing that without the large private investment promised by the New York Jets, who refused to consider a Queens location, the stadium could not be financed. Moreover, they pointed to a Jets-commissioned study that showed that a new Queens stadium would be just as expensive as a west side stadium, and because it was not linked to the Javits Convention Center, would not generate the "profit" that the NYSCC would. Finally, Mayor Bloomberg, in keeping with the notion of New York as a luxury city, insisted that the Olympics required a "world-class stadium" (Topousis 2004a) of greater "grandeur" (McIntyre 2005) than was possible in relatively hardscrabble Queens.

By rejecting a Queens alternative, NYC2012 and the administration had essentially created the situation of which it was trying to take advantage: a midtown Manhattan stadium became in fact the sine qua non of a successful New York City Olympic bid. Now, opposition to the stadium would indeed threaten the Olympic bid itself, along with all its purported benefits. However, there was still a way stadium opponents could evade this tightening rhetorical vise. Why not, they asked, delay approval of the stadium until after the IOC decided where the 2012 Summer Games would be held?

Deadlines, Deadlines, and More Deadlines

Critics of the NYSCC pointed out that it was more common for candidate cities for the Summer Games to make plans for new stadiums contingent upon approval. Bloomberg administration and NYC2012 officials insisted that this was not applicable in the context of the race for the 2012 Summer Games, since Paris, Moscow, and Madrid already had stadiums (London, the other candidate city and eventual victor, did not). NYC2012 and Bloomberg administration officials insisted that approving the NYSCC would convey to the IOC that New York City, in words used by a number of Olympic boosters, had "what it takes" to host the Olympics: a degree of political will and unity sufficient to overcome the development gridlock supposedly characteristic of the city.

Mayor Bloomberg and Deputy Mayor Doctoroff often cast this in intensely personalistic terms. Both seemed to feel that their standings as effective leaders were at stake, often eliding their own ability to "get things done" with the city's ability to do so. For example, Doctoroff said in early 2005 that "what's critical is that . . . we can look them in the eye and say we not only will get [the stadium] done, we did get it done" (Zinser 2005). Similarly, Mayor Bloomberg said in September 2004 that "I have to be able to look the IOC in the eye and say this stadium is going to be built" (Virasami 2004). In keeping with this supposed necessity, from early 2004, when Deputy Mayor Doctoroff claimed that not just the approval, but the *construction*, of the NYSCC needed to commence before the IOC made its selection in July 2005 (Bagli 2004b), the administration and NYC2012 officials pointed to a series of dates by which the crucial state portion of the funding for the NYSCC absolutely *had* to receive approval from the PACB. This process began with the claim that getting "shovels in the ground" (Williams 2004) by July 2005 would require the PACB to approve the stadium by early 2005. This deadline was made doubly important by the fact that an IOC evaluation commission would be visiting the city in late February. As that date neared, Mayor Bloomberg upped the ante considerably, threatening that "if we were to not get this stadium going very soon, we would have to drop out of the competition for the Olympics. If you don't have it, I've got to call the IOC and say don't come" (Colangelo 2004). Unsurprisingly, when the IOC's visit arrived and PACB approval was not forthcoming, Bloomberg did no such thing. Instead, it was now claimed that the PACB needed to approve the stadium before the IOC started writing its report summarizing what its members had found during their visit in April or May.

By the time of the IOC visit, two PACB members, State Senate Leader Bruno and Assembly Speaker Sheldon Silver, had indicated that they would happily approve the NYSCC — but only after the IOC selected New York City to host the 2012 Summer Games. Administration officials rejected conditional approval as insufficiently demonstrative of the city's resolve. Their insistence on this intensified after the press conference that ended the IOC delegation's visit, a whirlwind of site visits and white-glove treatment, including a fete attended by celebrities and city and NYC2012 officials at Mayor Bloomberg's Upper East Side townhouse. At that press conference, the head of the delegation stated that "for us it is important to have a stadium. . . . We need a stadium, and we received assurances the stadium will be there. We trust that between now and the end of March or even July an agreement will get done" (Jeansonne 2005; Satow 2005a).

Despite the ambiguity of this statement, administration and NYC2012 officials took these remarks and ran with them, portraying them as irrefutable evidence that the NYSCC had to be immediately approved for the city to have any chance to win the games and that opposition to the stadium was tantamount to opposition to the Olympics. Mayor Bloomberg, for instance, insisted that "their message was clear: no sports and convention center on the West Side, no Olympics. End of story. You can't have it both ways. If you're opposed to one, you're opposed to the other" (Saul 2005d).

Things were briefly complicated in mid-February, with the decision of the MTA to open up a formal bidding process for the development rights to the western portion of the Hudson rail yards. This was prompted by an unsolicited offer from Cablevision, an avowed opponent of the NYSCC, to buy those rights at a much higher price than had been offered by the Jets in its exclusive, ad hoc negotiations with the MTA. The approval process could not move forward until the bidding process was concluded—which it was in late March, when the MTA predictably granted the Jets the development rights for the yard. Soon afterwards, in mid-April, the ESDC approved the NYSCC funding and the GPP. Now, only the PACB, which would meet in mid-May, stood in the way of the NYSCC becoming a reality.

In the meantime, Sheldon Silver had taken center stage in the drama over the NYSCC. In early April, Goldman Sachs, which had earlier proposed to build a headquarters office tower downtown in Battery Park City, dropped its plans to do so, citing a lack of progress in the redevelopment of the former World Trade Center site. Silver was furious, arguing that this demonstrated the Bloomberg administration's neglect of downtown's recovery. The administration quickly acted to resolve a series of downtown development issues, acceding to important elements in the "Marshall Plan" for Lower Manhattan that Silver had demanded.

With these issues seemingly defused, the next meeting of the PACB, scheduled for May 18, became the deadline du jour. On April 15, Bloomberg said that the members of the PACB "have to . . . do it now. . . . Because if they don't, I don't know how we could keep going with our Olympic bid" (2005). Once again these threats proved hollow, as the May PACB meeting was postponed by Governor Pataki due to fears that Bruno would cast a final vote against the stadium if lawsuits regarding the MTA's sale of the development rights for the Hudson rail yards to the Jets were not resolved and if the still undetermined source of the public funding for the NYSCC was not identified.

Despite demands that the PACB vote had to be early enough that its outcome could be included in the IOC evaluation commission's report to be released in early June, Silver and Bruno refused to take action on the NYSCC until these lawsuits were resolved, which was not expected to occur until the first week of that month. Once again the deadline, and the rationale for it, changed. Now, it was necessary for the PACB to approve the stadium by June 6, when the report would be issued. Even if the NYSCC's approval was not included in the report, it was claimed, the publicity gained from its approval would outweigh any negative impressions from this omission and would prevent other candidate cities from using the lack of approval of an Olympic stadium against New York in their lobbying of IOC members.

So on May 27, Mayor Bloomberg, with urgency, if not desperation, in his voice, announced on his weekly radio address that the PACB vote would be scheduled for June 3, the day after decisions would be handed down in the lawsuits against the MTA. With time clearly running out, the administration stepped up its already frenzied negotiations with Silver, promising action on a number of downtown Manhattan projects that had been lagging. In addition, thinly veiled threats of political retribution against Silver should he not approve the funding for the NYSCC came from African American and Latino Democratic Assembly Democrats, as well as construction unions. USOC officials lobbied Silver and Bruno and the White House even got into the act, as Chief of Staff Andrew Card reportedly telephoned fellow Republican Joe Bruno and asked him to support the NYSCC. An internal NYC2012 memo outlining the dire threat posed by the lack of approval for the NYSCC was fortuitously leaked and then touted by Olympic supporters as evidence that the continuing failure to approve the NYSCC was undermining the bid.

On June 2, in a major victory for NYSCC proponents, all lawsuits against the MTA were dismissed. However, their joy quickly turned to unease when the PACB vote scheduled for June 3 was pushed back to June 6. This meant that the IOC evaluation commission would release its report before any action was taken by the PACB; it was feared that a negative appraisal of the bid would make stadium approval even less likely. A weekend of manic negotiations followed. On the early morning of June 6, the IOC issued its report, which ranked the city's bid in a tie with Madrid, behind Paris and London. In the hours between the release of the report and the scheduled vote of the PACB, NYC2012 and Bloomberg administration officials attempted valiantly to spin the report as unambiguously positive news for the bid. However, this all came to naught in the afternoon, when both Bruno and Silver refused to approve funding for the stadium. As of June 6, 2005, the NYSCC was dead.

The Broken Chain

Despite years of claims that a west side stadium was essential to the bid, and months of threats that the bid would have to be withdrawn if the stadium was not approved, the IOC allowed NYC2012 to submit an alternative plan. A new stadium would be built in partnership with the New York Mets baseball team, next to its current home, Shea Stadium. This exposed the falsity of the claim that no alternative site for an Olympic stadium was possible; indeed, the deal came together in a matter of weeks.[1]

The ongoing controversy over the stadium did damage the city's bid, though it was not ultimately a determinative factor.[2] Such dissension was common in Olympic candidate cities, an inevitable response to the large-scale urban development projects associated with hosting the games (Burbank, Andranovich, and Heying 2001). Even London, which eventually won the 2012 Summer Games, saw significant opposition to its eventually successful bid for the 2012 Games (Evans 2007, 307–308). In any case, it was clearly unnecessary for the stadium to be built or even approved before the IOC made its decision, as demonstrated by the fact London had made the construction of its Olympic stadium contingent upon winning the games.

Thus, the insistence that the absence of approval (or even the contingent approval) of the NYSCC would profoundly undermine perceptions of the city's ability to get things done was aimed primarily at matters (and people) close at hand. Why, if the IOC was of central concern, would NYC2012 and the Bloomberg administration take such pains to publicize and accentuate the most controversial element of its Olympic plan — the NYSCC — while downplaying the many elements of the plan that had in fact been approved or were moving quickly through the approval process? The answer was simple and had everything to do with the original justification for the city's Olympic bid: as of July 6, 2005, when the IOC made its decision, the Bloomberg administration and NYC2012 would likely, given the growing consensus that the 2012 Games would go to either Paris or London, lose the ability to use the Olympics as a "forcing mechanism" for the Hudson Yards plan and for the larger development agenda incorporated into the bid. By focusing so much attention on the NYSCC, and by refusing to consider, or even admit the existence of, alternative sites, the administration and NYC2012 attempted to maximize the leverage the bid provided even as doing so weakened the bid itself, making it more controversial and less flexible. In turn, agreeing to consider an alternative site or the contingent approval of the NYSCC might have strengthened the bid, but it would have undercut the administration's ability to argue that the fate of the Olympic bid hinged on getting the stadium before the IOC's decision.

Ultimately, this gambit not only failed, but backfired. Despite the administration's omnipresent claims that the Olympics were unquestionably in the best interests of the city, the level of support for the bid remained rather tepid compared to that in other candidate cities, and it actually fell during the period of time when these claims were the most volubly expressed (Saul 2005a). Polls also consistently showed that majorities of New Yorkers opposed a publicly subsidized stadium, suggesting that the efforts of the Bloomberg administration and NYC2012 to garner support for the NYSCC by linking it to the Olympic bid were in vain. Moreover, both Silver and Bruno expressed resentment at the use of "artificial deadlines," as Silver put it in early June (Satow 2005b), to create pressure to approve a project that, in the end, was unable to win their approval on its own merits.

MOBILIZING URBAN PATRIOTISM

This backlash can be attributed to a fundamental misconception on the part of both NYC2012 and the Bloomberg administration. Both assumed that their judgment that a New York City Olympics was in the best interests of the city as a whole was both unchallengeable and widely shared, and that the possibility of losing the Olympic bid because the NYSCC's approval was not forthcoming would push those who might otherwise question the stadium to put aside their doubts and act now. This led to a particular response to the continued unwillingness of many, including Bruno and Silver, to put aside their concerns about the NYSCC in the interests of the greater good of the city. NYC2012, and even more so Bloomberg administration officials, argued that those who opposed the NYSCC and thus the Olympic bid were opposed to the city itself: they were unpatriotic.

Like all patriotisms, the one mobilized by the administration and its allies represented an effort to "interpellate subjects as homogenous members of [an] imagined communit[y]" (Trouillot 2001, 132), though here community was imagined at the urban rather than national scale. Like all patriotisms, the homogenous subject so interpellated was not generic but imbued with certain characteristics, that is to say, with a certain identity. Good New Yorkers, then, were New Yorkers of a certain type, and the New York imagined by Bloomberg and others was the one they populated. This led inexorably to the imagining of a second, dystopian New York inhabited by "resident 'Others'" (Brodkin 2000, 248). Thus, like all patriotisms, this urban patriotism was both inclusive and celebratory, on one hand, and exclusive and denigrating on the other.

From the very beginning, a New York City Olympics was sold on this basis of a certain urban imaginary and urban identity. "We think what draws people to the Olympic Games is three things," Daniel Doctoroff said in a September 2004 speech. "Bringing the world together in one place; competition — anyone who's ever set foot in this city will tell you that this is the most competitive place on earth. But fundamentally what it's all about [is] athletes pursuing their Olympic dreams . . . against incredible odds, and it all coming down to a point or a fraction of a second. That's what New York is. New York is a city of dreamers. People come here from everywhere with big dreams and new ideas. That's what gives this city its special energy" (Doctoroff 2004a). The games were portrayed in keeping with a certain set of qualities ostensibly characteristic of New Yorkers and their city: competitiveness, ambition, boldness, innovativeness, and cosmopolitan diversity. This cluster of characteristics reflected how Doctoroff, Bloomberg, and the other postindustrial elites who led both the Bloomberg administration and NYC2012 viewed themselves and their city. In a conversation with me in late 2004, Anthony Borelli, CB4's district manager, summarized well the role that urban identity and imaginaries played in both the Hudson Yards plan and the Olympics, saying, "Doctoroff's Olympic desire — it's personal, not just political. Bloomberg's vision of a yuppie city — that's personal too. For him, it's just the way New York should be." This visceral and personal investment in a particular conception of "the way New York should be" accounted for the intensity with which the Bloomberg administration and others pushed the entire Hudson Yards plan, the NYSCC, and the city's Olympic bid. However, it was in the criticism of those who opposed the stadium, and thus the Olympics, that the specificities of the class identity underlying this urban imaginary became most clear.

While the celebratory and ostensibly inclusive aspect of this particular urban imaginary was prominently displayed in the words of Olympic boosters, it had a less savory flip-side. This became more and more evident throughout late 2004 and 2005, as the stadium's approval was delayed and imperiled by the legal and political machinations of its opponents. Opposition to the stadium (and thus, to the Olympics) evoked a fierce response: administration and NYC2012 officials portrayed opponents as bad New Yorkers. For example, the New York Jets, in coordination with the Bloomberg administration, launched a television ad campaign that professed to convey "What Real New Yorkers Have to Say about the New York Sports Convention Center," as indicated by the on-screen text that prefaced the testimony of a variety of politicians, far west side residents and business owners, and unionists about the benefits of the NYSCC. The insinuation, of course, was that those who opposed the stadium were *not* "real" New Yorkers.

The most heated rhetoric was aimed at Cablevision, which in the domed NYSCC saw a threat to the Manhattan monopoly on concerts and other large indoor events held by Madison Square Garden. The company provided media, financial, and organizational support to the campaigns opposing the stadium, and its unsolicited, if ultimately fruitless, last-minute bid for the development rights to the MTA-owned western Hudson rail yards delayed the PACB vote on the project. Despite Cablevision's support of the Olympics and its willingness to host the Olympics basketball tournament at Madison Square Garden should New York be granted the games, the company became a prime target of the wrath of Mayor Bloomberg and other stadium proponents. Mayor Bloomberg avowed that "we cannot allow a selfish monopoly to deny us the future we deserve" (City of New York 2004a), later saying that Cablevision "want[s] to take away the Olympics [and] the future of this city" (Virasami 2005).

Politicians, community groups, and other organizations opposed to the stadium were also repeatedly accused of trying to kill New York's "Olympic Dream" (Wilson 2004a). Sheldon Silver, who as a member of the PACB controlled the fate of the NYSCC, was the target of more oblique denigrations of his New York City patriotism. When Silver argued in May 2005 that since New York was widely judged to be trailing in the competition for the 2012 Summer Games the decision on funding the stadium should be deferred until after the site of the 2012 Games was selected, Mayor Bloomberg deplored "the defeatism here of not going out and trying! Let's all get together. . . . When did New York walk away from taking shots and trying to get things? Think about what society we're changing into here. We're giving up before we even start" (Saul 2005b). After Silver refused to approve the funding for the NYSCC, Mayor Bloomberg dropped his earlier restraint and repeatedly and explicitly condemned Silver, along with other stadium opponents, of being insufficiently committed to New York's future. The day after the funding was rejected, Bloomberg said:

> I think [the rejection of the NYSCC] was a major blow to this city. I think most people understand . . . that we have lost something. We've lost a little bit of our spirit to go ahead and our can-do attitude. If you adopt this kind of policy, we never would have built Carnegie Hall, we never would have built Radio City Music Hall, we never would have built the airports, or the Triborough Bridge or Central Park. . . . We have let down America. The United States Olympic Committee selected us, New York, to represent the country. New York won be-

cause people had confidence that New York would be able to do things. And it turned out that we, unfortunately, are not able to do things. (McIntyre and Rutenberg 2005)

The emphasis on action and efficacy echoed language that had been used earlier at other times in the debate over the Hudson Yards plan. For example, after the RPA and other planning groups came out against the stadium in 2004, they were subject to a litany of abuse. Some of it came from members of the city's real estate elite, who labeled critics of the stadium as reflexively antidevelopment NIMBY-ites. However, in his broadsides against the RPA and other plan opponents, Mayor Bloomberg shifted the emphasis away from opposition to development per se. For example, shortly after the release of the RPA's July 2004 position paper on the Hudson Yards plan, a mayoral spokeswoman condemned the report, saying: "Sadly, the RPA has been discussing the redevelopment of the Far West Side for more than 80 years. If the staff report's recommendations are adopted, they'll have the opportunity to just talk, rather than act, for another 80 years" (Cockfield 2004). And in a 2005 article, Bloomberg fumed about the obstinacy of stadium opponents:

> When I mentioned the stadium's opponents, Bloomberg bristled. "These people," he said dismissively. . . . "Most of the people that are criticizing it have never built anything in their lives, and they are not willing to put their own money up, so it leaves me a little cold. . . . It takes courage to go and build things. If you want to study it forever, you will study it forever, and you will never come to any agreement." . . . "It would be a tragedy if we let the naysayers stop us doing things," [Bloomberg] said. "What has always been great about New York has been that we've built the big things and taken the risks. People say, 'You were a business guy. You don't understand politics.' Yes. I was a very successful business guy because we took the risks in the business. We built for the future. You never know what the future is going to be like, but you have to build in advance. Running risks is exactly what you want to do. If you don't run any risks, you will never make any progress." (Cassidy 2005)

It was opponents' unwillingness to *act* in the face of risk that was most infuriating for the CEO mayor. Here was Bloomberg, CEO mayor, trying to take bold steps to ensure the city's future prosperity, and here were the RPA, Sheldon Silver, and other critics of the plan standing in the way.

The basis upon which Mayor Bloomberg and his compatriots were dividing New Yorkers into a "resident us" and a " resident other" was that of *performance*, so fundamental to the notion of the CEO mayor. In contrast to a New

York "not able to do things," full of "defeatist" opponents seemingly intent on "walking away," "giving up, " and "losing some of its can-do," Bloomberg's New York was one of achievement and ambition, populated by risk takers and those able to "do things." This language of performance was ultimately a language of class, legitimizing the wealth and power of New York City's postindustrial elite. The urban patriotism with which Bloomberg and his allies attacked opponents of the stadium and the Hudson Yards plan was a reflection of the class identity that shaped the Bloomberg Way. However, it did not go unchallenged.

CONTESTING URBAN PATRIOTISM

Opposition to the stadium came from many directions. But what I want to highlight here is the opposition that directly engaged with the efforts of the Bloomberg administration and its allies to mobilize urban patriotism in support of the Hudson Yards plan.

First, there were those who condemned not only the details of the Hudson Yards and Olympic plans but also the demand that New Yorkers abandon their own judgments of what was good for them and their city and defer to the judgment of Mayor Bloomberg, Deputy Mayor Doctoroff, and the leadership of NYC2012. These critiques explicitly challenged the use of urban patriotism as a means to circumvent debate over the wisdom of the stadium, the Olympics, or the Hudson Yards plan — and utterly rejected this rhetorical gambit. In fact, they often invoked their own characterizations of New York and New Yorkers in doing so. For instance, sportswriter Mike Lupica, a relentless opponent of the Olympic bid, the stadium, and the far west side redevelopment plan, wrote of Mayor Bloomberg, "Anybody who doesn't go along with him is painted as some kind of lousy New Yorker. If you don't think the real future of everything in New York is the 2012 Games, you are a bum. This is a lie" (2005). Likewise, one of the few politicians willing to publicly question the desirability of the city's Olympic bid, Manhattan Assemblywoman Deborah Glick, decried the fact that "few people have been willing to discuss if the Olympics are even a good idea for New York City, because Deputy Mayor Doctoroff has made opposition to the Olympics seem unpatriotic" (2004).

Some opponents of the stadium, including everyday New Yorkers, politicians, and media figures, went further, standing the logic of the Bloomberg administration on its head. They argued that the idea that New York needed the Olympics and the stadium was itself an insult to the city; some even ironically embraced their status as "bad New Yorkers." For example, one far west side resident I spoke to reacted to the stadium proposal and Olympic bid with derision. "A stadium for the Olympics?" he asked. "It's crazy! Why do we even need the Olympics? To put us on the map? To attract tourists? C'mon! Everybody knows New York City is the best! We don't need this!" Or, as journalist Juan Gonzalez put it, turning around the words of stadium proponents, who often argued that the city's status as "the greatest city in the world" was threatened by the fact it had never hosted the Olympics, "the plain fact is New York doesn't need the Olympics to be the greatest city in the world. It already is" (2005). Likewise, the cultural critic Kurt Anderson refused to permit the glory of the Olympic bid to overrule his conclusion that the redevelopment plan for the far west side was a throwback to mid-twentieth-century megaplanning and urban renewal schemes and was unworthy of "a city as sharp and self-aware as ours." He wrote, "I would be happy to have the Olympics here. . . . But I don't want to waste a glorious piece of Manhattan land on Bloomberg's big, dumb, old-school scheme. Therefore, at the risk of seeming a disloyal New Yorker, in July I'll be pulling for Paris or London or Moscow or Madrid—anyplace but here" (2005). These New Yorkers evoked the image of a city whose greatness was defined by the smarts and savvy of its populace. For them, the demand that they abandon their own judgment that was inherent in mobilization of urban patriotism was a slap in the face.

This critique raised the class underpinnings of the Hudson Yards and Olympic plans only obliquely, if it all. But other criticisms—particularly those of longtime residents of the far west side—took square aim at the class politics inherent in the plans and the urban imaginary and identity that animated them. In expressing their opposition to the stadium, these stadium opponents put forth visions of the city and their identities as New Yorkers that often stood in direct conflict with those put forward by the Bloomberg administration and its allies. Some described a New York welcoming to those of modest means, a city where one could live comfortably without being a stockbroker, a lawyer, or a commercially successful artist or writer. Others described a city hospitable to difference, and to those outside of the mainstream of white, middle-class American society. Still others described a city whose government provided a bevy of public services and amenities, from clean, well-run parks to affordable housing. While there was overlap between these oppositional visions of the city and urban identities, they differed nonetheless, often in ways that were structured by differences in race, class, sexuality, and gender. In any case, for these opponents of the plan, *their* city seemed to be giving way to the city of competition, ambition, cosmopolitanism, and innovation celebrated by Bloomberg, Doctoroff, and NYC2012, transformed into a zone of economic and cultural homogeneity increasingly hostile to all but well-paid members of the postindustrial elite. For instance, one longtime working-class resident of the far west side expressed this sense in August 2004 testimony before CB4. Despite calling for more government spending on affordable housing and education and less on office space, he seemed resigned to the city's continued transformation. "The struggle for the quality of life of the lower middle class," he said, "is futile." Another far westsider protested at a September 2004 community group meeting, "Bloomberg wants Manhattan only for the wealthy and the super wealthy — it's unjust!"

For far west side residents, the gentrification of the area, which was already well underway and would only be furthered and intensified by the Hudson Yards plan, threatened not just a loss of affordable housing but of an entire complex of businesses, institutions, residences, and shared and individual memories and meanings that had, despite its sometimes dilapidated appearance, made it a neighborhood. Three testimonials from far west side residents, all from a September 2004 CPC hearing, capture this.

> I love my neighborhood. . . . When I moved [here] 21 years ago . . . I found wonderful and affordable family-owned businesses: barber shops, a shoe repairman, butcher shops, a farmers' market, fish markets, spice shops, family-owned pharmacies, bodegas, bakeries and restaurants of all types. The family pharmacies are history now, and all the remaining family businesses here are already threatened, being replaced by banks, phone stores or yet another Starbucks. The West Side Stadium is a corporate-centric proposal and will clearly bring about the extinction of the rest of these one-of-a-kind businesses. Manganaro's Hero Boy will fall to Subway; O'Farrell's Bar is going to fall to TGI Friday's; Stile's in the Big Apple Market to the Food Emporium. . . . The damage to my community would be irreversible.

Whereas this relatively well-off white male professional stressed the deleterious effect of the plan on beloved small businesses on the far west side, a second white male resident, this one of relatively modest means, stressed the relationship between residential gentrification and the ability of the nonwealthy to live there:

> I discovered Hell's Kitchen 35 years ago. There are a lot of people that are discovering our neighborhood now. There are people discovering Chelsea, Clinton, West Side, call it Far West Side, whatever. We discovered it years and years ago, and we loved it. Why? I'm a member of the theatrical community. I'm an actor. I want to live near where I work. Thirty-five years ago we could all afford to live there. We are a huge number of people in the most important entertainment in-

dustry in the city. And our young people can't live there anymore because people are discovering us. The marketplace is discovering us. But the city is made up of more than fancy buildings and big businesses. Where are our young people going to live? An apartment that we used to rent for $450 so that we could afford to be a playwright and an actor is now renting in our building for $2,000 a month. This is craziness. City planning has to be more than about big development and big stadiums.

A third far west side resident, a female Puerto Rican antipoverty activist, stressed community and kinship:

> I'm a resident of Hell's Kitchen. . . . When I was born my mother was living in Chelsea. I returned to Chelsea to attend high school and attend college in Chelsea. . . . And as a resident of Hell's Kitchen, I worked in the community as a community worker. One of my children was born in Polyclinic Hospital, which no longer exists. It is now an apartment building and parking lot. . . . The stadium would be better served elsewhere. . . . This is not where this belongs. Congestion, pollution, traffic, and most important, the humanity of the project, there isn't any [*sic*]. . . . No more. We have to stop supporting the corporation [*sic*], destruction and gentrification of our communities.

These testimonials, by people of varying classes, genders, sexualities, and ethnicities, demonstrate that at stake here were not just questions of policy and economic interest but fundamental questions of urban meaning and belonging. For while these critics of the stadium in particular and of the Hudson Yards plan overall, especially those who were residents of the far west side, were undeniably acting and speaking in defense of their perceptions of their own economic interests, they were also asking a fundamental question articulated by one far west side resident as she testified before the CPC in September 2004: "What kind of city do we really want? That is what we really have to analyze."

THE BLOOMBERG WAY AND ITS OTHERS

The Bloomberg administration and NYC2012 had provided their own answer to this question, attempting to mobilize a vision of the city and a sense of urban identity stressing competition, innovation, and ambition, one that reflected the experiences and interests of the high-level professionals and executives prominent in these two organizations. However, these attempts failed precisely because they encountered the very different urban identities and imaginaries expressed by significant numbers of far west side residents and other New Yorkers: a conception of New York as a city true to its social democratic history; a city providing a comfortable life to those who were not wealthy, well credentialed, or ambitious; a city that provided a place for those outside the mainstream of American culture; a city that honored and cared for longtime residents and the neighborhoods they created. Ultimately, these visions of the city, especially those rooted in different, and in fact conflicting, class identities, could not be reconciled.

We have seen that even as it generated new lines of contestation, the Bloomberg administration's technocratic and corporate approach to governance was generally able to define the terms of debate in such a way that foreclosed discussion of the class politics that underwrote the Hudson Yards plan. In contrast, the administration's use of urban patriotism opened up this discussion, since the homogenized imagined community that its members evoked was one deeply rooted in class identity. This was the most potentially dangerous of the administration's ploys to garner support for the Hudson Yards plan, as it laid bare the class politics inherent in the plan, the luxury city development agenda it was a part of, and the Bloomberg Way overall. Moreover, it exposed the contradiction between the antipolitics inherent in the notion that the Olympics unproblematically represented the city's best interests and these class politics. Opponents of the plan who directly contested the use of urban patriotism acknowledged and even embraced the reality of social, political, economic, and ideological difference in the city, and thus they were able to acknowledge the centrality of the question of "what kind of city do we really want?"

The claim that the mayor and his allies could take the "standpoint of the city," to apply Marx's words to an urban, rather than national, scale, "mean[t] nothing more than the overlooking of the *differences* which express the *social relation*[s] . . . of bourgeois society" (Marx 1973, 264–265). The administration's antipolitical approach to urban governance was reinforced by its members' blindness to the partiality of their own vision of the city and its inhabitants, which they seemed to assume was shared by all. Once again, the administration was engaging in class politics while denying their legitimacy or even existence. The rancor and acrimony this denial generated, alongside that generated by the substance of the agenda being proposed, hardened the lines of division over the stadium portion of the plan during the first half of 2005, when the use of the Olympics and urban patriotism was most prominent. And as the outcome of the effort to leverage the (already tepid) support of the Olympics into support for the stadium indicates, it ultimately did not achieve its goal.

As potentially dangerous as this mobilization of urban patriotism was, in the end this potential was not fully realized. Though the stadium was the price paid for this, the broader Bloomberg Way was not badly damaged by its rejection from the PACB or by the increased focus on the class politics that animated it. While the class identity that undergirded this approach to governance made it vulnerable to critique, it also gave the approach a coherence, an ambition, and a potency it would not have otherwise had. In contrast, those who contested the mobilization of urban patriotism by the mayor and his allies ultimately consisted of a loose and diverse group, crosscut by axes of social differences. Elite white cultural critics and Latina antipoverty activists, rich white sportswriters and poor black people — these people might have been able to make common cause in opposing a stadium, but they were unlikely to agree on "what kind of city do we really want," let alone a development or governmental strategy that would provide a coherent alternative to the Olympics, the Hudson Yards plan, the stadium, or the Bloomberg Way. They could not propose a way to act, to build that city; they could only say no. If the flaws in the Bloomberg Way prevented it from winning the battle over the far west side stadium, its ability to articulate and aggressively pursue a positive and comprehensive approach to development and governance essentially allowed it to create its own others.

CONCLUSION

The Bloomberg Way cast the mayor as a CEO, the city government as a corporation, desirable businesses and residents as clients and customers, and the city itself as a product. This approach to urban governance linked entrepreneurial governing practices, a particular urban imaginary, and processes of class transformation in a way that drastically altered New York City's political terrain. Many of its constitutive elements were not without precedent, in New York City or elsewhere. But what was new was the role of class. The election of Michael Bloomberg and the construction of the Bloomberg Way saw an ascendant and assertive postindustrial elite, incubated in the hothouse of the post–fiscal crisis white-collar economy of New York City, assert its right to rule the city. Governance itself became a class project, a vehicle for the application of the postindustrial elite's skills, concepts, and expertise to the city's problems — and thus a legitimization of its power and wealth. The New York City imagined by the postindustrial elite — a city of ambition, achievement, elite sociality, and, above all, luxury — was a crucial mediator of this relationship between class and governance. It was this vision of New York that the postindustrial elite aimed to solidify and intensify through its engagement in New York City's governance.

Yet, the Bloomberg Way was not without flaws and contradictions. I conclude by taking stock of this form of urban governance in light of both the material discussed in this book and events since mid-2005, when the NYSCC and the Olympic bid met their demise. I first discuss the lessons of the Hudson Yards plan, then turn to the evolution of the Bloomberg Way during that subsequent period. I end with the implications of the Bloomberg Way for urban governance in New York City and for the analysis of urban neoliberalism in general.

THE LESSONS OF THE HUDSON YARDS PLAN

Much has been made in preceding chapters of the failures and frustrations of the Bloomberg Way in constructing and gaining approval for the Hudson Yards plan. Nevertheless, it is important not to lose sight of its successes. With the forceful Deputy Mayor Doctoroff at the helm, the EDC, DCP, and a number of other agencies worked together to transform the rough plan that NYC2012 had bequeathed to the administration. These efforts resulted in a coherent program of land-use changes, financing plans, and zoning mechanisms, much of which was successfully ushered through ULURP. And even though the stadium ultimately failed, it was no mean feat for the administration to bring it as far along as it did, especially coming so close on the heels of the failed west side stadium plans of the 1990s. Given the political, financial, and technical intricacies of the Hudson Yards plan, these were major achievements. Though NYC2012, the New York Jets, and the power of the city's real estate elite deserve credit, ultimately it was Mayor Bloomberg and his administration who laid the legal groundwork for the postindustrial transformation of the far west side. This was attributable to both the organizational capacity generated by the administration's efforts to "run the city like a business" and the strategic vision provided by the luxury city strategy.

Thus, it was not the managerial aspect of the Bloomberg Way — its ability to organize governmental bodies and have them act strategically — that was the major vulnerability of this approach to urban governance. The problem was its antipolitics, which clashed with the politics inherent in the Hudson Yards plan. The inability to acknowledge the existence and legitimacy of differing and conflicting interests and desires within the city led to the demise of the stadium and proved to be the biggest obstacle to the success of the Hudson Yards rezoning. The administration's technocratic insistence that its Hudson Yards plan was in accordance with the best principles of urban planning could not be squared with the actual details of the plan or the fact that it was clearly animated by political concerns. The logic of investment that shaped its financing precluded, until too late, the recognition of the contested nature of the ends of urban policy. Finally, the administration's mobilization of urban patriotism, aimed at unifying the city, actually divided it along the combustible lines of class, urban imaginary, and urban identity.

These antipolitics impacted not just opponents of the Hudson Yards plan but also those supportive of its broad goals and outline. Even as the administration had made the RPA and other planning groups more important, it rejected their friendly critiques of the plan. The administration's efforts to avoid legislative approval alienated potential supporters of the plan. So did its risky and costly financial scheme for the Hudson Yards plan, which alarmed many city council members and real estate elites, particularly those who had experienced firsthand the 1970s fiscal crisis. Finally, the administration's general neglect of political horse-trading, at least until late in the game, coupled with its attempt to avoid legislative approval, rendered useless the political support that the Jets were able to garner.

Yet if these antipolitics had harmful consequences, they were not too dire. Ultimately, the administration was, to a good degree, able to shape the contours of the debate: broader questions of class, the virtues of postindustrial development, and democratic process were marginalized. Community opposition to the plan, itself divided by class, generally condemned the Hudson Yards plan on its own terms, rather than challenging its basic premises. While tensions with the city's still-powerful real estate elites represented a potentially dangerous stumbling block, the power over development centralized in the person of Deputy Mayor Doctoroff discouraged vocal opposition from this direction. Fear of retribution was coupled with a growing realization that while the administration would not defer to the city's real estate elite, its luxury city development strategy, and its ability to implement it, provided ample opportunity for profitable development.

Moreover, the Bloomberg administration inherited a largely hospitable political terrain. The post–fiscal crisis years had seen the fragmentation of potential sources of opposition to the Hudson Yards plan, the normalization of privatism and private-sector intervention, the establishment of entrepreneurial governmental common sense, and the vitiation of viable alternatives to neoliberal governance. As a result, the city's labor movement and minority leadership were brought on board relatively easily. Plan opponents could only obstruct the plan or propose marginal changes, rather than challenge its basic logic — and then only with the aid of powerful actors like Sheldon Silver, Cablevision, and the RPA. Mayor Bloomberg's administration, his approach to governance, and his Hudson Yards plan all benefited from the "politics as usual" he deplored.

The ultimate lesson of the Hudson Yards plan for the Bloomberg administration was not just that antipolitics were futile but that they were unnecessary, even counterproductive. By late 2004, this lesson had begun to shape its approach to the Hudson Yards plan. The question moving forward was whether or not a move toward a more explicitly political stance would undermine the Bloomberg Way, in general, and the claim to class rule that it represented.

THE CEO MAYOR AS MASTER POLITICIAN

Mayor Bloomberg's move toward a more nakedly political approach to urban governance had ambiguous effects. On the one hand, the years since the failures of the stadium and the Olympic bid saw a remarkable consolidation of power on the part of Michael Bloomberg and the broader class alliance he led into city hall. By mid-2009 Mayor Bloomberg seemed the city's political master: he was owed fealty by virtually every interest group and politician, lauded by the mainstream media, and was able to have laws overturned for his own political benefit with a snap of his fingers. What's more, this transformation had not undermined the central animating feature of the Bloomberg Way, its class politics. Yet Mayor Bloomberg's seeming ability to dominate New York City politics obscured important vulnerabilities, which came to the fore in the mayoral election of November 2009.

Broadening the Bloomberg Coalition

As the administration followed the Jets' lead in procuring support for the stadium through the kind of direct bargaining with interest groups it had once eschewed, it was softening its antipolitics in other ways. Recognizing that the Hudson Yards plan's lack of a concrete affordable housing proposal had been a political liability, the administration included such proposals in all major city-sponsored development projects. It used the Jets' MWBE agreement as a model for citywide policy, ensuring that minority groups remained supportive of its ambitious development agenda. After taking a tough line with municipal unions early on, Mayor Bloomberg eased up after 2003. Finally, as Kim Moody points out, the administration "appeared to employ city contracts as a way of gaining widespread goodwill [by] spreading the largesse far more broadly and in smaller amounts" (2007, 162).

The move toward a more explicitly political approach to governance became even more apparent during the 2005 mayoral race. The mayor parlayed his support of the Hudson Yards plan and the ongoing construction boom in the city into strong construction-union support. Several other unions endorsed Bloomberg; others did not, but offered his Democratic opponent, Fernando Ferrer, only tepid support. Bloomberg's campaign aggressively courted a number of racial and ethnic groups, holding weekly meetings with African American and Caribbean American leaders, for example. Finally, Bloomberg made affordable housing a central plank of his reelection campaign, a tactic aimed at the city's struggling middle and working classes as well as community activists, progressive advocates, and urban policy organizations.

The broadening of the mayor's coalition was reinforced by a practice long central to Bloomberg's public persona: philanthropy. Using a variety of means, including his personal trust, the mayor guided vast sums of money toward cultural, community, educational, and nonprofit institutions. Whereas Bloomberg's private giving had once been narrowly focused, over his first term it grew in breadth, now targeting a broad array of nonprofits located in key areas and associated with key constituencies. All this helped Bloomberg make inroads into the social service and nonprofit sectors, usually hotbeds of Democratic support, and bought the silence, if not the outright support, of groups that might have otherwise criticized the mayor's generally pro-business policies.[1]

This deployment of private wealth was an extension of the massive campaign spending that had been crucial to his election in 2001 (and was again in 2005, when he spent $85 million). Yet it also represented something new. The targeting of important constituencies was an implicit acknowledgment of the diversity of interests constituting New York City's political field. If the mayor still believed that he had the ability to successfully identify the interests of the city as a whole, he was no longer willing to count on others' recognition of this or others' willingness to defer to his judgment. Faith in the mayor's leadership, while still important, was now backed up with cold, hard cash.

Cementing Elite Support

At the same time that Bloomberg was securing support among relatively marginalized social groups and geographical locales, he was solidifying his status as the leader of the city's elite. His administration's respect for technical expertise, along with his status as a supermanager and entrepreneur, not only drew professionals and corporate executives into city hall but also solidified and broadened his support among the city's postindustrial elite, who saw that people like them were now at the pinnacle of city government. As one aspiring professional said of the administration's approach, "it professionalizes the city" (Lowry 2007).

Bloomberg's first term also saw a shift of the political loyalties of a number of corporate executives. Steven Rattner, a prominent financier (and personal friend of Bloomberg), along with a number of other major investment bankers and media moguls who in the past had advised and raised funds for Democratic candidates, declined to give money to Ferrer; some even became active in a "Democrats for Bloomberg" campaign. The move toward Bloomberg among the city's superwealthy was so intense that Rattner could say, "I can't think of a single active Democrat in New York who's supporting Freddy Ferrer. And when I say active Democrats, I mean the people in our world, who help raise money for Presidential candidates and things like that" (Bruder 2005). For these plutocrats, class solidarity trumped party loyalty.

Perhaps the most important element in Bloomberg's emergence as the unquestioned leader of the city's elite was his growing support among the city's real estate elites. In 2001, copious amounts of real estate money flowed to Democratic candidates, and there was much anxiety among real estate elites about having a mayor independent of their political contribution–generated control. In 2005, despite tensions between the administration and some real estate elites, Ferrer found real estate's "deep pockets sewed up" (Cardwell 2005). In part, this was because real estate elites were smart enough to read the writing on the wall: even their most successful efforts to raise money for a Bloomberg challenger would likely be insufficient to overcome the advantage the mayor's private wealth provided. And if a public fight over the far west side stadium had raised fears of political retribution, the prospects of facing an angry Bloomberg reelected over the opposition of the city's real estate elites seemed even more unappealing. On a more positive note, the administration's aggressive development agenda, coupled with broader economic and political forces, had sparked a major boom in both construction and land values, with the real estate industry reaping the benefits. The administration had entered into a number of development partnerships with prominent developers like Jerry Speyer and Douglas Durst (both of whom were Ferrer contributors in 2001), giving these leaders of the city's real estate elite little incentive to make political waves. Finally, Bloomberg's appeal to real estate elites was enhanced by the globalization of the city's real estate industry, which had resulted in a growing contingent of "global" developers who shared many social and cultural characteristics with TCC members like Bloomberg and Doctoroff. This would become apparent in later years as developers like Stephen Ross of the Related Companies and Steven Roth of Vornado, who had strong social and business ties to the deputy mayor and mayor respectively, became favored partners of the administration (Angotti 2008, 52–54). In sum, by the end of Mayor Bloomberg's first term the city's real estate elite had accepted the political ascendancy of the city's TCC and also accepted the necessity to enter into a partnership — perhaps even a junior partnership — with its leading lights.

As of the 2005 mayoral election, the city's elite had unified behind the CEO mayor. They were joined by a remarkable cross-section of New Yorkers, resulting in Bloomberg's brutally decisive twenty-point victory over the hapless Ferrer. Joining conservative white Democrats, who had supported Republicans for two decades, every Democratic constituency joined the Bloomberg juggernaut, including labor, nonprofits, white liberals, almost half of the black electorate, and a third of the city's Latino voters, a particularly impressive showing considering that Ferrer would have been the city's first Latino mayor.[2] This dominance reflected the ability of the Bloomberg Way to structure the contours of political debate, to make the notion of a CEO mayor the new standard for political leadership in the city. But it was also attributable to the willingness of the mayor, his administration, and his campaign team to dive directly into urban politics, to spread around money, jobs, and favors in order to guarantee the support of particular constituencies. The CEO mayor had become a master politician.

The Lackluster Second Term

Bloomberg's first term saw the emergence and evolution of an ambitious and innovative approach to urban governance, the initiation of a coherent and comprehensive development strategy, the closing of major budget gaps without resort to major service reductions, the near success of the city's Olympic bid, and the major controversy over the west side stadium. It is perhaps unsurprising that his second term would prove anticlimactic.

There was one major new comprehensive planning initiative, PlaNYC 2030, which proposed a number of interventions to cope with the city's future growth, strengthen its infrastructure, and enhance its environmental sustainability. However, the administration's effort to implement a congestion pricing scheme for Manhattan, which was included in the plan, was beleaguered by problems similar to those that had beset the stadium. Faced with a dubious state legislature, which had to approve the plan, the administration refused to acknowledge that the plan would impose harsh costs on some New Yorkers (generally those outside of Manhattan and those of relatively modest means) while benefiting others (wealthy Manhattanites). It subjected skeptics to the same kind of derision it had aimed at stadium opponents: now it was not the city's Olympic dream that was at stake but the very future of the planet. In April 2008, after a year of acrimonious debate, the congestion pricing plan died before reaching the floor of the state assembly. Apparently the political lessons that the mayor had learned from his first term were only applied to matters close at hand, within the city; the mayor once again had difficulty when forced to deal with a governmental body that curtailed his autonomy to act in accordance with his judgment of the city's best interests, with once again deleterious consequences.

Congestion plan aside, the administration seemed satisfied with maintaining ongoing endeavors: a more political Bloomberg Way was also a less ambitious Bloomberg Way. When the administration did propose new programs, they tended to be smaller and less aggressive. And while they still reflected the corporate logic of the Bloomberg Way, they also were obviously geared toward particular constituencies.

One area in which this was particularly pronounced was social policy. This included the effort to expand affordable housing, which hit its stride after the mayor's reelection. Whereas its traditional advocates typically portrayed affordable housing as an issue of social justice or working-class interests, the Bloomberg administration placed affordable housing in the rubric of competitiveness. "Affordable housing is crucial to the future of economic development of this city," said Shaun Donovan, the head of the city's housing agency; the administration's plan "is really about how do we make sure that we keep workers in this city. . . . In this new economy, the cities that will compete and win are the cities that can build successful, mixed-income neighborhoods rather than the historic economic divide between city and suburb" (Scott 2006). Accordingly, many of the affordable housing units proposed by the administration were reserved for "middle-class" households making as much as twice the city's median household income. Furthermore, the administration engineered a new housing assistance program aimed to attract teachers from other areas who might otherwise be unable to afford to live in New York. This was affordable housing for the denizens of the luxury city.

The administration also focused on improving the lot of people of unambiguously limited material means. Soon after the 2005 election, the mayor created the Council on Economic Opportunity (known by the felicitous acronym "CEO"), led by acclaimed Harlem antipoverty activist Geoffrey Canada and Time Warner Chief Executive Richard Parsons. It was charged with formulating and implementing aggressive and innovative policies to reduce the city's poverty, which had risen substantially during Bloomberg's first term (Levitan 2006). Faced with a dearth of available resources as well as the desire of the mayor to quickly demonstrate measurable progress, the commission quickly cut back the scope of its proposals, targeting the working poor, young children, and young adults, but not the elderly, ex-prisoners, the unemployed, and the homeless. It put forward proposals for better coordination of existing city programs and started a number of public–private ventures, which were "more business- and results-oriented than broader strategies used in the past" (Cardwell 2006). Several of the new initiatives clearly reflected private-sector thinking, including one that paid people for behaving in certain ways. Announcing this program, Mayor Bloomberg said, "In the private sector, financial incentives encourage actions that are good for the company: working harder, hitting sales targets or landing more clients. . . . In the public sector, we believe that financial incentives will encourage actions that are good for the city and its families: higher attendance in schools, more parental involvement in education and better career skills" (Cardwell 2007).[3] Ultimately the antipoverty program was largely ineffective, and it was quietly scaled back in early 2009 (the financial incentive program was spared). Nevertheless, it burnished Mayor Bloomberg's image as someone concerned with those of a lower station in life than his own and earned him the loyalty of a chunk of the city's antipoverty advocacy community, while remaining consonant with the Bloomberg Way's commitment to private-sector logic.

After Bloomberg? The Fight for a Third Term

The failure of the congestion pricing plan and the fizzling of the antipoverty program, as well as the earlier defeats of the Olympic bid and the far west side stadium, seemed to leave the mayor at loose ends. Perhaps the novelty of leading the world's greatest city was wearing off for a man who often pointed out that, as a well-connected billionaire, his plan B should he leave politics was a lot better than most people's plan A. Perhaps the necessity to bend his approach to governance in accordance with the realities of urban politics, which was accompanied by a narrowing of scope of the administration's initiatives, lay uncomfortably with the mayor's highly cultivated image as a transformative figure who rose above politics. And perhaps the frustrating realization that even the CEO mayor might be stymied by state assemblymen and obscure state boards exasperated a man whose mythology — and class identity — centered on being "able to do things."

In any case, Bloomberg and his advisors had their sights set on an even bigger prize than the New York City mayoralty: the presidency of the United States. Bloomberg had been pushing into the national spotlight for some time, emerging as a spokesman for gun control and other urban issues. As 2007 wore on and no clear presidential frontrunner emerged in either party, there was growing speculation that the CEO mayor might make a move to become the CEO president (and one with a more legitimate claim to the title than George W. Bush). Early in 2008, Bloomberg, who had dropped his Republican affiliation in mid-2007, cochaired a much-ballyhooed panel celebrating bipartisanship with a bevy of centrist ex-senators, feeding this speculation. Bloomberg clearly enjoyed the attention and elevated public platform brought by his flirtation with running, as it landed him on the cover of both *Time* and *Newsweek* and made him a staple on Sunday morning political talk shows.

However, the ascension of Barack Obama to political stardom in 2008 dashed Bloomberg's presidential hopes. After the 2008 presidential nominees were determined, Bloomberg was considered a vice presidential possibility for both candidates. Despite a May 2008 promise made by his long-time advisor Kevin Sheekey that Bloomberg would contribute between "zero and a billion" dollars to the campaign that picked him (Barrett 2008), both Obama and Republican candidate John McCain made other choices. As the spotlight moved away, Bloomberg seemed disappointed and even angry—one article from the time noted that the mayor's always-mercurial temperament had worsened, calling him "short-tempered, scolding, even petulant" (Cardwell 2008). He began planning a memoir detailing his time in city hall, a second contribution to the CEO autobiography genre.

Others were thinking about life in New York City after Bloomberg. Especially concerned were his fellow CEOs, who feared a return to mayoral business-as-usual, especially given the slate of potential contenders, which included liberal Democrats such as west side councilwoman Christine Quinn, African American comptroller William Thompson, and Congressman Anthony Weiner, a Queens native and vocal Bloomberg critic. As early as 2006, a number of "tycoons who [saw] themselves as Mike Bloomberg–esque technocrats" were considering taking matters into their own hands and running for mayor (Gray 2006). Most prominent among them was none other than Richard Parsons, a liberal Republican who had worked for President Gerald Ford before entering business and who had the dual advantage of being African American and New York born and bred. However, Parsons eventually demurred, choosing instead to spend more time at his vineyard in Tuscany.

At the same time, another option was under consideration: repealing the city's term limits law, which imposed two-term limits on its mayors. In the eyes of many elites, this law, celebrated as a blow against politics as usual when it passed in the mid-1990s (with the financial support of another billionaire CEO, Ronald Lauder, who had made term limits his pet issue), now threatened to restore the status quo ante. In late 2006, Jerry Speyer and financier Henry Kravis, cochairs of the Partnership for New York City, ran the idea of a one-time term limit extension for Mayor Bloomberg by Lauder, who rejected it.

By mid-2008 the unsuccessful search for what Parsons described as not just a "businessman but a Bloomberg-type businessman, who is not beholden to special interests," had left the city's business elite feeling "significant trepidation over what comes after Bloomberg," according to Partnership for New York City head Kathy Wylde (Barbaro 2008). The city's TCC, along with members of the city's real estate elite, were resolved to have the mayoralty remain in the hands of one of their own, for reasons of both economic interest and class solidarity. For them, the notion of a CEO mayor, once a curiosity, was now a necessity.

Accordingly, the idea of overturning the term limits law was revived. Bloomberg, who as the prospects of a vice presidential nomination dimmed in early 2008 had asked a pollster to gauge voter reaction to the idea, remained publicly noncommittal. Nevertheless, he began lobbying Lauder, as well as owners of the city's major newspapers and a number of key politicians, to see if they would endorse a term-limit extension, and if so, what they saw as the best route to this end: the law could be overturned by a vote of the city council, but since it had been passed via public referendum, many argued that it should again go before the voters. By October 2008, Bloomberg had lined up a remarkable coalition in support of the extension, including city politicians, union leaders, activists, and the city's major papers. For his part, Lauder eventually acquiesced but vowed to work to reinstate the law after Bloomberg had reaped the benefits of its repeal. Despite near-universal acknowledgment among the media and politicians (and the opinion of nearly 90 percent of New Yorkers) that the term limits law should be repealed as it had been established, by a popular vote, it was overturned by the city council by a vote of 29–22 in early October 2008. Political expediency had trumped democratic niceties.

So had the exigencies of crisis, as the emerging financial crisis of late 2008 and its potential effects on the city's budget and economy were the primary public justifications for the law's repeal. It was argued that only Bloomberg had the managerial competence, vision, business expertise, and leadership skills to guide the city through crisis, as he had done after 9/11. An open letter from a number of business leaders (including Rattner, Parsons, Speyer, Kravis, and a number of financiers whom the financial meltdown was quickly making into household names, such as Jamie Dimon, John Mack, and Lloyd Blankfein), published in several newspapers just before the city council vote, argued that only "continuity of great leadership" would permit the city to move quickly past the crisis and to preserve the achievements of the past several years (Barger et al. 2008). As ex-Bloomberg advisor Mitchell Moss put it, "He is uniquely situated to understand this crisis and to cope with it" (Barbaro and Chen 2008b). Even those who opposed the means by which the term limits law was overturned endorsed the notion that Bloomberg, CEO mayor, was the only individual capable of dealing with the current situation: "There aren't a lot of people who have his experience, connections and gravitas," said Councilman Eric Gioia, who voted against the law's repeal (Barbaro and Chen 2008b). For his part, Bloomberg argued that despite his own past opposition to overturning the term limits law, the current situation called for nothing less. As his chief counsel testified to the city council, "Crisis has a way of . . . forcing us to put pragmatism first" (Chen and Barbaro 2008).

Where economic interest, class solidarity, and CEO mayor ideology did not reach, the mayor's attempts to generate political loyalty did. Indeed, many of those who now touted the indispensability of the mayor had condemned Rudy Giuliani when he attempted to extend his term as mayor after 9/11. Whereas Giuliani, no political slouch, was unable to leverage his post-9/11 goodwill to overcome the city's term limits law, Bloomberg's ability to do so was due to his ability to cash in his accumulated political capital. Many of the politicians, nonprofit leaders, union heads, and advocates that had benefited from the mayor's personal and governmental largesse now dutifully lined up behind the push for a third term, testifying in support of extending term limits in the media and to the city council, often after receiving "requests" to do so from city hall (Barbaro and Chen 2008a).[4]

Using a variety of political means, Mayor Bloomberg had procured the opportunity to remain in power after his second term ended. He quickly acted to ensure this work had not been in vain, snapping up Democratic campaign operatives and threatening to spend another eighty million dollars on his reelection campaign, including some twenty million dollars on negative advertising. Along with Bloomberg's incumbency and relatively high approval ratings, this deterred a number of potentially strong candidates, including Quinn and Weiner, from running. The only major candidate left was Comptroller Thompson, a weak candidate who was able neither to build a strong following among those who found themselves unwelcome in the luxury city nor to articulate a compelling alternative approach to governance, voicing instead a lukewarm anti-Bloomberg populism. Thompson's weaknesses were made all the more damaging by the fact that Bloomberg had already spent thirty-six million dollars on the campaign by mid-2009, well ahead of his 2005 pace and far above the amount that Thompson, under the rules of the city's public campaign financing system, would be able to spend in the entire campaign.

On the morning of November 4, the day after the 2009 mayoral election, New Yorkers woke up to a surprise. True, Bloomberg had been reelected. But despite spending over $100 million, he had won by a surprisingly narrow five-point margin. Some of the racial and class divisions Bloomberg had managed to overcome in earlier elections were reasserting themselves, as Thompson won three-quarters of the black vote and a majority of the votes of New Yorkers with incomes below fifty thousand dollars; Bloomberg won three-quarters of the votes of people making over two hundred thousand dollars (Powell and Bosman 2009). Moreover, there was evidence that many New Yorkers were disenchanted by Bloomberg's wildly disproportionate campaign spending and the tactics he had used in overturning the term limits law, rather than his leadership as mayor. His approval ratings remained high even as his electoral advantage declined (Powell and Bosman 2009), and the erosion of electoral support for Bloomberg was not accompanied by a commensurate increase in support for his opponent: Bloomberg received almost two hundred thousand fewer votes than in 2005, while Thompson received essentially the same number of votes as Ferrer had (Purnick 2010). As the election results sunk in, a growing chorus of criticism — of Bloomberg's imperiousness, of his favoritism toward the wealthy, of the unseemliness of his propensity to buy political support — emerged, often voiced by politicians and figures who so soon before had been loath to criticize the seemingly invulnerable mayor.

All this added up to a confusing and ambiguous situation. Before the election, Bloomberg's political position appeared impregnable. He had been hugely successful in cementing the support of organized political interests from poverty advocates to real estate developers. He had been able to overturn the city's popular term limits law with ease and to forestall effective electoral opposition. The citizenry seemed broadly supportive of his approach to urban governance; no real alternative to the Bloomberg Way had been articulated. Yet this seeming dominance, combined with $100 million of campaign spending and the power of incumbency, had translated into only the narrowest of victories over an ineffective and underfunded candidate. And voters seemed turned off by the very kind of personalization — the notion that the city's economic and fiscal health was absolutely dependent on Bloomberg's leadership, thus warranting fundamental changes to electoral processes — that had brought the CEO mayor into city hall in the first place. In order to understand this situation, we need to focus on the evolution of the class politics embedded in the Bloomberg Way.

Class and the Changing Bloomberg Way

As the Bloomberg Way softened its antipolitics, its class character grew more pronounced. The administration's political endeavors to broaden and deepen the mayor's support extended the class project inherent in the CEO mayoralty: they were premised on the idea that Bloomberg's mastery of the city, however achieved, was legitimate and beneficial to all. This was true even of the most tawdry of these efforts, the use of the mayor's money to gain the loyalty of nonprofits. As historian Fred Siegel pointed out, Bloomberg had "reversed the flow of money" in New York City politics: "The traditional politicians are bought by special interest groups, but Bloomberg buys special interest groups" (Barbaro and Chen 2008a). The use of money — the root of capitalist class power — as a political and policy tool became more pronounced in Bloomberg's second term. As it did so, it reinforced the mayor's claims to class leadership in two ways. First, even as Mayor Bloomberg dived into the world of interest group politics, his control over money, which, as the idiom goes, has no smell, permitted him to remain "above politics" while still able to wield class power. As in the realm of the market, the reduction of political relations to "the cash nexus" had the paradoxical effect of obscuring the compulsion inherent therein while at the same time laying bare the class relations at work (Marx and Engels 1994, 161). Just as the market transaction between capitalist and laborer appears as a free contract between differently endowed, yet equal, individuals that ultimately maximizes the wealth of all, the transactions between billionaire mayor cum political patron and his various clients were portrayed as necessary political steps to ensure that all of New York's citizens were moving together toward the fulfillment of the interests of the city as a whole. Second, the mayor's use of money symbolized and concentrated the character of the CEO as efficacy personified. Money, as David Graeber points out, "tends to be identified with the holder's generic, hidden capacities for action" (2001, 94). The ability to deploy money was the ultimate way to get things done, to take action, to cut through red tape and bureaucratic entanglements — to perform.

Both performance and the notion that the city, like a corporation, had an identifiable and unitary interest were crucial elements of the Bloomberg Way. Yet the administration's use of money as a political instrument, alongside the efforts of the city's elite to ensure that a "Bloomberg-type businessman" would remain in city hall, signaled a shift in the claims to class leadership inherent in the Bloomberg Way. Such claims were associated no longer with an antipolitics that obscured class even as it depended on it but rather with a more straightforward assertion of the rightness of class leadership. Bloomberg — along with the capitalists who had participated in his government, withdrawn their support from his rivals, and helped engineer the overturning of term limits — seemed comfortable asserting himself as part of a self-conscious group with the capacity, wisdom, skill, and right to rule the city in the interests of all.

This assertion of class leadership became more and more apparent in 2008 and early 2009, as the mayor's campaign to remain in office coincided with a national financial meltdown, recession, and revelations of excessive risk taking, self-dealing, and mismanagement among financial CEOs. Rather than display remorse or humility in the face of populist outrage and threats to regulate executive compensation, many CEOs, along with their apologists, reiterated the notion that their extraordinary qualities justified their high salaries, perks, and celebrity. Mayor Bloomberg and his compatriots were prominent participants in this defense of class privilege; indeed, the administration's willingness to cater to and celebrate corporate elites became more pronounced during this time.

This was evident in the administration's hiring practices, as the influx of private-sector personnel into city hall continued during Bloomberg's second term. In some cases, they took positions previously occupied by their former private-sector compatriots. For instance, when EDC president Andrew Alper left the administration in 2006 to start a hedge fund, Robert Lieber, a managing director of Lehman Brothers, succeeded him. Like Alper, Lieber had little experience with economic development issues; and also like Alper, Lieber had business connections with Deputy Mayor Doctoroff. Not long afterward, when Doctoroff stepped down and took over as president of Bloomberg LP, Lieber assumed the position of deputy mayor for economic development. In other cases, positions that had been filled in the first term by professionals with relevant experience now were going to Bloomberg's corporate brethren. So, during the administration's first term, positions related to social policy had typically been occupied by professionals drawn from the nonprofits, academia, or government. The second term saw this change. For example, in May 2009, John Rhea, yet another ex–Lehman Brothers managing director with no public-sector experience, was hired to head the New York City Housing Authority, which administered the city's 178,000 public housing units. Rhea's financial and management skills were touted as the right qualifications for the job given problems with the agency's budget and management. But the idea that Rhea's investment banking background prepared him for the complex and arcane domain of public-housing management was a stretch even by the standards of the Bloomberg administration. It seemed to be a sign that the CEO mayor's belief that private-sector skills and experience could be unproblematically transferred to the public sector was as strong as, if not stronger than, ever.

Moreover, there was little evidence that the financial crisis and its ill effects on New York City had undermined the idea that the city's postindustrial elites were the key to its economic future. In February 2009, at the same time his administration was refusing to use federal stimulus money to extend the time that single, able-bodied people were able to receive food stamps without entering a workfare program, the mayor announced a $45 million program aiding another group experiencing tough times: laid-off workers from the financial services sector. While administration officials insisted that the program was aimed at aiding financial service workers of all backgrounds, not just (formerly) highly paid investment bankers and traders, the latter were clearly its focus. The program provided "incubator space" for financial start-up companies, facilitated connections with venture capitalists, created an international business plan competition in partnership with top business schools aimed at enhancing the city's reputation for innovation, and provided funding for incentives to attract international banks to the city. Administration officials argued that these programs were necessary to retain these "very talented" individuals, whose "innovation, drive, and work ethic" would be essential to "winning [the] competition . . . for the jobs that the next revival of the financial services industry will bring" (City of New York 2009; McGeehan 2009b). The financial crisis and its deleterious effects on the city's economy had not altered the administration's belief that the high-level professionals and executives in the postindustrial sectors were crucial to the city's future prosperity.

Throughout 2009, as popular anger at the perceived entitlement and corruption of the richest Americans was growing, Mayor Bloomberg repeatedly expressed his solidarity with his wealthy peers. Rejecting the notion that New York City might grow more dangerous as recession took hold, Bloomberg stated (incorrectly, as a number of criminologists pointed out) that "people who go out and murder people don't read the *Wall Street Journal*" (Barbaro 2009a). He publicly praised former Lehman Brothers CEO Richard Fuld Jr., who oversaw the company's collapse, as well as high-level executives at AIG. Finally, condemning the rush to tax wealthy New Yorkers to close budget deficits, Bloomberg said on his radio program: "You know, the yelling and screaming about the rich — we want the rich from around this country to move here. We love the rich people" (Lisberg 2009). Despite the implied distinction between the "we" doing the loving and those being loved, this was, like the other examples listed here, a naked declaration of class solidarity.

By mid-2009, even as the overall climate was becoming less hospitable, the class project that animated the Bloomberg Way was only growing stronger. The notion that the city's prosperity and governance depended specifically on the skills, experience, leadership, and vision of the city's TCC and more broadly on its postindustrial elite was, if anything, being expressed more directly and unabashedly by the man whose political rise best emblematized that notion. Moreover, Bloomberg's use of money, the ultimate source of his class power, in governance had become more widespread and pronounced. With the softening of the Bloomberg Way's antipolitics, its claims to class leadership had become more direct and bold.

With this in mind, let us return to the mayoral election of 2009. The ambiguity surrounding Bloomberg's political status after that election was an indication that the class project informing his mayoralty had reached a critical point — and stalled. In the period running up to his decision to seek a third term, Bloomberg had managed to strike a fine political balance: between personalization and class, between politics and antipolitics, and between the CEO mayor and the master politician. The softening of the Bloomberg Way's antipolitics, along with his widely lauded stewardship of the city, allowed the class project informing his approach to governance to safely reveal itself. For a brief moment during Bloomberg's second term, the Bloomberg Way had successfully secured a new class hegemony in the city. His seemingly unchallengeable political dominance brought into being the political unity that was an assumption of the Bloomberg Way's antipolitics.

But as quickly as hegemony was achieved, its future was thrown into doubt. With the overturning of the term limits law and the scorched-earth tactics of the 2009 Bloomberg campaign, class leadership slid into class entitlement in the eyes of many New Yorkers. The balance was lost, and the mayor, never shy about touting his own extraordinariness, now seemed to consider himself indispensable. If the mantle of class leadership had been passed along to another "Bloomberg-type businessman," class hegemony might have been secured. Ironically, the Bloomberg Way's class project was checked by the very personalization that was its founding premise.

THE NEW RULES OF GOVERNANCE IN NEW YORK CITY

Despite the uncertain future facing both the mayor and the class project he spearheaded, one thing is clear: with Bloomberg's political ascension and the concomitant, if tenuous, establishment of the hegemony of the city's postindustrial elite came a restructuring of the rules of urban governance in New York City. By 2009, Bloomberg's approach to governance, once belittled as the vanity project of an entitled dilettante, had become the new governmental common sense in New York City. By 2009, Bloomberg himself, to apply Žižek's words in a new context, was "no longer . . . needed, since [his] message [was] incorporated into the mainstream" (2004, 69). The Bloomberg Way redrew the unwritten rules of neoliberal governance in New York City. However, just as the "new urban norms" (Sites 2003, 41) that emerged from the fiscal crisis created their own contradictions and weak points, so too did the new governmental norms embodied in the Bloomberg Way.

In terms of fiscal and development policy, the Bloomberg Way represented a decisive rejection of post–fiscal crisis orthodoxy. Previous administrations had consistently lowered taxes at the cost of services and infrastructure investment. Bloomberg reversed this, making the prioritization of value over cost the cornerstone of his development strategy. In addition, the Bloomberg Way revitalized the role of the local state in the economy, centralizing its development functions, enhancing its capacity for coordinated action, and permitting it to guide, rather than merely support, development. Despite the rough resemblance to pre–fiscal crisis urban liberalism, the broad aims of local state action — to enhance growth, strengthen the city's postindustrial sectors, and create an urban and governmental environment friendly to certain sectors of business — were consistent with neoliberal norms. Even if it did challenge the power of entrenched interests like real estate, the Bloomberg Way represented a reformulation, rather than a reversal, of post–fiscal crisis neoliberalization.

While providing certain political and ideological benefits, this continuity had its costs. Even before the global financial meltdown of 2008, it was apparent that the fundamental problem that had bedeviled New York City's economy since the late 1970s, an overreliance on financial and related postindustrial sectors, had actually worsened under Mayor Bloomberg, despite gestures toward economic diversification. The luxury city strategy also exacerbated problems of affordability, as now it was not just decent housing that was straining the budgets of even relatively well-off New Yorkers but everything from utility bills to the price of groceries. It also intensified geographic and wage inequality: the Manhattan-centric postindustrial sectors had boomed, with the familiar consequence of an increase in low-wage, low-skilled service work, on one hand, and an increase in the income of a highly skilled, well-educated few on the other. Relatively high-wage industries not requiring high levels of education, which tended toward outer-borough locations, suffered.[5]

As the effects of the 2008 crisis reverberated through the city's economy and treasury, the fiscal balance, high real estate values, and robust economic and job growth that had characterized the mid-2000s evaporated, with dire consequences for the city's economy and budget. Given the uncertain prospects of finance and the real estate market, the sources of the city's future prosperity seemed unclear at best. The administration's vision of a profusion of innovative start-ups founded by laid-off Wall Streeters taking the place of large financial institutions seemed less like the "fundamental shift in public policy" that its proponents described and more like a desperate and inadequate attempt to preserve the economic status quo (McGeehan 2009a). If the Bloomberg Way had managed to temporarily place the city on a more prosperous footing, it had not addressed the fundamental problems of the city's political economy. Neoliberalization was still failing to meet its own avowed goals of fiscal stability and sustained growth, to say nothing of generating broad-based benefits.

Ironically, given its original premises — that the antipolitical CEO mayor would use his business acumen to revitalize the city's economy — the Bloomberg Way had been much more successful in restructuring its politics. By 2009, the notion of a businessperson-mayor was not only accepted but had become the new standard for mayoral leadership in the city. Voicing a sentiment held by many New Yorkers across the political spectrum, one resigned leftist told me that "a good corporate technocrat is better than a bad one." In addition, by 2009, the position of the city's TCC, as well as the broader postindustrial elite, at the helm of city government and as the "target market" for city development policy had been cemented. The TCC had successfully established itself as the political superior of the city's real estate elite. And the city's liberal tradition, already weakened, was either marginalized completely or co-opted by the mayor's philanthropic and political constituency building.

The Bloomberg Way also redrew the relationship between the city's citizenry and its political leadership. Whether it was the evasion of legislative review of the Hudson Yards plan, the choice to have the submissive city council rather than the city's citizenry vote on the overturning of term limits, or efforts to defund community boards (Gross 2009) and reduce community control of schools (Medina 2009), Bloomberg was relentless in his determination to prevent democratic proceduralism from impinging on his autonomy as CEO mayor. Despite some protest, it seemed that much of the city's citizenry was willing to accept this new arrangement, to lessen their opportunities for political participation in exchange for managerial competence, strong leadership, and, in later years at least, some degree of governmental largesse.

The Bloomberg Way did have important political limits. As the failure of the far west side stadium and the congestion plan demonstrate, the CEO mayor's desire for autonomy clashed with the reality of significant state control over the city's destiny. The weakness of Bloomberg's 2009 mayoral showing was at least in part in reaction to the Bloomberg Way's antidemocratic tendencies, a fact that Bloomberg tacitly acknowledged by taking a more humble and conciliatory tone in the early days of his third term, though it was unclear if this represented anything more than a temporary and symbolic gesture.

The Bloomberg Way's class politics and material effects on life in the city generated and refocused oppositional politics on the left, especially outside of the city's mainstream Democratic Party and union movement. By the second Bloomberg term, a loose network of progressive and activist organizations, bloggers, cultural producers, and writers, along with a handful of politicians, had begun to articulate a trenchant critique of the Bloomberg administration's class politics, as well as of the imagined — but rapidly materializing — city of luxury, achievement, and ambition that animated its policies. For instance, the members of the Right to the City movement, an alliance of radical activist groups, community organizations, academics, and intellectuals, became an increasing presence in the city's politics, disrupting the mayor's 2009 State of the City address, holding movement-building meetings, producing and distributing videos, and developing policy proposals. Likewise, a series of bloggers, documentary filmmakers, and writers angrily documented the "Vanishing New York" (Senko and DeRosa 2009) of small business, affordable housing, class and racial diversity, low-rent aesthetics, and radical difference in the face of what one blogger, using the name of a famous, high-end chef, labeled the "Vongerichtification" of the city (Moss 2008): its transformation into the luxury city. Importantly, these forms of opposition directly engaged the Bloomberg Way at the level of class and the urban imaginary. However, they often did so in a backward-looking and reactive manner through sentimental evocations of New York City's postwar "golden age" or quasi-perverse celebrations of the very fiscal crisis–era disorder (and cultural ferment) whose reemergence the Bloomberg Way explicitly sought to prevent. What a more just city of the future might look like was unclear, though some groups, like the Right to the City alliance, recognized the need to develop and articulate an alternative vision of the city and its governance.

The Bloomberg Way also generated opposition from the right. Conservatives of various stripes decried Bloomberg's social liberalism, his ostensible cultural elitism, and the deleterious effects of the luxury city strategy on small business, the middle class, and taxpayers (Kotkin 2009; McMahon 2005; Riley 2008). This raised the possibility of a rebirth of Giuliani-style tax-cutting revanchism. But it also presented novel political potentialities: the critiques of conservative defenders of middle-class interests and values, stressing affordability and condemnations of Bloomberg's elite status, strongly echoed those coming from the left, if they differed in terms of urban imaginary, policy prescriptions, and the class and racial interests they represented. One could envision some kind of left-right anti–Bloomberg Way alliance, consisting of white outer-borough residents from the working and middle classes on one hand, and minorities, the poor, and white leftists on the other. In fact, one 2009 mayoral candidate, Tony Avella, whom the reader might remember leading the huzzahs for the Hudson Yards rezoning plan as cochair of the city council's Zoning and Franchising Subcommittee, changed his political stripes and ran just this kind of campaign in 2009, though with negligible success.

In sum, if the Bloomberg Way restructured the rules of politics in New York City, it has also created the potential for its own overcoming. As the election of 2009 demonstrated, the bald assertions of class power essential to its success also created seams of vulnerability. If the broader mood of discontent with economic elites intensifies, if the city's economy does not recover as Mayor

Bloomberg has promised it will, and if the disenchantment with Bloomberg's political tactics continues, there will be political space for an emerging movement able to link class, urban imaginary, and governance. While a New York version of the anti-Obama right-wing populist backlash is possible (especially given revanchism's success during the 1980s and 1990s), New York's ethnic and racial diversity, as well as its ever-more-tenuous liberal tradition, reduces its likelihood. If a new political movement directly challenging the Bloomberg Way and its class politics does arise, one would expect — and hope — that it would reassert, to use the words of Thomas Bender, "the broader political culture of the city — grounded upon an experience marked by the reality of difference" toward the end of "bring[ing] economic decisions within the sphere of democratic politics" (2002, 192).

THE BLOOMBERG WAY AND URBAN NEOLIBERALISM

Despite its contradictions and vulnerabilities, the Bloomberg Way represented a potent new form of neoliberal urban governance. Like earlier mutations of neoliberalism implemented in different places and at different scales — Reagan and Thatcher's muscular antiwelfarism or the urban revanchism of Rudy Giuliani — the Bloomberg Way associated an effort to assert upper-class power with a claim to represent the greater good. Reaganism, Thatcherism, and revanchism accomplished this through misdirection, using the demonization of some set of actors (unions, welfare mothers, squeegee men, and others) to push for policies more to the liking of elite economic interests. In contrast, the Bloomberg Way, especially after the softening of its antipolitics, made more direct claims to class power. It is from this centrality of class that the two key implications of the Bloomberg Way for broader understandings of neoliberalism flow.

Full-Spectrum Neoliberalism

The first draws on the argument set forth in the introduction to this book that neoliberalism must be understood as operating on political, cultural, and social levels. That is to say, neoliberalism (at least potentially) entails a certain approach to governance (generally one reserving a central role for the market and private-sector logics), a certain imagining of the self and society (generally focusing on the self's entrepreneurial capacities and a "desocialized" idea of society), and a certain class politics (the restoration of upper-class power). Translating all this in the terms used and at the scale addressed in this book, neoliberalism is at its most potent when it is able to link class, urban imaginaries, and urban governance. It was this linkage that made the Bloomberg Way powerful in New York City. In gauging the broader impact of the Bloomberg Way, the question is whether or not projects elsewhere will be successful in linking governance, urban imaginary, and class to the same degree.

Many of the governing practices that the Bloomberg administration cobbled together are in wide use. Among them are standard features of entrepreneurial urban governance like branding and private-sector management techniques. However, given the "fast policy transfer" that interurban competition engenders (Peck and Tickell 2002, 397), it is certain the Bloomberg administration's refinement and intensification of many of these practices will be noted and replicated elsewhere: indeed, this process has already begun. For instance, the mayor's particular approach to the city's public school system, centered on strong mayoral control, professionalization, and the use of private-sector techniques, has shaped educational reform efforts in other cities, as indicated by well-publicized information-gathering visits by the mayors of Washington, D.C., and Los Angeles (Hemphill 2009; Henig 2009). Bloomberg's "post-welfare" approach to battling poverty, which itself drew on practices in other cities, quickly became a model for similar efforts in Chicago, Miami, San Antonio, Savannah, and Seattle, especially after Bloomberg, along with San Francisco mayor Gavin Newsom, founded a national organization, Cities for Financial Empowerment, to spread such ideas (Cohen 2009). Mayor Bloomberg also has become a national spokesperson for cities, active in the annual U.S. Conference of Mayors and drawing attention to a number of urban issues, including sustainability, public transit, guns, poverty, and the necessity for sound managerial practices. In fact, a number of figures closely identified with Mayor Bloomberg joined the Obama administration, which showed more interest in urban issues than any other in recent memory. The Bloomberg Way has become a touchstone of neoliberal urban governance nationwide.

The Bloomberg Way also helped solidify the particular political position that the mayor espoused, that is, social liberalism combined with fiscal conservatism and a repudiation of old-style economic liberalism. While this sort of "third-way" politics is not new, the Bloomberg Way helped keep it alive during the 2000s, when it seemed that the dominance of conservative ideology was unlikely to be challenged anytime soon, and helped push it to the forefront when conservatism hit hard times late in the decade. The perceived success of the Bloomberg Way bolstered "post-partisanship," which posited competence, pragmatism, technocracy, and managerialism as the best approach to governance, endorsing the competent implementation of "what works" over the pursuit of "tired ideology." In addition, the Bloomberg Way solidified the notion of a post–liberal activist state and helped undermine anti-tax orthodoxy. Thus, Mayor Bloomberg, along other politicians, some of whom explicitly cited him as an inspiration, helped legitimize a kind of "liberal" neoliberalism, a second Third Way, that added an activist state to the familiar mix of social tolerance, fiscal conservatism, and business-friendliness. Among these politicians were mayors like Cory Booker of Newark, Adrian Fenty of Washington, D.C., Thomas Menino of Boston, and Shirley Franklin of Atlanta, as well as those on a larger stage: President Barack Obama has celebrated Bloomberg's "extraordinary leadership," his rejection of "old ideological battles," and his search for "pragmatic solutions" (Ambinder 2008). The Bloomberg Way helped cement this softer version of neoliberalism as the "liberal" alternative to hard-right conservatism, thus dramatically narrowing the bounds of mainstream political discourse.

Returning to the urban arena, the governmental practices associated with the Bloomberg Way have often been married to an urban imaginary quite similar to the one it was animated by. In a development inconceivable in the 1970s context of urban decline and disorder, cities are now imagined as centers of innovation, ambition, leisure, cultural diversity, cosmopolitanism, and wealth. This urban imaginary has become a central driver of urban policy in the United States, as cities across the country have attempted to spur entrepreneurialism and create urban environments attractive to "the best and the brightest." In cities from Providence to Toledo to Tacoma, urban managers have developed and circulated visions of their cities as hubs of creativity, innovation, and excitement.

While the Bloomberg Way's constituent governmental strategies and urban imaginary are relatively widespread, it is more difficult to find cases in which the final link in the chain, class, is present. Despite Richard Sennett's claim that "the new global elite, operating in cities such as New York, London, and Chicago, avoids the urban political realm [and] wants to operate in the city but not rule it" (2000), there are numerous examples of new global elites, that is, members of the TCC, engaging in urban governance. Some of these examples preceded Mayor Bloomberg: financier Richard Riordan, who served as mayor of Los Angeles from 1993 to 2001 (Kaufmann 2003), and, farther afield, the late billionaire Rafik Hariri, who led the reconstruction of war-torn Beirut while serving as Lebanon's prime minister from 1998 to 2004 (Sawalha 1998). More recently, Microsoft cofounder Paul Allen has been a prominent figure in the redevelopment of Seattle (Ritter 2005). In Dallas, political neophyte and retired head of Turner Construction Tom Leppert was elected in 2006 on the promise to "treat the job like a CEO" and soon became the dominant political figure in that city (Crain 2009). Again considering more distant locales, Lee Myung-bak, former CEO of Hyundai Construction and Engineering, was elected mayor of Seoul in 2002 and, five years later, president of South Korea. In both positions, like Bloomberg, he deployed private-sector techniques and concepts, particularly in the context of aggressive economic and urban development campaigns (Veale 2008). Finally, scholars have demonstrated the efforts of "new economy" capitalists in California to enhance the area's all-important "quality of life" (Lee 2005; Nevarez 2003), as well as the role of Bank of America executives in encouraging gentrification in Charlotte, North Carolina, as a way to attract well-educated workers and enhance its own image (Smith and Graves 2005).

Such elite engagement in urban governance was made possible by the rise of the figure of the charismatic CEO and the rehabilitation of the image of business discussed in chapter 2. In this sense, it reflects the formation of a TCC whose members have sufficient place commitments and status to be willing and able to convert their business success into political success. What is not evident in these cases is that urban governance served as a vehicle for class mobilization, as was the case with the Bloomberg Way. Nor do we see the sort of extreme claim to class rule that underwrote the efforts to ensure the continuing presence of a CEO mayor in New York City. It may be that the mix of globality and intensity of local life found in New York City formed a unique antidote to the sort of placelessness inherent in transnational capitalism that many scholars see as precluding the linkage of class mobilization and urban governance that constituted the Bloomberg Way. Or it may be that future research will uncover parallel processes taking place in other cities. In any case, it is safe to say that the growing number of global business elites engaged in urban affairs represents a necessary but not sufficient condition for this sort of linking of class mobilization and urban governance.

Elements of the Bloomberg Way, then, are present in other cities besides New York. But in no other case have they been linked in as coherent and sustained a manner; in no other case has such a linking led to the kind of restructuring of the rules of urban governance as was seen during Mayor Bloomberg's first two terms. For now, at least, the Bloomberg Way's potent reconstruction of neoliberalism is a unique case. However, it is certainly conceivable and perhaps even likely, given the importance of cities to the transnationalization of capitalism, that the linking of class formation, governance, and urban imaginary that made the Bloomberg Way so powerful will be replicated elsewhere.

Neoliberalization, Politics, and the Future of the City

If this does happen, what emerges is likely to resemble the Bloomberg Way in its broad contours but not its specifics. This brings us to a second important implication of the Bloomberg Way for our understandings of neoliberalism. As discussed in the introduction to this book, a number of analysts of neoliberalism, urban and otherwise, have insisted that neoliberal projects emerge out of specific contexts and build on existing political, economic, cultural, and social processes and practices. Moreover, such scholars have argued that neoliberal projects are typically forced to accommodate these ongoing processes and practices. In keeping with this, I described how the Bloomberg Way emerged from the history of post–World War II New York. I also demonstrated, in my analysis of the debate over the Hudson Yards plan, the ways in which the Bloomberg Way was forced to accommodate existing realities. However, I also insisted that in its rearticulation of existing practices and its incorporation of new elements, the Bloomberg Way represented an important departure from previous governmental practice. In particular, I argued that the merging of the ongoing processes of class formation and the neoliberalization of governance amounted to something distinctly different than what had gone before and that this class character was key to understanding the emergence, implementation, tribulations, and, ultimately, the success of the Bloomberg Way.

Thus, as a number of analysts have argued, neoliberalism entails not a radically new form of governance but one that entails the *reconstruction* and *reinvention* of existing institutions, concepts, and practices. In this case, this meant, among other things, that branding became not just an appurtenance of development policy but also its guide; postindustrial development became a means to competitiveness rather than real estate profits alone; antipoverty activists became indebted to the billionaire mayor; and labor unions became strong allies of capitalists in city hall. The Bloomberg Way's success in the post–Hudson Yards period illustrates that in order to succeed neoliberals must embed themselves in and reengineer existing realities in a way that curtails potential sources of opposition and provides benefits to a relatively broad array of interests. In other words, this notoriously depoliticizing approach to governance must be willing to directly engage with the messy realities of politics. It must be willing to acknowledge the reality of difference and, ultimately, its own positionality. In short, neoliberalism must acknowledge that it is a project aimed at restoring class power.

The restoration of class power that neoliberalism ultimately seeks cannot work through the ideological coercion of antipolitics, at least in well-formed democratic polities like the United States and New York City; it can only work by obtaining the consent of the governed through political means broader than elections alone. Just as municipal socialists of yore attempted to win support for the working class by delivering concrete benefits to urbanites of a variety of classes, neoliberal urban managers — and the capitalist classes that they may represent, seek to attract, or overlap with — must be willing and able to take the necessary steps to deliver relatively broad-based benefits.

The fact that the softening of the Bloomberg Way's antipolitics and the concomitant acknowledgment of its rooting in upper-class power only cemented its dominance of New York City's politics represents an object lesson for those who imagine a more just urban order. The battle for the future of the city will be won not by unmasking the class politics at the core of neoliberalism but by articulating and, if given the chance, demonstrating the effectiveness of an alternative linking of governance, urban imaginary, and class that defines and achieves a radically new form of the good of the city as a whole.

NOTES

INTRODUCTION

1. This phrase is of course a play on the construction common to the titles of CEO biographies; for an example, see Slater 1999.

2. Scholars have addressed the articulation of neoliberalism with other processes, including environmental sustainability (Heynen et al. 2007), professionalization (Bondi and Laurie 2005), the construction of gender (di Leonardo 2006; Kingfisher 2002b; Morgen and Gonzales 2008; Wright 2006), racial or ethnic struggles (Dávila 2004; Gregory 1998; Maskovsky 2001), post-9/11 securitization (Ruben and Maskovsky 2008), and modernization (Wilson 2008b).

3. These include business trainers (Ong 2006), penal policy professionals (Wacquant 1999), and other elites (Harper 1998; Ho 2005; Larner and Butler 2007; Miyazaki 2007a, Miyazaki 2007b; Ong 2006; Peck 2005; Phelps, Power, and Wanjiru 2007; Riles 2004; Schwegler 2008; Shore and Nugent 2003; Strathern 2000; Ward 2003, 2004, 2007a; Zaloom 2006).

4. For various works outlining these critiques of class see Clark and Lipset 2001; Gibson-Graham, Resnick, and Wolff 2001; Joyce 1995; Laclau and Mouffe 2001; and Wood 1986.

5. To clarify my use of a related term, I will use "elite" to refer to the cross-class group formed by those who occupy powerful roles in economic, cultural, and political institutions.

6. The literature on intersectionality is too large to cite exhaustively. For some key works, see Andersen and Hill Collins 2007; Boellstorff 2007; Brodkin 2000; di Leonardo 1984; Hartigan 1999; McCall 2001; Mullings 1997; and Williams 1989.

7. This vein of scholarship also includes work showing how class, whiteness, and regional or urban identities are linked in mutually constitutive ways (Adams and Gorton; Durrenberger and Doukas 2008; Hartigan 1999); how spatial practices like home ownership and neighborhood "improvement" express class divisions among African Americans and other racial and ethnic minorities (Gregory 1998, 1999; Pattillo 1999; Taylor 2002b; Williams 1988); and how exclusionary spatial practices, such as the residences in gated communities or efforts at suburban secession, are linked to the formation of class and race differences (Davis 1992, 151–264; Low 2003).

8. The definition, coherence, and even the existence of a "new middle class" of professionals and managers have been the subject of a great deal of debate in the social

sciences. For some key works advancing the concept, see Aronowitz 1979; Bruce-Biggs 1979; Ehrenreich and Ehrenreich 1971; Gouldner 1979; Mills 2002; Poulantzas 1978; and Wright 1985. See Smith 1996, 93–98, and Bell 1980 for critiques coming from very different theoretical perspectives. Much of the theoretical work on the new middle class conflates cultural attitudes, occupation, income, and status, a result of a multiplicity of understandings of class. Nonetheless, there are still theoretical and empirical reasons to believe that the twentieth century, and especially its second half, saw the growth of a relatively privileged stratum of salaried workers mediating between the capitalist class and the working class, whose labor involved either cultural or intellectual production or the management of the labor of others (Ehrenreich and Ehrenreich 1971; Wright 1985). This class is neither internally homogenous nor sharply distinct from other classes, nor is it constituted in isolation from other forms of identity and consciousness. My position is that the PMC concept serves a useful analytic purpose, allowing us to identify a social grouping, which, while diverse, complex, and difficult to define with theoretical and empirical precision, has nevertheless clearly become a marked and important presence in contemporary social life — and in particular, in contemporary urban life.

9. See Brenner 1997, 1999, 2001; Cox 1997; Herod and Wright 2002; Marston 2000; Sheppard and McMaster 2004; Smith 1992, 2000, 2008 [1984]; and Swyngedouw 1997.

10. See Friedmann 1995; Friedmann and Wolff 1982; Hannerz 1996, 127–139; Sassen 2001 [1991]; and Smith 2000.

11. For some examples of such work, see Beaverstock 2002, 2005; and Willis, Yeoh and Fakhri 2002.

12. For works that explicate and employ the notion of an urban imaginary, see Brash 2006a; Cinar and Bender 2007; di Leonardo 2006; Greenberg 2000; Huyssen 2008; King 2007, 1; Leitner, Peck, and Sheppard 2007b; LiPuma and Koelble 2005; Ruben 2001; Rutheiser 1996; Taylor 2002a; and Zukin et al. 1998.

13. A second such area was education reform, as Mayor Bloomberg, like many business leaders in the city, was concerned that the city's educational system was failing to prepare students for "the demands of the 21st century, knowledge-based economy" (2004b).

14. To be clear, what I mean by *political* here is not what the term is usually taken to mean in popular and media discourse: that is, as having to do with the struggles of partisans (i.e., party-affiliated politicians and/or activists) to gain electoral advantage or advantage within the state apparatus. What I take the term to denote is a broader form of struggle among a variety of social, economic, and political groupings over wealth, power, and meaning, a struggle that often involves the state apparatus but is by no means limited to it.

15. Here, I am using this much-debated term in the relatively straightforward sense that Giovanni Arrighi uses it: as opposed to sheer domination, "hegemony is the *additional* power that accrues to a dominant group by virtue of its capacity to *lead* society in a direction that not only serves the dominant group's interests but is also perceived by subordinate groups as serving a more general interest" (2007, 149).

CHAPTER 1. THE NEOLIBERALIZATION OF GOVERNANCE IN NEW YORK CITY

1. My own writing has heretofore followed this pattern (2003, 2004, 2006b).

2. For works that document both the consistencies and shifts in the makeup and power of this alliance over time, see Angotti 2008, 38–46; Fainstein 2001a; Fitch 1993; and Shachtman 2000.

3. The RPA is a nonprofit regional planning group founded in 1922.

4. Along with Fitch, see Angotti 2008, 42–44; Schuerman 2007; and Schwartz 1993, 296.

5. For details of the fiscal crisis period, see Alcaly and Mermelstein 1977; Bailey 1984; Freeman 2000, 256–290; Lichten 1986; Moody 2007, 9–61; Shefter 1992; Sites 2003, 35–42; and Tabb 1982.

6. For details of this agenda and its development, see Freeman 2000, 256–287; Lichten 1986, 127–148; Shefter 1992, 124–148; and Tabb 1982, 21–35.

7. Examples include investment bankers Peter Solomon and Barry Sullivan, who served as a deputy mayors for economic development under mayors Koch and Dinkins, respectively; Charles Millard, a former managing director of Lehman Brothers who served as the head of the EDC under Mayor Giuliani; and Norman Steisel, Dinkins's first deputy mayor, charged with daily administration of the city's budget and operations.

8. To stretch the psychoanalytic metaphor, austerity's superego took the form of the high-minded and moralizing calls for "sharing the pain" and for various interests to cooperate in order to "save the city" (Brash 2003; Tabb 1982, 29).

9. For examples of cultural resistance, see Dickinson 2008; Greenberg 2003; Mele 2000; and Smith 1993. For examples of neighborhood-level activism, see Chesluk 2008, 134–187; Gregory 1998; and Sites 2003, 101–135. For ethnic organization, see Dávila 2004; Sanjek 1998; and Sze 2006. For new forms of unionism, see Moody 2007, 243–283.

10. The EDC was known as the Public Development Corporation until 1991.

11. ULURP was established in the mid-1970s to enhance community participation in planning in the wake of the depredations of Robert Moses and federal urban renewal programs. ULURP gave local community planning boards (called "community boards") and borough presidents the right to make nonbinding recommendations and decisions on particular land use changes. The City Planning Commission (the majority of whose members were appointed by the mayor) was given a binding vote on such projects, which would be ultimately subject to be approved or rejected by the city council.

12. As we will see, many of the individuals involved in the development of the 1969 comprehensive plan under Mayor Lindsay would reappear in the various planning efforts that emerged in the late 1990s, as momentum built among members of the city's elite for a more proactive and comprehensive approach to economic and urban development.

13. For a sampling of analyses of gentrification in post–fiscal crisis New York City, see Abu-Lughod 1994; Dávila 2004; Lees 2003; Mele 2000; Prince 2003; Smith 1996; Smith and Williams 1986; and Zukin 1989.

14. Details of Doctoroff's biography are drawn from a number of sources, including Bennett 2005; Golson 2004; Horowitz 2004; Lieber 2004a, 2004b; Robbins and McIntyre 2004; and Robbins 2005a.

15. NYC2012 was originally called "NYC2008," as its original intent was to bring the 2008 Olympic Games to New York. The name was changed in 1997 after the city's bid was deferred for four years, to 2012. For the sake of clarity, I will refer to the organization as NYC2012.

CHAPTER 2. ELECTING THE CEO MAYOR

1. While this work focuses on the class aspects of the charismatic CEO, this figure is defined by other social identities as well. Despite the existence of female CEOs, the overwhelming majority of *celebrity* CEOs have been and are male (Capelli and Hamori 2005); one observer writes that the gateway qualification for those aspiring to enter such rarified ranks is to "be born a man" (Rothkopf 2008, 289). Moreover, CEOs and corporate activity have generally been described and understood in hypermasculine terms, and displays of masculinity have been an important part of the self-presentation and bonding of corporate executives (Collinson and Hearn 1996; Guthey 2001; Schoenberger 2001). In addition, despite the avowals of corporate multiculturalism, corporate elites are still overwhelmingly white (Frederickson 2003, 148). Indeed, the strong belief in meritocracy so prevalent among the corporate elites can obscure the continuing reality of racial inequality and its function in the workings of capitalism (Gordon 1995, 15–17; Mullings 2005, 679). Finally, according to Rakesh Khurana (2002, 68), the "cult of the CEO" is "distinctly American." Thus, the focus here is on the United States.

2. While I first applied Max Weber's notion of charisma to contemporary CEOs in early versions of this work independently of Khurana, I have used his work to flesh out my thoughts on the subject.

3. See Bates 2005; Benton 1996, 2001; and the Web site www.ceomom.com.

4. Anna Tsing has noted the importance of the dual sense of performance to "investment-oriented entrepreneurship" (2000, 118).

5. In his biography, Michael Bloomberg scolds "those decrying the disparity between the haves and the have-nots, and those in government desirous of redistributing wealth" to "take note" of the fact that "it is from the rich . . . that philanthropic organizations get a disproportionate percentage of their funding" (Bloomberg and Winkler 2001, 234).

6. Philanthropy and class have long had a tight relationship, of course. Many of the functions of CEO philanthropy described here — establishing networks, preempting state action, and co-opting or shaping priorities of recipient institutions — are not new (Silver 2007, 537). However, the deepening inequalities that were a result of neoliberalization as well as the emergence of a new global elite both spurred and altered philanthropic activity (Sawaya 2008; Sklair 2001, 149–197).

7. Note that this is the publicly available version of Bloomberg's biography: I am more concerned with its cultural function than with its literal truth.

8. These biographical details are drawn from Bloomberg and Winkler 2001; Bumiller 2001a; BusinessWeek 2001; Kolbert 2001; Loomis 2007; Lowry 2001a, 2001b, Lowry 2007; Smith 2005; and Wolff 2001a, 2001b.

9. Bloomberg won 47 percent of the Latino vote, just behind Green's 49 percent. Though Green won 71 percent of the black vote, this was well below the 90 percent level Democrats had enjoyed in recent elections (Cooper and Barbanel 2001).

10. This seems especially likely given the fact that the city's first minority mayor, African American David Dinkins (1990–1993), was widely condemned as "incompetent," as had been white liberal John Lindsay, whose 1966–1973 mayoralty rested on an alliance between African Americans and liberal whites (Cannato 2001). Scholars have noted the tendency for whites to blame black mayors for the ill effects of structural changes as well as to hold them to unrealistically high standards that, when not met, lead to charges of incompetence (Rich 2007, 17–18; Thompson 2005, 14).

CHAPTER 3. RUNNING GOVERNMENT LIKE A BUSINESS

1. It is also related to the gendering of this identity (Guthey 2001; Schoenberger 2001).

2. Private aviation — both riding in and flying private planes — seems to have a prominent place in the self-image of many members of the TCC (Rothkopf 2008, 24–28).

3. The contrast with the previous administration was stark: during the early days of the Giuliani administration, political supporters of the new mayor called in favors and flooded city hall with resumes, where they were reviewed by twenty-three-year-old Tony Carbonetti, a former campaign staffer and son of a Giuliani childhood acquaintance. "Of course we are hiring supporters," Giuliani said at the time, "who else would we appoint" (Kirtzman 2001, 99)?

4. The Department of Education, which as mentioned above, was headed by former Bertelsmann corporate counsel Joel Klein, was also a site of the implementation of such practices (Hemphill 2009, 194).

CHAPTER 4. THE LUXURY CITY

1. There is a large literature on place marketing and boosterism in urban studies. For some empirical works, see Gold and Ward 1994; Kearns and Philo 1993; Short 1999; Short and Kim 1998; and Ward 1998a, 1998b. For key theoretical discussions of the role of place marketing in capitalist urbanization, see Harvey 1989, 150; and Logan and Molotch 1987, 62–63.

2. Other documented examples, with their own limitations, include New Orleans (Gotham 2007b), Atlanta (Rutheiser 1996), and Las Vegas (Hannigan 1998).

3. During the period from 1969 to 2000, the number of jobs in the city had actually declined, even as it rose in the metropolitan region, New York State, and the country as a whole. The decline in the city's share of the region's and the nation's high-paying jobs

in the FIRE and business services sectors was especially pronounced. Despite this, the city's economy had grown more dependent on these sectors as a result of the precipitous decline in manufacturing and wholesale trade jobs in the city (Bowles and Kotkin 2003).

4. The study was never publicly released. It was made available to a reporter for the *Economist*, who used it to generate a survey article on New York City in the February 19, 2005 issue of that magazine. This description of the study and its conclusions is based on interviews with economic development experts, their public statements on the subject, and newspaper reports. See Economist 2005a, 2005b, 2005c; and Temple-Raston 2004b.

5. Much to the consternation of progressive economic development advocates, manufacturing and light industry were left off this list until 2005, when a much-delayed manufacturing strategy was released. However, its neglect of the key issue of land use rendered it largely useless.

6. Sectoral development had at times been discussed in the context of reducing economic inequality in the city by cultivating the growth of industries that, unlike finance and business services, had a history of unionization, provided opportunities to workers with a broader array of education and skill levels, and/or provided opportunities for career advancement (Fiscal Policy Institute 2002b; Zandniapour and Conway 2001). Whether or not sectoral development was used as a steadying fiscal and economic influence and a source of new jobs and city revenues or as a means to mitigate economic inequality and provide economic opportunities to a broader portion of the city's population was very much dependent on which industries were targeted. It was quite possible to push to diversify the city's economy without addressing issues of economic inequality or increased opportunity if the career and compensation structures of targeted industries were not taken into account. And in fact, this is generally how the Bloomberg administration proceeded, targeting industries based on the city's "value proposition" rather than on the contributions they might make to reducing inequality or enhancing economic opportunity.

7. In Bloomberg's first term in office, the city hosted the 2004 Republican National Convention as well as *The Gates*, a massive art installation in Central Park by the artists Christo and Jeanne-Claude.

8. City Comptroller William Thompson sued the administration over the Snapple deal, arguing that it had been improperly reviewed. A judge later found that there had been irregularities, but refused to nullify the deal. More to the point, the deal, which the administration initially said would bring some $166 million into city coffers over five years, generated significantly less money than had been projected. This was to some degree the result of a small but noteworthy instance of new governmental strategies generating new forms of conflict: students in city schools, angry that their choices were being limited to one, high-cost, sugary beverage, brought their preferred beverages to schools, which in turn resulted in some schools banning the possession of outside beverages (Andreatta 2004; Lucadamo 2004; Michaud 2004; Saltonshall 2004).

9. Most of the city's subsidies were nondiscretionary, granted automatically to any company meeting certain criteria. Most discretionary deals were with small private firms and nonprofits and did not usually rise in dollar amounts above the tens of thousands, and thus they were not particularly controversial. It was the discretionary subsidies involving many millions of dollars made to large, successful companies that drew the most criticism and were the most difficult to justify. The smaller subsidy deals continued under the Bloomberg administration and were largely unaffected by the shifts in policy described here, which generally affected the large financial and media firms that had received the lion's share of the dollar benefits from past retention deals.

10. The city made some concessions to Bear Stearns in order to avoid alienating a major New York City employer, but they were minor and did not involve the granting of any new tax incentives.

11. A number of additional caveats should be noted here. First, the relatively loose and cheap commercial real estate market in the city during 2002 and 2003 reduced cost pressures and lowered the number of companies demanding subsidies. Second, the availability of federal development assistance after the terrorist attacks of September 11, 2001 also reduced the demand for city-funded corporate retention deals. Much of this assistance was used in ways only tenuously related to post-9/11 reconstruction. See Good Jobs New York 2004.

12. Bloomberg again pushed to raise taxes as a part of dealing with the fallout from the 2008 financial crisis, again invoking the lessons of the 1970s in doing so (Chen 2008)

13. For a similar, if unelaborated, version of this argument see Peck 2005, 765.

14. Bloomberg LP was located in Midtown, as was the company's new headquarters building, which was under construction when Bloomberg became mayor. In addition, Daniel Doctoroff had invested in Midtown and far west side real estate.

15. The administration would be remarkably successful in implementing much of its development agenda. During Mayor Bloomberg's first term, Deputy Mayor Doctoroff's reorganized economic and urban development apparatus successfully pushed a series of major rezonings and development projects through the approval process, including plans for downtown Brooklyn, Williamsburg/Greenpoint, West Chelsea, Park Slope, Harlem, and Long Island City, as well as plans for the downzoning of a number of upscale residential neighborhoods throughout the five boroughs. Significant progress was also made on plans for the East River waterfront in Lower Manhattan, for the completion of a greenway circumnavigating the Manhattan waterfront, for the redevelopment of Flushing, and for the Fresh Kills Park in Staten Island. In all these endeavors, coordination between the EDC, charged with developing the economic development aspects of these plans, and the DCP, charged with developing land use, urban design, and physical plans for these areas, proved essential.

16. For more on this aspect of the politics of branding, see Gotham 2007a, 142–196; and Greenberg 2008, 12.

CHAPTER 5. THE BLOOMBERG WAY

1. As the discussion of internal corporate politics in chapter 4 indicates, this radically understates the actual internal complexity of corporations, the multiplicity of interests within them, and the various claims made on their income and assets. But the analogizing of business and urban governance depends on this oversimplification.

2. Despite their touting of "rewarding and fulfilling" jobs, administration officials did little to ensure the quality of the jobs brought into the city, evidently assuming that any job was a good job (Jonas 2009).

3. Peterson defines the "city, taken as a whole" in this way: "Cities consist of a set of social interactions structured by their location in a particular territorial space. . . . Although social roles performed within cities are numerous and conflicting, all are structured by the fact that they take place in a specific spatial location that falls within the jurisdiction of some local government" (1981, 20–21).

4. The faith in scalar providence that flows from the notion that the city is a bounded entity has a second implication: that the benefits of efforts to make the city competitive will not just flow to all residents but, to a significant degree, *only* to residents. This assumption that benefits and costs can be, for the most part, internalized is what makes the application of neoclassical economic principles to urban governance possible, yet as Harvey (2001, 353–354) notes, the scale of the benefits of particular urban interventions tend to often overflow jurisdictional bounds.

5. For two excellent overviews of critical state theory, see Barrow 1993 and Sharma and Gupta 2006.

6. Critical state theory's central subject has been the vexing relationship between capital and the state. The Bloomberg administration essentially cut through this Gordian knot: now capital was the state, or at least had occupied much of the upper ranks of the local state. To put it glibly, things get quite a bit simpler when it is not that the "executive of the modern State is but a committee for managing the common affairs of the whole bourgeoisie" (Marx and Engels 1994, 161), but rather that the highest levels of the modern state actually consist of a committee of bourgeois executives.

CHAPTER 6. FAR WEST SIDE STORIES

1. A "downzoning" is a zoning change that reduces or limits the amount of space that can be built on a particular plot of land; an "upzoning" increases this amount.

2. For more on the development of Midtown and the west side, see Chesluk 2008; Fainstein, Fainstein, and Schwartz 1989; Fainstein 2001a; Reichl 1999; Sagalyn 2001; and Schwartz 1993.

3. See City of New York 1969; Fitch 1993; Johnson 1996, 265–266; and Regional Plan Association 1969.

4. The early 1970s also saw the beginning of the battle over Westway, the proposed

replacement for the West Side Highway, which eventually resulted in the death of the project at the hands of environmental regulations and federal litigation in the late 1980s.

5. Alexander Garvin served as NYC2012's chief planner and Jay Kriegel its executive director. Alexander Cooper and Jacquelin Robertson's firm would create the first urban design plan of the Hudson Yards plan.

6. The term "Hudson Yards" is confusingly used both to refer to these rail yards *and* the entire area west of Eighth Avenue between Twenty-eighth and Forty-second streets. I use the phrase "Hudson Yards" to refer to this larger area, and the term "Hudson rail yards" to refer to the rail yards themselves.

7. The USOC is the governing body for all Olympic-related activities in the United States, and is one of the 205 member organizations of the IOC, which coordinates the bidding for and conduct of the various Olympic Games. In picking host countries for the games, the IOC tends to cycle through continents in a fairly consistent and predictable way. Given that Atlanta had the summer games in 1996 and Salt Lake City had been awarded the winter games for 2002, it seemed unlikely that IOC would choose a U.S. city for the games in 2008.

8. See Sanders 2002 and 2004 on this convention center building boom.

9. For a listing of the commission's members, see Group of 35 2001.

10. Such projects traditionally have been funded by government bonds issued after the legislative approval of a state and/or city capital budget. The assumption on the part of government officials and lenders is that these projects will enhance the *overall* ability of the government to secure tax revenues, out of which project costs and/or bond repayments are paid. However, with the decline of federal urban aid, often used in the past for such capital improvements, and the overall pressures on local government's budgets, financing schemes that directly tie a project's funding (usually in the form of project-specific bonds) to the revenues it is expected to generate have become more widespread (Weber 2002, 533–536).

11. These efforts were largely unsuccessful, as Pataki's advisors, though indicating that he would not publicly oppose a west side stadium, doubted its political feasibility. Shortly after becoming deputy mayor under Mayor Bloomberg, Doctoroff would successfully repair the relationship between city hall and the governor. Key to this was an implicit but widely recognized deal that gave Pataki de facto control over the redevelopment of the World Trade Center site and the Bloomberg administration de facto control over the redevelopment of the far west side (Steinhauer 2004). Ultimately, Pataki would become an active and public supporter of the Hudson Yards plan.

12. This strategy — generating money through the creation of development rights in one spot and their transfer to another spot — had previously been used in a recent rezoning scheme for nearby Eighth Avenue (Chesluk 2008, 165–187).

13. TIF is a specific kind of self-financing mechanism that permits the additional tax revenue generated by a spatially delimited development to be dedicated to paying back

the bonds floated to make infrastructure improvements that make development possible. See New York City Independent Budget Office 2002; and Weber 2002, 533–536.

14. Details of the Hudson Yards Coalition's meetings are drawn from Bagli 2001.

CHAPTER 7. WHY THE RPA MATTERED

1. Under New York City's zoning resolution, the level of permissible density is governed by the application of a Floor Area Ratio, which consists of the ratio of the total square footage of development on a site to the site's area.

2. One knotty question concerning this financing scheme not addressed in the Document was that of ownership. The MTA owned the entirety of the rail yards, and the right to develop them, and thus had a right to proceeds from any transfer of development rights. Nothing required the MTA to fund the extension of the Number 7 Subway line, and in fact the MTA, while generally cooperative, had not identified the Number 7 line as a high priority. The only way to get around this problem would be for the city to acquire the development rights for the eastern rail yards, as NYC2012's Hudson Yards plan had proposed, and assume responsibility for funding the subway extension. But the likelihood of this happening, as of early 2003, was still unclear.

3. For her part, Jane Jacobs condemned the stadium as "an awful way to use valuable land in Manhattan" (Doig 2005).

4. Cablevision pushed the Jacobs angle hardest, and most cynically. It was put together by Alex Krieger, a Harvard planner, architect, and self-described disciple of Jacobs, and was dubbed "Hudson Gardens" in an effort to evoke Ebenezer Howard's Garden City movement. Krieger's presentations of the plan continued this reference to planning history, as they were sprinkled with references to planning icons like Jacobs and Lewis Mumford and with the language of human-scale urbanism. In fact, the plan was mixed use in the same superficial way as the Hudson Yards plan, and the rows of towers surrounding a wedge of green space it proposed evoked no one more than Le Corbusier, whose "towers in the park" urbanism was one of the favorite targets of the Jacobs-led backlash against modernist planning.

5. The Newman plan included a stadium as an option but not a necessity.

CHAPTER 8. THE LOGIC OF INVESTMENT

1. All dollar amounts used here are in constant 2003 dollars. PILOTs are generally used when private developers are permitted to build on publicly owned land, which is exempt from property taxes.

2. Ultimately, the mayor would accede to a city council review of how PILOTs were used as part of a deal over the 2006 budget.

3. Scholarly analyses of these sorts of economic impact studies have concluded that they are "bogus" (Noll and Zimbalist 1997, 84–85) and "remarkabl[y] divorce[d] from reality" (Sanders 2002, 209).

4. In part, this was the result of the tacit but generally acknowledged deal between the mayor and Governor Pataki, which left the far west side to the mayor and Lower Manhattan to the governor (Steinhauer 2004).

5. The evidence for this was rather thin. While some firms, like Bank of America, refused to consider a downtown location, others, like Goldman Sachs, whose protracted search for new space bounced back and forth between Midtown and downtown, seemed perfectly willing to consider both locations.

CHAPTER 9. THE BLOOMBERG WAY AND ITS OTHERS

1. Olympic boosters liked to talk about the enviable "legacy" that the games would leave the city in the form of new development; one rather less desirable legacy was the obligation to subsidize this stadium, as in their haste to come up with a feasible alternative stadium site, Bloomberg administration officials committed to a plan to subsidize a new Mets stadium whether or not the Olympics came to New York City.

2. More important was the fact that North America had hosted a number of other recent Olympic Games, and was scheduled to do so in the near future. The international unpopularity of President George W. Bush likely played a role as well.

CONCLUSION

1. See Colford and Singleton 2005; Lueck 2005; Moody 2007, 162–164; and Roberts and Rutenberg 2005.

2. See Engquist and Michaud 2005; Roberts 2005; and Rutenberg 2005.

3. The administration also strove to "reincentivize" educational achievement by developing programs to pay students who did well on tests and by developing a marketing plan to "rebrand" education as "cool" by giving (mostly minority and poor) students in selected schools cellular phones that could be used as a conduit for text messages or calls celebrating academic success from celebrities like rapper Jay-Z or basketball star Lebron James. "Hustling 101" was one of the names considered for this program, which was eventually dubbed "Million" and implemented in early 2008 (Medina 2007, 2008).

4. Moreover, as Wayne Barrett has detailed, a number of other public and media figures who supported the extension had business ties to Bloomberg LP and Bloomberg's investment funds, which might have made them hesitant to resist the drive for a third term (2008). While the mayor had no day-to-day control over Bloomberg LP or his investments, they were in loyal hands: Daniel Doctoroff had become Bloomberg LP's president in early 2008 after leaving government, and Bloomberg's chief investment advisor was none other than Steven Rattner.

5. For these effects of the luxury city strategy, see Bowles et al. 2009; Moody 2007, 243–283; and Steinhauer 2006.

REFERENCES

Aaker, D. A. 2002. Foreword to *Brand Asset Management: Driving Profitable Growth through Your Brands*, ed. S. Davis. San Francisco: Jossey-Bass.

Aaker, D. A., and E. Joachimsthaler. 2000. *Brand Leadership*. New York: Free Press.

Abrams, P. 2006. Notes on the Difficulty of Studying the State. In *The Anthropology of the State: A Reader*, ed. A. Sharma and A. Gupta, 112–130. Malden, Mass.: Blackwell.

Abu-Lughod, J., ed. 1994. *From Urban Village to East Village: The Battle for New York's Lower East Side*. Cambridge, Mass.: Blackwell.

Adams, J., and D. Gorton. 2006. Confederate Lane: Class, Race, and Ethnicity in the Mississippi Delta. *American Ethnologist* 33:288–309.

Alcaly, R. E., and D. Mermelstein. 1977. *The Fiscal Crisis of American Cities: Essays on the Political Economy of Urban America with Special Reference to New York*. New York: Vintage Books.

Alper, A. 2002a. Testimony. Hearing on Corporate Subsidies, Committee on Economic Development, New York City Council. New York. June 11.

———. 2002b. Testimony. Hearing on Proposed Fiscal Year 2003 Economic Development Budget, Committee on Economic Development, New York City Council. New York. March 12.

———. 2003a. Testimony. Hearing on Proposed Fiscal Year 2004 Economic Development Budget, Committee on Finance and Committee on Economic Development, New York City Council. New York. May 11.

———. 2003b. Testimony. Hearing on Proposed Fiscal Year 2004 Economic Development Budget, Committee on Economic Development, New York City Council. New York. March 7.

———. 2004. Testimony. Hearing on Proposed Fiscal Year 2005 Economic Development Budget, Committee on Economic Development, New York City Council. New York. March 8.

———. 2007. Interview with author. New York. July 26.

Alschuler, J. 2004. *Urban Stadia: Pittsburgh, San Diego, Cleveland*. New York: Hamilton, Rabinovitz, and Alschuler.

Ambinder, M. 2008. Obama: Bloomberg Is "Extraordinary." *The Atlantic*. http://marcambinder.theatlantic.com/archives/2008/03/obama_bloomberg_is_extraordina.php. (accessed March 29, 2009).

Andersen, M. L., and P. Hill Collins, eds. 2007. *Race, Class, and Gender: An Anthology.* Belmont, Calif.: Thomson/Wadsworth.

Anderson, K. 2005. Too Big Not to Fail. *New York Magazine.* April 25.

Anderson, R. 2004a. Testimony. Public Hearing on the Hudson Yards Rezoning Plan and Draft Generic Environmental Impact Statement. New York. September 23.

——. 2004b. West Side Stadium: Good Regional Planning. *New York Post.* July 30.

Andranovich, G., M. J. Burbank, and C. H. Heying. 2001. Olympic Cities: Lessons Learned from Mega-Events Politics. *Journal of Urban Affairs* 23:113–131.

Andreatta, D. 2004. School Drink Stink. *New York Post.* December 24.

Angotti, T. 1997. New York City's "197-A" Community Planning Experience: Power to the People or Less Work for Planners. *Planning Practice and Research* 12:70.

——. 2008. *New York for Sale: Community Planning Confronts Global Real Estate.* Cambridge, Mass.: MIT Press.

Applebome, P. 1996. So, You Want to Hold an Olympics. *New York Times.* August 4.

Arnstein, S. 1969. A Ladder of Public Participation. *Journal of American Institute of Planners* 35:216–224.

Aronowitz, S. 1979. The Professional-Managerial Class or Middle Strata. In *Between Labor and Capital,* ed. P. Walker. Boston: South End Press.

Arrighi, G. 2007. *Adam Smith in Beijing: Lineages of the Twenty-First Century.* New York: Verso.

Ashworth, G. J., and H. Voogt. 1994. Marketing and Place Promotion. In *Place Promotion: The Use of Publicity and Marketing to Sell Towns and Regions,* ed. J. R. Gold and S. V. Ward, 39–52. New York: Wiley.

Avlon, J. P. 2004. Committing to Hudson Yards. *New York Sun.* February 12.

Bagli, C. 2000. New York Olympic Stadium Plan Masks Shaky Political Coalition. *New York Times.* October 2.

——. 2001. Support for Development, but Maybe Not a Stadium. *New York Times.* May 14.

——. 2002. Big Real Estate Groups Mobilizing against Proposed Jump in Property Taxes. *New York Times.* November 21.

——. 2004a. Albany Votes to Expand Javits Center. *New York Times.* December 8.

——. 2004b. City Sees Gain of $12 Billion from Landing 2012 Olympics. *New York Times.* January 17.

——. 2004c. Plan for Financing West Side Development Is Called "Extremely Risky." *New York Times.* October 21.

——. 2004d. Sweating over Gold. *New York Times.* November 21.

——. 2005a. Jets Unveil a Redesign for a Less Imposing Football Stadium. *New York Times.* February 3.

——. 2005b. Suddenly, Developers Yearn for the Gritty Far West Side. *New York Times.* February 14.

Bagli, C., and M. Cooper. 2005. Olympic Bid Hurt as New York Fails in West Side Stadium Quest. *New York Times.* June 7.

Bailey, R. W. 1984. *The Crisis Regime: The MAC, the EFCB and the Political Impact of the New York City Financial Crisis*. Albany: State University of New York Press.

Barbaro, M. 2008. Titans Seek New York Mayor in Bloomberg's Mold. *New York Times*. July 7.

———. 2009a. How Bloomberg Knows Who's Not a Killer. *New York Times*. April 14.

———. 2009b. Top Democratic Talent Agonizes, Then Goes to Work for Bloomberg. *New York Times*. March 7.

Barbaro, M., and D. W. Chen. 2008a. Bloomberg Enlists His Charities in Bid to Stay. *New York Times*. October 18.

———. 2008b. Term Limits Get Notice in Crisis. *New York Times*. September 17.

Barger, D., et al. 2008. An Open Letter. *New York Daily News*. October 2.

Barnett, C. 2005. The Consolations Of "Neoliberalism." *Geoforum* 36:7–12.

Barrett, W. 2008. The Transformation of Mike Bloomberg. *Village Voice*. November 19.

Barron, C. 2005. Remarks on Hudson Yards Plan. Stated Council Meeting, New York City Council. New York. January 19.

Barrow, C. W. 1993. *Critical Theories of the State: Marxist, Neo-Marxist, Post Marxist*. Madison: University of Wisconsin Press.

Bates, S. 2005. *Speak Like a CEO: Secrets for Commanding Attention and Getting Results*. New York: McGraw-Hill.

Beauregard, R. A. 2003. *Voices of Decline: The Postwar Fate of U.S. Cities*. New York: Routledge.

Beaverstock, J. V. 2002. Transnational Elites in Global Cities: British Expatriates in Singapore's Financial District. *Geoforum* 33:525–538.

———. 2005. Transnational Elites in the City: British Highly-Skilled Inter-Company Transferees in New York City's Financial District. *Journal of Ethnic and Migration Studies* 31:245–268.

Bell, D. 1980. The New Class: A Muddled Concept. In *Winding Passage: Essays and Sociological Journeys*, 144–164. Cambridge, Mass.: ABT Press.

Bender, T. 2002. *The Unfinished City: New York and the Metropolitan Idea*. New York: New Press.

Bennett, C. 2005. Who Is Dan Doctoroff? The Man Behind NYC's Bid for the 2012 Olympics. *amNewYork*. February 23.

Benton, D. A. 1996. *How to Think Like a CEO: The 22 Vital Traits You Need to Be the Person at the Top*. New York: Warner Books.

———. 2001. *How to Act Like a CEO: 10 Rules for Getting to the Top and Staying There*. New York: McGraw-Hill.

Berman, R. 2007. McCain Touts Bloomberg on Education. *New York Sun*. December 13.

Bloomberg, M. 2002a. Speech to the Partnership for New York City. New York. April 10.

———. 2002b. Press Conference. New York. January 15.

———. 2002c. State of the City Address. New York. January 30.

———. 2003a. Investing in New York: The City of Opportunity. Speech to the Association for a Better New York. New York. October 21.

———. 2003b. State of the City Address. New York. January 23.

———. 2004. State of the City Address. New York. January 8.

Bloomberg, M., and J. Gambling. 2004. *Live from City Hall with Mayor Mike and John Gambling.* WABC. March 26. http://www.nyc.gov:80/html/om/html/2004a/abcrs032604.asx. (accessed June 18, 2005).

———. 2005. *Live from City Hall with Mayor Mike and John Gambling.* WABC. April 15. http://www.nyc.gov/html/om/html/2010a/media/04-16-10-worrs.asx. (accessed June 18, 2005).

Bloomberg, M., and M. Winkler. 2001. *Bloomberg by Bloomberg.* New York: John Wiley and Sons.

Boellstorff, T. 2007. Queer Studies in the House of Anthropology. *Annual Review of Anthropology* 36:17–35.

Boggs, C. 2000. *The End of Politics.* New York: Guilford Press.

Bondi, L. 2005. Working the Spaces of Neoliberal Subjectivity: Psychotherapeutic Technologies, Professionalisation and Counseling. *Antipode* 37:497–515.

Bondi, L., and N. Laurie. 2005. Introduction: Working the Spaces of Neoliberalism: Activism, Professionalisation and Incorporation. *Antipode* 37:393–401.

Boschken, H. L. 2003. Global Cities, Systemic Power, and Upper-Middle-Class Influence. *Urban Affairs Review* 38:808–830.

Boschken, H. L., and S. B. Hoagland. 1998. The Upper-Middle-Class Genre and Its Influence on Policy Outcomes. *Social Science Quarterly* 79:412–431.

Bousquet, M. 2008. *How the University Works: Higher Education and the Low-Wage Nation.* New York: New York University Press.

Bowles, J., and J. Kotkin. 2003. *Engine Failure.* New York: Center for an Urban Future.

Bowles, J., J. Kotkin, and D. Giles. 2009. *Reviving the City of Aspiration: A Study of the Challenges Facing New York City's Middle Classes.* New York: Center for an Urban Future.

Box, R. C. B. 1999. Running Government Like a Business: Implications for Public Administration Theory and Practice. *American Review of Public Administration* 29:19–43.

Boyd, M. 2005. The Downside of Racial Uplift: The Meaning of Gentrification in an African American Neighborhood. *City and Society* 17:265–288.

Boyer, M. C. 2002. Meditation on a Wounded Skyline and Its Stratigraphies of Pain. In *After the World Trade Center: Rethinking New York City*, ed. M. Sorkin and S. Zukin, 109–120. New York City: Routledge.

Brash, J. 2003. Invoking Fiscal Crisis: Moral Discourse and Politics in New York City. *Social Text* 76:59–84.

———. 2004. The Work of 9/11: Myth, History and the Contradictions of the Post-Fiscal Crisis Consensus. *Critique of Anthropology* 24:75–99.

———. 2006a. Anthropologies of Urbanization: New Spatial Politics and Imaginaries.

Urban Anthropology and Studies of Cultural Systems and World Economic Development 35:341–354.

——— . 2006b. Re-Scaling Patriotism: Competition and Urban Identity in Michael Bloomberg's New York. *Urban Anthropology and Studies of Cultural Systems and World Economic Development* 35:387–423.

Brecher, C., and R. Horton. 1991. The Public Sector. In *Dual City: Restructuring New York*, ed. J. H. Mollenkopf and M. Castells, 103–128. New York: Russell Sage Foundation.

Brenner, N. 1997. State Territorial Restructuring and the Production of Spatial Scale: Urban and Regional Planning in the Federal Republic of Germany, 1960–1990. *Political Geography* 16:273–306.

——— . 1999. Beyond State Centrism? Space, Territoriality, and Geographical Scale in Globalization Studies. *Theory and Society* 28:39–78.

——— . 2001. The Limits to Scale? Methodological Reflections on Scalar Structuration. *Progress in Human Geography* 25:591–614.

Brenner, N., et al. 2003. State Space in Question. In *State/Space: A Reader*, ed. N. Brenner et al., 1–26. Malden, Mass.: Blackwell.

Brenner, N., and N. Theodore. 2002. Cities and the Geographies Of "Actually Existing Neoliberalism." *Antipode* 34:349–379.

——— . 2005. Neoliberalism and the Urban Condition. *Cities* 9:101–107.

Brint, S. 1992. Upper Professionals: A High Command of Commerce, Culture, and Civic Regulation. In *Dual City: Restructuring New York*, ed. J. Mollenkopf and M. Castells, 155–176. New York: Russell Sage Foundation.

——— . 1994. *In an Age of Experts: The Changing Role of Professionals in Politics and Public Life*. Princeton, N.J.: Princeton University Press.

Brodkin, K. 2000. Global Capitalism: What's Race Got to Do with It? *American Ethnologist* 27:237–256.

Bruce-Biggs, B. 1979. *The New Class?* New Brunswick, N.J.: Transaction Books.

Bruder, J. 2005. The Plutocrats of Democrats Go Bloomberg. *New York Observer*. October 10.

Brunzema, M. 2004. Interview with author. New York. August 23.

Bumiller, E. 2001a. Bloomberg Cites Polygraph in a Denial of Harassment. *New York Times*. March 3.

——— . 2001b. With Attention Money Can Buy, Bloomberg Kicks Off Campaign. *New York Times*. June 7.

Burbank, M. J., G. Andranovich, and C. H. Heying. 2001. *Olympic Dreams: The Impact of Mega-Events on Local Politics*. Boulder, Colo.: Lynne Rienner.

Burden, A. 2004. Reshaping New York: Major Land Use Developments in NYC. Presentation to the Center for New York City Law, New York Law School. New York. April 23.

Burrows, E. G., and M. Wallace. 1999. *Gotham: A History of New York City to 1898*. New York: Oxford University Press.

BusinessWeek. 2001. What Makes Mike Run: A Short History of the Man and His Company. April 23.

Butler, T. 1997. *Gentrification and the Middle Classes.* Ashford: Ashgate.

Calthorpe, P. 1993. *The Next American Metropolis: Ecology, Community, and the American Dream.* New York: Princeton Architectural Press.

Cannato, V. 2001. *The Ungovernable City: John Lindsay and His Struggle to Save New York.* New York: Basic Books.

Cantor, I. 2004. Remarks. New York City Planning Commission Meeting. New York. November 23.

Capelli, P., and M. Hamori. 2005. The New Road to the Top. *Harvard Business Review* 83:25–32.

Cardwell, D. 2003. Mayor Says New York Is Worth the Cost. *New York Times.* January 8.

———. 2005. Ferrer Camp Finds City's Deep Pockets Sewed Up. *New York Times.* October 11.

———. 2006. To Cut Poverty, Panel Advises a Narrow Focus. *New York Times.* August 26.

———. 2007. New York City to Reward Poor for Doing Right Thing. *New York Times.* March 30.

———. 2008. As Term Wanes, Bloomberg's Temper Boils Up. *New York Times.* May 20.

Cardwell, D., and J. C. McGinty. 2007. Money Rubs Off for City Aides Close to Mayor. *New York Times.* December 14.

Carlson, M. A. 1996. *Performance: A Critical Introduction.* New York: Routledge.

Caro, R. A. 1975. *The Power Broker: Robert Moses and the Fall of New York.* New York: Vintage Books.

Cassidy, J. 2005. Bloomberg's Game. *New Yorker.* April 4.

Castells, M. 1996. *The Rise of the Network Society.* Malden, Mass.: Blackwell.

Chakrabarti, V. 2004a. Presentation of the Hudson Yards Plan. Meeting of Land Use Committee, Manhattan Community Board Four. New York. July 13.

———. 2004b. Speech. Envisioning the West Side. New York. August 5.

Chen, D., and M. Barbaro. 2008. Passions High on Term Limits in City Council. *New York Times.* October 17.

Chen, D. W. 2008. Council Approves 7% Property Tax Increase. *New York Times.* December 19.

Chesluk, B. 2008. *Money Jungle: Imagining the New Times Square.* New Brunswick, N.J.: Rutgers University Press.

Cinar, A., and T. Bender. 2007. Introduction: The City: Experience, Imagination, and Place. In *Urban Imaginaries: Locating the Modern City,* ed. A. Cinar and T. Bender, xi–xxvi. Minneapolis: University of Minnesota Press.

City of New York. 1969. *Plan for New York City, 1969: A Proposal.* Cambridge, Mass.: MIT Press.

———. 2002a. Mayor Michael R. Bloomberg Announces Six Appointments. Press Release. New York. January 15.

———. 2002b. *The Mayor's Management Report, Fiscal 2002: Executive Summary*. New York: Mayor's Office of Operations, City of New York.

———. 2003a. Chief Marketing Officer Will Leverage City's Image and Assets to Generate New Revenue Streams for New York City. Press Release. New York. April 2.

———. 2003b. Mayor Michael R. Bloomberg Hosts Summit on New York City Economic Development for Top CEOs and City Leaders. Press Release. New York. January 7.

———. 2004a. Mayor Michael R. Bloomberg Calls on Cablevision to Stop the Lies. Press Release. New York. November 14.

———. 2004b. No Time Like the Present to Invest in Our Future. Press Release. New York. March 31.

———. 2005. Mayor Michael R. Bloomberg Discusses Administration's Efforts to Promote Economic Development and Affordable Housing. Press Release. New York. February 27.

———. 2009. Mayor Bloomberg Outlines 11 Initiatives to Support New York City's Financial Services Sector and Encourage Entrepreneurship. Press Release. New York. February 18.

Clark, K. 2004. *Brandscendence: Three Essential Elements of Enduring Brands*. Chicago: Dearborn Trade Publishers.

Clark, T. N., and S. M. Lipset, eds. 2001. *The Breakdown of Class Politics: A Debate on Post-Industrial Stratification*. Washington, D.C.: Woodrow Wilson Center Press.

Clarke, J. 2004. *Changing Welfare, Changing States: New Directions in Social Policy*. London: Sage.

Cockfield, J., and A. Errol. 2004. Planning Group Opposes New Jets Stadium. *New York Newsday*. July 20.

Cohen, A. 2009. Cities Break Out the Piggybank. *Next American City*. http://americancity.org/buzz/entry/1260/. (accessed July 2, 2009).

Colangelo, L. 2003. Plan for New York's West Side Goes on Display. *New York Daily News*. February 11.

———. 2004. Mike on Stadium: L-E-T-S G-O! *New York Daily News*. September 13.

Colford, P., and D. Singleton. 2005. Mike Generous to Tune of $139m. *New York Daily News*. November 19.

Collinson, D., and J. Hearn. 1996. *Men as Managers, Managers as Men: Critical Perspectives on Men, Masculinities and Managements*. Thousand Oaks, Calif.: Sage.

Comaroff, J., and J. L. Comaroff. 2001. Millenial Capitalism: First Thoughts on a Second Coming. In *Millenial Capitalism and the Culture of Neoliberalism*, ed. J. Comaroff and J. L. Comaroff, 1–56. Durham, N.C.: Duke University Press.

Compton, L. 2004. Testimony. Public Hearing on the Hudson Yards Rezoning Plan and Draft Generic Environmental Impact Statement. New York. September 23.

Conard, M., and D. Smiley. 2002. *Hell's Kitchen South: Developing Strategies*. New York: The Design Trust for Public Space and the Hell's Kitchen Neighborhood Association.

Cooper, A., and J. Robertson. 2005. An Icon of Urbanism. *New York Times*. February 13.

Cooper, M. 2002. Mayor Adds Six Members to His Team. *New York Times*. January 16.

Cooper, M., and J. Barbanel. 2001. Gains among Hispanic, Black and Liberal Voters Helped Push Bloomberg to Victory. *New York Times*. November 10.

Cox, K. R., ed. 1997. *Spaces of Globalization: Reasserting the Power of the Local*. New York and London: Guilford Press.

Crain, Z. 2009. Tom Leppert Is Now Dallas' First Strong Mayor. *D Magazine*. June.

Crain's New York Business. 2000. West Side's Role in City's Future. September 25.

Crain's New York Business. 2004a. The RPA's West Side Fallacies. July 26.

Crain's New York Business. 2004b. W. Side Plans a Step Forward. February 16.

Crain's New York Business. 2005. West Side Will Help Downtown. April 18.

Cross, J. 2004. Testimony. Hearing on the New York Sports and Convention Center, Committee on Economic Development, New York City Council. June 3.

Currid, E. 2007. *The Warhol Economy: How Fashion, Art, and Music Drive New York City*. Princeton, N.J.: Princeton University Press.

Damiani, B. 2004. Interview with author. New York. May 24.

Das, V., and D. Poole, eds. 2004. *Anthropology in the Margins of the State*. Santa Fe: School of American Research Press.

Dávila, A. M. 2004. *Barrio Dreams: Puerto Ricans, Latinos, and the Neoliberal City*. Berkeley: University of California Press.

Davis, M. 1992. *City of Quartz: Excavating the Future in Los Angeles*. New York: Vintage Books.

Davis, S. 2002. *Brand Asset Management: Driving Profitable Growth through Your Brands*. San Francisco: Jossey-Bass.

Dean, M. 1999. *Governmentality: Power and Rule in Modern Society*. Thousand Oaks, Calif.: Sage.

DeDapper, J. 2004. Interview with Dan Doctoroff. *News Forum*. WNBC. April 11.

DeFilippis, J. 2004. *Unmaking Goliath: Community Control in the Face of Global Capital*. New York: Routledge.

Demause, N. 2000. Athenian Dreams or Trojan Horse? *Village Voice*. December 19.

———. 2004. Unemployment-Lover! *Field of Schemes*. http://www.fieldofschemes .com/news/archives/000557.html. (accessed May 8, 2004).

di Leonardo, M. 1984. *The Varieties of Ethnic Experience: Kinship, Class, and Gender among California Italian-Americans*. Ithaca, N.Y.: Cornell University Press.

———. 2006. There's No Place Like Home: Domestic Domains and Urban Imaginaries in New Haven, Connecticut. *Identities* 13:33–52.

———. 2008. The Neoliberalization of Minds, Space, and Bodies: Rising Global Inequality and the Shifting American Public Sphere. In *New Landscapes of*

Inequality: Neoliberalism and the Erosion of Democracy in America, ed. J. Collins, M. di Leonardo, and B. Williams, 191–208. Santa Fe: School for Advanced Research Press.

Dickinson, M. 2008. The Making of Space, Race and Place: New York City's War on Graffiti, 1970–the Present. *Critique of Anthropology* 28:27–45.

Doctoroff, D. 2002. Testimony. Hearing on the NYC2012 Plans for 2012 Summer Olympic Games, Committees on Economic Development, Committee on Transportation, and Select Committee on Waterfront, New York City Council. New York. December 17.

———. 2004a. Speech. *Crain's New York* Business Breakfast Forum. New York. September 29.

———. 2004b. Speech. Envisioning the West Side. New York. August 5.

———. 2004c. Testimony. Hearing on the Hudson Yards Financing Plan, Committee on Finance, New York City Council. New York. December 15.

———. 2004d. Testimony. Hearing on the New York Sports and Convention Center, Economic Development Committee, New York City Council. New York. June 3.

Doig, J. 1993. Expertise, Politics, and Technological Change. *Journal of the American Planning Association* 59:31–45.

———. 2002. *Empire on the Hudson: Entrepreneurial Vision and Political Power at the Port of New York Authority*. New York: Columbia University Press.

Doig, W. 2005. Jacobean Drama. *New York Magazine*. April 4.

Dowling, R. 2009. Geographies of Identity: Landscapes of Class. *Progress in Human Geography* 33:833–839.

Drennan, M. 1991. The Decline and Rise of the New York Economy. In *Dual City: Restructuring New York*, ed. J. Mollenkopf and M. Castells, 25–42. New York: Russell Sage Foundation.

Duggan, L. 2003. *The Twilight of Equality?: Neoliberalism, Cultural Politics, and the Attack on Democracy*. Boston: Beacon Press.

Dumenil, G., and D. Levy. 2004a. *Capital Resurgent: Roots of the Neoliberal Revolution*. Cambridge, Mass.: Harvard University Press.

———. 2004b. Neoliberal Income Trends: Wealth, Class, and Ownership in the USA. *New Left Review* 30:105–133.

Dunlap, D. 2003. The Design Image vs. The Reality. *New York Times*. September 28.

———. 2005. The Sky Is No Longer the Limit on Far West Side Buildings. *New York Times*. January 13.

Durrenberger, E. P., and D. Doukas. 2008. Gospel of Wealth, Gospel of Work: Counterhegemony in the U.S. Working Class. *American Anthropologist* 110:214–224.

Economic Research Associates and Cushman and Wakefield. 2003. *Hudson Yards Redevelopment: Economic Overview and Demand Forecast*. New York.

Economist. 2005a. After the Fall. February 19.

Economist. 2005b. The Town of the Talk. February 19.

Economist. 2005c. Under the New Management. February 19.

Edozien, F. 2003. West Side Glory: Team Mike Bares Master Redesign Plan. *New York Post.* October 24.

Ehrenreich, B., and J. Ehrenreich. 1971. The Professional-Managerial Class. *Radical America* 11:7–31.

Eisenman, P. 2004. Speech. Architecture and Stadiums. Center for Architecture, New York. July 20.

Eisinger, P. K. 1988. *The Rise of the Entrepreneurial State: State and Local Economic Development Policy in the United States.* Madison: University of Wisconsin Press.

Elliott, D. 2004. Testimony. Public Hearing on the Hudson Yards Rezoning Plan and Draft Generic Environmental Impact Statement. New York. September 23.

England, K., et al. 2007. Neoliberalizing Home Care: Managed Competition and Restructuring Home Care in Ontario. In *Neoliberalization: States, Networks, Peoples,* ed. K. England and K. Ward, 169–194. Malden, Mass.: Blackwell.

Engquist, E., and A. Michaud. 2005. Bloomberg Listens to Blacks, Gets Vote. *Crain's New York Business.* November 21.

Evans, G. 2007. London 2012. In *Olympic Cities: City Agendas, Planning, and the World Games, 1896–2012,* ed. J. R. Gold and M. M. Gold, 298–317. New York: Routledge.

Fainstein, N. I., and S. S. Fainstein. 1984. The Politics of Urban Development: New York City since 1945. *City Almanac* 17:1–25.

Fainstein, N. I., S. S. Fainstein, and A. Schwartz. 1989. Economic Shifts and Land Use in the Global City: New York, 1940–1987. In *Atop the Urban Hierarchy,* ed. R. Beauregard, 45–85. Totowa, N.J.: Rowman and Littlefield.

Fainstein, S. S. 2001a. *The City Builders: Property Development in New York and London, 1980–2000.* Lawrence: University Press of Kansas.

———. 2001b. Competitiveness, Cohesion, and Governance: Their Implications for Social Justice. *International Journal of Urban and Regional Research* 25:884–888.

Ferguson, J. 1990. *The Anti-Politics Machine: "Development," Depoliticization, and Bureaucratic Power in Lesotho.* Minneapolis: University of Minnesota Press.

Ferguson, J., and A. Gupta. 2002. Spatializing States: Towards an Ethnography of Neoliberal Governmentality. *American Ethnologist* 29:981–1002.

Fields, C. V. 2004. Remarks. Meeting of the Manhattan Borough Board. New York. September 15.

Finnegan, W. 2005. The Terrorism Beat. *New Yorker.* July 25.

Fiscal Policy Institute. 2002a. *Learning from the '90s: How Poor Public Choices Contributed to Income Erosion in New York City.* New York: Fiscal Policy Institute.

———. 2002b. *Sectoral Approaches to Economic Development Research in New York City: Key Themes and Issues.* New York: Fiscal Policy Institute.

Fitch, R. 1993. *The Assassination of New York.* New York: Verso.

Florida, R. L. 2002. *The Rise of the Creative Class: How It's Transforming Work, Leisure, Community and Everyday Life.* New York: Basic Books.

Forbes. 2001. The *Forbes* Four Hundred. September 27.

Forester, J. 1999. *The Deliberative Practitioner: Encouraging Participatory Planning Practice*. Cambridge, Mass.: MIT Press.

Foucault, M. 1991. Governmentality. In *The Foucault Effect: Studies in Governmentality*, ed. G. Burchell, C. Gordon and P. Miller, 87–104. Chicago: University of Chicago Press.

Frank, T. 1997. *The Conquest of Cool: Business Culture, Counterculture, and the Rise of Hip Consumerism*. Chicago: University of Chicago Press.

———. 2000. *One Market under God: Extreme Capitalism, Market Populism, and the End of Economic Democracy*. New York: Doubleday.

Frederickson, G. M. 2003. *Racism: A Short History*. Princeton, N.J.: Princeton University Press.

Freeman, C. 2007. The "Reputation" of Neoliberalism. *American Ethnologist* 34:252–267.

Freeman, J. 2000. *Working-Class New York: Life and Labor since World War II*. New York: New Press.

Friedmann, J. 1995. Where We Stand: A Decade of World City Research. In *World Cities in a World System*, ed. P. L. Knox and P. J. Taylor, 21–47. Cambridge: UK: University of Cambridge Press.

Friedmann, J., and G. Wolff. 1982. World City Formation: An Agenda for Research. *International Journal of Urban and Regional Research* 6:309–344.

Fuchs, E. 1992. *Mayors and Money: Fiscal Policy in New York and Chicago*. Chicago: University of Chicago Press.

Gardiner, J. 2007. City Seeks to Gauge "Customer Satisfaction." *New York Sun*. July 24.

Garvin, A. 2002. *The American City: What Works, What Doesn't*. New York: McGraw-Hill.

Gastil, R. 2002. *Beyond the Water's Edge: New York's New Waterfront*. Princeton, N.J.: Princeton Architectural Press.

Geertz, C. 1973. *The Interpretation of Cultures: Selected Essays*. New York: Basic Books.

George, S. 2000. A Short History of Neoliberalism: Twenty Years of Elite Economics and Emerging Opportunities for Structural Change. In *Global Finance: New Thinking on Regulating Capital Markets*, ed. W. Bello, N. Bullard, and K. Malhotra, 27–35. London: Zed Books.

Gibbs, N. 2005. The 5 Best Big-City Mayors. *Time Magazine*. April 17.

Gibson-Graham, J. K., S. A. Resnick, and R. D. Wolff. 2001. *Re/Presenting Class: Essays in Postmodern Marxism*. Durham, N.C.: Duke University Press.

Gimein, M. 2002. Mayor Mogul: Mike Bloomberg Wants to Be New York City's CEO; Too Bad He's Only Mayor. *Fortune*. April 1.

Gioia, E. 2002. Testimony. Hearing on the NYC2012 Plans for 2012 Summer Olympic Games, Committees on Economic Development, Committee on Transportation, and Select Committee on Waterfront, New York City Council. New York. December 17.

Giuliani, R. 2000. State of the City Address. New York. January 13.

Glaeser, E. L., M. G. Resseger, and K. Tobio. 2008. *Urban Inequality*. Cambridge, Mass.: National Bureau of Economic Research.

Gledhill, J. 2004. Neoliberalism. In *A Companion to the Anthropology of Politics,* ed. D. Nugent and J. Vincent, 332–348. Malden, Mass.: Blackwell.

Glick, D. 2004. West Side Story. *Villager.* July 14.

Gobe, M. 2001. *Emotional Branding: The New Paradigm for Connecting Brands to People.* New York: Allworth Press.

Gold, J. R., and M. M. Gold, eds. 2007. *Olympic Cities: City Agendas, Planning, and the World Games, 1896–2012.* New York: Routledge.

Gold, J. R., and S. V. Ward. 1994. *Place Promotion: The Use of Publicity and Marketing to Sell Towns and Regions.* New York: Wiley.

Goldberger, P. 2000. A Place to Play: Is Manhattan Ready for 80,000 Football Fans? *New Yorker.* February 14.

Goldin, H. 2005. Interview with Deputy Mayor Daniel Doctoroff. *Inside City Hall.* NY1. February 22.

Goldstein, D. M. 2001. Microenterprise Training Programs, Neoliberal Common Sense, and the Discourses of Self-Esteem. In *The New Poverty Studies: The Ethnography of Power, Politics, and Impoverished People in the United States*, ed. J. Goode and J. Maskovsky, 236–272. New York: New York University Press.

Goldstein, E. 2004. Speech. The Hudson Yards Plan: Issues and Alternatives. New York. November 23.

Golson, B. 2004. Doctoroff Olympiad. *New York Observer.* November 29.

Gonzalez, J. 2005. It Was One Vote He Couldn't Buy. *New York Daily News.* June 7.

Good Jobs New York. 2004. *The LMDC — They're in the Money; We're in the Dark: A Review of the Lower Manhattan Development Corporation's Use of 9/11 Funds.* New York.

Goode, J., and J. Maskovsky. 2001. Introduction. In *The New Poverty Studies: The Ethnography of Power, Politics and Impoverished Peoples in the United States*, ed. J. Goode and J. Maskovsky, 1–36. New York: New York University Press.

Gordon, A. 1995. The Work of Corporate Culture: Diversity Management. *Social Text* 44:3–30.

Gordon, C. 1991. Governmenal Rationality: An Introduction. In *The Foucault Effect: Studies in Governmentality*, ed. G. Burchell, C. Gordon, and P. Miller, 1–51. Chicago: University of Chicago Press.

Gotham, K. F. 2007a. *Authentic New Orleans: Tourism, Culture, and Race in the Big Easy.* New York: New York University Press.

———. 2007b. Destination New Orleans: Commodification, Rationalization, and the Rise of Urban Tourism. *Journal of Consumer Culture* 7:305–334.

Gottdeiner, M. 1997. *Theming of America: Dreams, Visions, and Commercial Spaces.* Boulder, Colo.: Westview Press.

Gottfried, R. 2004. Testimony. Hearing on the Hudson Yards Financing Plan, Committee on Finance, New York City Council. New York. December 15.

Gough, J. 2002. Neoliberalism and Socialisation in the Contemporary City: Opposities, Complements, and Instabilities. *Antipode* 34:405–426.

Gouldner, A. W. 1979. *The Future of Intellectuals and the Rise of the New Class: A Frame of Reference, Theses, Conjectures, Arguments, and an Historical Perspective on the Role of Intellectuals and Intelligentsia in the International Class Contest of the Modern Era.* New York: Seabury.

Graeber, D. 2001. *Toward an Anthropological Theory of Value: The False Coin of Our Own Dreams.* New York: Palgrave.

Gray, G. 2006. Is Parsons the New Bloomberg? *New York Magazine.* August 14.

Greenberg, M. 2000. Branding Cities: A Social History of the Urban Lifestyle Magazine. *Urban Affairs Review* 36:228–263.

——— . 2003. The Limits of Branding: The World Trade Center, Fiscal Crisis, and the Marketing of Recovery. *International Journal of Urban and Regional Research* 27:386–416.

——— . 2008. *Branding New York: How a City in Crisis Was Sold to the World.* New York: Routledge.

Gregory, S. 1998. *Black Corona: Race and the Politics of Place in an Urban Community.* Princeton, N.J.: Princeton University Press.

——— . 1999. The Changing Significance of Race and Class in an African American Community. In *Theorizing the City: The New Urban Anthropology Reader*, ed. S. Low, 37–66. New York: Routledge.

Gross, C. 2009. Endangered Community Boards. *Gotham Gazette.* http://live .gothamgazette.com/article/communitydevelopment/20090608/20/2936. (accessed August 12, 2009).

Group of 35. 2001. *Preparing for the Future: A Commercial Development Strategy for New York City.* New York: Group of 35.

Gupta, A. 1995. Blurred Boundaries: The Discourse of Corruption, the Culture of Politics, and the Imagined State. *American Ethnologist* 22:375–402.

Guthey, E. 1997. Ted Turner's Media Legend and the Transformation of Corporate Liberalism. *Business and Economic History* 26:184–199.

——— . 2001. Ted Turner's Corporate Cross-Dressing and the Shifting Images of American Business Leadership. *Enterprise and Society* 2:111–142.

Hackworth, J. 2002. Postrecession Gentrification in New York City. *Urban Affairs Review* 37:815–843.

——— . 2006. Neoliberalism, Contingency and Urban Policy: The Case of Social Housing in Ontario. *International Journal of Urban and Regional Research* 30:510–527.

——— . 2007. *The Neoliberal City: Governance, Ideology, and Development in American Urbanism.* Ithaca, N.Y.: Cornell University Press.

Hackworth, J., and N. Smith. 2001. The Changing State of Gentrification. *Tijdschrift voor Economische en Sociale Geografie [Journal of Economic and Social Geography]* 92:464–477.

Hall, T., and P. Hubbard. 1998a. The Entrepreneurial City and the "New Urban Politics." In *The Entrepreneurial City: Geographies of Politics, Regime, and Representation*, ed. T. Hall and P. Hubbard, 1–26. New York: Wiley.

——, eds. 1998b. *The Entrepreneurial City: Geographies of Politics, Regime, and Representation*. New York: Wiley.

Hankinson, G. 2001. Location Branding: A Study of the Branding Practices of 12 English Cities. *Journal of Brand Management* 9:127–142.

——. 2004. Relational Network Brands: Towards a Conceptual Model of Place Brands. *Journal of Vacation Marketing* 10:109–121.

Hanna, K. 2000. The Paradox of Participation and the Hidden Role of Information. *Journal of the American Planning Association* 66:398–410.

Hannerz, U. 1996. *Transnational Connections: Culture, People, Places*. New York: Routledge.

Hannigan, J. 1998. *Fantasy City: Pleasure and Profit in the Postmodern Metropolis*. New York: Routledge.

——. 2003. Symposium on Branding, the Entertainment Economy and Urban Place Building: Introduction. *International Journal of Urban and Regional Research* 27:352–360.

Harper, R. 1998. *Inside the IMF: An Ethnography of Documents, Technology and Organisational Action*. San Diego, Calif.: Academic Press.

Hartigan, J. 1997. Locating White Detroit. In *Displacing Whiteness: Essays in Social and Cultural Criticism*, ed. R. Frankenberg, 180–213. Durham, N.C.: Duke University Press.

——. 1999. *Racial Situations: Class Predicaments of Whiteness in Detroit*. Princeton, N.J.: Princeton University Press.

Harvey, D. 1989. *The Urban Experience*. Baltimore, Md.: Johns Hopkins University Press.

——. 2001. From Managerialism to Entrepreneurialism: The Transformation in Urban Governance in Late Capitalism. In *Spaces of Capital: Towards a Critical Geography*, 345–369. New York: Routledge.

——. 2003. *Paris, Capital of Modernity*. New York: Routledge.

——. 2005. *A Brief History of Neoliberalism*. New York: Oxford University Press.

Healy, P. 1993. The Communicative Work of Development Plans. *Environment and Planning B* 20:83–104.

Hemphill, C. 2009. Parent Power and Mayoral Control: Parent and Community Involvement in New York City Schools. In *When Mayors Take Charge : School Governance in the City*, ed. J. P. Viteritti, 187–205. Washington, D.C.: Brookings Institution Press.

Henig, J. R. 2009. Mayoral Control: What We Can and Cannot Learn from Other Cities. In *When Mayors Take Charge: School Governance in the City*, ed. J. P. Viteritti, 19–45. Washington, D.C.: Brookings Institution Press.

Herod, A., and M. Wright, eds. 2002. *Geographies of Power: Placing Scale*. Malden, Mass.: Blackwell.

Heynen, N., et al., eds. 2007. *Neoliberal Environments: False Promises and Unnatural Consequences*. New York: Routledge.

Ho, K. 2005. Situating Global Capitalism: A View from Wall Street Investment Banks. *Cultural Anthropology* 20:68–96.

Hoffman, L., M. DeHart, and S. J. Collier. 2006. Notes on the Anthropology of Neoliberalism. *Anthropology News* 47:9–10.

Holcomb, B. 1994. City Make-Overs: Marketing the Post-Industrial City. In *Place Promotion: The Use of Publicity and Marketing to Sell Towns and Regions*, ed. J. R. Gold and S. V. Ward, 115–131. New York: Wiley.

Holston, J. 1989. *The Modernist City: An Anthropological Critique of Brasília*. Chicago: University of Chicago Press.

Holt, D. B. 2004. *How Brands Become Icons: The Principles of Cultural Branding*. Boston: Harvard Business School Press.

Horowitz, C. 2004. Stadium of Dreams. *New York Magazine*. June 21.

Hu, W., and C. Bagli. 2005. Obstacle Rises for Bloomberg on West Side Stadium Plan. *New York Times*. March 3.

Huyssen, A., ed. 2008. *Other Cities, Other Worlds: Urban Imaginaries in a Globalizing Age*. Durham, N.C.: Duke University Press.

Hyatt, S. B. 2001. From Citizen to Volunteer: Neoliberal Governance and the Erasure of Poverty. In *The New Poverty Studies: The Ethnography of Power, Politics, and Impoverished Peoples in the United States*, ed. J. Goode and J. Maskovsky, 201–235. New York: New York University Press.

Iacocca, L., and W. Novak. 1984. *Iacocca: An Autobiography*. New York: Bantam.

Inda, J. X., and R. Rosaldo. 2002. Introduction: A World in Motion. In *The Anthropology of Globalization: A Reader*, ed. J. X. Inda and R. Rosaldo, 1–34. Malden, Mass.: Blackwell.

Innes, J. 1996. Planning through Consensus Building: A New View of the Comprehensive Planning Ideal. *Journal of the American Planning Association* 62:460–472.

Isin, E. F. 1998. Governing Cities, Governing Ourselves. In *Governing Cities: Liberalism, Neoliberalism, Advanced Liberalism*, ed. E. F. Isin, T. Osborne, and D. Rose, 38–59. Toronto: Urban Studies Programme, Division of Social Science, York University.

Jackson, K. T. 1987. *Crabgrass Frontier: The Suburbanization of the United States*. New York: Oxford University Press.

Jacobs, J. 1992. *The Death and Life of Great American Cities*. New York: Vintage.

Janison, D., and W. Murphy. 2005. Convention-Center Wisdom in Question. *New York Newsday*. January 24.

Jeansonne, J. 2005. IOC: No Stadium, No Games. *New York Newsday*. February 25.

Jessop, B. 1998. The Narratives of Enterprise and the Enterprise of Narrative: Place Marketing and the Entrepreneurial City. In *The Entrepreneurial City: Geographies of Politics, Regime, and Representation*, ed. T. Hall and P. Hubbard, 77–102. New York: Wiley.

Johnson, D. A. 1996. *Planning the Great Metropolis: The 1929 Regional Plan of New York and Its Environs*. London: E & FN Spon.

Jonas, J. 2009. Bloomberg on Poverty: A War or Small Skirmishes? *Gotham Gazette*. October 23.

Joyce, P., ed. 1995. *Class*. New York: Oxford University Press.

Katz, C., and M. Saul. 2001. Mayoral Foes Begin the Insults. *New York Daily News*. October 13.

Katz, P. 1994. *The New Urbanism: Toward an Architecture of Community*. New York: McGraw-Hill.

Katznelson, I. 1982. *City Trenches: Urban Politics and the Patterning of Class in the United States*. Chicago: University of Chicago Press.

———. 2005. *When Affirmative Action Was White: An Untold History of Racial Inequality in Twentieth-Century America*. New York: W. W. Norton.

Kaufmann, K. M. 2003. The Mayoral Politics of Los Angeles and New York. In *New York and Los Angeles: Politics, Society, and Culture*, ed. D. Halle, 314–340. Chicago: University of Chicago Press.

Kavaratzis, M. 2004. From City Marketing to City Branding: Towards a Theoretical Framework for Developing City Brands. *Place Branding* 1:58–73.

———. 2005. Place Branding: A Review of Trends and Conceptual Models. *Marketing Review* 5:329–342.

———. 2007. City Marketing: The Past, the Present and Some Unresolved Issues. *Geography Compass* 1:695–712.

Kavaratzis, M., and G. J. Ashworth. 2005. City Branding: An Effective Assertion of Identity or a Transitory Marketing Trick? *Tijdschrift voor Economische en Sociale Geografie [Journal of Economic and Social Geography]* 96:506–514.

———. 2007. Partners in Coffeeshops, Canals and Commerce: Marketing the City of Amsterdam. *Cities* 24:16–25.

Kearns, G., and C. Philo. 1993. *Selling Places: The City as Cultural Capital, Past and Present*. New York: Pergamon Press.

Keller, K. L. 1997. *Strategic Brand Management: Building, Measuring, and Managing Brand Equity*. Upper Saddle River, N.J.: Prentice Hall.

Khurana, R. 2002. *Searching for a Corporate Savior: The Irrational Quest for Charismatic CEOs*. Princeton, N.J.: Princeton University Press.

Kim, J. 2004. Virgin HQ Will Bring 700 Jobs. *Crain's New York Business*. June 7.

King, A. D. 2007. Boundaries, Networks, Cities: Playing and Replaying Diasporas and Histories. In *Urban Imaginaries: Locating the Modern City*, ed. A. Cinar and T. Bender, 1–14. Minneapolis: University of Minnesota Press.

Kingfisher, C. 2002a. Neoliberalism I: Discourses of Personhood and Welfare Reform. In *Western Welfare in Decline: Globalization and Women's Poverty*, ed. C. Kingfisher, 13–31. Philadelphia: University of Pennsylvania Press.

———, ed. 2002b. *Western Welfare in Decline: Globalization and Women's Poverty.* Philadelphia: University of Pennsylvania Press.

Kingfisher, C., and J. Maskovsky. 2008. The Limits of Neoliberalism. *Critique of Anthropology* 28:115–126.

Kirtzman, A. 2001. *Rudy Giuliani: Emperor of the City.* New York: Perennial.

Klein, N. 2000. *No Logo: Taking Aim at the Brand Bullies.* New York: Picador.

Kolbert, E. 2001. Big Ticket Item: Why Does Michael Bloomberg Want to Be Mayor? *New Yorker.* September 9.

Kolker, R. 2001. The Power of Partnership. *New York Magazine.* November 26.

———. 2002. City Father's Son. *New York Magazine.* February 11.

Kotkin, J. 2009. The Luxury City vs. The Middle Class. *The American: The Journal of the American Enterprise Institute.* May 13.

Kriegel, J. 2002a. New York's Olympic Plan. Speech to the Council on Foreign Relations. New York. July 10.

———. 2002b. Testimony. Hearing on New York City's 2012 Olympic Bid, Committees on Economic Development, Transportation, and Waterfronts, New York City Council. New York. December 17.

———. 2004. Testimony. Hearing on the New York Sports and Convention Center, Economic Development Committee, New York City Council. New York. June 3.

Laclau, E., and C. Mouffe. 2001. *Hegemony and Socialist Strategy: Towards a Radical Democratic Politics.* New York: Verso.

Larner, W. 2003. Neoliberalism? *Environment and Planning D* 21:509–512.

Larner, W., and M. Butler. 2007. The Places, People, and Politics of Partnership: After Neoliberalism in Aotearoa New Zealand. In *Contesting Neoliberalism: Urban Frontiers*, ed. H. Leitner, J. Peck, and E. S. Sheppard, 71–90. New York: Guilford.

Larner, W., and R. Le Heron. 2004. Global Benchmarking: Participating "At a Distance" in the Globalizing Economy. In *Global Governmentality: Governing International Spaces*, ed. W. Larner and W. Walters, 212–232. New York: Routledge.

Lee, Y.-J. 2005. Governing Quality of Life: Corporate Citizenship. Annual Meetings of the American Anthropological Association. Washington, D.C. December 3.

Leeds, A. 1994. *Cities, Classes and the Social Order.* Ithaca, N.Y.: Cornell University Press.

Lees, L. 2003. Super-Gentrification: The Case of Brooklyn Heights, New York City. *Urban Studies* 40:2487–2509.

Lefebvre, H. 2003. *The Urban Revolution.* Minneapolis: University of Minnesota Press.

Leitner, H., J. Peck, and E. S. Sheppard. 2007a. Squaring up to Neoliberalism. In *Contesting Neoliberalism: Urban Frontiers*, ed. H. Leitner, J. Peck, and E. S. Sheppard, 311–327. New York: Guilford.

Leitner, H., J. Peck, and E. S. Sheppard. 2007b. Contesting Urban Futures: Decentering Neoliberalism. In *Contesting Neoliberalism: Urban Frontiers*, ed. H. Leitner, J. Peck, and E. S. Sheppard, 1–25. New York: Guilford.

Levin, A. H. 2004a. Interview with author. New York. September 27.

Levin, B. 2004b. Testimony. Public Hearing on the Hudson Yards Rezoning Plan and Draft Generic Environmental Impact Statement. New York. September 23.

Levitan, M. 2004. *A Crisis of Black Male Employment: Unemployment and Joblessness in New York City, 2003*. New York: Community Service Society.

———. 2006. *Poverty in New York City, 2005: More Families Working, More Working Families Poor*. New York: Community Service Society.

Levy, J. 2003a. Bill for Far West Side Development Could Reach Olympian Heights. *New York Sun*. October 24.

———. 2003b. City Throws London Party to Draw Euro Business. *New York Sun*. March 19.

Ley, D. 1996. *The New Middle Class and the Remaking of the Central City*. Oxford: Oxford University Press.

———. 2004. Transnational Spaces and Everyday Lives. *Transactions of the Institute of British Geographers* 29:151–164.

Lichten, E. 1986. *Class, Power, and Austerity: The New York City Fiscal Crisis*. South Hadley, Mass.: Bergin and Garvey.

Lieber, J. 2004a. Athens Games Energize New York's Bid Leader. *USA Today*. August 30.

———. 2004b. No Longer Just a Dreamer. *USA Today*. May 10.

LiPuma, E., and T. Koelble. 2005. Cultures of Circulation and the Urban Imaginary: Miami as Example and Exemplar. *Public Culture* 17:153–179.

Lisberg, A. 2009. Mayor Bloomberg: "We Love the Rich People." *Daily News*. March 6.

Liu, L. Y. 2006. Counterhegemony and Context: Racial Crisis, Warfare, and Real Estate in the Neoliberal City. *Urban Geography* 27:714–721.

Lloyd, R. D. 2006. *Neo-Bohemia: Art and Commerce in the Postindustrial City*. New York: Routledge.

Logan, J. R., and H. L. Molotch. 1987. *Urban Fortunes: The Political Economy of Place*. Berkeley: University of California Press.

Loomis, C. 2007. Bloomberg's Money Machine. *Fortune*. April 5.

Low, S. 2000. *On the Plaza: The Politics of Public Space and Culture*. Austin: University of Texas Press.

———. 2003. *Behind the Gates: Life, Security and the Pursuit of Happiness in Fortress America*. New York: Routledge.

Lowry, T. 2001a. The Bloomberg Machine. *BusinessWeek*. April 4.

———. 2001b. Hizzoner, Mayor Bloomberg? *BusinessWeek*. April 23.

———. 2007. The CEO Mayor. *BusinessWeek*. June 25.

Lucadamo, K. 2004. Snapple Rule Eats at Students. *New York Daily News*. December 24.

Lueck, T. 2005. What's Up and Spans City? Bloomberg's Philanthropy. *New York Times*. August 17.

Lukas, S. A., ed. 2007. *The Themed Space: Locating Culture, Nation, and Self*. Lanham, Md.: Lexington Books.

Lupica, M. 2005. Political Football: It's Time to Flag Mike for Jets Stadium Blitz. *New York Daily News*. June 3.

Lyon-Callo, V., and S. B. Hyatt. 2003. The Neoliberal State and the Depoliticization of Poverty: Activist Anthropology and "Ethnography from Below." *Urban Anthropology and Studies of Cultural Systems and World Economic Development* 32:175–204.

Macchiarolla, F. J. 1986. Managing Partnerships: A CEO's Perspective. In *Public–Private Partnerships: Improving Urban Life*, 127–136. New York: Academy of Political Science.

Magill, K. 2004. Virgin-Branded Low-Fare Airline Selects New York for Headquarters. *New York Sun*. June 8.

Magnet, A. 2005. Doctoroff: Mayor's Support Unwavering for Rebuilding of Ground Zero. *New York Sun*. October 26.

Malanga, S. 2003. Bloomberg to City: Drop Dead. *City Journal* 13:27–35.

———. 2005. Gotham Stalls Out. *City Journal* 15:50–57.

Malmendier, U., and G. Tate. 2005. Superstar CEOs. Unpublished paper.

Mankoff, W. 2004. Testimony. Public Hearing on the Hudson Yards Rezoning Plan and Draft Generic Environmental Impact Statement. New York. September 23.

Marcuse, P. 2002. What Kind of Planning after September 11? The Market, the Stakeholders, Consensus — Or . . . ? In *After the World Trade Center: Rethinking New York City*, ed. M. Sorkin and S. Zukin, 153–163. New York: Routledge.

Marston, S. A. 2000. The Social Construction of Scale. *Progress in Human Geography* 24:219–242.

Martin, R. 2002. *Financialization of Everyday Life*. Philadelphia: Temple University Press.

Marx, K. 1973. *Grundrisse*. New York: Penguin.

———. 1990. *Capital: A Critique of Political Economy*. New York: Penguin Books in association with *New Left Review*.

Marx, K., and F. Engels. 1994. The Communist Manifesto. In *Karl Marx: Selected Writings*, ed. L. Simon, 157–186. Indianapolis, Ind.: Hackett.

Maskovsky, J. 2001. The Other War at Home: The Geopolitics of U.S. Poverty. *Urban Anthropology and Studies of Cultural Systems and World Economic Development* 30:215–238.

McAvoy, G. E. 1999. *Controlling Technocracy: Citizen Rationality and the Nimby Syndrome*. Washington, D.C.: Georgetown University Press.

McCall, L. 2001. *Complex Inequality: Gender, Class, and Race in the New Economy*. New York: Routledge.

McDonogh, G. 1999. Discourses of the City: Policy and Response in Post-Transitional

Barcelona. In *Theorizing the City: The New Urban Anthropology Reader*, ed. S. Low, 342–376. New Brunswick, N.J.: Rutgers University Press.

McGeehan, P. 2009a. After Reversal of Fortunes, City Takes a New Look at Wall Street. *New York Times*. February 23.

———. 2009b. City Will Help Retrain Laid-Off Wall Streeters. *New York Times*. February 19.

McGovern, S. J. 2009. Mobilization on the Waterfront: The Ideological/Cultural Roots of Potential Regime Change in Philadelphia. *Urban Affairs Review* 44:663–694.

McIntyre, M. 2004. As Mayor Sees a Better City, Numbers Show a Mixed Report. *New York Times*. September 16.

———. 2005. Mayor Says Shea Isn't Fit for the Olympics. *New York Times*. February 23.

McIntyre, M., and J. Rutenberg. 2005. After Stadium Bid Fails, a Disheartened Bloomberg Worries for City. *New York Times*. June 8.

McKenzie, J. 2001. *Perform or Else: From Discipline to Performance*. New York: Routledge.

McMahon, E. J. 2005. *Pricing The "Luxury Product": New York City Taxes under Mayor Bloomberg (Civic Report 47)*. New York: Center for Civic Innovation at the Manhattan Institute.

McMahon, E. J., and F. Siegel. 2005. Gotham's Fiscal Crisis: Lessons Unlearned. *Public Interest* 158:96–110.

Medina, J. 2007. Reaching Out to Students When They Talk and Text. *New York Times*. November 13.

———. 2008. For " A" Students in Some Brooklyn Schools, a Cellphone and 130 Free Minutes. *New York Times*. February 28.

———. 2009. Debate on Mayoral Control of Schools Is Renewed. *New York Times*. January 29.

Mele, C. 2000. *Selling the Lower East Side: Culture, Real Estate, and Resistance in New York*. Minneapolis: University of Minnesota Press.

Michaud, A. 2004. Snapple Ruling Calls for More Transparency. *Crain's New York Business*. July 30.

Mills, C. W. 2002. *White Collar: The American Middle Classes*. Oxford: Oxford University Press.

Mitchell, M. 2002. *Labor Market Trends and Issues in the New York City Securities Industry*. New York: Fiscal Policy Institute.

Miyazaki, H. 2007a. Arbitraging Faith and Reason. *American Ethnologist* 34:430–432.

———. 2007b. Between Arbitrage and Speculation: An Economy of Belief and Doubt. *Economy and Society* 36:396–415.

Mnookin, S. 2008. Bloomberg without Bloomberg. *Vanity Fair*. December.

Mollenkopf, J. 1992. *A Phoenix in the Ashes*. Princeton, N.J.: Princeton University Press.

———. 2003. New York: Still the Great Anomaly. In *Racial Politics in American Cities*, ed. R. P. Browning, D. R. Marshall, and D. H. Tabb, 115–142. New York: Longman.

———. 2005. How 9/11 Reshaped the Political Environment in New York. In *Contentious City: The Politics of Recovery in New York City*, ed. J. Mollenkopf, 205–222. New York: Russell Sage Foundation.

Moody, K. 2007. *From Welfare State to Real Estate: Regime Change in New York City, 1974 to the Present*. New York: New Press.

Morgen, S., and L. Gonzales. 2008. The Neoliberal American Dream as Daydream. *Critique of Anthropology* 28:219–236.

Moss, J. 2008. Beatrice Vongerichtified. *Jeremiah's Vanishing New York*. http://vanishingnewyork.blogspot.com/2008/03/beatrice-vongerichtified.html. (accessed March 3, 2009).

———. n.d. *Jeremiah's Vanishing New York*. http://vanishingnewyork.blogspot.com. (accessed September 22, 2010).

Mullings, L. 1997. *On Our Own Terms: Race, Class, and Gender in the Lives of African American Women*. New York: Routledge.

———. 2005. Interrogating Racism: Toward an Antiracist Anthropology. *Annual Review of Anthropology* 34:667–693.

Murphy, D. 2001a. Bloomberg Expands on Economic Plans. *New York Times*. October 18.

———. 2001b. Bloomberg Stresses Private Business as Key to Revival. *New York Times*. November 1.

Murphy, D., and R. C. Archibold. 2001. Starting Race against Green, Bloomberg Stresses His Business Past. *New York Times*. October 13.

Murphy, J. 2005. Stopping a Stadium. *Village Voice*. June 7.

Nagourney, A. 2001. Bloomberg and Green Clash over Capability in Debate. *New York Times*. November 2.

Nevarez, L. 2003. *New Money, Nice Town: How Capital Works in the New Urban Economy*. New York: Routledge.

New York City Department of City Planning. 2001. *Far West Midtown: A Framework for Development*. New York.

———. 2003. *Hudson Yards Master Plan: Preferred Direction*. New York.

New York City Department of City Planning and Metropolitan Transportation Authority. 2003. *Draft Scoping Document: Proposed No. 7 Subway Extension — Hudson Yards Rezoning and Development Program CEQR No. 03dcp031m Draft Generic Environmental Impact Statement*. New York.

New York City Economic Development Corporation. 2002. NYC Economic Development Corporation President Andrew Alper Announces Corporate Restructuring. Press Release. April 2.

New York City Independent Budget Office. 2000. *Big City, Big Bucks: NYC's Changing Income Distribution*. New York.

———. 2002. *Learning from Experience: A Primer on Tax Increment Financing.* New York.

———. 2004a. *A Guide to the Capital Budget.* New York.

———. 2004b. *The Long-Term Costs and Benefits of the New York Sports and Convention Center.* New York.

———. 2004c. *Supply and Demand: City and State May Be Planning Too Much Office Space.* New York.

———. 2004d. *West Side Financing's Complex, $1.3 Billion Story.* New York.

New York Daily News. 2004. Private Profit, Public Falsehoods. September 5.

New York Jets. 2004. *Preliminary Estimates of Economic and Fiscal Impacts of a Proposed Multi-Use Athletic and Exhibition Facility, Hudson Yards District, New York City.* New York.

New York Post. 2002. Taxing in the Dark. November 26.

New York State Advisory Panel on Transportation Policy for 2025. 2004. *Transportation — Trouble Ahead.* New York: University Transportation Research Center.

New York State Financial Control Board. 2004. *Review of Fiscal Years 2005–2008 Budget Plan.* Albany, N.Y.

New York Sun. 2003. Doctoring the Economy. November 26.

New York Times. 2001. Mark Green for Mayor. October 29.

———. 2005. An Endorsement for Mayor. October 23.

Newfield, J., and P. DuBrul. 1981. *The Permanent Government: Who Really Runs New York?* New York: Pilgrim Press.

Noll, R. G., and A. S. Zimbalist. 1997. The Economic Impact of Sports Teams and Stadiums. In *Sports, Jobs, and Taxes: The Economic Impact of Sports Teams and Stadiums,* ed. R. G. Noll and A. S. Zimbalist, 55–91. Washington, D.C.: Brookings Institution Press.

Nonini, D. M. 2008. Is China Becoming Neoliberal? *Critique of Anthropology* 28:145–176.

Noonan, P. 2004. Interview with author. New York. October 18.NYC2012. 2001. *Hudson Yards: A Proposal for the West Side Rail Yards.* New York.

Ojito, M. 2001. No Ferrer, So Latinos Hold Nose and Choose. *New York Times.* November 2.

Ong, A. 2002. The Pacific Shuttle: Family, Citizenship, and Capital Circuits. In *The Anthropology of Globalization: A Reader,* ed. J. X. Inda and R. Rosaldo, 172–197. Malden, Mass.: Blackwell.

———. 2006. *Neoliberalism as Exception: Mutations in Citizenship and Sovereignty.* Durham, N.C.: Duke University Press.

Osborne, D., and T. Gaebler. 1993. *Reinventing Government: How the Entrepreneurial Spirit Is Transforming the Public Sector.* New York: Plume.

Osborne, T., and N. Rose. 1998. Governing Cities. In *Governing Cities: Liberalism,*

Neoliberalism, Advanced Liberalism, ed. E. F. Isin, T. Osborne, and D. Rose, 1–32. Toronto: Urban Studies Programme, Division of Social Science, York University.

Ouroussoff, N. 2004. Sobering Plans for Jets Stadium. *New York Times*. November 1.

Page, M. 2004. Testimony. Hearing on the Hudson Yards Financing Plan, Committee on Finance, New York City Council. New York. December 15.

Partnership for New York City. 2005. Our Partners. http://www.nycp.org/ourpartners .asp. (accessed November 10, 2005).

Pasanen, G. 2004. The Mayor's Management Report Skimps on Information about Education and Everything Else. *Gotham Gazette*. http://www.gothamgazette.com/ article/finance/20041006/8/1139. (accessed October 10, 2006).

Pasotti, E. 2010. *Political Branding in Cities: The Decline of Machine Politics in Bogotá, Naples, and Chicago*. New York: Cambridge University Press.

Pattillo, M. E. 1999. *Black Picket Fences: Privilege and Peril among the Black Middle Class*. Chicago: University of Chicago Press.

Peck, J. 2002. Political Economies of Scale: Fast Policy, Interscalar Relations, and Neoliberal Workfare. *Economic Geography* 78:331–360.

———. 2004. Geography and Public Policy: Constructions of Neoliberalism. *Progress in Human Geography* 28:392–405.

———. 2005. Struggling with the Creative Class. *International Journal of Urban and Regional Research* 29:740–770.

———. 2006a. Liberating the City: Between New York and New Orleans. *Urban Geography* 27:681–713.

———. 2006b. Response: Countering Neoliberalism. *Urban Geography* 27:729–733.

Peck, J., and A. Tickell. 2002. Neoliberalizing Space. *Antipode* 34:380–404.

Pederson, W. 2004. Architecture and Stadiums. Speech at Center for Architecture, New York. July 20.

Peterson, P. E. 1981. *City Limits*. Chicago: University of Chicago Press.

Phelps, N. A., M. Power, and R. Wanjiru. 2007. Learning to Compete: Communities of Investment Promotion Practice in the Spread of Global Neoliberalism. In *Neoliberalization: States, Networks, People*, ed. K. England and K. Ward, 83–109. Malden, Mass.: Blackwell.

Piketty, T., and E. Saez. 2004. The Evolution of Top Incomes: A Historical and International Approach. *American Economic Review: Papers and Proceedings* 96:200–205.

Pogrebin, R. 2004. An Aesthetic Watchdog in the City Planning Office. *New York Times*. December 29.

Poulantzas, N. 1978. *Classes in Contemporary Capitalism*. New York: Verso.

Powell, M., and J. Bosman. 2009. Mayor No Longer Seems Invincible. *New York Times*. November 4.

Prince, S. 2003. *Constructing Belonging: Class, Race, and Harlem's Professional Workers*. New York: Routledge.

Purnick, J. 2009. *Mike Bloomberg: Money, Power, Politics*. New York: Public Affairs Books.

———. 2010. Bloomberg's No Shows. *Huffington Post*. http://www.huffingtonpost .com/joyce-purnick/bloombergs-no-shows_b_345860.html. (accessed February 15, 2010).

Quinn, C. 2004. Speech. Envisioning the West Side. August 5.

Ravitch, R. 2004a. Testimony. Hearing on the Hudson Yards Financing Plan, Committee on Finance, New York City Council. New York. December 15.

———. 2004b. The West Side Stadium: An Effective Stimulus or an Unaffordable Subsidy? Speech to the City Club. New York. November 9.

Rayman, G. 2004. Wall Street Worries. *New York Newsday*. May 31.

Rayman, G., and J. Robin. 2004. Dueling West Side Stories: Locals' Plan Lacks Stadium City Wants. *New York Newsday*. February 2.

Regional Plan Association. 1969. *Urban Design Manhattan*. New York: Viking Press.

———. 2004. *Fulfilling the Promise of Manhattan's Far West Side*. New York.

Reichl, A. J. 1999. *Reconstructing Times Square: Politics and Culture in Urban Development*. Lawrence: University Press of Kansas.

Renwick, T. 2008. *Pulling Apart in New York: An Analysis of Income Trends in New York State*. New York: Fiscal Policy Institute.

Rich, W. C. 2007. *David Dinkins and New York City Politics: Race, Images, and the Media*. Albany: State University of New York Press.

Riles, A. 2004. Real Time: Unwinding Technocratic and Anthropological Knowledge. *American Ethnologist* 31:392–405.

Riley, J. 2008. New York Will Survive without Bloomberg. *Wall Street Journal*. October 16.

Ritter, J. 2005. Billionaire's Plan in Seattle Sets Off Furor. *USA Today*. June 8.

Ritthichai, C. 2003. A New Executive Order: Don't Ask, Don't Tell. *Gotham Gazette*. http://www.gothamgazette.com/article/Immigrants/20031001/11/535. (accessed September 22, 2005).

Robbins, L., and M. McIntyre. 2004. A True Champion of Grand Plans and Tiny Detail: With the Zeal of an Athlete, Doctoroff Pursues Olympics. *New York Times*. May 16.

Robbins, T. 2005a. The Deputy Mayor for the Olympics. *Village Voice*. February 1.

———. 2005b. Stadium Fear Factor. *Village Voice*. February 15.

Roberts, S. 2005. Mayor Crossed Ethnic Barriers for Big Victory. *New York Times*. November 10.

———. 2006. Mayor's Big Campaign Bonuses Raise Questions Later in Office. *New York Times*. March 6.

Roberts, S., and J. Rutenberg. 2005. With More Private Giving, Bloomberg Forges Ties. *New York Times*. May 23.

Robin, J., and G. Rayman. 2002. West Side Banking on Bright Future. *New York Newsday*. July 29.

Robinson, W. I. 2004. *A Theory of Global Capitalism: Production, Class, and State in a Transnational World*. Baltimore: Johns Hopkins University Press.

Rofe, M. W. 2003. "I Want to Be Global": Theorising the Gentrifying Class as an Emergent Elite Global Community. *Urban Studies* 40:2511–2526.

Rogers, J. 2002. Downtown Officials Question Olympic Plan. *Downtown Express*. November 13.

Rohatyn, F. G. 1983a. Time for a Change. *New York Review of Books*. August 18.

———. 1983b. *The Twenty-Year Century: Essays on Economics and Public Finance*. New York: Random House.

———. 2009. *Bold Endeavors: How Our Government Built America, and Why It Must Rebuild Now*. New York: Simon and Schuster.

Rose, J. 2000. Comments. Midtown-West Conference: Options for Mid-Manhattan's Last Frontier. New York. December 8.

Rose, N. S. 1999. *Powers of Freedom: Reframing Political Thought*. New York: Cambridge University Press.

Ross, I. 1987. In Demand: Wall Street's Liberals. *Fortune*. April 27.

Rotenberg, R. 2007. End of Term Reminder II. *SUNTA Teacher*. http://suntateacher .blogspot.com/2007/05/end-of-term-reminder-ii.html. (accessed October 23, 2007).

Rotenberg, R., and G. McDonogh, eds. 1993. *The Cultural Meaning of Urban Space*. Westport, Conn.: Bergin and Garvey.

Rothkopf, D. 2008. *Superclass: The Global Power Elite and the World They Are Making*. New York: Farrar, Straus, and Giroux.

Ruben, M. 2001. Suburbanization and Urban Poverty under Neoliberalism. In *The New Poverty Studies: The Ethnography of Power, Politics and Impoverished Peoples in the United States*, ed. J. Goode and J. Maskovsky, 435–469. New York: New York University Press.

Ruben, M., and J. Maskovsky. 2008. The Homeland Archipelago: Neoliberal Urban Governance after September 11. *Critique of Anthropology* 28:199–217.

Rutenberg, J. 2005. Rich Democrats Are Lining Up with Mayor. *New York Times*. July 26.

Rutheiser, C. 1996. *Imagineering Atlanta: The Politics of Place in the City of Dreams*. New York: Verso.

Sagalyn, L. 2001. *Times Square Roulette: Remaking the City Icon*. Cambridge, Mass.: MIT Press.

———. 2004. Speech. Make No Small Plans: The Far West Side and Its Impact on the Region. New York. April 16.

Saltonshall, D. 2004. Snapple Cash Still Slow Drip. *New York Daily News*. November 30.

Sanders, H. 2002. Convention Myths and Markets: A Critical Review of Convention Center Feasibility Studies. *Economic Development Quarterly* 16:195–210.

———. 2004. *Space Available: The Realities of Convention Centers as Economic Development Strategy*. Washington, D.C.: Brookings Institution.

Sanjek, R. 1998. *The Future of Us All: Race and Neighborhood Politics in New York City.* Ithaca, N.Y.: Cornell University Press.

Sargent, G. 2003a. After a Huddle, Jets Start Rush for West Side. *New York Observer.* February 24.

———. 2003b. Mayor Bloomberg Opens His Manor to London Lucre. *New York Observer.* March 2.

Sassen, S. 1997. Cities, Foreign Policy, and the Global Economy. In *The City and the World: New York's Global Future,* ed. M. E. Crahan and A. Vourvoulias-Bush, 171–187. New York: Council on Foreign Relations Press.

———. 2001 [1991]. *The Global City: New York, London, Tokyo.* Princeton, N.J.: Princeton University Press.

Satow, J. 2005a. IOC Evaluators Call Stadium "Important" For 2012. *New York Sun.* February 25.

———. 2005b. Mayor, Jets Get a Victory on Stadium. *New York Sun.* June 3.

Saul, M. 2001. Bloomy and Badillo Trade Slaps. *New York Daily News.* September 1.

———. 2004. Mike's True to Stadium Plan. *New York Daily News.* December 3.

———. 2005a. City Olympic Spirit Sags — Poll. *New York Daily News.* March 3.

———. 2005b. Mike Pooh-Poohs Games Doubters. *New York Daily News.* May 24.

———. 2005c. Mike Won't Rule Out New Tax Hike. *New York Daily News.* March 2.

———. 2005d. No Stadium, No Olympics, Swears an Angry Mike. *New York Daily News.* March 2.

———. 2005e. W. Side Stadium Gets Al Amen. *New York Daily News.* March 27.

Savitch, H. V. 1988. *Post-Industrial Cities: Politics and Planning in New York, Paris, and London.* Princeton, N.J.: Princeton University Press.

Sawalha, A. 1998. The Reconstruction of Beirut. *City and Society* 10:133–147.

Sawaya, F. 2008. Capitalism and Philanthropy in the (New) Gilded Age. *American Quarterly* 60:201–213.

Schoenberger, E. 2001. Corporate Autobiographies: The Narrative Strategies of Corporate Strategists. *Journal of Economic Geography* 1:277–298.

Schuerman, M. 2007. The Rise of Real Estate and the Decline of the Industrial City. In *The Suburbanization of New York,* ed. J. Hammett and K. Hammett, 129–141. New York: Princeton Architectural Press.

Schwartz, J. 1993. *The New York Approach: Robert Moses, Urban Liberals, and the Redevelopment of the Inner City.* Columbus: Ohio State University Press.

Schwegler, T. 2008. Take It from the Top (Down)? Rethinking Neoliberalism and Political Hierarchy in Mexico. *American Ethnologist* 35:682–700.

Sciame, F. 2004. Testimony. Manhattan Borough President Hearing on the Hudson Yards Rezoning Plan and Draft Generic Environmental Impact Statement. New York. September 13.Scott, J. 2006. Mayor Rethinks Need for Housing Tax Breaks. *New York Times.* February 24.

Scott, J. C. 1998. *Seeing Like a State: How Certain Schemes to Improve the Human Condition Have Failed.* New Haven, Conn.: Yale University Press.

Seifman, D. 2005. Mike: No Vow on Tax Hikes. *New York Post*. March 2.

Senko, J., and F. DeRosa. 2009. *Vanishing New York: The Documentary*. November 6.

Sennett, R. 2000. Cities without Care or Connection. *New Statesman*. June 8.

Shachtman, T. 2000. *Skyscraper Dreams: The Great Real Estate Dynasties of New York*. Lincoln, Nebr.: iUniverse.com.

Sharma, A., and A. Gupta, eds. 2006. *The Anthropology of the State: A Reader*. Malden, Mass.: Blackwell.

Shearmur, R. 2008. Of Urban Competitiveness and Business Homelessness. *Urban Geography* 29:613–615.

Shefter, M. 1992. *Political Crisis/Fiscal Crisis: The Collapse and Revival of New York City*. New York: Columbia University Press.

Sheppard, E. S., and R. B. McMaster, eds. 2004. *Scale and Geographic Inquiry: Nature, Society, and Method*. Malden, Mass.: Blackwell.

Sherman, R. 2007. *Class Acts: Service and Inequality in Luxury Hotels*. Berkeley: University of California Press.

Shore, C., and S. Nugent, eds. 2003. *Elite Cultures: Anthropological Perspectives*. New York: Routledge.

Short, J. R. 1999. Urban Imagineers: Boosterism and the Representation of Cities. In *The Urban Growth Machine: Critical Perspectives, Two Decades Later*, ed. A. E. G. Jonas and D. Wilson, 37–54. Albany: State University of New York Press.

Short, J. R., and Y.-H. Kim. 1998. Urban Crises/Urban Representations: Selling the City in Difficult Times. In *The Entrepreneurial City: Geographies of Politics, Regime, and Representation*, ed. T. Hall and P. Hubbard, 55–76. New York: Wiley.

Shoval, N. 2002. A New Phase in the Competition for the Olympic Gold: The London and New York Bids for the 2012 Games. *Journal of Urban Affairs* 24:583–599.

Silver, I. 2007. Disentangling Class from Philanthropy: The Double-Edged Sword of Alternative Giving. *Critical Sociology* 33:537–549.

Sindin, S., and A. H. Levin. 2003a. Letter to DCP, Re: DCP's "Preferred Direction" for Hell's Kitchen/Hudson Yards. New York. March 24.

———. 2003b. Letter to MTA-NYC Transit and DCP, Re: No. 7 Subway Extension—Hudson Yards Area Rezoning Draft Scoping Document. New York. June 13.

Sites, W. 2003. *Remaking New York: Primitive Globalization and the Politics of Urban Community*. Minneapolis: University of Minnesota Press.

Sklair, L. 2001. *The Transnational Capitalist Class*. Malden, Mass.: Blackwell.

Slater, R. 1999. *Jack Welch and the GE Way: Management Insights and Leadership Secrets of the Legendary CEO*. New York: McGraw-Hill.

Sleeper, J. 1991. *Closest of Strangers: Liberalism and the Politics of Race in New York*. New York: W. W. Norton.

Smith, C. 2005. The Mayor and His Money. *New York Magazine*. September 26.

Smith, H., and W. Graves. 2005. Gentrification as Corporate Growth Strategy: The Strange Case of Charlotte, North Carolina and the Bank of America. *Journal of Urban Affairs* 27:403–418.

Smith, N. 1992. Geography, Difference and the Politics of Scale. In *Postmodernism and the Social Sciences*, ed. J. Doherty, 57–79. London: MacMillan.

———. 1993. Homeless/Global: Scaling Places. In *Mapping the Futures: Local Cultures, Global Change*, ed. J. Bird et al., 87–119. New York: Routledge.

———. 1996. *The New Urban Frontier: Gentrification and the Revanchist City*. New York: Routledge.

———. 2000. New Globalism, New Urbanism: Uneven Development in the 21st Century. *Working Papers in Local Governance and Democracy* 99:4–14.

———. 2002. New Globalism, New Urbanism: Gentrification as Global Urban Strategy. *Antipode* 34:427–450.

———. 2008 [1984]. *Uneven Development: Nature, Capital, and the Production of Space*, 3d ed. Athens: University of Georgia Press.

Smith, N., and P. Williams, eds. 1986. *Gentrification of the City*. Boston: Allen and Unwin.

Smith, P. 2007. *Primitive America: The Ideology of Capitalist Democracy*. Minneapolis: University of Minnesota Press.

Sorkin, M., ed. 1992. *Variations on a Theme Park: The New American City and the End of Public Space*. New York: Hill and Wang.

———. 2002. The Center Cannot Hold. In *After the World Trade Center: Rethinking New York City*, ed. M. Sorkin and S. Zukin, 197–207. New York: Routledge.

Spiro, L. N. 1997. In Search of Michael Bloomberg. *Business Week*. May 5.

Steinhauer, J. 2002a. A Survey Asks Companies for Opinions of New York. *New York Times*. April 10.

———. 2002b. What Kind of Businessman Raises Your Taxes? *New York Times*. December 1.

———. 2004. The West Side's Yours, Ground Zero Mine. *New York Times*. March 27.

———. 2005. Requiem for a Stadium: Overtures Came Too Late. *New York Times*. June 8.

———. 2006. As Manhattan Booms, Inflation Squeezes Rest of New York. *New York Times*. January 25.

Strathern, M., ed. 2000. *Audit Cultures: Anthropological Studies in Accountability, Ethics, and the Academy*. New York: Routledge.

Sugrue, T. J. 2005. *The Origins of the Urban Crisis: Race and Inequality in Postwar Detroit*. Princeton, N.J.: Princeton University Press.

Surowiecki, J. 2002. Blame Iacocca: How the Former Chrysler CEO Caused the Corporate Scandals. *Slate*. http://slate.msn.com/?id=2068448. (accessed July 22, 2007).

Swyngedouw, E. 1997. Neither Local nor Global: "Glocalization" and the Politics of Scale. In *Spaces of Globalization*, ed. K. R. Cox, 137–166. New York: Guilford Press.

Swyngedouw, E., F. Moulaert, and A. Rodriguez. 2002. Neoliberal Urbanization in Europe: Large-Scale Urban Development Projects and the New Urban Policy. *Antipode* 34:542–577.

Sze, J. 2006. *Noxious New York: The Racial Politics of Urban Health and Environmental Justice*. Cambridge, Mass.: MIT Press.

Tabb, W. 1982. *The Long Default: New York City and the Urban Fiscal Crisis*. New York: Monthly Review Press.

Tagliabue, P. 2002. New York's Olympic Plan. Speech to the Council on Foreign Relations. New York. July 10.

Taylor, C. 2002a. Modern Social Imaginaries. *Public Culture* 14:91–124.

Taylor, M. M. 2002b. *Harlem between Heaven and Hell*. Minneapolis: University of Minnesota Press.

Temple-Raston, D. 2004a. Bloomberg Sees Little Opposition to Stadium Plan. *New York Sun*. February 4.

———. 2004b. Bridging the Public-Private Divide: Interview with Andrew Alper. *New York Sun*. December 6.

———. 2004c. Mayor Eyes a Compromise in Scheme to Finance West Side Development. *New York Sun*. November 19.

Thompson, E. P. 1964. *The Making of the English Working Class*. New York: Pantheon.

Thompson, J. P. 2005. *Double Trouble: Black Mayors, Black Communities, and the Call for a Deep Democracy*. New York: Oxford University Press.

Tierney, J. 2001. An Outsider Comes Inside to Run Things. *New York Times*. November 8.

Tobin, A. 1953. Authorities as a Governmental Technique. Conference of the Bureau of Governmental Research. Rutgers University, New Brunswick, N.J. March 23.

Todd, G. 1995. Going Global in the Semiperiphery: World Cities as Political Projects: The Case of Toronto. In *World Cities in a World System*, ed. P. L. Knox and P. J. Taylor. Cambridge, U.K.: University of Cambridge Press.

Topousis, T. 2004a. Cheers and Jeers: 700 in Fierce W. Side Debate. *New York Post*. September 24.

———. 2004b. City Tab for Jets' Stadium Could Double. *New York Post*. November 5.

Trouillot, M.-R. 2001. The Anthropology of the State in the Age of Globalization: Close Encounters of the Deceptive Kind. *Current Anthropology* 42:125–138.

Trueman, M. M., M. Klemm, and A. Giroud. 2004. Can a City Communicate? Bradford as a Corporate Brand. *Corporate Communications: An International Journal of Brand Management* 9:317–330.

Tsing, A. 2000. Inside the Economy of Appearances. *Public Culture* 12:115–144.

———. 2002. The Global Situation. In *The Anthropology of Globalization*, ed. J. X. Inda and R. Rosaldo, 453–486. Malden, Mass.: Blackwell.

Uchitelle, L. 2007. The Richest of the Rich, Proud of a New Gilded Age. *New York Times*. July 15.

University of Chicago Graduate School of Business. 2004. Distinguished Alumni Award, 2004: Andrew Alper. http://www.chicagobooth.edu/alumni/daa/alper.aspx. (accessed February 21, 2010).

Useem, M. 1999. *Investor Capitalism: How Money Managers Are Changing the Face of Corporate America.* New York: Basic Books.

Veale, J. 2008. Can South Korea's President Deliver? *Time.* February 25.

Virasami, B. 2004. Mayor on Stadium: 2012 Bid's Fate Tied to Jets. *New York Newsday.* September 13.

———. 2005. Mayor Says Cablevision Wants to Derail Olympics. *New York Newsday.* February 10.

Vitale, A. 2008. *City of Disorder: How the Quality of Life Campaign Transformed New York Politics.* New York: New York University Press.

Wacquant, L. 1999. How Penal Common Sense Comes to Europeans: Notes on the Transatlantic Diffusion of the Neoliberal *Doxa. European Societies* 1:319–352.

Waldinger, R. 2000. *Still the Promised City: African-Americans and New Immigrants in Postindustrial New York City.* Cambridge, Mass.: Harvard University Press.

Ward, K. 2003. UK Temporary Staffing: Industry Structure and Evolutionary Dynamics. *Environment and Planning A* 35:889–909.

———. 2004. Going Global? Internationalization and Diversification in the Temporary Staffing Industry. *Journal of Economic Geography* 4:251–273.

———. 2006. "Policies in Motion," Urban Management and State Restructuring: The Trans-Local Expansion of Business Improvement Districts. *International Journal of Urban and Regional Research* 30:54–75.

———. 2007a. Temporary Staffing, "Geographies of Circulation," and the Business of Delivering Neoliberalization. In *Neoliberalization: States, Networks, People*, ed. K. England and K. Ward, 110–136. Malden, Mass.: Blackwell.

Ward, K., and K. England. 2007. Introduction: Reading Neoliberalism. In *Neoliberalization: States, Networks, Peoples*, ed. E. Kim and K. Ward, 1–22. Malden, Mass.: Blackweel.

Ward, K. G. 2000. Front Rentiers to Rantiers: "Active Entrepreneurs," "Structural Speculators," and the Politics of Marketing the City. *Urban Studies* 37:1093–1107.

Ward, S. 1998a. Place Marketing: A Historical Comparison of Britain and North America. In *The Entrepreneurial City: Geographies of Politics, Regime, and Representation*, ed. T. Hall and P. Hubbard, 31–55. New York: Wiley.

———. 1998b. *Selling Places: The Marketing and Promotion of Towns and Cities, 1850–2000.* New York: Routledge.

———. 2007b. Promoting the Olympic City. In *Olympic Cities: City Agendas, Planning, and the World Games, 1896–2012*, ed. J. R. Gold and M. M. Gold, 120–137. New York: Routledge.

Ward, S. V., and J. R. Gold. 1994. Introduction. In *Place Promotion: The Use of Publicity and Marketing to Sell Towns and Regions*, ed. J. R. Gold and S. V. Ward, 1–17. New York: Wiley.

Weber, M. 1947. *The Theory of Social and Economic Organization.* New York: Oxford University Press.

———. 1958. The Sociology of Charismatic Authority. In *From Max Weber: Essays in Sociology,* ed. H. H. Gerth and C. W. Mills, 245–252. New York: Oxford University Press.

Weber, R. 2002. Extracting Value from the City: Neoliberalism and Urban Redevelopment. *Antipode* 34:519–540.

Weikart, L. A. 2001. The Giuliani Administration and the New Public Management in New York City. *Urban Affairs Review* 36:359.

Wheeler, W. 2004. Testimony. Public Hearing on the Hudson Yards Rezoning Plan and Draft Generic Environmental Impact Statement. New York. September 23.

Whyte, W. H. 1980. *The Social Life of Small Urban Spaces.* Washington, D.C.: Conservation Foundation.

Williams, B. 1988. *Upscaling Downtown: Stalled Gentrification in Washington, DC.* Ithaca, N.Y.: Cornell University Press.

———. 1989. A Class Act: Anthropology and the Race to Nation across Ethnic Terrain. *Annual Reviews of Anthropology* 18:401–444.

Williams, T. 2002. Bloomberg Says Giuliani Plan to Move Stock Exchange Is "Not Viable." *New York Newsday.* May 24.

———. 2004. New York Mayor Stakes Political Capital on Olympic Stadium. *New York Newsday.* December 12.

Willis, K., B. Yeoh, and S. M. A. K. Fakhri. 2002. Transnational Elites. *Geoforum* 33:505–507.

Wilson, D. 2004a. Bloomberg Plays Nice, but Plays for Keeps. *New York Times.* December 4.

———. 2004b. Toward a Contingent Urban Neoliberalism. *Urban Geography* 25:771–783.

———. 2008a. Review of Contesting Neoliberalism: Urban Frontiers. *Annals of the Association of American Geographers* 98:498.

Wilson, P. C. 2008b. Neoliberalism, Indigeneity and Social Engineering in Ecuador's Amazon. *Critique of Anthropology* 28:127–144.

Wolff, M. 2001a. Bloomberg News. *New York Magazine.* August 27.

———. 2001b. Chairman Mike. *New York Magazine.* September 10.

Wollman, H. 2004. Presentation of Newman Center Plan to Manhattan Community Board Four. New York. November 8.

Wood, E. M. 1986. *The Retreat from Class: A New "True" Socialism.* New York: Verso.

Wright, E. O. 1985. *Classes.* New York: Verso.

Wright, M. W. 2006. *Disposable Women and Other Myths of Global Capitalism.* New York: Routledge.

Yaro, R. 2004. Speech. Envisioning the West Side. New York. August 5.

Yglesias, M. 2008. Bloomberg's Future. *The Atlantic.* http://matthewyglesias

.theatlantic.com/archives/2008/06/bloombergs_future.php. (accessed December 17, 2009).

Zaloom, C. 2006. *Out of the Pits: Traders and Technology from Chicago to London.* Chicago: University of Chicago Press.

Zandniapour, L., and M. Conway. 2001. *Closing the Gap: How Sectoral Workforce Development Programs Benefit the Working Poor.* Washington, D.C.: Aspen Institute.

Zinser, L. 2005. New York Will Soon Make Its Case for 2012 Olympics. *New York Times.* February 15.

Žižek, S. 2004. *Iraq : The Borrowed Kettle.* London and New York: Verso.

———. 2008. *Violence: Six Sideways Reflections.* New York: Picador.

———. 2009. *First as Tragedy, Then as Farce.* New York: Verso.

Zukin, S. 1989. *Loft Living: Culture and Capital in Urban Change.* New Brunswick, N.J.: Rutgers University Press.

———. 2002. Our World Trade Center. In *After the World Trade Center: Rethinking New York City,* ed. M. Sorkin and S. Zukin. New York: Routledge.

Zukin, S., et al. 1998. From Coney Island to Las Vegas in the Urban Imaginary: Discursive Practices of Growth and Decline. *Urban Affairs Review* 33:627.

INDEX

Abrams, Philip, 139
accountability: and Bloomberg Way, 18,
    132–133, 208–209, 229–230, 272; and
    CEO mayor, 77–80; of NYC2012, 83,
    160–161; and private-sector participa-
    tion in governance, 30, 31, 34; and
    public-private partnerships, 41; and
    running government like business, 75
affordable housing: and Bloomberg
    administration's second term, 261; and
    Bloomberg's 2005 mayoral campaign,
    257; in Hudson Yards plan, 171–172,
    193, 207, 223, 224; in Olympic plan,
    237
African Americans: and development
    policy, 41, 226; economic position of,
    226–227; and electoral politics, 35,
    72–73, 259, 265, 285n9; and postwar
    liberalism, 27
Allen, Paul, 276
Alper, Andrew: and Bloomberg, 87; and
    Bloomberg administration, 84–87,
    94, 268; and Doctoroff, 86–87; and
    Economic Development Corporation,
    97–98, 142; on flight of jobs to New
    Jersey, 106; on Giuliani's relationship
    with business elites, 31; and London
    trip in 2003, 114; and Partnership for
    New York City, 109; philanthropy of,
    87; on rebranding New York, 100, 107,
    108, 113; on strategic plans, 96; and tax
    incentive policy, 117–119; wealth of, 93
Anderson, Kurt, 249
Anderson, Richard, 175

Angotti, Tom, 52
Arrighi, Giovanni, 282n15
Association for a Better New York, 31, 32
austerity, 4, 28, 32–39 passim, 283n8. *See
    also* fiscal crisis of 1970s
Avella, Tony, 224, 273
aviation, 87, 285n2

Bank of America, 118, 277
Barron, Charles, 224, 227
Battery Park City, 88, 207, 241
Battery Park City Authority, 207, 208
Beame, Abe, 81
Bear Stearns, 118, 142, 205, 287n10
benchmarking, 61, 79, 80, 98, 100, 133.
    See also measurement; performance
Bender, Thomas, 274
Bloomberg, Michael: and Alper, 85, 87;
    on alternative stadium locations, 239;
    approval ratings of, 266; biography
    of, 66–67, 90; and Burden, 88; busi-
    ness background of, 2, 16, 67, 110, 113,
    210; as CEO mayor, 75, 77, 94, 210,
    272; and charismatic CEO, figure of,
    55, 65–74, 90; class solidarity of, 269;
    on development policy, 121–122; and
    Doctoroff, 83–84, 165; and expertise,
    20, 71, 80–81, 90–93 passim, 196, 234;
    on far west side stadium, 228–229,
    240, 241, 242; on far west side stadium
    opponents, 246, 247; and financial
    crisis, 264; on fiscal crisis of 1970s,
    119–120; on Hudson Yards plan, 123,
    174, 179, 217–218; lack of political

325

GEOGRAPHIES OF JUSTICE AND SOCIAL TRANSFORMATION

CPSIA informati
Printed in the US
238802LV

820 336817

DEMCO